JUDAISM AND HEALTH

Also by Jeff Levin

Healing to All Their Flesh: Jewish and Christian Perspectives on Spirituality, Theology, and Health
(Edited with Keith G. Meador)

Divine Love: Perspectives from the World's Religious Traditions
(Edited with Stephen G. Post)

Faith, Medicine, and Science: A Festschrift in Honor of Dr. David B. Larson
(Edited with Harold G. Koenig)

Religion in the Lives of African Americans: Social, Psychological, and Health Perspectives
(with Robert Joseph Taylor and Linda M. Chatters)

God, Faith, and Health: Exploring the Spirituality-Healing Connection

Essentials of Complementary and Alternative Medicine
(Edited with Wayne B. Jonas)

Religion in Aging and Health: Theoretical Foundations and Methodological Frontiers
(Edited)

Also from Jewish Lights and the Kalsman Institute on Judaism and Health

Healing and the Jewish Imagination: Spiritual and Practical Perspectives on Judaism and Health
Edited by Rabbi William Cutter, PhD

Midrash & Medicine: Healing Body and Soul in the Jewish Interpretive Tradition
Edited by Rabbi William Cutter, PhD
Preface by Michele F. Prince, LCSW, MAJCS

JUDAISM AND HEALTH

A Handbook of Practical, Professional and Scholarly Resources

Edited by
Jeff Levin, PhD, MPH
Institute for Studies of Religion, Baylor University
Michele F. Prince, LCSW, MAJCS
Kalsman Institute on Judaism and Health, Hebrew Union College
Foreword by Rabbi Elliot N. Dorff, PhD

For People of All Faiths, All Backgrounds
JEWISH LIGHTS PUBLISHING
Woodstock, Vermont

Judaism and Health:
A Handbook of Practical, Professional and Scholarly Resources

2013 Hardcover Edition, First Printing

Page 399 constitutes a continuation of this copyright page.

Library of Congress Cataloging-in-Publication Data
Judaism and health : a handbook of practical, professional, and scholarly resources/[edited by] Jeff Levin, Michele F. Prince.
pages cm
Includes bibliographical references and index.
ISBN 978-1-58023-714-7
1. Health—Religious aspects—Judaism. 2. Healing—Religious aspects—Judaism. 3. Medicine—Religious aspects—Judaism. I. Levin, Jeffrey S. editor. II. Prince, Michele F., 1966- editor.
BM538.H43J83 2013
296.3'76—dc23
2013021754

10 9 8 7 6 5 4 3 2 1

Manufactured in the United States of America
Cover and Interior Design: Kelley Barton

For People of All Faiths, All Backgrounds
Jewish Lights Publishing
A Division of LongHill Partners, Inc.
Sunset Farm Offices, Route 4, P.O. Box 237
Woodstock, VT 05091
Tel: (802) 457-4000 Fax: (802) 457-4004
www.jewishlights.com

For Sam Karff, my first rabbi (J.L.)

For my beloved husband, Jeffrey Prince (M.F.P.)

Contents

Part V
Jewish Communal, Organizational, and Policy Perspectives

Foreword

Rabbi Elliot N. Dorff, PhD

As the title of this book indicates, its subject is Judaism and health. But why should we expect Judaism to have anything distinctive to say about health? What is wrong with American secular understandings of health?

There is nothing particularly wrong with American secular understandings of health. One should recognize, though, that what passes as the secular viewpoint in Western nations is not, as is often assumed, therefore objective and true. Instead, what we call "secular" is actually the perspective of Western liberalism, influenced by philosophers like John Locke, Jean Jacques Rousseau, and Claude Montesquieu. Like every other perspective on life, the Western liberal perspective has its strengths and its weaknesses, and it is not any more objective than any of the other ways of thinking about our world, ourselves, and, specifically, our health.

Every religion and secular philosophy (such as Western liberalism, existentialism, and communism) offers its particular lens on life with its own distinctive understanding of who we are as individuals and as a community and what kind of persons and communities we should strive to be. Even though all the viewpoints we know were created by human beings and seek to describe human beings, there is a remarkable diversity in how the various religions and philosophies of the world depict both what kind of being we are and what kind we should strive to be. For example, is the ideal person married? In some religions the ideal person is celibate (for example, Buddhist and Catholic priests and monastics); in others (like Judaism), the ideal person is married; and in yet others (for example, some forms of current American secularism), that is a matter of individual choice with no moral judgment one

Rabbi Elliot N. Dorff, PhD, is rector and Sol & Anne Dorff Distinguished Service Professor in Philosophy at American Jewish University in Los Angeles, California.

way or the other. Is the ideal person educated? In some religions (like Mormonism or Buddhism) and some secular philosophies, only the elite are to know the secrets of the religion or ideology and the community attached to it; in others (like Judaism), every person is to strive to learn the entirety of the tradition, and parents have the duty to initiate their children into that process, a process that continues one's whole life. Is the individual at the center of value or is the community? American liberalism would assert the former; communism would assert the latter; and Judaism would assert the importance of both.

These differences in general viewpoint have a direct impact on how the various religions and philosophies of the world understand the role of medicine and health. The differences are rooted in each tradition's fundamental understanding of the human being in the first place.

For example, Western philosophy (beginning with Plato) makes a sharp distinction between body and mind: the body is the animal in us and the mind the distinctly human in us. Christianity sees a similar dichotomy between body and soul. If one begins with either of those views, the body is simply a machine that supports the mind or soul, and caring for the body is at best an instrumental value, something one does in order to have the physical abilities to accomplish some other goal (learning accurate ideas and developing the life of the mind in the case of Plato; saving the soul from its sinfulness in the case of Christianity). If one begins instead, as Judaism does, with the view that the body, mind, emotions, and will (the latter three constituting a person's identity or "soul") are all integrated within us and each affects the other constantly, then care of the body immediately involves care of the soul as well, and care of the person becomes an absolute value.

Are medical interventions a forbidden human attempt to change what God or nature has wrought, as in Christian Science and some forms of natural law theory? Or are healthcare personnel nothing less than the agents and partners of God in the ongoing act of healing, as they are in Judaism? Furthermore, if one sees individuals as isolated beings, each with "unalienable rights," as the U.S. Declaration of Independence states, then healthcare should focus on the welfare of each individual instead of the health of the familial or communal context in which that person lives, except as it affects a particular patient. If on the other hand one sees the individual as enmeshed in a web of tight and often irrevocable relationships with family and community, as Judaism does, then the family and the whole society must be taken into account in all healthcare decisions for any individual, and we as a community have a duty to each other to provide both preventive and curative healthcare.[1]

Judaism has a distinctive view of healthcare, not only because of the long history of Jews valuing and engaging in healthcare, but also because of deep ideological commitments that shape the Jewish approach to life in general and to health and medicine in particular. These Jewish convictions are very much in evidence in each chapter of this book, as the editors have brought together essays that describe not only a Jewish approach to medical care of the body but also how Judaism would have us care for the soul and for each other.

They begin with attention to the body, for in Judaism the body is created by God as much as any other part of us is; it is not of instrumental value alone. Jews have historically been eager to avoid diseases when possible and to cure them when not, and part 1 informs us of how Judaism understands the results of those efforts for us living today. Part 2, on pastoral care, draws the reader's attention to the pastoral needs not only of the patient but also of the caregiver, whether a healthcare professional, friend, or family member; and it provides good advice for anyone on the giving or receiving end of pastoral care. Part 3, on coping with disease and suffering, is a graphic example of how a Jewish approach to healthcare differs from much of Western medicine. It explores how we can cope with suffering and pain when pills and even surgeries are not effective or only partially so, through specific personal, familial, and communal strategies that can effectively respond to pain and suffering. Part 4 draws attention to the psychological components of assuring health in the first place and of restoring health when a person is ill or addicted. I found the empirical research on the relationship between Judaism and health that is included in this section absolutely fascinating. Finally, part 5 turns the reader's attention to communal, political, and policy issues in healthcare, and wisely so. In our time almost no one can afford all the medical interventions that are possible, and so we all need health insurance, but even the government cannot afford to cover everything, nor should it. Most other Western democracies realized this long ago and shaped their healthcare delivery system to make difficult triage decisions; we Americans are only now facing this issue squarely, for the staunch individualism at the heart of the American perspective on life has so far made it impossible to decide communally what kind of healthcare can and should be offered. Other democracies are achieving much better results in virtually all parameters of health and wellness than the United States is, and at half the cost, so attention to the political aspect of healthcare is crucial.

Through this broad selection of essays, the editors of *Judaism and Health* have grasped the core Jewish commitments of seeing ourselves as organisms that integrate body and soul and that live in the context of a family and a community. Because these underlying Jewish commitments are time-tested and full of wisdom, both Jews and non-Jews would do well to think about health and healthcare in line with them. I dare to hope that this book will make that possible for us all.

Acknowledgments

… *v'higiyanu laz'man hazeh*—and enabled us to reach this special occasion.

Completing this project does indeed seem like a "special occasion," one that merits a *Shehecheyanu*. This book was two and half years in the making, dating back to conversations with Stuart Matlins before and after the Kalsman Institute's Research Roundtable retreat at Brandeis-Bardin Institute in 2011. We are so grateful to Stuart for lending us an ear and green-lighting a pretty huge collaborative project that, at times, made us wonder if we were guilty of overreach.

But, actually, this book was about five years in the making, dating to our original meeting at the inaugural conference of the Society for Spirituality, Theology, and Health in Durham, North Carolina, in 2008. We owe that introduction to our mutual friend, Gila Silverman, who provided the entrée. The three of us spent much of the conference sitting around over coffee plotting all sorts of projects, many of which subsequently came to fruition: the Kalsman Roundtable on Judaism and Health Research, a successfully funded grant from the Templeton Foundation, multiple journal articles and other writing projects, and ultimately, *Judaism and Health*.

But, then, this book was really about twenty-five years in the making, dating to those exciting times in the late 1980s when so many of the threads discussed in this book—Jewish pastoral care, Jewish chaplaincy, new Jewish healing liturgy, Jewish communal programming in health and aging, Jewish bioethics, and research on the mental and physical health of Jews—all began to coalesce into a Jewish healing movement. Many of the contributors to *Judaism and Health* were also significant contributors to the emergence of Judaism and health—to the coming-together of varied professional communities and affinity groups into a self-identifying "field."

But, to be honest, and not to overstate, this book was probably about a thousand years in the making, dating to the Golden Age, an era of great rabbi-physicians: the Rambam, Judah Halevi, Ibn Ezra, the Ramban, among others. These intellects set in motion centuries of writing, philosophical and halakhic, including tens of thousands of rabbinic responsa, regarding applications of Jewish law to the practice of medicine and the healing arts. (Dr. Julius Preuss's monumental *Biblical and Talmudic Medicine*, first published in 1911, aptly summarized this prodigious body of writing.)

Whatever great divide may have separated religion and medicine across time and throughout the other faith traditions of the world—although the presence of historical correlations of the *Sānkhya* philosophy and *Āyurveda*, of Islam and *Unani*, and of Taoism, Buddhism, and Confucianism and traditional Chinese medicine call such a tacit divide into question—the relations between religion and medicine and among its practitioners were never as conflicted for Jews as within, say, Christianity. Still, by the mid-twentieth century, with over a hundred years of Jewish rational enlightenment behind us, liberalized religious observance, growing assimilation and secularism, and ascendancy of scientism as an intellectual ideal, one could be forgiven for failing to notice much of an intersection between the Jewish religion, Jewish life, or the Jewish people on the one hand, and medicine, health, healing, or healthcare on the other—save for the cultural stereotype of the overachieving Jewish doctor.

An important marker of things to come appeared in 1959, with the publication of *Jewish Medical Ethics* by Rabbi Immanuel Jakobovits. This one publication set in motion many developments in academic, institutional, and congregational Judaism; these occurred, significantly, within and across the various Jewish movements. By the 1980s, consciousnesses sufficiently raised, new Jewish voices began to be heard on a variety of themes related to healing, wellness, and spirituality—personally and individually as well as communally and institutionally. There were Conservative voices, Reconstructionist voices, Orthodox voices, Reform voices, Renewal voices, and voices of socially committed non-affiliated Jews. New generations of Jewish medical, religious, communal, academic, and human services professionals began to weigh in on vital issues related to what Judaism, in all its flavors, might have to say about health and healing, broadly defined. We are two of those new voices.

Since this is an acknowledgments section and not a prologue or introduction, we will save further exploration of these topics for the book. But, as Jews, we are sensitive to the Rabbinic mandate to cite sources (*Pirkei Avot* 6:6; Talmud, *Chullin* 94a). *Judaism and Health* did not spring forth from a vacuum. When we met, in 2008, both of us and Gila noted that our coming together felt like it was *beshert* (fated), something that we still acknowledge. There was work to do, and in putting together this book it feels like we have fulfilled, in part, a sacred charge by honoring and building on the work of all the great Jewish sages and contemporary colleagues whose efforts constitute the foundation stones for the field of Judaism and health.

It is a cliché, but there are so many people to thank that it is hard to know where to start. Serendipitously, many of them are formally associated with this book, as contributors or through their endorsements. These are the folks who built this meta-field of Judaism and health through their leadership in the various component fields and disciplines that are rapidly being assembled into a whole. They are the heroes of this project; we have simply fit the pieces together that they had already so carefully crafted.

We are grateful to Stuart Matlins, Emily Wichland and Rachel Shields at Jewish Lights Publishing, for their support and encouragement. This book is written in a mix of voices for a mix of audiences and for a mix of expressed purposes, including being partly a professional handbook. We recognize that Stuart has taken a leap of faith in signing on, and for that we are thankful. We are also especially thankful for all the professionals at Jewish Lights who worked with us throughout the various phases of production.

We also wish to acknowledge our work colleagues for their support of us, tangible and emotional, as we undertook this project. They, too, have "enabled us to reach this special occasion."

Michele is thankful for the unexpected opportunities to provide leadership to the Jewish community during her eight-year tenure with the Kalsman Institute at Hebrew Union College–Jewish Institute of Religion. Much gratitude goes to Michele's staff and board of directors at OUR HOUSE Grief Support Center and to colleagues currently or previously part of the Kalsman network: Adi Bodenstein, Scarlet Newman-Thomas, Josh Holo, Dvora Weisberg, Leah Hochman, Jay Abarbanel, Joel Kushner, and particularly Kalsman's founder, Rabbi William Cutter, a dear colleague and teacher.

Jeff is grateful for the support of Byron Johnson and Rodney Stark, co-directors of the Baylor Institute for Studies of Religion (ISR), and of colleagues and staff at ISR, including Philip Jenkins, Gordon Melton, Thomas Kidd, David Jeffrey, Frances Malone, Cameron Andrews, Leone Moore, and Josh Jang. Thanks also to Baylor colleagues Ken Starr, Elizabeth Davis, and Charlie Beckenhauer. And a special thank you to Rabbi Gordon Fuller, who provided guidance and assistance to Jeff in tracking down and verifying rabbinic references during the months of editing and copyediting the manuscript.

Finally, we would like to thank our families for their patience and support as we worked long hours on this project. Editing a book in many ways is a more difficult task than writing one outright. Fortunately, we instituted a useful division of labor: in the lingo of the publishing world, Michele was the "acquisitions editor" and Jeff was the "copyeditor," and we shared other duties. This made the best use of our respective strengths without being too overwhelming for either of us. Thankfully, our spouses, Lea Steele Levin and Jeffrey Prince, were beacons of loving-kindness and kept us grounded throughout our work.

In closing, it is our prayer that *Judaism and Health* will continue to build the field of Judaism and health by inspiring and preparing a new generation of Jewish leaders to sensitively and capably help congregants and community members to deal with the critical issues that they face throughout their lives.

Introduction
Judaism and Health

Jeff Levin, PhD, MPH, and
Michele F. Prince, LCSW, MAJCS

Connecting health/medicine with religion is not difficult, even if many moderns have forgotten how they intertwine.
MARTIN E. MARTY [1]

Religion and Medicine

The intersection of religion, broadly defined, and the institution of medicine, again broadly defined, has been a topic of considerable discussion over the past three decades. This is due in large part to the proliferation of published studies suggesting statistical relations between expressions of faith (e.g., attendance at worship services) and certain health outcomes (e.g., lower rates of depression).[2] As these studies have become widely publicized, long-standing conflicts between religion and science or religion and medicine have come to the fore. Books, conferences, news stories, and thousands of scholarly papers have dissected this issue and have spawned numerous side debates, such as on the propriety of doctors or nurses conducting spiritual assessments, of clinicians praying with their patients, and of the individual versus the communal consequences of religious practice.[3] The majority of scholarly and popular writing on this subject has come from Christian medical professionals or writers and has focused on themes and issues that are constructed primarily in a Christian context.[4] A smaller, but substantial, minority of work in this area has a new-age or metaphysical focus.[5]

Since the late 1980s, the research and writing on this subject has begun to coalesce into a veritable academic field. University research centers, academic journals, and distinguished professorships are devoted to the interconnections between religion or spirituality and health, large research grants are given out by the U.S. National Institutes of Health and the John Templeton Foundation, and content matter on these broad interconnections has made its way into the curricula of 90 percent of medical schools in the United States.[6] If at one time the idea of scholarship at the intersection of religion and medicine would have seemed unlikely or at least marginal, that is no longer the case today.

As Jews, standing to the side and observing this rapidly growing academic and popular discourse, we are struck by two things. First, relatively little of this work applies to us. The themes, constructs, language, and presumptions—they just do not apply, at least not in the same way as they do to non-Jews.[7] Second, issues that seem to be a source of tension in other faith traditions—for example, in Western Christianity since the Enlightenment[8]—are not so heated for us. Throughout our entire history, there were much closer relations between medicine and science, on the one hand, and religion and the rabbinate, on the other. In many instances, rabbi and physician were one and the same.

> In the beginning of Jewish history, religion and healing were inseparable because the priest and physician were one and the same person.... The advent of scientific medicine in the middle of the nineteenth century nearly completely separated medicine from religion. Nevertheless, Jewish physicians traditionally consider their vocation to be spiritually endowed and not merely an ordinary profession.[9]

The most notable and familiar example for us in the Common Era is, of course, Moses Maimonides, the Rambam. According to medical professor Fred Rosner, the Rambam's "attitude towards the practice of medicine came from his deep religious background, which made the preservation of health and life a divine commandment."[10] The idea that one's commitment to a Jewish religious life might have something relevant to say about one's obligations regarding the practice or receipt of medical care is not just a historical notion; it is as true for us in the present day as in the time of the Rambam and, later, in the time of Sforno and other great rabbi-physicians. Motivated by affirmation of Torahitic or Rabbinic principles, it is not unheard of for contemporary Jews to find in their respective families, and family trees, both doctors and rabbis, sometimes in one and the same person.

In Rosner's *Pioneers in Jewish Medical Ethics*, there is a chapter containing profiles of the most prominent contemporary experts.[11] Rosner's comment is notable: "Several are rabbis, several are physicians, and several are both."[12] In his foreword to the book, leading Jewish medical ethicist Shimon Glick elaborates a possible reason: "Throughout the millennia, Judaism and medicine have marched hand-in-hand as allies, not as rivals."[13]

For Jews, religion and medicine (and science) are not inherently in conflict, even within the Torah-observant community,[14] but, rather, can be friendly partners in the pursuit of wholesome ends, such as truth, healing, and the advancement of humankind. It may be a stretch to say that this is a *uniquely* Jewish phenomenon. Albert Schweitzer, for example, comes to mind. But *characteristically* Jewish? Certainly.

The late chief rabbi of the British Commonwealth Lord Immanuel Jakobovits provides some insight into this convergence:

> Of all the sciences, it is preeminently medicine that enjoys a natural kinship with Judaism historically and intellectually. For many centuries, rabbis and physicians, often merging their professions into one, were intimate partners in a common effort for the betterment of life.[15]

What form did this "common effort" take? For centuries, a book with the title *Judaism and Health* would have implied a sourcebook of medical *halakhah*—an application of Jewish law to matters of physician and patient decision making regarding medical care and prevention of illness. This is still a main preoccupation of writing on Judaism and health today, across the Jewish movements, but in the past quarter century the phrase "Judaism and health" has come to designate an expansively multidimensional field of study and action. This field is at once practical, professional, and scholarly, and it incorporates and affects the work of academics, of healthcare, communal, and rabbinic leaders, and of Jewish laypeople.

From Judaism and Health to *Judaism and Health*

This book is entitled *Judaism and Health*, and not simply *Jews and Health*. Why? And is there a difference?

The latter might suggest one of two things: for one, a book about the contribution of individual Jews to medicine or medical research or to the study and practice of the healing arts—for example, an elaboration of the history just recounted, of the Rambam and all the rabbi-physicians who followed. Perhaps, too, it might imply a book of scientific findings containing the latest information on the health or mental health of people of Jewish descent. Such works, including scholarly books and papers, as noted, already exist.[16]

Judaism and Health, by contrast, is focused on the contributions of Jewish spirituality and the Jewish religion—personally, communally, institutionally—to health, healing, medicine, and healthcare. We, the editors of this book, are starting from a basic premise: that the Jewish religious tradition speaks to health and healing and that Jewish teachings, Jewish professionals, Jewish institutions, and Jewish life can be resources for healing and wellness, both personally and communally.[17] While the presence of long-standing traditions of halakhic writing on medicine and of rabbi-physicians serving our people is well documented, as noted, the identification of this broader intersection between Judaism and health as a focus for academic, professional, and communal work is of very recent vintage.[18] It is currently evolving from a cobbling together of several disparate fields and areas of scholarly and popular writing whose roots extend back to various points in time:

- The many centuries of rabbinic writing on medical *halakhah* (Jewish legal rulings)
- Many decades of *t'shuvot* (rabbinic responsa) and academic writing on topics in Jewish bioethics
- Two-plus decades of health policy advocacy and community organizing on the part of rabbinic and denominational bodies
- The quarter-century-old field of Jewish healthcare chaplaincy and organized efforts in pastoral care and education
- Burgeoning community and congregational programming over the past two decades focusing on myriad personal and public health concerns, as well as considerable liturgical innovation across the Jewish movements
- Three decades of contemporary scholarly and popular writing at the interface of Jewish spirituality, healing, and

wellness, with emphases on personal growth and self-actualization, on life transitions, on aging and caregiving, on Jewish psychology and meditation, and on kabbalistic themes related to health and healing

- Two decades of published study results on the physical and mental health of practicing Jews, both in Israel and the United States, including social, behavioral, epidemiologic, clinical, ethnographic, and health services research

Yet despite all of these labors, each facet of this work has been pursued mostly in isolation from the others. The principal figures rarely interact and may not be familiar with each other's efforts, and there has not yet been a single published resource that brings these strands together into a single tapestry. It is for this reason that *Judaism and Health* was conceived: as the first comprehensive published resource seeking to meld these disparate elements into a community of scholars, a truly multidisciplinary *k'lal* (collective), thus enhancing the work within each area and creating new possibilities for synergy across disciplines, streams of Jewish life, and substantive topics for the benefit of the Jewish people. Just as recent books on Jewish pastoral care,[19] Jewish aging,[20] and Jewish and multi-faith spiritual care,[21] all published by Jewish Lights, have served to coalesce and advance these respective areas of professional work and scholarship, so, too, does *Judaism and Health* bring together each of the pieces identified above into a single resource that can reach and impact all of the audiences that constitute this new field.

Judaism and Health encompasses the physical, psychological, communal, and spiritual dimensions and expressions of health and features chapters invited from among the leading Jewish contributors to the emerging field of Judaism and health. Most of these contributors are part of a network of professional partners associated with the Kalsman Institute on Judaism and Health at Hebrew Union College–Jewish Institute of Religion (HUC–JIR). Founded in 2000, the Kalsman Institute serves as a catalyst for interaction, discussions, and partnerships among spiritual leaders, healthcare providers, and Jewish community professionals and members.[22] While serving as a department of HUC–JIR and affiliated with the Reform movement, Kalsman is explicitly transdenominational in outlook. In the present book, rabbinic contributors, especially, span the various Jewish movements. This is by intention.

But *Judaism and Health* also expresses another type of diversity. The emerging field of Judaism and health encompasses basic and applied research and scholarly writing on scientific, clinical, bioethical, pastoral, and educational themes, as well as communal and liturgical programming focusing on health, healing, medicine, and healthcare. Accordingly, *Judaism and Health* is part professional handbook, part scholarly resource, and part source of practical information for Jewish medical and healthcare providers, nonprofit professionals, educators, rabbis, researchers, academic scholars, congregational leaders, and educated lay leaders with an interest in the exciting developments in this new field. Chapters include summary overviews of recent research studies, first-person narrative accounts by rabbis or clinicians, and professional or personal advice of many types for many audiences. The diversity of voices, styles, and formats that characterize these chapters is also by design and reflects the innate and cherished diversity of the field.

For Jews, diversity is a foundational virtue—a good in and of itself. As the editors of *Judaism and Health*, we take this value to heart and have striven to give voice to a wide range of constituencies, each of whom represents a significant and valued contributor to the larger Judaism-and-health discussion that has been evolving rapidly over the past several years.

Judaism and Health: An Overview

As noted, *Judaism and Health* contains a diversity of voices addressing the intersection of Judaism and health in myriad contexts, documenting the dialogue between the Jewish spiritual path and the domain of health and healing in a variety of narrative styles. We were challenged to organize the two dozen chapters into thematic categories, and the resulting outline contains five substantive sections.

Part 1, "Judaism, Medicine, and Healing," consists of five chapters emphasizing issues confronting physicians, rabbis, and Jewish patients in the medical care arena. Dr. Fred Rosner ("History of Jews in Medicine and Healthcare") provides an insightful historical overview of Jews in medicine. He especially focuses on the origins of the field of Jewish medical ethics. Rabbi Simkha Y. Weintraub ("At the Bedside in the Babylonian Talmud: Reflections on Classical Rabbinic Healers and Their Approaches to Helping the Suffering") lucidly and passionately summarizes Talmudic narratives of Rabbinic healers. He emphasizes themes of suffering, touch, relationship, wounding, and vulnerability. Rabbi David A. Teutsch ("An Overview of Jewish Bioethics") provides a comprehensive outline of Jewish bioethical perspectives on key health-related matters. These include not only the usual clinical topics included in Jewish medical ethics discussions (e.g., euthanasia, abortion, contraception, autopsy), but significant issues regarding health and culture, body and spirit, and healthcare policy in light of scarce resources. Rabbi William Cutter and Dr. Ronald M. Andiman ("Words Worth Healing") survey how prominent Jewish poets have written about healthcare and patienthood. Taking the form of a dialogue between friends, they elaborate on the poetry of Carmi, Zelda, Abba Kovner, Malka Shaked, and others. Finally, Dr. Elizabeth Feldman ("Spiritual Resources for Jewish Healthcare Professionals") offers a practical guide to spiritual resources for physicians and other clinicians. She emphasizes the vital importance of making time for spiritual sustenance and provides helpful guidance for Jewish medical care providers.

Part 2, "Jewish Pastoral Care and Caregiving," contains six chapters providing complementary perspectives on the Jewish pastoral role. Rabbi Naomi Kalish ("Jewish Healthcare Chaplaincy: Professionalizing Spiritual Caregiving") contributes a thorough overview of the Jewish healthcare chaplaincy profession. This includes descriptions of its historical origins and the current state of the field. Rabbi Mychal B. Springer ("Jewish Pastoral Care") offers a heartfelt narrative on themes in Jewish pastoral care. Her chapter contains insights from poetry, Torah, the Rabbinic literature, Jewish liturgy, clinical cases, and her own personal journey. Rabbi Nancy Wiener and Dr. Barbara Breitman ("Pastoral Care in a Postmodern World: Promoting Spiritual Health across the Life Cycle") reflect on issues in Jewish pastoral care that arise in the context of normative life transitions. They especially focus on pastoral responses to modernity, to premodern and postmodern Jewish life, and to feminism. Rabbi Wiener along with Rabbi Julie Schwartz and Michele F. Prince ("Seminary-Based Jewish

Pastoral Education") thoroughly describe the history and current state of Jewish pastoral education within the seminary environment. While focusing on curriculum, skills training, and supervision, they also explore themes related to personal integration, self-reflection, and the encounter with cultural and social change. Rabbi Stephanie Dickstein ("Judaism and Caregiving") describes the broad interface of Judaism and caregiving. Her chapter carefully examines halakhic obligations, the demographics of caregiving in today's world, spiritual issues that arise for Jewish care providers, and resources and tools that are available for spiritual care. Finally, Rabbi Stephen B. Roberts ("The Jewish Professional as Personal Caregiver") discusses the unique challenges of serving as a caregiver that confront Jewish professionals. Drawing on personal and professional experiences and insights, he provides a detailed and practical account of identifying and dealing with compassion fatigue.

Part 3, "Jewish Approaches to Coping with Challenge," comprises six chapters on how Jews experience and deal with physical and psychological challenges. Rabbi Richard Address ("Tradition, Texts, and Our Search for Meaning") offers a lucid take on what Judaism says about the search for meaning. He expands on biblical perspectives about wisdom, spiritual growth, life transitions, and the choices that we make as we age. Rabbi Rachel Adler ("Bad Things Happen: On Suffering") contributes a profound and scholarly essay on the concept of suffering in Jewish context. A highlight is her critique of explanations commonly given for why bad things happen. Rabbi Lynne F. Landsberg and Shelly Thomas Christensen ("Judaism and Disability: *R'fuat Hanefesh*—The Healing of Our Souls, Individual and Communal") present two personal narratives on Judaism, disability, and healing. One story is of an unexpected and life-altering physical challenge; the other is of the developmental challenge of a loved one. Rabbi Shira Stern ("Judaism and Resiliency") writes with great insight about Judaism and resiliency. After presenting some case examples, she carefully elaborates on therapeutic and spiritual responses, drawing on the biblical accounts of Isaac, Joseph, and Miriam. Rabbi Anne Brener ("Doing *Kaddish* to Turn Mourning into Dancing") offers a concise and creative overview of Jewish mourning rituals. Her chapter constitutes both an extended sermon and a scholarly discourse on the

Kaddish and is both inspiring and practical. Finally, Judith Margolis ("Creativity and Healing in a Jewish Context") presents a beautiful and very personal narrative on art as a vehicle for Jewish healing. She illustrates the story of the loss of her husband with many of her own works of visual art, as well as with the words and stories of artist colleagues who also have been faced with personal loss or challenge.

Part 4, "Judaism, Psychology, and Health" contains four chapters summarizing theoretical perspectives and ongoing studies of mental- and physical-health-related outcomes. Rabbi Dr. Abraham J. Twerski ("Judaism and Addiction") writes with great wisdom and authority on Judaism and addictive behavior. Drawing on decades of clinical expertise, he discusses a range of topics: the dynamics of Jewish families, psychiatric insights, the successes of Alcoholics Anonymous, the dangers of the Internet, and recent research findings. Dr. David Pelcovitz ("Gratitude: Perspectives from Positive Psychology and Judaism") provides an overview of Jewish perspectives on gratitude and positive psychology. His chapter summarizes theory and research on gratitude in relation to health, coping, and values education, as well as on ingratitude and habituation, also drawing on material from Jewish sources and from positive psychology. Dr. David H. Rosmarin, Devora Greer Shabtai, Steven Pirutinsky, and Dr. Kenneth I. Pargament ("Jewish Religious Coping and Trust in God: A Review of the Empirical Literature") provide a comprehensive overview of empirical research on Jewish religious coping and trust in God. This chapter is a veritable encyclopedia of current research and writing on the mental health and well-being of Jews, drawing especially on the contributors' own work. Finally, Dr. Jeff Levin ("Population Research on Judaism, Health, and Well-Being") summarizes results from population-based research on the health impact of Jewish observance. Also drawing on his own recent studies, this chapter provides a current state-of-the-field look at social and epidemiologic research on religion and health among Israeli and Diaspora Jews.

Finally, part 5, "Jewish Communal, Organizational, and Policy Perspectives," consists of three chapters that elaborate on the communal, rather than personal-psychological, implications of a putative Judaism-health link. Michele F. Prince ("A Program Assessment of the Field of Judaism and Health: Program Review and Key Stakeholder Interviews") summarizes the comprehensive assessment of Judaism and health programming throughout the United States that she conducted while directing the Kalsman Institute. Based on program reviews and interviews with key stakeholders, this is the most comprehensive summary to date of what is happening in Jewish agencies, synagogues, and medical centers, and it offers a series of field-building recommendations. Rabbi Nancy Epstein and Dr. Adina Newberg ("Three Jewish Lenses for Work and Health") expertly discuss what makes for healthy Jewish organizations. They focus especially on leadership challenges and offer three intentional strategies for creating healthy work settings: accepting and embracing others, engaging and building relationships through dialogue, and having rest, refreshment, and pleasure. Finally, Dr. Jeff Levin ("Jewish Ethical Themes That Should Inform the National Healthcare Discussion: A Prolegomenon") outlines Jewish ethical principles that should inform the ongoing healthcare discussion in the United States, a legislative debate that is far from finished. He also summarizes policy-related, economic, political, and moral challenges that confront those involved in engaging this issue.

It is our intent for *Judaism and Health* to serve as a sourcebook that provides an up-to-date look at this new and rapidly coalescing field. We hope that it will jump-start a larger discussion within institutional Jewish life around the themes touched on in the book. Any of the sections of this book could be elaborated into entire volumes, and indeed, several of the contributors have already written book-length treatments of their particular topic. In the years to come, we anticipate new themes and new subjects coming to the fore in the Judaism and health field, especially as a result of more systematic evaluations of programmatic efforts in the Jewish community and more focused research studies on health and well-being among Jewish populations. Some authors secretly hope that their book will be known as "the first and last word" on a given topic. Our hope, instead, is that *Judaism and Health* will represent a beginning and will point the way to more future paths—and publications—than we can currently imagine.

❖

Part I

Judaism, Medicine, and Healing

History of Jews in Medicine and Healthcare

Fred Rosner, MD, MACP

As noted by Dr. Shimon Glick in his foreword to my book *Pioneers in Jewish Medical Ethics*:

> Throughout the millennia, Judaism and medicine have marched hand-in-hand as allies, not as rivals. The mainstream of Jewish tradition has placed an enormous value on human life and health, has given human beings an obligation to preserve life and health, and has pursued a dual track of encouraging recognized medical therapy together with faith in the Almighty. Judaism has also, for the most part, rejected all varieties of dualism and of dualism and rivalries between the body and the spirit, maintaining rather that spiritual progress can be enhanced by a healthy body. Our ancients already had insights, as well, into preventive medicine and behavioral medicine.[1]

Still, we are reminded that the study of Judaism and medicine is not a recent phenomenon. Jews have been studying, writing about, and practicing ethical medicine for thousands of years. The Jewish tradition dates back to Mount Sinai and is perhaps the longest unbroken tradition that is still followed by its adherents.

Because Judaism and medicine enjoy historical and intellectual kinships, it is only natural that Jewish law is best qualified to apply its reasoned pragmatic rules of morality to the practice of medicine. In the words of Rabbi Lord Immanuel Jakobovits:

> For many centuries rabbis and physicians, often merging their professions into one, were intimate partners in a common effort

---

Fred Rosner, MD, MACP, is a professor of medicine at Icahn School of Medicine at Mount Sinai in New York, New York.

> for the betterment of life. The perplexities of our age challenge them to renew their association in the service of human life, health and dignity. Indeed, they challenge Judaism itself to reassert its place as a potent force in the moral advancement of humanity.[2]

Originally, medical and spiritual diagnosticians in Judaism were one and the same, namely priests. As the separation of these functions progressed with time, we had physicians and rabbis. In the Talmud, such dual figures are cited, the most famous of whom are Mar Samuel the physician and Todos the physician. In the Middle Ages, several very prominent Jews were both physicians and rabbis. Among the most renowned are Moses Maimonides and his son Abraham, Nachmanides (also known as Ramban), and Rabbi Judah Halevi.[3]

The reason so many Jews chose medicine as a profession was that nearly all other fields were closed to them by papal decree or by outright anti-Semitism.[4] Only in the last two or three centuries have banking and business become available to Jews to choose as professions. Jewish Nobel Prize winners in medicine and other sciences far outnumber their proportion of the world's population, beginning with Karl Landsteiner, for his discovery of blood groups in 1910, and subsequently the fugitive from Nazi Germany Albert Einstein, for his theory of relativity. Many other Jewish physicians and scientists are Nobel laureates.

Historical Background

In a recent article, Jeff Levin and Michele F. Prince reflect on Judaism and health as an emerging scholarly field, and they describe the recently formed Kalsman Institute on Judaism and Health in Los Angeles. These authors trace the history of discourse on health and healing within Judaism, from the biblical and Rabbinic eras to contemporary research and writing on Jewish bioethics, pastoral care, communal services, and aging, including congregational and community planning and programming related to health and illness and the emergence of the Jewish healing movement.[5] Other recent reviews expand on these themes.

Norman R. Goodman, Jeffrey L. Goodman, and Walter I. Hofman review some of the religious writings, legal precedents, and forensic authorities that may assist the medical examiner or coroner when confronted with a Jewish decedent.[6] The authors conclude that the final consent for autopsy and interpretation of the rules, laws, traditions, and customs will rest with the courts and local rabbinic authorities.

Marios Loukas and colleagues review surgery in early Jewish history.[7] The authors conclude from their review that ancient Hebrew texts pay particular attention to the possible use of anesthetics, the environment, and equipment used in surgery, as well as indicating knowledge of infection and hygienic practices. A knowledge and understanding of human morphology was necessary for many of these surgical practices.

Gary H. Brandeis and Daniel J. Oates discuss the Judaic-Christian origin of nursing homes.[8] These authors explore the basis of Jewish and Christian thought in providing background for religiously based nursing homes. Although the underlying principles are similar, conclude the authors, differences exist in approach and execution in the formation of such homes.

Y. Michael Barilan's article entitled "From *Imago Dei* in the Jewish-Christian Traditions to Human Dignity in Contemporary Jewish Law" surveys and analyzes the roles in Judaism of the value of *Imago Dei*/human dignity, especially in bioethical contexts.[9] Two main topics are discussed: first, a comparative analysis of *Imago Dei* as an anthropological and ethical concept in Jewish and Western thought; second, the role of *Imago Dei* as a moral value relative to others. The Rabbinic Judaism respect for human dignity, concludes the author, is not the primary moral maxim; it is secondary to the value of neighborly love and sometimes to other moral laws and values.

Goedele Baeke, Jean-Pierre Wils, and Bert Broeckaert's article with the provocative title "There Is a Time to Be Born and a Time to Die (Ecclesiastes 3:2a): Jewish Perspectives on Euthanasia" reviews the publications of prominent American rabbis who have extensively published on Jewish biomedical ethics.[10] The authors conclude that there is a diversity of opinion within Judaism and its branches.

Daniel B. Sinclair wrote an article whose main theme is the tension between the obligation to preserve life and the value of timely death.[11] Rabbi Sinclair concludes that preventing suffering in relation to a dying person by praying for his or her death is permitted. Preventing suffering is also discussed by Benjamin O. Gesundheit and colleagues in the article "Treatment of Depression by Maimonides (1138–1204): Rabbi,

Physician, and Philosopher."[12] The authors conclude that potent ethical values, such as patient autonomy and medical obligations versus religious commandments, are found in Maimonides's "Medical Letter," and they detail many of these ethical issues.

Donna Evleth examines the way in which the Jewish question was handled in Vichy France, in 1940–1944.[13] She discusses the circumstances that led to the inevitable defeat of the "Superior Council."

The Grovingen Protocol, introduced by P. J. Sauer in 2005, proposes criteria allowing active euthanasia for seriously ill, not necessarily terminal, newborns with incurable conditions and poor quality of life in order to spare them unbearable suffering.[14] Gesundheit and his colleagues discuss the protocol and the views of its defenders and critics. They point out that this protocol violates numerous Jewish laws, and they urge their colleagues in the Netherlands to reconsider it and revise or withdraw it.

Still other reviews touch on important historical issues and themes. Zohar Amar and Efraim Lev provide an "Early Glimpse at Western Medicine in Jerusalem 1700–1840."[15] Fred Rosner discusses the ethical dilemmas of an observant Jewish physician working in a secular ethical society.[16] William P. Cheshire, Jr. discusses the ethical origins of the hospital in the Jewish and Christian traditions, from the biblical Abraham's hospitality through the biblical "Love your neighbor as yourself" (Leviticus 19:18), the New Testament ministry of healing in the Christian tradition, the monastic hospitals in the Christian Middle Ages, and the modern day, where tertiary care hospitals represent the "very crown of medical achievement."[17] In these multispecialty centers, rigorous education is combined with innovative research, as altruistic men and women skillfully apply cutting-edge technology to the care of patients in the ongoing fight against disease.

Finally, one of the greatest Talmudic scholars of the twentieth century was Rabbi Shlomo Zalman Auerbach, of blessed memory. Many of his medical halakhic decisions have been assembled by his disciple Rabbi Dr. Abraham Steinberg.[18] These decisions were always rendered in accord with classical sources in Judaism. Several major texts on Jewish medical ethics from a halakhic perspective have been published in recent years for the interested reader.[19]

Jewish Medical Ethics

The emergence of Jewish medical ethics as a distinct subspecialty within Jewish thought is a relatively recent phenomenon. Jakobovits's doctoral dissertation at the University of London in 1955, published as *Jewish Medical Ethics* by New York's Philosophical Library in 1959, was the first use of the phrase "Jewish medical ethics."[20] This landmark monograph was a revolutionary publication, not merely because the term or concept of Jewish medical ethics was unknown at that time, but because the subject itself had been entirely unexplored and left without any literary or scholarly expression in any Western language. Physicians, medical students, and other interested parties had no writings to consult to familiarize themselves with Jewish views even on such elementary subjects as abortion, contraception, euthanasia, and autopsy. Only a handful of people, mostly rabbis, could consult the original Hebrew and/or Aramaic sources scattered in Rabbinic writings.

Rabbi Jakobovits was also outspoken in the House of Lords, where he preached the traditional values of religion and morality, the importance of ethical conduct, the dignity of labor, and the primacy of family. He was a brilliant communicator with an elegant command of the English language, which matched his majestic physical appearance.

In a widely reported speech he delivered in the House of Lords against a plan to allow commercial activities on Sundays, Rabbi Jakobivits said, "The loss of the Sabbath will deprive Britain of the last visible vestige of national spirituality and sanctification." The silence in the House of Lords was broken by an Anglican admirer who shouted down from the gallery, "But it takes a Jew to tell you that."[21]

At the establishment of the Rabbi Immanuel Jakobovits Center of Jewish Medical Ethics at Ben-Gurion University in Beer Sheva, Israel, in 1983, Rabbi Jakobovits said, in part:

> Jewish doctors ought to have some idea of where Jewish teachings differ from commonly accepted norms of medical practice; for instance, the reluctance to inform patients of a fatal diagnosis if there is the slightest fear that such information may cause a physical or mental trauma; or the need to set the saving of life above the patient's consent; or the limits of professional secrecy when overriding third party or public interests are at stake, such

> as undisclosed genetic defects in a person planning marriage, or suppressed medical records liable to cause grave public hazards through violence, crime, or illness. In all these cases, the teachings of Jewish ethics are quite distinct, and Jewish doctors ought to be aware of them.[22]

The secular medical literature also reports on various aspects of Jewish medical practice and ethics.[23] A more detailed discussion of Jewish medical ethics can be found in Rabbi David A. Teutsch's chapter, "An Overview of Jewish Bioethics."

Conclusions

Since antiquity, throughout the history of mankind, and especially since the Middle Ages when such illustrious rabbi-physicians as Maimonides, Nachmanides, and Judah Halevi flourished, Jews have always held medicine and public health to be cornerstones of the Jewish tradition and medical practice. The material briefly summarized in this chapter demonstrates the high esteem and value placed by Jews on the practice of medicine and on medical ethics.

For much of history, as noted earlier, Jews were excluded from many professions because of discrimination and anti-Semitism. For the past two centuries, doors have opened wide to give Jews access to many endeavors, including, of course, the study and practice of medicine, which are based on biblical and Rabbinic laws and mandates. Especially important has been the inauguration of Jewish medical ethics as a distinct field by Jakobovits in the classic *Jewish Medical Ethics*. Alongside evolving Roman Catholic and secular medical ethical systems, emphasizing the general principles of autonomy, beneficence, non-malfeasance, and justice, among others, the new field of biomedical ethics has been catapulted to the forefront by scientific and technological advances occurring in recent years. This is a challenge for theologians and biomedical ethicists, who have not yet caught up in their ethical assessment with rapid scientific and technological advances in neonatal care, end-of-life care, resuscitative measures, organ transplants, and assisted reproduction. These are just a few of the topics that require intense religious, moral, theological, philosophical, and legal discussion and analysis.

Continued scholarly interest in the history of Jews and medicine and of Jewish medical ethics is evidenced by the ongoing publication of notable review articles. These include titles such as "Medicine and Judaism: An Overview,"[24] "The Physician in the Talmudic Period: Between Technie and Halakhah,"[25] "Milestones in Jewish Medical Ethics: Medical Halachic Literature in Israel, 1948–1998,"[26] "Halakhic Dilemmas in Modern Medicine,"[27] "The Embryo in Ancient Rabbinic Literature: Between Religious Law and Didactic Narratives; An Interpretive Essay,"[28] "Abortion—The Breath of Life,"[29] and "Hippocrates, Maimonides and the Doctor's Responsibility."[30]

Any history of Jewish contributions to medicine and healthcare would be incomplete without mention of the deontological oaths and prayers composed by such renowned physicians as Judah Halevi,[31] Jacob Zahalon,[32] and Abraham Zacuntus,[33] as well as the physician's prayer attributed to Moses Maimonides.[34] These are deeply moving and pious prayers of gratitude for divine help and recognition that *Adonai* in heaven is the Ultimate Healer of the sick who granted Jewish physicians a divine right to heal the sick.

At the Bedside in the Babylonian Talmud

Reflections on Classical Rabbinic Healers and Their Approaches to Helping the Suffering

Rabbi Simkha Y. Weintraub, LCSW

The Rabbis of the Talmud and the Midrash had many roles: scholars and teachers, communal and political leaders, scribes and interpreters. While many devoted their lives almost exclusively to Torah and education, the yeshivot of old encouraged students to pursue an occupation, if only not to be dependent on the community for support. Gamliel III, the second- to third-century Palestinian *tanna* and the oldest son of Rabbi Yehudah HaNasi, is quoted as saying, "It is good to combine the study of Torah with a worldly occupation, for the two together can keep one from sin."[1]

Some *tanna'im* and *amora'im* were supported by wealthy families, others had their own profitable ventures, and most seem to have earned a modest living as laborers or artisans. The list of skills and occupations is surprisingly diverse: engineer, wine merchant, farmer, gravedigger, beer brewer, shoemaker, carpenter, tailor, and even gladiator, to name just a few.

But certain sages—whatever their source of livelihood—seem to have excelled in the role that we might call "healer." There were, to be sure, a good number of rabbis who were physicians (Shmuel, second- to third-century Babylonian *amora* was arguably the most distinguished) and cuppers (e.g., Abba Umana, fourth-century Babylonian

Rabbi Simkha Y. Weintraub, LCSW, is rabbinic director of the National Center for Jewish Healing, a program of the Jewish Board of Family and Children's Services in New York, New York.

amora), but it is striking that no class of "healing rabbis" seems to have been identified as such—or at least we have no record of such a group or label. Nonetheless, *aggadot* about the visits and interactions of great "healers" with suffering individuals (including colleagues) resonate many centuries later, because of their success in caring if not in curing, in strengthening the spirits of those confronting painful, debilitating illnesses if not in bringing about physiological improvement. It behooves us to closely read these stories and draw out their models and guidance for our own rabbinic counseling and spiritual care of those who suffer.

Let's begin with three narratives from the Talmud that involve Rabbi Johanan:

> Rabbi Hiyya bar Abba fell ill, and Rabbi Johanan went in to visit him. He [Rabbi Johanan] said to him, "Are your sufferings welcome/beloved to you?" He replied, "Neither they nor their reward." He said to him, "Give me your hand." He gave him his hand and he [Rabbi Johanan] raised [healed] him.
>
> Rabbi Johanan once fell ill, and Rabbi Hanina went in to visit him. He [Rabbi Hanina] said to him, "Are your sufferings welcome/beloved to you?" He replied, "Neither they nor their reward." He said to him, "Give me your hand." He gave him his hand and he raised him. *Why could not Rabbi Johanan raise himself?* They replied, "The prisoner cannot free himself from jail."
>
> Rabbi Elazar fell ill, and Rabbi Johanan went in to visit him. He [Rabbi Johanan] noticed that he was lying in a dark room, and he [Rabbi Johanan] bared his arm and light radiated from it. Thereupon he noticed that Rabbi Elazar was weeping, and he said to him, "Why do you weep? *Is it because you did not study enough Torah?* Surely we learned: The one who sacrifices much and the one who sacrifices little have the same merit, provided that the heart is directed to heaven. *Is it perhaps lack of sustenance?* Not everybody has the privilege to enjoy two tables. *Is it perhaps because of the lack of children?* This is the bone of my tenth son!" He replied to him, "I am weeping on account of this beauty that is going to rot in the earth." He said to him, "On that account you surely have a reason to weep," and they both wept. In the meanwhile he said to

him, "Are your sufferings welcome/beloved to you?" He replied, "Neither they nor their reward." He said to him, "Give me your hand," and he gave him his hand and he raised him.[2]

These three *aggadot* involving Rabbi Johanan, the third-century Palestinian *tanna*, certainly one of the leading "healers" in the Talmud, became the "Bible" of the Jewish healing movement in its earliest years, abounding in lessons for those seeking to help. The three sages who appear with Rabbi Johanan are very much a part of his life—Rabbi Hiyya bar Abba and Rabbi Elazar left Babylonia and became students of Rabbi Johanan, and Rabbi Hanina, also originally from Babylonia, migrated to Israel and became Rabbi Johanan's teacher. The fact that these three stories entail generations surrounding Rabbi Johanan adds to a sense of wholeness and completeness; it is, *l'havdil* (with some difference), like having a "patriarchal" thread linking Abraham, Isaac, and Jacob.

Permit me here just to summarize some of the many, many Jewish spiritual care lessons implicit in these rich narratives, specifically concerning the provision of rabbinic and spiritual care to those who are suffering.

Showing Up with an Eye to Uplifting

The first story—very terse, and serving as a narrative template for the other two—opens with the "healer" zooming in to visit a colleague who is ill. The Aramaic phrase used in these (and other) narratives for "coming to visit the sick" is *al legabeih*, which idiomatically means "entered" but echoes the Hebrew *alah*, "went up." This is striking, since we know that the very ill were typically on bed-like platforms that were down below, close to the ground (and not raised up or elevated, as our contemporary hospital beds provide)—so what we have is the active, moving visitor "going up" to see the one who is actually "down there." The visit, which might technically be portrayed as a "descent," is instead described or choreographed as an "ascent." That is touching in itself, but we will soon see that each of these three stories ends with a "raising" by the visitor, so it is not too much to extrapolate that the lifting up—of spirits, if not of red blood cell counts—was furthered by a conscious, respectful approach. That is, rather than envisioning an encounter that drags him down, we may imagine that

Rabbi Johanan is able to consider, and even to consciously reach for, growth and climbing, some sort of elevation, advancing, bringing up.

Open to the Truth of the Sufferer

This zealous approach to *bikkur cholim* is laudable, of course, since we have other narratives in which the neglect of this *mitzvah* is denounced as akin to homicide![3] But caring requires not just a physical "showing up," but a true presence and engagement, and it is in that light that we hear the first words from Rabbi Johanan's mouth, a provocative question: *Are your sufferings welcome/beloved to you?* To our ears, the query may initially be a bit confusing or off-putting, until we consider that on the previous page of the Gemara, sages were exploring the question of why there is suffering. Among the ideas discussed is that sufferings represent *yissurin shel ahavah* ("chastisements of [God's] love"), including the possibility that sufferings are a form of love, as they atone for sins and hence pave the way for redemption. Rabbi Johanan asks his colleague a question that relates to these deliberations. This question is deceivingly simple (is it about meaning? coping? spirit? perhaps sarcasm?), but immediately it yields an honest reply: these sufferings are *not acceptable*, even if they may yield some major reward. Stunningly, we see that the responder need not feign some accepted understanding or false piety; he is allowed, truly encouraged, to tell it like it is. This affirmation betrays the speaker's membership in what Dr. Ruhama Weiss has termed the "Underground against Suffering,"[4] and it frees him to rejoin with the living in an honest manner, without artifice or masquerade.

Cementing the Joining through Touch

With that joining—a spiritual companionship defined by the absence of forced acquiescence and not requiring insincere submission—Rabbi Johanan next offers the possibility of connecting through touch; he does not impose this on his ill colleague, but recommends it (we can imagine him extending his hand as he speaks). Through the added dimension of touch and physical relationship—a "post-verbal" or "meta-verbal" rapport—some kind of healing, some "raising" takes place. Space does not allow for much discussion about healing/therapeutic touch in these pages, but this hand-holding seems to have "sealed the deal," furthering reassurance and comfort, if not a physiological transfer of positive, healing energy.

Touch, of course, conveys most directly that one is not alone, that even though our bodies are discrete, our spirits interflow. Perhaps the "raising" or "lifting up" was a restoration to the land of the living or at least a temporary transcending of the isolation and disconnection that serious illness so often yields.

The Wounded Healer and Liberation via Honest Relationship

How useful that in the second story, the "healer" himself falls ill. Although we will soon be reminded (in the third paragraph) that he has been no stranger to suffering, here, in the middle, he simply falls ill. Nothing more and nothing less, like those before and, alas, those after. We are struck by the starkness of this, and it echoes the dismantling of the hierarchy/choreography of "the well hovering over the ill" suggested by the previous story. Now, if you will, Rabbi Johanan is living on the same plane as Rabbi Hiyya bar Abba was previously, and in this state, his response actually becomes identical to his student's. And it makes sense that the one to minister to him now is his own teacher, Rabbi Hanina, who actually has no new question to ask. In the end, it is not going to be about words, certainly not about magical "fix-it" words; what is critical is presence, fellow travelers, allies, witnesses—*truth*.

The Talmud asks a question that helping people certainly need to revisit periodically: why couldn't the great healer heal him- or herself? And the answer points to *a*, maybe *the*, major point in Jewish healing, and that is, "The prisoner cannot free him- or herself from jail"—meaning, yet again, that community, connection, and relationship are of the essence. It is not this or that practice or this or that script that helps, but sensing divine care and compassion through the divine image, through fellow human beings. The keys to the prison cell are, in a certain sense, in the hands of fellow inmates![5]

Bringing Our Wounded Selves Fully

The third paragraph breaks the narrative mold, but before saying anything else, it is important to underscore that every reading of a text is a midrash, a commentary, on it—and so this writer can only truly attest to what he sees/reads in the text. Humility demands that I affirm that there may be very different takes on this paragraph, but, to my mind, the weeping of his devoted student, Rabbi Elazar, was particularly challenging for Rabbi Johanan and caused him to want to fix things—an understandable but also problematic and, alas, persistent pitfall in spiritual care. Nervously, I believe, Rabbi Johanan asks about—perhaps, *projects*—three concerns that, in classical Judaism, were the subjects of personal prayer: Torah, livelihood, and children.

With the first two, he dismisses them by offering a teaching, an aphorism, to countervail any imagined inadequacy or felt failure; we might generously see it as "cognitive therapy" or reframing.[6] But when he gets to the third concern, about children, Rabbi Johanan is catapulted into his own inner reality, his personal narrative, his own struggles and resources, and he apparently pulls out the small bone (from his tenth child who died) that he is known to have carried on him. *The healer, in other words, shares his own ghastly (and open?) wound with the patient.* Although we do not know precisely what Rabbi Johanan was experiencing—did the serious illness of another young student/colleague trigger a rekindling of his own intolerable losses?—we know that the visitee now responds to him with profound honesty, directness, and power: "I am weeping on account of this beauty that is going to rot in the earth." This is a dust-to-dust statement, an existential assertion—about mortality and the human condition, about the very nature of life—which brings them very, very close to each other.

Mutual Weeping and Fellow Traveling: Sharing Vulnerability

With Rabbi Johanan having dug deeply into himself, and Rabbi Elazar responding with clarity and depth, a profound emotional meeting has transpired. Instead of "cleaning up" or "explaining away" the weeping, Rabbi Johanan now affirms that there is, indeed, good reason to weep, and so they move beyond left-brain cogitation and into fraternal bonding, perhaps mirroring. Joining on a deeply human level, they are truly present for each other, and the categories of "healer" and "healee" have melted away into the shared status of fragile, ephemeral mortal.

My teacher, colleague, and friend Rabbi Tsvi Blanchard once taught from Maimonides that the essence of *bikkur cholim*, the heart of reaching out to those who suffer, is *shared vulnerability*—the mutual connection of visitor and visitee, not necessarily in having the same troubles, the same diagnoses, the exact same experiences, but rather a common link of mortality, of exposure, of need, and of concern, love, and support.[7] It is precisely because Rabbi Johanan ultimately brings himself so fully to the visit that Rabbi Elazar can do the same, and the two, almost as a "healing *chavruta*," can move together to both grieving and healing.

Chronic Suffering

Let us shift now to another classical narrative involving these great "healers" for some additional guidance about rabbinic and spiritual care, this time from a later midrashic source, commenting on a line of biblical love poetry:

> *"My beloved is mine, and I am his; he pastures his flock among the lilies"* [Song of Songs 2:16]: Rabbi Johanan had the misfortune [lit., "was chastised," from heaven] to suffer from gallstones for three and a half years. Once Rabbi Hanina went to visit him. He said to him, "How do you feel?" He replied, "My sufferings are worse than I can bear!" He said to him, "Don't speak so, but say, 'The faithful God.'" When the pain was very great he used to say, "Faithful God," and when the pain was greater than he could bear, Rabbi Hanina used to go to him and utter an incantation that gave him relief. Subsequently Rabbi Hanina fell ill, and Rabbi Johanan went to see him. He said to him, "How do you feel?" He replied, "How grievous are my sufferings!" He said to him, "But surely the reward for them is also great!" He replied, "I want neither them nor their reward." He said to him, "Why do you not utter that incantation that you pronounced over me and that gave me relief?" He replied, "When I was out of trouble I could be a surety for others, but now that I am myself in trouble do I not require another to be a surety for me?" He said to him, "It is written, 'pastures ... among the lilies': this means that the rod of the Holy One, blessed be He, lights only upon men whose heart is pliant like lilies."[8]

Though elements of this story echo our previous narratives from the Talmud, we might note some significant differences and new directions.

The Efficacy of Words?

The first part of our story focuses on Rabbi Johanan's experience of painful suffering that persisted for three and a half years; the Aramaic original uses the verb *ityaser*, "was chastised," echoing the discussion mentioned earlier about the notion of *yissurin shel ahavah*, "chastisements of [God's] love." Although the visitor's question this time is a bit more open-ended and perhaps less provocative (more like, "How do you feel?" and not, "Are your sufferings beloved to you?"), the truth is that the patient, Rabbi Johanan, is as direct and straightforward as before and shares honestly that his sufferings are "off the charts." This time, the rabbi in the healing position, Rabbi Johanan's teacher, Hanina, *instructs*; he recommends (prescribes?) a mantra of sorts, which apparently helps when the pain is very great. But when the pain soars beyond a "10," more than Rabbi Johanan can bear, Rabbi Hanina utters a *milah*, a "word" or an incantation, which somehow provides relief.

This surprises us, as we may have gleaned from the previous Talmud stories that healing, in fact, is distinctly unrelated to words and often derives more from hand-holding or mutual weeping. How/why do words seem to work here? Though we do not know precisely, of course, (and we may be shocked that a visitor appears to tell a sick individual—his student—not to speak his mind/heart), it seems that Rabbi Johanan is receptive to the suggestion and finds it useful, at least some of the time. Some ideas for how this might have helped:

- Perhaps this intervention of Rabbi Hanina's speaks to his refocusing Rabbi Johanan, not unlike the "reframing" of cognitive-behavioral therapy: "Don't focus on the unbearable sufferings, but on the faithful God."
- The healing may have been more in the music than in the lyrics, not unlike the use of *niggunim* (chants), which can helpfully impact breathing, inspire or distract patients, restore a connection to the community and to the present moment, and empower the sufferer.
- Studies about effective placebos have suggested that they often work in/thanks to a particularly trusting relationship between the patient and prescribing physician; here,

> the student (Johanan) believes in the teacher (Hanina) and so can benefit from his direction.

In any event, we can see these were not as a one-size-fits-all prescription but a sincere and personalized gift: "Here's something I hope can be of help to you."

Standing In for the Suffering

As in the Talmud stories, the healer becomes the patient and vice versa in our present narrative, and the pious acceptance of the suffering's "reward" is similarly rejected. Whereas in the Talmud story the Gemara taught, in response to why the healer could not heal himself, that "the prisoner cannot free himself from jail," here the question is posed in terms of the healing tool: why could not the now-ill healer use the incantation for his own self, just as he had successfully used it with others before? It makes sense that in our present story, in which a particular incantation proved efficacious, the question is framed in terms of that very intervention, but once again the response stresses that the healing takes place *in terms of relationship*, and a very particular one at that: that of an *eiravon*, the visitor as a "pledge" or "security." This Hebrew word, in fact, is loaded with associations, among them a guarantee, a deposit, a bond, and even a "stand-in."[9]

So we've now articulated a new dimension, a new (but very old) possibility in rabbinic counseling and spiritual care. Whereas before we spoke of, if you will, standing *with* or *next to* the one who is suffering, now we are considering standing *in*. Obviously we cannot (and should not pretend or attempt to) take on an individual's illness or pain, but we can certainly represent his or her interests and advocate both on earth and vis-à-vis heaven for the person's well-being and healing (again, spiritually if not physiologically or materially). Perhaps this is how "one-sixtieth of suffering is removed"[10]—by one spirit's willingness to present itself as a pledge, a deposit for the other.

The Potential of Prayer

The reader might at this point be wondering what are the tools of the trade—what do classical narratives present as spiritual apparatuses to utilize, assuming the critical positions of mutuality and advocacy are in place? One, of course, is prayer, so let us consider one of a number of *aggadot* in the Talmud that relate to healing prayer in rabbinic counseling and spiritual care.

> Our Rabbis taught: Once the son of Rabban Gamliel fell ill. He sent two scholars to Rabbi Hanina ben Dosa to ask him to pray for him. When he saw them, he went up to an upper chamber and prayed for him. When he came down, he said to them, "Go, the fever has left him." They said to him, "Are you a prophet?" He replied, "I am neither a prophet nor the son of a prophet, but I learned this from experience. If my prayer is fluent in my mouth, I know that he is accepted; but if not, I know that he is rejected." They sat down and made a note of the exact moment. When they came to Rabban Gamliel, he said to them, "By the temple service! You have not been a moment too soon or too late, but so it happened: at that very moment the fever left him and he asked for water to drink."
>
> On another occasion it happened that Rabbi Hanina ben Dosa went to study Torah with Rabbi Johanan ben Zakkai. The son of Rabbi Johanan ben Zakkai fell ill. He said to him, "Hanina my son, pray for him that he may live!" He put his head between his knees and prayed for him, and he lived. Said Rabbi Johanan ben Zakkai, "If Ben Zakkai had stuck his head between his knees for the whole day, no notice would have been taken of him." Said his wife to him, "Is Hanina greater than you are?" He replied to her, "No; but he is like a servant before the king, and I am like a nobleman before a king."[11]

Jewish tradition instructs that a critical component of supporting those who are suffering is prayer; indeed, we have not fulfilled our obligations in *bikkur cholim* if we have not prayed on behalf of the one who is ill.[12] But *how*? It is beyond the scope of this chapter to fully develop this, but we can observe from this narrative that essential to this piece of the puzzle are the elements of sincerity, fluency, focus, humility, and, yet again, relatedness. As Rabbi Johanan ben Zakkai explains to his wife, Hanina ben Dosa, because of his constant "service to the king," is heard and listened to regularly, whereas one who is a nobleman, perhaps ironically, has less fluid, informal access to the king. Related, then, to the "wounded healer" idea is that rabbis and spiritual care providers, when they pray for those who are suffering, must assume the stance of the *eved lifnei HaMelekh*, the servant before the King, rather than the *sar lifnei HaMelekh,* the nobleman before the King. Our words must be part of humble service, not the entitled petition of an aristocrat!

But Torah Is Where It's At ...

As important as prayer is, the model of Rabbi Joshua ben Levi (third-century Palestinian *amora*) illustrates a very particular, and very Jewish, element in the rabbinic pastoral toolbox. On one page of the Talmud, there is a very graphic description of a horrible disease called *ra'atan*, followed by a truly harrowing description of the treatment that was offered some eighteen hundred years ago. Then we read the following:

> Rabbi Johanan announced: Beware of the flies of one afflicted with *ra'atan*. Rav Zera never sat [with such a sufferer] in the same draft. Rabbi Elazar never entered his tent. Rav Ammi and Rav Assi never ate any of the eggs coming from the alley in which he lived. Rabbi Joshua ben Levi, however, attached himself to these [sufferers] and studied the Torah [with them]; for he said, "'Let her be like a loving hind and a graceful doe' [Proverbs 5:19].[13] If [the Torah] bestows grace upon those who study it, would it not also protect them?"[14]

Painfully, the individuals suffering from *ra'atan* seem to have been highly isolated and even stigmatized, so that even some very great rabbis avoided them and anything near them. But Rabbi Joshua ben Levi—who is subsequently rewarded by God, who directs the Angel of Death to show him his ultimate, reserved place in paradise!—"attached himself to these [sufferers] and studied the Torah [with them]." We, who generally do not have to be concerned about contagion thanks to scientific understandings and medical procedures, nonetheless confront the physical, social, or spiritual isolation, and shame, of those who suffer, and we know that so many want and need Torah, which is our Tree of Life. The description of Rabbi Joshua ben Levi and the sufferers of *ra'atan* remind us to always turn to Torah in our rabbinic counseling and spiritual care, even when it might seem irrelevant or far-fetched. Note that no specific texts, topics, or lessons are itemized; it seems that the very process of joining in Torah study is what is "healing."

Concluding with a Cautionary Tale

All the preceding stories stem from Talmudic or midrashic sources no later than the fifth to sixth century. Let us stretch just a couple of centuries closer to our times for a cautionary tale:

> Rabbi Shimon bar Yohai used to visit the sick. He once met a man who was swollen and afflicted with intestinal disease, uttering blasphemies against God. Said Rabbi Shimon, "Worthless one! Pray rather for mercy for yourself!" Said the patient, "May God remove these sufferings from me and place them upon you."[15]

This is a spiritual "do no harm" admonition if ever there was one! It features the great Rabbi Shimon bar Yohai, the second-century Palestinian *tanna* who was both a major scholar and, reputedly, a miracle worker. Despite his learning, ethical sensibilities, and political courage, we see that he—and how much more so we—needed this reminder that people afflicted with serious illness may well utter blasphemies against God, and the rabbinic counselor or spiritual care provider must not demean but listen to their cries. God, after all, can defend Godself! To further emphasize this, let us end with a teaching of the Sassover Rebbe, just two hundred years ago:

> *Even the denial of God can serve God.*
> *If a person should come to you and ask for help,*
> *you should not put him off with pious words, saying,*
> *"Have faith and take your troubles to God,"*
> *but you should act as if there were no God at all,*
> *as if there was only one person in the world*
> *who could help this person—*
> *yourself.*[16]

❖

An Overview of Jewish Bioethics

Rabbi David A. Teutsch, PhD

Everyone sooner or later has ethical questions about maintaining health and about medical decisions. Secular bioethics deals with those questions. However, the responses to many questions will differ depending on the values, norms, definitions of key terms, and decision-making methods that decision makers bring to bear. Jewish bioethics is distinctive because of the resources developed over the centuries within Jewish tradition and culture that Jewish bioethicists apply. The commitments to preserving life and maintaining human dignity and the definition of life as beginning at birth (and not before) are examples of the Jewish approach that have major ramifications for bioethics.

It is helpful for Jews to familiarize themselves with key ideas and practices of Jewish bioethics and the reasons for them so that the resulting insights can guide their personal choices and shape how they interact around these questions with their families. For social workers, nurses, doctors, and chaplains, learning about Jewish bioethics can help them interact more helpfully with Jewish patients who look to them for guidance. And, of course, such learning may also deepen the thoughtfulness of such professionals, whether they are Jewish or not, around the difficult questions that they confront in their work. With those purposes in mind, what follows is a brief summary of Jewish bioethics. All the topics surveyed below are dealt with in great depth in the current Jewish bioethics literature.

Rabbi David A. Teutsch, PhD, is the Louis and Myra Wiener Professor of Contemporary Jewish Civilization; chair of the Department of Contemporary Jewish Civilization; and director of the Levin-Lieber Program in Jewish Ethics at Reconstructionist Rabbinical College in Wyncote, Pennsylvania.

The Importance of Health

Health (*b'riyut*) is one of our most valued gifts, and preserving life (*pikuach nefesh*) is one of the highest duties in Jewish tradition. Virtually any activity or *mitzvah* should be set aside in order to save a life. Closely related to this obligation is the duty to heal, the duty to restore oneself and others to health. Another duty, that of self-care, stems from the idea that the world is God's, as is everything in it (*l'Adonai ha'aretz um'loah*; Psalm 24:1). According to classical Rabbinic thought, our existence as creatures carries an obligation to do the will of the Creator. Acknowledging the interdependence of our lives generates an obligation to care for ourselves as part of our obligation to others.

Jewish tradition regards healing (*r'fuah*) as a duty that one has both to oneself and to others. By contrast, North American culture talks about the right to healthcare without recognizing a duty of individuals to provide healing, which complicates the ongoing American debate about who is responsible for how much healthcare provision. Seeing healing as a duty would shift the American debate. Jewish tradition sees the duty to heal as incumbent on every individual, as well as on society as a whole.

The positive attitude of Judaism toward science supports the idea that through what we learn we can all become God's partners as healers (*rofeh cholim*). As medical science steadily becomes more efficacious in responding to illness and injury, the work of medical professionals becomes ever more central to the *mitzvah* of healing.

The concepts of *b'riyut*, *pikuach nefesh*, and *r'fuah*, together with the possibilities of medical science, frame Jewish medical ethics, which must be applied in the best interest of the patient (*l'tovato*). But who decides what is *l'tovato*? When people are clearheaded and well informed, they are the best arbiters of what is *l'tovato/a*, in their individual best interest. Only they have the feelings, attitudes, experiences, and relationships that shape their personal decisions about best interests. When patients' decision-making capacities are impaired, their agents seek their best interest. Acting in another's best interest requires extensive conversation while the person is clear-minded, so that the patient's perspective has been fully explored.

How best to decide what is in a patient's best interest is the subject of the ethical exploration of medical issues that follows.

Cultural Differences

The context for this discussion is early twenty-first-century American Jewry. The availability of advanced healthcare, the educational sophistication of most American Jews, and the high value placed on autonomy in our culture all shape the approach taken here. In different times and places, and especially in different cultures, the weighting of values and their application could be considerably different. No timeless, pure medical ethics exists. Any ethic has a context within which its application works well and other contexts within which that application would be dysfunctional.

Maintaining Health

Judaism mandates protecting our own health. Maintaining a nutritious diet without overeating, sleeping sufficiently, exercising regularly, using prophylactic measures during sexual activity, and obtaining regular medical and dental care are part of self-maintenance. Ordinarily doing something that might put our lives at risk violates the prohibition against taking a life. Avoiding such destructive behaviors as drinking to excess and smoking tobacco plays a part in the fulfillment of this *mitzvah*. Preserving our health allows us to enjoy our lives and accomplish our tasks in the world.

The Patient-Physician Relationship

Excellent healthcare requires sound communication. Learning how to talk openly not only aids the free flow of information. It also empowers the patient, who is most able to make healthcare decisions in his or her best interest (*l'tovato*).

Creating a dialogue among patient, physician, and other healthcare workers is a mutual responsibility. It is important for patients to find physicians with whom communication is comfortable, as this supports asking questions, raising issues, and exploring treatment alternatives. It is also vital to have physicians and healthcare workers who explain both the medical situation and its treatment in ways that are fully comprehensible to patients. The importance of communication stems from the Jewish values of truth (*emet*), compassion (*rachamim*), and healing (*r'fuah*). Similar motivations underlie the mandate for informed consent in secular bioethics. Helping people to maintain dignity (*kavod*) and to feel in control empowers them and supports healing.

Telling the Truth

Is full disclosure about health situations always the best approach? One strand of Jewish tradition suggests that in cases of life-threatening illness, the patient should be shielded from the truth about the seriousness of the situation, lest the impact of the news be so great that it disrupts the patient's will to live (*teiruf hada'at*). However, deception and concealment can also create unease and disrupt relationships. Negotiating these challenges requires honesty with the patient about symptoms, prognosis, and possible courses of treatment without specific predictions about the future. Predictions often turn out to be wrong, so making negative predictions to a terminally ill patient often works against everyone's interest.

It is appropriate, however, to suggest that "just in case," every patient should make sure to have an up-to-date will and well-ordered financial affairs and that these should be discussed with appropriate family members or friends.

Patients reach the conclusions that they are ready to absorb as a result of such conversations. Over time, patients can progress through a series of emotional stages and insights that help them and their loved ones to face whatever comes. Meanwhile, the patient should be encouraged to spend as much time as possible with loved ones. It is never wrong to urge a person to make every day count.

Curing

Through surgery, medication, radiation, rehabilitation, and other therapies, patients can return to health after many common illnesses and accidents. Therefore curing is the primary goal of medical intervention, and it should be aggressively pursued as long as there is a reasonable possibility of a return to health.

Once a cure becomes unlikely due to the nature of the specific health problem and/or to irreversible deterioration, the focus should shift to palliative care. Medical experts differ about when the shift from curing to palliating should occur. The goals of preserving any possibility of life and avoiding needless suffering are sometimes in tension with each other. After consultation with the caregiver, the patient or proxy must ultimately make that decision by weighing burdens and benefits in conjunction with personal values. A much fuller exploration of these issues can be found in *Behoref Hayamim*, published by the Reconstructionist Rabbinical College Center for Jewish Ethics.[1]

Body and Spirit

Jewish thought generally treats a living person's body and soul as fully intertwined. What affects the body has an impact on the spirit, and one's spiritual state affects one's health. Preserving the health of others is not solely about the body. One reason that *bikkur cholim* (visiting the sick) is a *mitzvah* is that it is a part of our duty to heal. Lifting a person's spirits can strengthen the body and aid in healing. Prayer can also be an important part of healing. The *Mi Shebeirakh L'cholim* (prayer for the ill) asks for complete healing (*r'fuah sh'leimah*), healing both for the spirit (*nefesh*) and for the body (*guf*).

Sometimes a distinction is made between curing, a medical description, and healing, which includes the spiritual. Healing can take place regardless of the success or the stage of curing. Hospice care focuses effectively on healing when a cure is not possible. Preserving dignity (*kavod*), minimizing pain, and maintaining familial and communal relationships (*mishpachah*, *k'hilah*) are all values that hospice care is designed to uphold. Hospice care has great moral and morale value once the patient or proxy decides that achieving a cure is either impossible or undesirable (usually because the likely suffering from the treatment outweighs its likely benefit).

Pain Management

Minimizing a patient's pain is a highly valuable medical task and a legitimate goal for medication and surgery.

When the course of disease cannot be arrested, palliative care that minimizes pain and maximizes patient comfort is an important goal—and, for many patients at that stage, the most important one. Some patients will balance this goal with their desire to communicate with loved ones, since eliminating pain sometimes requires doses of medication that induce sleep or semiconsciousness. At this stage there is a trade-off between pain mitigation and the patient's mental clarity. When that is the case, the patient's wishes are paramount in deciding how to medicate. Medication that is sufficient to stop the pain can result in a loss of consciousness that precedes death.

When the intent of increasing the dosage of medication for a patient with advanced irreversible illness is to minimize pain, increasing the dosage is the proper thing to do even if this may hasten death.

Euthanasia

The Jewish emphasis on preserving life led to a strong prohibition against suicide, which some Rabbinic sources see as self-inflicted murder. This prohibition extends to euthanasia as well. However, removing impediments that are interfering with the dying process is permitted when it is certain that the patient is dying. Impediments to dying can include the use of respirators and feeding tubes. Hastening death through large doses of pain medication is not considered euthanasia if the intent is pain control. A person certain to die within seventy-two hours is known as a *goseis*; a dying person who might not die in that time frame is called *t'reifah*. There is no obligation to make an effort to delay the death of a *goseis*, but the patient's wishes should guide caregivers' behavior.

Occasionally a baby is born with such severe medical problems that the chances of survival without constant medical intervention are negligible, and the infant's future is likely to be one of constant pain. In such a case, withholding or withdrawing extraordinary medical measures that would preserve the infant's life is the merciful, though tragic, thing to do. That is in the parents' interest and in the community interest, and is *l'tovato*, in the infant's interest. This approach can be applied in the days following birth as medical facts become known; however, after thirty days the infant is seen as a fully viable person who must be treated in a way aimed at sustaining the infant's well-being. One must weigh the benefit of invasive treatments against comfort measures to determine the infant's best interest.

Confidentiality

Jewish advocacy of community coexists with a strong commitment to keeping personal information private. An appropriate level of confidentiality helps to make community more comfortable and workable. Information is shared based on the person's need for others to know. Patient information used to be known only to the patient, doctors, nurses, and, with the patient's permission, family. Now it is known to insurance company personnel, researchers, third-party billing firms, and often the government and a variety of others. The patient's right to privacy, seriously eroded by these changes, deserves community advocacy. At the same time, patients and their families would do well to ensure that their health situations are known to rabbis with whom they have relationships. Many hospitals and nursing homes have a rabbinic chaplain who is available to patients and their families. Chaplains can provide emotional and spiritual support for patients and their families.

Decision Making on Behalf of a Patient

Sometimes patients cannot make decisions for themselves. Dementia, coma, high pain levels, sudden injury, and the effects of medications and anesthesia are some of the reasons for this. Furthermore, very young children are never competent decision makers (although some of them develop that capacity at a surprisingly young age). In such situations, others must step in to make decisions. Family members usually play this role. Individuals can issue a legal document called a durable power of attorney for healthcare (DPAHC) to designate in advance who should make decisions in any situation where they are unable to do so. The potential patient (and we are all potential patients) should confer in advance with the person named in the DPAHC so that the designee can make decisions that the patient perceives as being in his or her "best interest." The potential patient has a moral obligation to have such a conversation for self-protection.

When such a conversation about the patient's understanding of his or her best interest has not taken place, which is almost always the case when the patient is a very young child and frequently the case with adults, the decision makers must use their own judgment. This substituted judgment requires the decision makers to decide based on their own thinking—an option that should be exercised only when guidance from the patient is not available.

One way to avoid substituted judgment is by executing an advance directive in the form of a treatment directive or living will. These provide written guidance regarding how to handle some circumstances. There are so many variables, however, that such a document (now often made available by hospitals and nursing homes) is usually insufficient by itself. It helps when conversations flesh out values and perspectives in advance. Some of these can be written down as well. Copies of these documents must be provided each time a patient moves to a new hospital, nursing home, or rehabilitation facility.

Contraception

Sexual pleasure (*onah*) is valued as a divine gift in Jewish tradition provided that its context is permitted, an issue more fully discussed in the section on sexual and family ethics in my book *A Guide to Jewish Practice*.[2] Sexual ethics and abstinence are discussed there. In Jewish tradition, sexual activity can certainly be enjoyed without having procreation as its goal. Examples of long-accepted uses of contraceptives mentioned in Jewish sources include uses by couples who already have several children and cannot afford more and by couples who are aware that pregnancy would have major ill effects on the woman. Today many Jews take contraceptive measures.

The prevalence of sexually transmitted diseases (STDs) has influenced preferences about contraceptive measures. The Jewish emphasis on preserving health makes condoms the preferred choice outside of a covenanted relationship, because condoms are an effective method of avoiding STDs. Historically, Jewish tradition has rejected onanism, the discharge of semen anywhere other than directly in the vagina, but this view is not held by most contemporary Jews. Masturbation is a normal, pleasurable activity. Therefore we reject the traditional concern with spilling seed (*hash'chatat zera*). We encourage the use of condoms because their use now has a double purpose—preventing conception and protecting from disease. We have an obligation to protect ourselves and our partners from STDs. We are also obliged to protect the rights of those who are HIV-positive.

Other methods of contraception—the use of a diaphragm, spermicide, pills, intrauterine device (IUD), patches, and injections, as well as surgical procedures—must each be evaluated according to health risks, reversibility, and effectiveness. A physician's recommendations should be evaluated in terms of these criteria. Methods meeting these criteria can then be evaluated for comfort, convenience, and aesthetics. Since new methods and medical information continue to emerge, a permanent hierarchy of methods cannot be listed here, but the shifting health risks associated with implants and pills ought to be considered. While Jewish tradition prohibits castration and some traditional authorities object to vasectomy on these grounds, a values-based analysis rejects this consideration, since vasectomy for men is the functional equivalent of tubal ligation for women. Both are sound choices for those certain they will not want to have another child.

If a physician recommends birth control because of a health risk to the woman or to a nursing child, the patient should obey, since *pikuach nefesh*, and even a small possibility of saving a life (*safek pikuach nefesh*), is of high priority.

Infertility and Assisted Reproduction

Many couples who wish to have children discover that they cannot do so without help. Pursuit of a diagnosis of the causes of a couple's infertility is a legitimate medical undertaking. The use of medication and such artificial means as in vitro fertilization to aid in conception is legitimate as long as the risks are carefully examined. Since the conception involves no sexual activity, there is no issue of sexual impropriety.

The use of donor eggs or sperm is an acceptable measure, but a couple considering this step should obtain thorough counseling, since psychological issues are often of concern under these circumstances. Hiring a surrogate mother is an acceptable method of dealing with infertility only when a woman cannot carry a pregnancy to term and the surrogate is prepared for the personal emotional cost of her role. Childbearing should not be commercialized; a reputable agency and legal contracts should be utilized.

A lesbian couple or a single woman may also seek assisted conception, often involving artificial insemination. Potential mothers carefully consider the full implications of childbearing because of the expenditure of effort and financial resources required, and their decision deserves the support of medical personnel, rabbis, families, and Jewish communities.

The obligation to "be fruitful and multiply" does not extend to these measures. They should only be undertaken when people are certain they wish to do so. Adoption is a time-honored alternative for becoming a parent. Some couples choose to remain childless under these circumstances, and they deserve communal support.

Genetic Testing

Several methods of genetic testing now exist, and the number of concerns covered by testing continues to grow rapidly. Testing before marriage or pregnancy can warn of the potential for such diseases as Tay-Sachs in future offspring. A full test for potential disorders can provide information that supports good planning and decision making, particularly when accompanied by genetic counseling. While the negative results of such screening can affect matchmaking in the ultra-Orthodox world, it has little effect on partner selection among other Jews.

Genetic testing can be performed on eggs and sperm to ensure their suitability for use. When a pregnant woman's age or the results of genetic screening suggest its advisability, in utero embryonic testing can take place early in a pregnancy. This testing can help parents to prepare emotionally and practically for the birth of a child who will need special care, such as one with Down syndrome. It can sometimes open the door to in utero surgery that can save the future infant's life. It can also lead to difficult decisions about how to handle the situation when a fetus suffers from a disease like Tay-Sachs. (See the next page for a discussion of abortion.)

Genetic testing can also reveal the likelihood of future disease. For example, the high likelihood of breast cancer for those shown to have a genetic predisposition (BRCA1/2) raises a question as to the advisability of prophylactic mastectomy. Genetic testing can also predict the future onset of Huntington's disease.

Genetic testing is generally a valuable source of information that supports decision making, but the data that it produces need expert interpretation and often supportive counseling to be used properly. Used appropriately, the collection of this data has significant moral and practical value. However, it also carries the danger of misuse if it is employed to determine sex, intelligence, eye color, or the like. (See "Enhancement" below.)

Requiring the genetic testing of employees or for health-insurance screening can be destructive not only to individuals but also to the social fabric. Attempts to require genetic testing should be resisted both individually and on the level of social policy, because such testing can result in employment discrimination, denial of insurance applications, and other forms of social and economic mistreatment.

Abortion

In Jewish tradition, the fetus is taken seriously as a potential life, but Jews have never criminalized abortion. Considering whether to have an abortion is a difficult and emotional experience; having one is sometimes traumatic. Women rarely take abortion lightly. Yet the trauma of some abortions is worse than others. The later in pregnancy an abortion occurs, the more difficult it is. The difficulty intensifies because of the nature of the procedure needed, the physical changes in the woman's body, the development of the fetus, and the woman's emotional attachment to it. Jewish tradition reflects this reality by describing the fetus in the beginning weeks of pregnancy as "water" and in the later stages as "a limb of its mother." According to Jewish tradition, the status of a fetus becomes that of a person only when the fetus becomes visible during the birthing process.

Because of these definitions, the health of the mother takes precedence over preserving the fetus. Indeed, when the fetus threatens the life of the mother, it is considered a *rodeif*, a "pursuer," and any action to help the mother is warranted. While abortion during the "water" stage is preferable, abortion is required at any stage to save the mother's life, and it is permitted to save her from serious injury. Given the complex interaction between physical and mental health, a threat to the mother's emotional well-being can provide a justification for abortion as well, though the impact of the abortion itself requires careful consideration. Cases involving rape or incest also fall into the psychologically devastating category where abortion is permissible.

When a child would have a very short and highly painful life, as is the case with Tay-Sachs disease, abortion is preferable at the earliest possible stage of pregnancy to minimize suffering.

When there are several children in a family and an additional child has the potential to economically destabilize the family or damage the marriage, this, too, is recognized by some traditional authorities as sufficient grounds for an abortion. This reasoning has sometimes been applied when a diagnosis of Down syndrome is made. Since some people with this syndrome lead happy, meaningful lives, the existence of Down syndrome in a fetus is not by itself a sufficient justification for abortion, but other maternal or familial concerns may justify one.

Contemporary women often face difficult decisions if they become pregnant while they are single or establishing their careers. Jewish tradition takes seriously the potential for life in a fetus and rejects these considerations as grounds for abortion by themselves, although the "morning-after pill," which is used before the egg and sperm have joined, can be understood as permitted contraception rather than abortion. In other circumstances, contemporary women can use the framework above, taking psychological and economic hardships into consideration along with the possibility of allowing a child to be adopted.

Enhancement

Most medical practice is aimed at maintaining and restoring health. Repairing a harelip, for example, is as much about health as is clearing a blocked artery. In recent years, medical capabilities have advanced in ways that allow not only the restoration of health but physical enhancement through plastic surgery, manipulation of DNA, the use of drugs such as steroids, and other means.

Jewish tradition teaches appreciation for the full diversity in our world—diversity of species, ages, sizes, shapes, and capacities. Efforts to artificially reduce this wondrous diversity raise questions about motives. While cosmetics have always been used by Jews and can be understood as enhancements, they are by nature temporary and reversible. Most medical enhancements are far from simple to reverse. Some of them carry substantial risk for no medical gain.

Plastic surgery can repair scars and injuries; such interventions constitute healing. Breast augmentation and wrinkle removal exemplify enhancement, although sometimes the line between reconstruction and enhancement is thin. We live in a culture that idealizes some aspects of physical appearance. While physical fitness improves individual appearance, its primary goal is improved health and stamina. Do we want to reinforce the contemporary obsession with physical appearance?

Jews have always honored those who have grown in wisdom and accomplishment through long lives well lived. This reflects a fundamentally different approach from the contemporary idealization of youthful appearance. The costs and risks of most enhancements are difficult to justify. Since the education of physicians and the maintenance of the health system is heavily subsidized by public funds, this is not simply a question of people spending their own money. The pursuit of enhancement has societal costs. The growing use of enhancements creates ever stronger pressure on people to employ them, and many Jews do. Nonetheless, the negative aspects of their use deserve serious consideration.

Medical interventions that create or restore functional capacities, preserve health, or remove disfigurements are not included in this critique of enhancement. This important distinction applies to genetics as well. The genetic testing of embryos to avoid life-shattering deformities and diseases such as Tay-Sachs is a valuable medical measure. Testing to ensure that an embryo is the "right" sex or has some other desired characteristic with the intent of otherwise aborting it is a form of seeking enhancement. Such testing ought to be avoided, and even if the results become known, they should not shape subsequent decisions.

Complementary Treatment

While medical advances are rooted in scientific research, the practice of medicine contains an element of art as well. Virtually any method that cures or heals is permitted. While thoughtful people will differ about the effectiveness and proper use of osteopathy, massage, chiropractic, acupuncture, herbal treatments, and other such interventions, they are permitted as long as the patient believes them to be helpful. They must not be used in place of conventional medical treatments that are usually successful nor used if they are known to have serious side effects. These determinations ought to be made through careful consultation with reliable medical professionals, since informed judgment is critical.

Western scientific explanations for the success of some of these alternative treatments may emerge later. In the meantime, hundreds and, in some cases, thousands of years of experimentation have legitimated some of these methods, as have contemporary American users. An ethical decision to use alternative healing methods must be preceded by an investigation of both conventional and alternative medical techniques: their effectiveness, side effects, and compatibility with each other. Not infrequently the conventional method and complementary treatment can be combined to achieve an optimal outcome.

If the investigation has been thorough and the patient has made a choice with a clear mind, family members and friends should support that choice, since their support will help in the patient's healing.

Another area of controversy is the decision made by some parents to avoid vaccinating their children. Since the duty to heal is communal, this choice is ethical only when parents believe that no one should be vaccinated or when the vaccine poses a grave health risk to a particular child.

Organ Donation

The duty to heal others, Jewish tradition teaches, rests on all of us. *Pikuach nefesh* takes precedence over all but a tiny handful of other obligations. In our time, organ donation can save lives. One person's body can supply a heart, lungs, liver, kidneys—enough to save several lives. Thus contemporary Jewish ethics recognizes an obligation (*mitzvah*) to carry an organ donor card, which would facilitate organ removal for transplantation in case of sudden death.

At an earlier stage of medical technology, organ transplants were extremely risky, in part because treatments suppressing immune reactions were not yet advanced. It was not clear in those early days that harvested organs could actually be put to good use. In light of the long lists of people currently waiting for lifesaving organs and the availability of effective medical procedures, Jewish medical ethicists from across the ideological spectrum have come to agree on the imperative to donate organs at death. Earlier definitions of death involved the cessation of respiration and heartbeat. Technological change made these definitions ineffective. Currently there is broad agreement among Jewish bioethicists that cessation of brain activity is the legitimate determination of death. This definition is critical for harvesting organs.

Is it permitted for a living person to donate an organ he or she can probably live without to save the life of another? May a person donate a kidney, for example, to save a sibling's life? All surgery carries some risk. For example, the donor might develop kidney disease in the remaining kidney. There is always a substantial risk to the living donor, and the potential donor must be fully informed of the risk. While there is clearly no obligation to do so, a reasonable person may choose to accept some pain and risk to save the life of another person. This moral choice is a complex one, and there is no simple right or wrong answer. The potential donor often benefits from consulting a rabbi and medical professionals but in the end must be allowed to make this momentous decision as free as possible from pressure and guilt.

Scarce Resources

Medical equipment, personnel, supplies, and drugs are often in short supply. Sometimes this is caused by a war, epidemic, or natural disaster, but it can also be the result of a decision not to invest beyond a certain point in expensive medical measures. With so many legitimate social needs, only a certain percentage of expenditures can go toward healthcare. Thus medical scarcity is an ongoing challenge.

Two basic and widely agreed-upon policies have emerged in both Jewish and secular bioethics to deal with medical scarcity:

1. Once a patient's treatment has begun, it should not be interrupted as long as it has a reasonable chance of success.
2. If several people suffer from a condition needing treatment and the treatment is most likely to save one of them, that person should be the first treated. This conforms to the method of triage, which focuses medical treatment neither on the *t'reifah* nor on the person who will heal without treatment, in order to help the seriously ill or injured person who can be restored to health.

The application of these two policies leaves many scarcity conflicts unresolved. Jewish ethics emphatically rejects resolving these conflicts by auctioning medical resources to the highest bidder. While this is accepted for luxury goods, in life-threatening situations it is a violation of the principle that every human life is *b'tzelem Elohim*, of infinite worth as a reflection of the divine image.

Traditional Jewish scholars have made several suggestions about whom to choose when resources are insufficient. Suggestions have included using the criteria of greater education, greater communal leadership, or greater age. These have generally been rejected in our time. Currently the most common method of distribution in the case of organ transplants is a waiting list of qualified recipients, with preference going to the person longest on the list provided that person's health remains good enough to qualify. This works because organ waiting lists are regional rather than local.

When a hospital or physician must choose which of two patients to treat, their physical condition, commitment to self-care, and future capacity to function legitimately weigh into the equation. Race, religion, gender, and ethnicity ought to be irrelevant. When there is sufficient time, the hospital's ethics committee may provide guidance, but such decisions usually must be made quickly. It is critically important for physicians to keep in mind the appropriate criteria for making such decisions.

Psychiatry and Psychotherapy

Mental illness ought to be treated, as should any other illness. Any treatment method acceptable to the patient that is considered efficacious by qualified mental health professionals is permitted. Therapy has many useful functions. Often pharmaceutical interventions and the use of residential facilities are beneficial in conjunction with therapy.

The long-term use of medication is becoming increasingly common to stabilize mental health. Such indefinite use of psychotropic drugs raises questions that deserve careful discussion on a regular basis between patient and therapist.

Psychotherapy can be an important source of insight, and many people benefit from it. Those who seek therapy should carefully explore the values and approach of any therapist that they consider seeing. Therapy is not a substitute for family or community support. Much of the isolation or dislocation that pushes some people into therapy or keeps them there stems from the lack of deep engagement with other people that is common in North America. Jews place a high value on community and on anchoring relationships. Our relationships stabilize us and shape our sense of ourselves and the world. Therapy can help people prepare to engage more deeply with others. That, in turn, can bring the next stage in their healing and their return to full living. Every effort should be made to remove the stigma sometimes attached to mental illness. Jewish organizations have a responsibility to undertake education in this area.

Autopsy

Several reasons exist for performing autopsies. They can determine the cause of death, including the possibility of foul play or medical malpractice. This is sometimes important to the family and to governmental processes. Determining the cause of death can also be valuable for identifying hereditary health-risk factors of which descendants of the deceased should be aware. Autopsies can also aid medical research, providing information that can save lives in the future.

Traditional Judaism has had several objections to autopsy. *K'vod hamet*, honoring the deceased, is a value exercised by the speedy burial of an intact body, and some views of resurrection of the dead (*t'chiyat hametim*) hold that the body parts must all be in the grave.

Contemporary autopsies are generally done without delay and with respect for the body. The reasons for allowing autopsy outweigh traditional concerns. Refrigeration permits a slight delay in burial without the disrespect associated with decay, autopsies have greater value than in the past, and liberal Jewish theology rejects the doctrine of bodily resurrection. Autopsies should be performed if there is a substantial reason to do so. Families giving permission for an autopsy would do well to stipulate that minimally invasive procedures be used and that the body be returned for burial promptly with as many body parts as possible.

Medical Research

The wonderful capacity of current healthcare is the product of a long history of medical research. Pursuing such research is a natural extension of the duty to heal, and supporting that research is a valuable goal of government grants and individual giving.

Several forms of research deserve special attention. Some experiments require the use of control groups. This is generally accepted as long as the control group is not being denied access to treatment known to be effective. The moment a treatment is shown to be helpful, it should be made available to the control group.

Questions have been raised about stem cell research. Research on adult stem cells can be conducted in a manner similar to all other research. Embryonic stem cell research is permitted as long as embryos are not created for that purpose. Embryos no longer needed by fertility clinics are frequently destroyed; these should be available for research purposes. As long as the embryos are treated with respect, this use to further human life is permitted.

The use of animals in medical research has produced results that have saved countless lives. When such research is considered, its potential benefit must be balanced by concern for *tza'ar baalei chayim* (preventing pain in living creatures). When another method of research can effectively be substituted for animal research, or when animal research will be of only modest benefit, such research should be avoided.

Healthcare Policy

The current healthcare system involves a complex interaction among hospitals, physicians, and other healthcare workers, medical schools, research institutes, state and federal government, insurance companies, pharmaceutical companies, and others. As the system's ability to cure disease, ease suffering, and extend life continues to increase, the costs increase as well. This has resulted in a lack of access to many kinds of care for a significant number of people.

Given the high cost of healthcare, few can afford insurance that has no restrictions. Governments, employers, and individuals must make choices regarding healthcare plans. As long as basic services are provided, these choices can be made by considering all the advantages and disadvantages of each alternative.

While some medical rationing is inevitable, resources must be distributed fairly. The duty to heal requires that a reasonable level of medical care be available to all. This requires changes in governmental policy that Jews ought to help achieve. A satisfactory level of healthcare ought to be available to every resident in countries where such healthcare exists for some.

Words Worth Healing

Rabbi William Cutter, PhD, and
Ronald M. Andiman, MD

A Rabbi's Introduction

I have been talking about poetry for many years with my friend Ronald Andiman. Dr. Andiman is a neurologist and one of our city's beloved physicians, a man with an aesthetic striving that helps him understand the relationship between the intricacies of the brains he treats as a neurologist and the (perhaps) vaster intricacies of language out of which meanings are made. Ron Andiman reads daily the maps of his patients' minds and their moods. But he also reads a poem a day, and with almost every poem he remarks on the miracle of words that work together. I have little knowledge of clinical medicine but have worked for several generations helping my students learn about the spirit that resides in the sickroom, where patients "incline"—which may be the root of the word "clinic." This chapter is an opportunity for a public dialogue between us, a chance to share some favorite poems, and an inaugural public flight of sharing the discovery that poetry inspires. Our joint contribution here is a book launching, we hope, but for now we offer an example of our dialogue around some important poems—mostly written originally in Hebrew—that bring insight and foster dialogue about the harmonies and the disharmonies of the sickroom.

Dialogue

Dear Ron,

I am writing to begin a dialogue between a rabbi and a physician about health, healing, and the human spirit. We have frequently shared

---

Rabbi William Cutter, PhD, is Steinberg Professor Emeritus of Human Relations and founding director of the Kalsman Institute on Judaism and Health at Hebrew Union College–Jewish Institute of Religion in Los Angeles, California. Ronald M. Andiman, MD, is director of the Headache Clinic, Department of Neurology, Cedars-Sinai Medical Center in Los Angeles, California.

poems we love, and especially poems that illuminate our particular professional experiences—you as a skilled physician, and me as a "visitor of the sick." I will rely on your decades of experience, and the idea here is that you will be willing to engage my nonmedical experience of being with people in their sickrooms, rejoicing in their healing, and even accompanying some of them in their deaths. The prejudice of some chaplains like me is that doctors are not attentive to the many nonmedical needs of their patients. I hope that you will share your prejudices with me in your responses to what I write.

As a patient myself, I am aware of the rich possibilities and disappointments that are part of communication between a doctor and a patient. Doctors in their offices try to speak with great clarity and objectivity, lest the patient leave with doubts as to why procedures are necessary or what will be the nature of a procedure. Stifled by some understandable anxiety, the patient can become uncertain as to what he or she has heard. The physician must seek a simplicity in the midst of the complexity with which he or she lives. Poetry, on the other hand, is partially the art of rich ambiguities, and it may be an opportunity to express deep personal feelings in the midst of objective fact. In the immediate moments of treatment, few people have time for poetry; but in the time between crises, poetry is its own kind of healer: what John Keats had in mind when he said, "... sure a poet is a sage; /A humanist, physician to all men."[1]

For example what did the poet T. Carmi mean when he compared his ailing body to a hotel?

EMPTY FOR THE TIME BEING

Empty for the time being
The moment, the second,
But surely
It will soon be a full occupancy. [The Hebrew captures a unique oxymoron, unavailable in English.]
So what shall one do?
Leave a light on at the doorway?
Get the beds ready?
It's a time to remember
(the taste of coffee) [taste and significance are a pun in Hebrew]

> *It's a time to forget*
> *(The taste of dust)* [i.e., the "reason for dust"]
> *It's a time to die (it will surely come)*
> *The time to die*
> *(has come).*[2]

I have always enjoyed the ambiguity of this poem and would love to have your response to it. Quite obviously, Carmi is playing with the famous lines of Ecclesiastes: "There is a time for everything under the sun" (Ecclesiastes 3:1). When I teach this poem in relaxed classroom circumstances, I let my audiences ruminate on it, rather than give them my straightforward linear analysis—it's always more interesting that way. What do you think?

Dear Bill,

It seems to me that the poem sees the body as a "hotel"—that is, a place meant for guests, usually welcome guests. It is empty only for the time being—the implication is that the poet is dealing with the recurrence of cancer and soon will be at full occupancy, that is, filled with metastases. The mood is almost one of welcoming anticipation, or at least considering the possibility of having a welcoming attitude in the face of the inevitable: "What shall one do? Leave the lights on in the doorway? Get the beds ready?"

But before the guests arrive, remember the taste of coffee, for the taste of dust will surely come. (Ecclesiastes's idea of a time for everything is ambiguous anyway; is it a good thing or a bad thing?)

Dear Ron,

I think the notion of "almost welcoming" is brilliant and risky—perhaps a bit overstated. I see a kind of sarcasm from what must have been a fleeting association about emptiness. Surely you know that patients can get sarcastic when faced with their immediate deaths. The metaphor of body as hotel is, as you suggest, quite disjunctive—two parts of a proposition that don't fit. In this case, the lack of fit serves the poem's ironies. Then the sudden jump to Ecclesiastes, which serves him as a concluding point: the time to die has come. This is one of ten poems that Carmi composed near the end of his long passage to dying. In another poem, the poet quotes his doctor saying, "I'm afraid 'it' will return." And the poet morbidly responds, "Well he didn't mean the Messiah." (He could make that joke because the word for "it" and "he" are not distinguished in Hebrew.)

Carmi was a great poet, but one who is less familiar to American readers because of the density of his verse and because he used a lot of classic Jewish references that could be obscure to an American audience. (In the above witticism about the Messiah, he is citing a Talmudic passage that says that when the Messiah comes, the world will be topsy-turvy anyway. Maybe that's when a cancer-filled body can become a hotel.)

Let me share with you a more direct poem about time in the hospital with a loved one. I know you have just finished being a "visitor to the sick," rather than a physician, when your wife had surgery, and I know that you often visit friends in the very hospital where you are on staff. I thought you might like to see a poem about *bikkur cholim*, or visiting the sick.

FINAL ORDERS

Kiss her on her mouth,
Lightly without delay.
Don't let her know with your moving lips
That the night tortured your sleep.
That you gulped nightmares
And that the shade over your eyes
Slowly became like
A whispering oxygen mask.
Kiss her gingerly
And swiftly.
Don't breathe into her
Your darkness.[3]

Dear Bill,

As you know, Felice [Dr. Andiman's wife] had surgery last seek. Our experience was "time out of time." Between visits of nurses, clinical partners, menu leavers and picker-uppers, cleaning personnel, PTs, OTs, and the doctor, the hospital room is quiet, so quiet until the bed alarm, the IV alarm, and all the many technical sounds down the hall break the silence. It is a quiet bedlam where patients wait silently, expectantly.

As the visitor, you place burdens on yourself, deluding yourself into thinking that you have some critical responsibility. You create clinical questions to address: Should I let her sleep ... is she sleeping too long ... ask the nurse if she should be awakened. No, I can make this decision ... but what if something is wrong? Is she breathing okay? Should I be concerned?

Dear Ron,

Wow, Ronald. I so appreciate the intimate power your words bring here—as a visitor to your beloved, and not as a physician. You also employ a common poetic technique—the oxymoron—to capture the topsy-turvy nature of things ("quiet bedlam"). Above all, and whatever doubts the visitor may have, I might suggest that you "don't breathe into her your darkness." A little deception is called for, in other words.

But let me share with you another poem about visiting the sick—before we move on to an additional question suggested by your letter: the imposing quality of the hospital setting. In the following poem by Malka Shaked, deception also plays a part in the visit, and a classic Jewish reference gives a remarkable and even humorous direction to the idea of visiting the sick: the mask of the visitor. (This is my translation, and I'm still working on it, but you will see what I'm trying to do with the hard and soft sounds of the "s" in the spelling c-l-o-s-e and with the pun about pain.)

A RECIPE FOR VISITING THE SICK

Close off close to all
the chambers of your heart,
And sweep to the sides
the pain that took pains
to gather
Like a pile of dust.
Wipe it away.
Every last speck.
Then cook it.
Do the Hocus-Pocus.

And arm it with
unseen armor.
Drive out any leftover
Feelings.
Then realize.
Reduce and refine.
Heat (the reduction) at a low temperature.
Then cool.
And now, decorate your tongue
with a crown of fibs.
To be extra certain
(for not every day is Purim),
Wrap your body
And inscribe: "Fragile."[4]

Both Carmi and Shaked invite the visitor to restrain their feelings in the presence of their ill loved one. Is this something you think about as a doctor?

Dear Bill,

I like this poem, although the intensity might be a bit exaggerated; and I love the metaphor of visiting the sick as a recipe. I'm still trying to figure out whether there is more to the Purim reference than the simple idea of a mask. I actually have found that in many cases I can be a good visitor by talking about neutral matters. In that way, people feel that they are part of the regular functioning world and not totally defined by their illness.

Dear Ron,

Sure, but it's a delicate balance, isn't it, since people don't like their illness to be trivialized into news about the baseball standings. I think what she means is that Purim is a time when we get complete license, and no one expects the "truth" to be spoken. (Of course, behind the masks of Purim sometimes lies an even greater truth—how we are really feeling, etc.) She might have said: Visiting the sick is a little like Purim—we get to behave in fanciful ways and be someone else, but actually people know that the someone we are imagining is the real self, whereas what seems like reality can be a mask, and what seems like a mask may be reality ... so, in that sense, perhaps visiting the sick should be like Purim. Of course, sometimes we seek a unique authenticity that is just the opposite of Purim. Here's a poem by Israeli poet Zelda that I have been teaching for a long time to my chaplaincy students. Through it I hope they might understand the intimacies that some of their patients experience. (It has one biblical reference, from the book of Amos, about the very lowest part of the world: the seafloor.)

THEN MY SOUL CRIED OUT

Then my soul cried out—
"Scorched lips,
you are on one side,
the world on the other,
the whole world on the other side."
For in that room
flooded with sun,
I stood so close to her
that my mouth touched her face,
which had changed in the throes of death.
She spoke my name
in a voice
that dwelt on the floor of the sea [Amos is referenced here];
in a distant, muffled voice
that shattered to bits
the silver mirrors,
her smoldering lips
spelled out my name.[5]

I won't pretend that the "story line" of this poem is perfectly obvious, but surely one can imagine a scene between two people who are very close, and surely we have all heard that bare muffled voice that sounds as if it comes from the bottom of the sea. It is quiet and yet so significant that "it can shatter glass."

Dear Bill,

Thanks for taking me to this level of serious poetry and reflections on things that I have just recently experienced. My wife was certainly not "in extremis," and yet the moments of intimacy were there, the feeling that we were on one side with the world on the other, and a fresh appreciation of our closeness emerged that is hard to experience except in rare circumstances. Actually we had wonderful treatment in the hospital, so the world wasn't always "on the other side"—at least not in the negative sense.

But in responding to my last letter, you left out one important paragraph from my first note to you—the part about the size of the hospital. Remember what I wrote at the beginning of my note about the burdens of the visitor:

> As Felice prepares to go to the hospital she says to me, "I feel like I'll be swallowed up" in the vastness of the hospital.

The hospital does swallow one up. You become one of the cogs in the machine—subsumed by it, enveloped by it. You are swept along by its pace. Restrictions are imposed on you, what to eat, how to move, what precautions to take.

Do you have some poems that capture that feeling of bigness and feeling of alienation in the face of that bigness?

Dear Ron,

Boy, do I ever. You've probably forgotten, but I sometimes feel that way even when I visit your much smaller medical office building: the halt and the lame lumbering in to see the doctor; slow elevators, no place to sit, no handles to support the broken-legged. One of Israel's leading historical figures, Abba Kovner, wrote several poems about the size of the Sloan-Kettering Hospital, where he was treated for what turned out to be a fatal cancer. He found rich metaphors to describe the endless hallways, the elevators, and the symbolic size of the doctors. Let me first tell you about Kovner himself.

Kovner died about twenty-five years ago from (what appears to have been) laryngeal cancer. His long series of poems captures several aspects of this final experience of his life at the awesome hospital. His life's end was especially severe for the modern Jew who knew about him as a hero and one of the great leaders of the partisan fighters who navigated the forests of Lithuania and led people to safety in brutal circumstances. He plays on that past in a pretty straightforward way by noting the ironies of his life: escape from the Nazi hell along with his people, but finally alone with his beloved wife, Vitka, a hero herself, now knitting and waiting for the doctor to appear out of the depths of this gigantic institution.

Drawing on the name of the hospital, Kovner added to the sense of alienation he described in this short poem by his spelling with Hebrew letters the untranslatable name of the hospital. (The Hebrew transliteration of the long English name, in other words, highlights the feeling of strangeness.) I had my own experience with the monster Sloan-Kettering myself, and I have been a patient in other gigantic medical centers, where just a little opening on the street level takes you into a tremendous palace of sterile apparatus, incredibly busy people, and urgency. I'm so appreciative that you experienced and understood the bigness of our own Cedars-Sinai Hospital in Los Angeles. You should try Hadassah in Ein Kerem, where the entrance is a series of shops and huge escalators, restaurants of all kinds, and a bus station.

Here is the great Kovner:

SLOAN-KETTERING

Sloan-Kettering (its full name: Memorial
Sloan-Kettering Cancer Center)
is a large and growing building
and all who come within its walls
to strip
naked,
jointly and separately,
suddenly find themselves
in a cage, captive, exposed
and the silence astounds on all
its many floors
and when a patient
cut off from his supervisor
finds himself running
from room to room
with no idea where to turn
first, peering down the glaring corridors,

half-open doors and half-
shut,
Sloan-Kettering is a personal encounter
with a pathless wilderness
between yellow arrows
and blue signs
something obscure is going on
in the feverish cells
of your brain
at the entrance to a triple elevator
that has not yet
opened its maw
like a desert
beginning to take shape
from within.[6]

It has seemed to me that desert imagery has special meaning for an Israeli writer, with historical reference to the biblical wilderness, and an ever-present consciousness of the empty-feeling terrain that surrounds Jerusalem and proceeds southward to Eilat. But, Ron, Kovner's Sloan-Kettering poems relate the experience of one especially sensitive patient. Although Kovner once in a while slips into sarcasm about life in the hospital (the chaplain brings the patient a copy of the prayer for humility at the High Holy Days—*oy!*), his primary art in the fifty or so Sloan-Kettering poems is his personal rumination about a life lived between the Holocaust and laryngeal cancer. On another occasion, I will want to introduce you to an American doctor-poet, Marc Strauss, who talks about bigness in more critical terms.

Yes, Ronald, I have had contradictory experiences. I see that some of my doctors don't know how to bring intimacy to their work, while others (and I think you are one of them) bring the magic of an individual personality. I think perhaps that your love of poetry both demonstrates that and may even be one of the things that creates your ability to believe that you are treating the patient, not just curing the illness. Zelda once described feeling like an object in the marketplace:

WHEN A HORSE IS SOLD IN THE MARKETPLACE

When a horse is sold in the marketplace,
no one asks the horse-soul
if it will allow a strange hand
to open the horse's mouth,
To touch its limbs.
They set my shamed flesh
before the dragon of science
without asking my soul.
Ten heads of the lofty dragon
observed my misery
without asking my soul.[7]

Also by Zelda is a very short and seemingly innocent poem whose meanings kind of sneak up on you. Zelda, the poet, was known only by her first name. She was a descendant of the distinguished and pious Hasidic family the Schneersons. Her poetry is often laden with kabbalistic imagery, but not always easily accessible—even to the "insiders." Her Hebrew is not only laden with references to Jewish mystical tradition, but—where that is absent—thoughts of religious tradition always await just behind her poems.

In this poem that I want to share with you, Zelda mixes a sense of simple prayer with the "class" simplicity of one of the people one meets most frequently in the hospital:

WHEN THE WOMAN

When the brown-faced woman—
who was, at that moment,
polishing the floor—
heard the doctor's words,
she said to me,
"I will pray for you."
A sudden, new friend
said to me,
"I will pray for you."[8]

Dr. Mordecai Mushkat, of that same giant Hadassah Hospital, likes to have his young doctors imagine the poem as a scenario in which each character is a particularized individual whom the young doctors "role-play" with a particular behavior. Perhaps it is oversimplified to attach significance to this poem, but I'm eager to know what you think. Wherever I have read this poem—with doctors, with nurses, with laypeople—they have imagined a remarkable number of scenarios for what "really happened," proving the complex potential even within a simple poem: the doctor's haughty style, the eavesdropping care of the woman cleaning the floor, the ethnic distinction, and the simple fact of prayer.

Dear Bill,

Hospitals are very diverse. But the social-class distinctions remain a feature of our hospitals, as staff come from the Philippines, Somalia, Jamaica, the Dominican Republic, Sweden, Russia, Canada, Mexico, India, Pakistan, and everywhere in between. Of course not all of the support staff are "brown-faced," but there is a tendency to have immigrants not from the white, comfortable mainstream serving in such capacities as Zelda's brown-faced woman.

Dear Ron,

Matter of fact, in the Kovner Sloan-Kettering sequence, another dark-faced woman appeared, and I couldn't help but be struck by the appearance as angels of mercy: first of all, women, and, second of all, people from apparently more modest social class than many of the patients. Among Kovner's caretakers is "Norma," identified as the black Puerto Rican nurse to whom he asks the question (in poetry):

> *How many years*
> *Have you been cleaning*
> *the filth*
> *of others?*[9]

or:

> *His scarred tissue was lapped*
> *By waves of salt water*
> *And he screamed mightily*
> *And only the sudden appearance of the Puerto Rican nurse*
> *Who stood between the doorway and the screen,*
> *Embarrassing, unreal, asking*

"Did you ring the emergency bell, sir?"
Obliged him to ask: "What time is it?"[10]

NINE O'CLOCK. NORMA
Nine o'clock. Norma brings a pill to sweeten his sleep
If you can say sweet dreams on a night of strain
Exhausted by a wild dream that recurs
With minor changes, like caressing
The stern of a foul-smelling ship
That brought them to safety on the dockside
Before the harbor was sealed off at two in the morning.[11]

Of course, Kovner's dreams are different from those of most patients, as he is constantly conflating his hospital nightmare with the grand historical nightmare that informed the earlier part of his life. But in the midst of his terror, his poetry pauses to mention the acts of kindness that made his hospital stay a tolerable and even humanizing experience. And it occurred to me that just as the nurses and other helpers in the hospital need a little science to guide them through the medical thicket in which they are working, so perhaps the more established medical professionals could use an orientation to humanness that is reflected in so many of the non-physician staff.

Dear Bill,

Our correspondence has been an interesting process, because each of us in our own way is interested in finding meaning in the personal experiences *we* experience. You, as you see patients and read poems; I, as a physician. Ideally the physician is a seeker, an explorer of the unknown. Every new patient encounter is an opportunity to make an exploration into a new continent. Though other doctors may have seen this patient, she or he is being referred to the consultant for a fresh perspective or insight. In the course of interviewing the patient, the doctor is trying to derive meaning from information that the patient proffers. This is often meaning that the other doctors missed or of which they failed to see the significance. Finding meaning in what the patient has to say ultimately brings meaning from the patient encounter to the physician. I am constantly trying to "read" my patients for new insights—reading first into their medical condition so that I might be of some help; but, secondly, into an understanding of the human condition. You once read Amichai's poem "The Precision of Pain and the Blurriness of Joy" to me, and I remember the final line: "I learned to speak among the pains."[12]

Dear Ron,

Now you are moving into an area that I have enjoyed working with doctors on. Somehow I got to doctors before I got to my own students—whom I also have to read if I am going to be of any help to them. Some of my students don't appreciate "being read," but that is the reality of being a good teacher-mentor. I don't like to compare my students to patients in need, and doing so might lead to a kind of instrumental relationship—the opposite of the old Buberian "I-Thou." Yet, there is it.

Let me talk about physicians first, in the shadow of that most poetic of physicians, and most physician of poets: William Carlos Williams. Many physicians have found in poetry a partner in discovery, and when you and I find the time for the book that will grow from this essay, it will be "discovery" that marks our path. Names like the American doctors Marc Strauss and Raphael Campo will join with the less artistically skilled but no less sincere healing professionals with whom I have worked to demonstrate how that act of discovery works.

In these letters I hope to share with you some of the "games" that I have played with doctors and nurses to get them to compose some of their own poems of discovery. Sometimes those discoveries are harsh, but they always contribute to the greater humanness of the doctor. I ask doctors to create little two-line couplets, find exaggerated metaphors for their patients, write alternate stanzas about themselves and their patients, and so forth. I remind the doctors whom I encourage to write little poems about William Carlos Williams. Williams was not a simple man, although he liked to write of unmediated experiences, and was not a self-conscious poet with complex technique. He apparently did not love every moment of his life, and so his appreciation of the medical encounter was not one of unadulterated pleasure. But he loved discovery, and I like to think that this love of discovery is in the spirit of the opening of this chapter. Here is what his biographer says of him:

> For Williams, day after day, each encounter with a patient could lead to uncertainty, ennui, friction, and inescapable signs of his own limits; but even the humdrum brought unexpected windfalls of pleasure and insight. The physician plays many roles: spy, skeptic, social worker, novelist, anatomist. With characteristic humility, Williams describes him "observing, weighing, comparing value of which neither he nor his patients may know the significance."[13]

Note, too, this quote about Robert Coles, the great writer and himself a teacher of poetry:

> When invited as a medical student to accompany the older doctor on his house calls, the writer Robert Coles reported being deeply affected by the older man's heightened alertness to everything around him in the neighborhood he was summoned to—"where people eat, get home supplies, get some aspirin or bandages and adhesive tape, or maybe a holiday card, or a drink that sizzles"—even before he had knocked on the patient's door and begun listening to a recital of symptoms.... This curiosity about the local is the cornerstone of Williams's poetics and prose.[14]

That was a sentiment that demanded the link between the healing arts and the therapies of poetry.

Williams's biographer reminds us how much the poet-doctor loved immediacy and tried to avoid murky abstractions. I think it's immediacy that Zelda captures in her encounter with the brown-faced woman, or that moment in which visitor and ill friend are on one side of the world, and that Carmi and Shaked capture in their consideration of the visit to the sick. When I compare that immediacy in the hospital room with difficult experiences and harsh anxieties, with the relative ease and ambience involved when I am sitting in my study reading a poem, I am sometimes embarrassed at the comfort that I am living in.

As a rabbi, I am too comfortable in my physical life, and I must work on entering the suffering and struggles of patients I visit; and—I would argue as a critic of our medical system—every doctor should try to imagine what really goes on in patients' lives when they are seriously suffering, and truly living "on the edge," dependent on a caretaker who once made love to them. A visit to the movie *Amour* would help, and in the meantime, I invite all physicians, as I invite you, dear Ronald, to keep reading those poems that make us think about the life lived among the ill.

I've just gotten off the phone with a patient who is facing a re-surgery for a major tumor, and my reassuring comments sometimes seem flat compared to her sensation of uninterrupted turmoil. Yet here I am reading and commenting on poems. But, once I overcome my sense of awkwardness and even a little guilt that I'm not within the turmoil, I realize that it may be the poet who makes me aware of the power of those immediate moments. If they aren't part of my personal or family life just now (and thank God they are not), then at least a good poet can bring me there "suddenly" and with greater intimacy than I can appreciate just contemplating the experience from the outside as a murky abstraction. And so I head off to visit a young former student of mine who is suffering from pancreatic cancer, and she reminds me that just this past November she sat in a hotel auditorium in New Jersey and heard me read poems about death and dying. And now she faces death and dying in the quite unpoetic environment of a large urban hospital.

Spiritual Resources for Jewish Healthcare Professionals

Elizabeth Feldman, MD

I am a Jewish physician—I practice clinical medicine and am a practicing Jew. What do being Jewish and being a healthcare professional have to do with each other? In this chapter, I discuss the connections between Jewish concepts, values, texts, and practices and the healthcare profession. Next, I address the personal and the communal relevance of these connections. Finally, I share resources to facilitate such connections for other Jewish healthcare professionals.

Serving as a healthcare professional providing acute and chronic medical or mental healthcare can be highly stressful. We face the challenge of trying to address the many needs of patients or clients. We are called upon to diagnose acute or long-standing problems; to hear tales of suffering and to address fear, anxiety, and worry; to witness and try to ameliorate physical or emotional pain; and to balance the needs of a patient's various family members—all without taking it home at the end of the day. As healthcare professionals, we try a variety of ways to deal with this stress, to recharge our batteries, nourish ourselves. We engage in physical activity, read, play or listen to music, meditate, travel, cook, garden, or spend time with friends and family. Some providers identify spiritual resources—prayer, meditation, a solitary nature walk, religious services—while others think about methods of self-care, stress reduction, or simply relaxation.

For some Jewish healthcare providers, elements of our Judaism are important to our lives. We may find comfort and meaning in different

---

Elizabeth Feldman, MD, is medical coordinator for the Sheriff's Alternative Programs with Cermak Health Services of Cook County, a department of Cook County Health and Hospitals System in Chicago, Illinois.

Jewish traditions and rituals, in Israeli dance or Hebrew music, in contemplative prayer or membership in a Jewish community, in chicken soup with matzah balls. Some are nourished by Torah text study or by gathering together with family and friends at the Passover seder table or Chanukah party. We find meaning in involvement with synagogues, Jewish social justice organizations, or other Jewish institutions. For some, our work as a healthcare professional may take place in the context of a Jewish hospice, nursing home, or other healthcare organization.

Of course, we need not utilize specifically Jewish mindfulness practices, writings about ethical issues, social justice values, or communal efforts. Clearly, caring providers from all faith traditions, or no specific tradition, provide profoundly meaningful healing to patients and engage in self-care and restorative activities to nourish themselves. But if you feel that you resonate with Jewish spirituality, have a profession in the healthcare fields, and wish to explore the integration of these two elements in your life, then I invite you to embark on the journey with me. May these efforts enrich our professional lives and sustain us as healers and caregivers.

Connections: Jewish Life and the Healthcare Profession

As a family physician with long-standing active involvement in a *chavurah*, or small "do-it-yourself synagogue," I have spent several decades participating in various Jewish activities without ever thinking about how my Jewish life might connect with my healthcare work. I was raised in a Reform Jewish home, and my involvement slowly grew: I became a Jewish songleader, taught Sunday school, started keeping kosher, learned to read Torah and lead traditional egalitarian davening (services), joined lay-led participatory *minyan*s, celebrated Shabbat and the holiday cycle, danced the hora at my wedding, and began to raise Jewishly involved children. These activities took place throughout college, medical school, family medicine residency, and faculty development fellowship training. They continued and expanded as I joined a primary care practice, became a residency faculty member, received specialty certification in adolescent medicine, and entered into my practice life.

In the late 1990s, I attended a Harvard Medical School conference on spirituality and medicine. I sought out the few Jews in the audience and joined a breakout discussion group facilitated by a rabbi. As we explored the conference topics from a Jewish perspective, I was excited to learn about traditional Jewish texts on health and healing and to think about the idea of a Jewish "healing service"—songs and prayers that would focus on health and healing. I began to explore the concept of "mindfulness" and to think about my healing intentions as a physician.

During my experiences in academic family medicine, I explored ways of teaching residents to become better listeners, to value the therapeutic worth of "just listening" to patients, and to integrate their own family and personal issues along the path to becoming better physicians. Colleagues and I discussed issues relating to end-of-life care and helping families cope with illness. But I had not looked closely at the resources my Jewish tradition might have to offer in this area. I discovered that I had two separate identities, as a physician and as a committed Jew. Gradually, I became aware of a desire to integrate these two important aspects of my life. Why is it important to do so? There are several possible reasons:

1. Resources that nurture my spirit will increase meaning in my work, reduce burnout, and increase my job satisfaction. Many studies link burnout to decreased quantity and quality of patient care.[1]
2. Integrating different parts of my life helps me to feel more whole and more fulfilled as a human being and deepens my life experience. When I am present in my Jewish world—celebrating Shabbat or holidays, participating in both joyous and sad life-cycle events—my identity as a doctor is still part of me, and it feels good for that part to feel engaged and welcome in the spiritual and communal moments.
3. Studying with and learning from other Jewish healthcare professionals who are also addressing issues of meaning, suffering, or healing enriches my own personal day-to-day experience.
4. Jewish texts and sources have addressed many concerns, such as ethical dilemmas, end-of-life issues, and the

> provider-patient relationship, in ways that can help me be a better physician.[2]

I believe there is "value added" for Jewish healthcare providers to address the big questions about their work from a Jewish perspective. Whether or not we choose to think of these as spiritual questions, we all have sought to alleviate suffering in our patients, addressed decisions about the end of life, and tried to listen empathetically and deeply to our patients who are in physical and emotional distress. We have encountered ethical dilemmas in our practices. We deal frequently with people in the most vulnerable, fear-filled moments of their lives. We may be privy to unbearable tragedy, chaos, pain, and sometimes tremendous joy. We may have the responsibility of leading teams of supporting individuals through births and deaths. At times, profound (and sometimes unrealistic) hopes and expectations are placed on our shoulders. Our patients and their families may want to vest us with powers or capacities we do not truly have. Availing ourselves of Jewish spiritual resources can be helpful in dealing with these stressful elements of our work. They can support and nurture us in our dual identity as healthcare providers and Jews, both individually and as members of the Jewish community.

Relevance: Spirituality for Jewish Healthcare Professionals

Early in my journey, I was fortunate to be invited to join the Kalsman Institute on Judaism and Health at the Los Angeles campus of the Hebrew Union College–Jewish Institute of Religion. The Kalsman Institute is a center for training, collaboration, and dialogue on healthcare, healing, and spirituality at the intersection of Judaism and health, which brings together Jewish religious leaders, healthcare providers, and community members. There I was introduced to traditional Jewish texts and sources that explored the nature of suffering, healing, and end-of-life and related issues. Dr. Rachel Naomi Remen led an experiential workshop about setting our conscious intention before we began to engage with patients. I learned about Jewish meditation. Later, I co-led a workshop with Rabbi Dr. Eleanor Smith (before she attended medical school and was then "just" a rabbi) in which we addressed the interaction of rabbis and physicians in the care of our congregants/patients. The very concept of one's personal clergy and healthcare provider joining the same "care team" was new and meaningful. Excited by this learning, I began to ask questions about the ways Jewish healthcare providers could bring specific mindfulness techniques or spiritual issues into their clinical practice.

In the Talmud, Rabbi Hanina asserts that he has learned the most from his students, even more than from his teachers or his colleagues.[3] One year, during intern orientation in my family medicine residency training program, I introduced the concept of taking a spiritual history or assessment, utilizing a spiritual assessment tool developed by family physician Howard Silverman, MD, a fellow Kalsman Institute partner. In one informal lunchtime session, I asked trainees and faculty to address our own spiritual issues. To model this self-disclosure, I began by speaking about my feeling that my personal Jewish religious life was disconnected from my daily clinical practice, wondering aloud about ways to link them. I spoke a bit about the potential use of centering and mindfulness techniques. One of the interns, Cindy Griebler, MD, who is also Jewish, commented that since hand-washing was a religious ritual performed at various times in Jewish life and since it was also a regularly employed practice during patient care, perhaps we could add a mindfulness moment as we washed our hands before turning to examine a patient.

What a significant moment for me! Over the ensuing months, I experimented with the practice. As I turned to the sink, I would silently recite the traditional Jewish blessing for hand-washing or offer up the hope that I would be a channel for healing and would be fully present with the patient I was about to examine. At times, this has had a profound impact on me. What remains a challenge, however, is maintaining the necessary mindfulness to recall my desire to perform the ritual during a busy afternoon of patient care.

Several years ago, I conducted a qualitative survey of Jewish friends and colleagues in the healthcare professions, asking them to share their mindfulness or centering practices prior to entering the encounter with a patient or client. Is there a *kavanah* (spiritual intention) that they set before engaging in the encounter? Their words were enlightening.

One physician responded:

To be very honest, at least 99 percent of the time I push from one patient to another without any sort of spiritual preparation. I sometimes do some brief praying if I am feeling particularly apprehensive about a particular visit or about my day in general. For instance, the first page I get when I'm on call always jumps up my anxiety level, or seeing that I have a particularly packed schedule.... So most often my prayer goes something like this: "Please grant me the clarity of mind to access all of the knowledge that I have, and the humility to ask for help if I need it." Sometimes I use a phrase from Maimonides's prayer for the physician: "May I never see in the patient anything else but a fellow-creature in pain" (this is especially useful with "hateful" patients!).

A physical therapist commented:

I make my office into a container for healing. There is a mezuzah at the door of the office. I have a very special framed picture of hands with stars of David growing out of them. I often say the "my soul is pure" prayer to slow myself down; and when I do not have clarity, I say Moses's prayer to heal Miriam: "*El na r'fa na lah*" [please, God, heal her]. I always wash my hands with consciousness. In shul, I often silently add my patients to the healing part of the service.

One nurse recites the following as she changes into her scrubs before her shift:

Ribbono shel olam [Master of the universe], let it be a good day. Help me to make it a good day. Let me be a kind, compassionate, and competent caregiver to my patients and their loved ones. Let me be a strength and support to my coworkers. And let me remember to balance their needs with mine.

An emergency physician noted:

The one thing I have been able to do consistently is say, "*Barukh dayyan emet*" (blessed is the True Judge) after calling a code and setting the time of death.... When a list of names is recited in shul for *misheberach* for *cholim* (prayer for the sick) on Shabbat, I try to remember to add the phrase "*kol elu sheba'u tachat yadai*" (all those that have come under my hands).

A psychotherapist responded:

I am a meditator and so I try to meditate for twenty to thirty minutes daily first thing in the morning. I know that I proceed through my day differently when I do this. I am more present and calmer. Sometimes I say a little prayer, which is usually about strength, guidance, healing, and that I stay compassionate without being consumed. I also have some simple rituals that I do after a grief group or an emotionally draining meeting.

Another psychologist said:

I try to give myself a bit of downtime before each appointment so that I go in a bit refreshed. I think I use my spirituality most when I am trying to help someone who is feeling hopeless or despairing. That is when I most use my own and Jewish learning/convictions to try to help the person persevere, feel that it matters to transcend his or her difficulties and go on, and that there is meaning in the small daily things of life—to have hope.

Several respondents mentioned utilizing breath awareness:

I take one to three deep breaths, in through my nose and out my mouth. I imagine white warm light coming into me and filling me. I try to stay present in the here and now.

I try to take some time to do some breathing—follow my breath. One of my goals is to be receptive. I might chant or sing *Halleluyah* or *Kadosh Kadosh* or repeat a psalm. The breath is key—God breathed our soul into us.

My general practice is to stop and spend a minute or two in meditative reflection. I find it difficult to be fully present without these moments. Sometimes I will focus on a simple Jewish text about breath and perhaps even hum a melody that is associated with that text.

Finally, one physician shared a desire to add a mindfulness practice to patient visits:

> Your question has inspired me to begin doing some spiritual centering before seeing a patient. I must admit that despite my desire and the importance of doing so, I do not regularly prepare myself for each therapeutic encounter. What I consistently do is review my records, prepare mentally for what I expect to be discussed, and make sure I have some of the potentially important clinical information at my fingertips. I would very much appreciate hearing any ideas that surface that might inspire more of us to add such a holiness-enhancing practice to our work.

These examples offer an invitation for any healthcare professional to add their own centering practice or mindfulness elements into their clinical encounters. The Jewish notion of *kavanah*, or spiritual intention, may be helpful. Breath awareness is one possibility. Using a single word such as "peace," "one," *shalom* (peace), *olam* (world), *rachamim* (compassion), or *chesed* (loving-kindness) is an option. Identifying a phrase from Psalms or from the traditional prayer liturgy or an existing blessing is another choice. You might use the opening "May I" or "Allow me to" to individualize the intention for each patient. A behavioral cue, such as turning to the sink to wash your hands, may engender a thought or intention.

Resources: How to Integrate Judaism into Healthcare Work

I recently conducted an online informal survey of Jewish healthcare professionals, asking about their own experiences at the intersection of their Judaism and their healthcare work. I asked about any Jewish underpinnings to their chosen profession and if there were Jewish resources they identified as being helpful in their daily work lives. Several themes emerged. I offer these along with my own reflections in the hope that they will be helpful for others engaged in similar work. One theme is the idea that Jewishly identified values bring meaning to our healthcare work.

The concept of *tikkun olam* (repairing the world) is a very real *raison d'etre* for many in the healing profession. Some identify this as following the familiar Jewish admonition to "be a mensch," based on the Torah precept to "love your neighbor as yourself" (Leviticus 19:18), in their relationship with patients. Closely linked to this is the idea of viewing humans as created in the image of the Divine (Genesis 1:27), which leads to an ethical obligation to ensure fairness, justice, dignity, and respect for each person.[4] For some, it directly enjoins choosing a practice that involves caring for disadvantaged and vulnerable populations, linking to a social justice or activism value. I view my medical care for incarcerated women in this light. Several colleagues volunteer regularly for "medical missions" to the developing world, offering their skills and experience to heal and teach others. Even when participating as part of a church mission, some specifically articulate this work as their efforts to promote repair of the world, citing the Talmudic concept that "he who saves a single life is as if he saved the entire world."[5] For others, the concept of *tikkun olam* underscores the importance of valuing and affirming the life of each individual patient, the "choose life" dictum (Deuteronomy 30:19). Related to this is the urge to help create hope out of despair.

Many providers cite a Jewish injunction to behave with compassion and kindness. The Rabbinic midrashic commentary *Sifre Deuteronomy*, citing divine qualities as delineated in Exodus 34:6, urges, "Just as God is gracious and compassionate, you too must be gracious and compassionate.... As the Holy One is loving, you too must be loving."[6] Remembering to see the face of the Divine in each of my patients helps me to maintain an empathetic and nonjudgmental attitude, especially when caring for those who suffer from serious substance abuse disorders that have led to poor life choices. Closely related is the injunction to forgive others as an aspect of this behavioral imperative, one that may also guide our professional attitude toward those we care for.

Efforts to promote the repair of the world, engagement in *tzedakah* (charitable efforts), and doing various *mitzvot* (good deeds) can also give meaning to our work when the activities take place outside of the healthcare arena. Spending an evening alongside fellow *chavurah* members engaged in feeding homeless individuals at the JUF Uptown Café,[7] devoting an afternoon to packing and delivering Rosh Hashanah and Passover food baskets, attending a deportation center vigil, and contributing to social justice organizations all offer nourishment for my spirit, inspiring me to more zealous efforts in my medical work. Judaism is a religion that highlights the performance of actions such as *mitzvot* over particular dogma or beliefs. It is these *mitzvot* that can enhance meaning in our healthcare profession.

Participation in Shabbat observance nourishes many healthcare professionals on both individual and communal levels. When possible, we may use the twenty-four-hour period from sundown Friday to just after sundown Saturday as a respite from our busy work lives. For some, this "sanctuary in time" described by Rabbi Abraham Joshua Heschel[8] involves turning off pagers, cell phones, and computers; allowing for rest and relaxation, family time, and ritual activities; and disconnecting from stresses of the work world. Our family's commitment to a special weekly Friday night dinner, often with guests and always with decadent dessert and singing, has served as the cornerstone of our home Jewish observance. I prioritize the need to cook and prepare for Shabbat. As our daughters became teenagers, they invited their friends to join us for "*Shabbos* dinner" before they went on to other activities. The chance to attend synagogue services or study sessions is an opportunity to engage with friends, family, and colleagues in a social setting. Sometimes, communal prayer and singing on Shabbat allows to me "recharge my batteries." Other weeks, it is a Saturday lakefront jog or meditative yoga class that has the same effect.

One particularly Jewish activity that has proved extremely meaningful to me and many colleagues over the past decade is involvement in a *chevra kadisha*, or Jewish burial society. A small team of members is called upon to wash, purify, and dress a body for burial. While engaged in the specific tasks, prayers, and rituals of the *taharah* (purification), the team maintains two overarching principles: honoring the dead and comforting the mourners. Doing *taharah* is understood as the ultimate *mitzvah*, an act done without expectation of any reward,[9] as the individual being cared for has already died, and the family members are not to know who specifically performed the loved one's *taharah*.

For me, participation in a *taharah*—joining with three or four other women, leaving my pager and cell phone outside, entering the *taharah* room and joining as a holy community to collaborate in gently washing, drying, and dressing the *metah* (dead woman)—is a deeply and profoundly transformative spiritual task. As a physician, I have been called to "pronounce" (to verify and note the time of death) a patient whom I have never seen before, and I have sat at the bedside alongside family members of longtime patients as they died. When we join in the task of *taharah*, however, I experience a transcendent sense of sacred time and space. I am nurtured by engaging in the caring acts along with a group of other women. Many other therapists, nurses, and physicians echo this sense: being involved in the *chevra kadisha* brings us back to our individual essence, allows us to take off the clinical blinders or professional trappings and to be part of a holy act. There is also a timeless factor: we are a part of that essence, by tapping into an ancient tradition and all of its continuity.

Many of us identify various Jewish sources that help with health-care work. One traditionally Jewish activity is the study of religious texts, probing the ancient words for new meanings, fresh perspectives. The words of the Torah, the Talmud, the book of Psalms, or *Pirkei Avot* can offer tremendous solace and meaning when we read them to ourselves. With a *chavruta* (partner) or in group study in which we grapple collectively with the words, their many-layered meanings offer additional concrete and metaphysical inspiration and assistance. One provider mentioned the many lessons to be learned in studying the *parashat hashavua* (the weekly Torah portion) on topics such as empathy, listening, family dynamics, and styles of conflict resolution.

For many Jews, reciting the words of the *siddur* (prayer book) or expressing personal prayers individually or communally offers an opportunity to engage with God—to talk to God, to ask from God—in whatever way they understand or conceptualize God, *Adonai*, the Divine, the All, the Source, Being Itself. Specific prayers and liturgical elements, recited in English or Hebrew, can provide sustenance and inspiration. For me, chanting the words, "*Elohai n'shamah shenata bi t'horah hi*" (God, the soul you have given me is pure),[10] and, "*Kol han'shamah t'hallel Yah*" (Let everything that has breath praise God),[11] feels profoundly comforting. Colleagues cited the Maimonidean prayer for physicians, the *Mi Shebeirakh* prayer, the Priestly Blessing, and reciting *Kaddish* when a patient dies as other liturgical sources of meaning.

Several Jewish healthcare professionals in my survey expressed a desire for contact with others. For example: "I would love to have a support group of Jewish providers who see the same brokenness I see, to learn how they balance their work and beliefs. I hope to get some tips about how to merge my Jewish and work life—how to use Judaism to be less pessimistic." Another hoped we might "create a network of Jewish physicians, and others in clinical practice, who can share ideas regarding the impact in their lives and Judaism." As healthcare professionals, we spend many work hours caring for patients and completing the associated administrative tasks. We may become isolated from any colleagues, and we certainly rarely experience the opportunity to interact with other Jewish healthcare professionals.

When I participated in the Kalsman Institute physician's educational initiative, ASSAF: Judaism, Health and Healing for Physicians,[12] a gathering and online study program, I felt moved and inspired by the discussions, text study, singing, and praying that we shared together. Some synagogues have held retreats for healthcare professionals to offer similar experiences. Jewish healing networks in some communities may offer similar opportunities.

When asked in what additional ways they hoped that Judaism could help in their clinical work, providers asked for educational opportunities, support from mentors, meeting with Jewish chaplains, discussions with rabbis, and the opportunity to study texts. One colleague hoped for assistance "simply to help me stay humble and sincere." Jewish healthcare professionals who belong to a synagogue or other organized Jewish communal institution can serve a special role in that organization's life, in a way that may offer them fulfillment and meaning. Bringing one's experience and resources as a healthcare provider—leadership, patience, teaching skills, compassion—that is, lessons learned in clinical circumstances—can be helpful, both to share with each other and to offer to the larger community. Some synagogues may have a Jewish pastoral care initiative, and most have need of members who will visit ill and elderly congregants (*bikkur cholim*) who are either homebound or hospitalized. Many communities have *g'milut chesed* (acts of loving-kindness) and social action committees. Healthcare professionals may find it fulfilling to serve a mentoring role for young people in the community, describing educational choices and paths to becoming a healthcare provider.

One colleague articulated the nature of the connection between being Jewish and being a healthcare professional:

> My Judaism and my healthcare work are interwoven. They inform one another. They both present questions and mysteries, and they both challenge me to distinguish between puzzles to be solved and mysteries to be experienced.

The words of a well-known song lyric from Psalms say, "Behold, how good and how pleasant it is for brothers [and sisters] to dwell together—*gam yachad*—in unity, in togetherness, in integration" (Psalm 133:1). We know that our patients and their families seek wholeness and integration in their healing. I believe that it is "good and pleasant" for us as Jewish healthcare professionals to be *gam yachad* in our lives. May we find integration in our lives as we seek to address the questions and experience the mysteries.

Part II

Jewish Pastoral Care and Caregiving

Jewish Healthcare Chaplaincy

Professionalizing Spiritual Caregiving

Rabbi Naomi Kalish, BCC

A Historical Snapshot

Judaism, like virtually all religions and cultures, encourages the care of those who are sick, hospitalized, dying, and bereaved. Jews trace the value of visiting the sick to Genesis 18:1, in which God visits Abraham after his circumcision,[1] and to the millennia-old Jewish practice of *bikkur cholim* (visiting the sick). The Talmud classifies the commandment of *bikkur cholim* as incumbent upon all Jews, certainly not only rabbis.[2] In the latter half of the twentieth century and the beginning of the twenty-first century, Jews in North America dramatically changed their practice of caregiving through creating and professionalizing the field of Jewish healthcare chaplaincy.

Initially rabbis assumed positions as chaplains through the military and then in healthcare settings. Those who held positions of religious leadership in hospitals, prisons, nursing homes, and universities were referred to as "chaplains," a term etymologically dating back to the fourth-century legend of Saint Martin of Tours, which connects to the conversion of a Roman soldier to Christianity after an act of compassion.[3] Since that time, the term "chaplain" has been the standard term for all clergy providing for the pastoral needs of people when they are away from their normative home religious environment.[4] Chaplains

---

Rabbi Naomi Kalish, BCC, is coordinator of pastoral care and education at New York–Presbyterian / Morgan Stanley Children's Hospital in New York, New York.

have been the clergy who administered chapels, houses of worship that were away from the main sanctuary. Today, chaplains are found in liminal spaces—battlefields, prisons, universities, nursing homes. The first rabbis who served as military chaplains in the United States date back to the Civil War, and the first known Jewish healthcare chaplain was Rabbi Samuel Isaacs, an Orthodox rabbi, who worked from 1852 to 1878 at New York's Jews' Hospital, later renamed Mount Sinai Hospital.[5] Other non-Christian faith groups have also assumed the term "chaplain," including Muslims and Buddhists.

In the mid-1920s, Protestant ministers and physicians birthed a radical form of education for "theological students," which would later prompt the establishment and professionalization of the entire field of chaplaincy. Their classes took place in the clinic as opposed to the academy, and they applied scientific methods, such as the case study, to their training of seminarians. When Dr. Richard Cabot, the innovator of the case study in medical education and the founder of medical social work, brought a clinical approach to religious education, he helped found the field of clinical pastoral education (CPE).[6]

Jews created the field of Jewish healthcare chaplaincy by both joining and differentiating from broader general fields of chaplaincy. This transition occurred amid the popularization of psychology and the changing attitudes toward diversity in the general society. World War II and its aftermath were a watershed era, with its cultural triumph of science that has permeated virtually all realms of North American society, including religion and health. Psychology became a reference point and means of validation in fields across American society, including education and business administration. During and after World War II, the prevailing religious ethos of the United States was interfaith—a perspective that prioritized the areas of commonality among different religious groups. During the war, the U.S. military significantly expanded its chaplaincy and created quotas for representation from the Protestant, Catholic, and Jewish religions. Additionally, it mandated the provision of religious services. This was an important juncture for the recognition and inclusion of Jews in the broader American religious life. Sociologist Will Herberg wrote of the change from a previous vision of America as one melting pot in which identities mixed and merged to an America with these faiths constituting a "tripartite" division of American civil religiosity.[7] Yet, despite differences, chaplains were also expected to provide emotional counseling and support across religious boundaries. Stories are even told of chaplains conducting religious services for other faith traditions, such as one Episcopal priest and chaplain, who had studied Hebrew in seminary, who led a Jewish Passover seder when there was no one Jewish who was able to.[8]

This period also witnessed a rise in professionalizing. The concept of "the professions" emerged in the nineteenth century and specifically referred to the fields of medicine, law, and ministry.[9] After World War II, numerous other fields began to become professionalized, including psychology, psychiatry, and social work and, in the Jewish community, the fields of Hillel, Jewish day school and supplemental education, and Jewish studies in higher education. The fields of chaplaincy and CPE began to blossom during this period, and religious leaders from underrepresented groups, including the Jewish community, began to enroll in CPE in small numbers. Believing that their religious studies were not adequately preparing them for the rabbinate, they pursued additional training. Rabbi Fred Hollander played a pioneering role for the Jewish community, entering this field during this era. In 1948, recently ordained at Yeshiva University, he transformed a volunteer position at Bellevue Hospital in New York City into an employment position and continued on to become the first Jew "accredited" to teach chaplaincy.

By the 1980s and 1990s, the prevailing ethos in the chaplaincy field had shifted to multiculturalism, in which the contrasts between religious groups were emphasized and (hopefully) respected. During this era, Jews began to enter the fields of healthcare chaplaincy and CPE in greater numbers. Jewish chaplains sought to establish their work as a profession with its various trappings. With the leadership of its founding president, Rabbi Jeffrey Silberman, in 1990 they established an association, the National Association of Jewish Chaplains (NAJC), which has become the premier professional association for Jewish chaplains.[10] Since its founding, NAJC has established credentialing through board certification, requirements for clinical training, a journal (*The Jewish Chaplain*, later renamed *Jewish Spiritual Care*), a loose body of specialized knowledge, an annual conference, and a code of ethics. NAJC emerged as part of a trend of new organizations that sought to create a context for their religiously or culturally distinctive group.[11]

One characteristic of the first decade of the twenty-first century has been a rise in interest and an ethos of spirituality. The Joint Commission, the leading accrediting agency for healthcare institutions in the United States, standardized the requirement of spiritual care services for patients—for example, "Each patient has the right to have his or her cultural, psychosocial, spiritual, and personal values, beliefs, and preferences respected"; "The hospital accommodates the right to pastoral and other spiritual services for patients."[12] This has both supported the profession of healthcare chaplaincy as well as sparked interest in other disciplines regarding their own role in the provision of spiritual care. In the past decade, there was a startling increase in the number of publications in spirituality and spiritual care in medical literature.[13]

"Spirituality" is an elusive term, and its definition and distinction from (or relationship to) religiosity remain an area in chaplaincy and healthcare that lacks clear definition. In 2009, a group of national leaders in palliative care met for a consensus conference and formulated the following definition: "Spirituality is the aspect of humanity that refers to the way individuals seek and express meaning and purpose and the way they experience their connectedness to the moment, to self, to others, to nature, and to the significant or sacred."[14] Chaplains are frequently in the position of needing to make the case for their funding within the hospital or other healthcare setting (as a value-added service, as opposed to a reimbursable service that produces revenue). The report of the Consensus Project framed the role of chaplain as the "spiritual care specialists" among a team of generalists.[15]

In 2004, NAJC joined with other pastoral care and education organizations in the United States and Canada and formed the Spiritual Care Collaborative, establishing common standards for pastoral care education, certification, and ethics. Jewish healthcare chaplaincy, like the broader chaplaincy field, is not government regulated. Credentialing includes clinical training and board certification; however, the field does not have government licensure and is not eligible for insurance reimbursement. In these ways, healthcare chaplaincy is similar to the field of child life and different from the fields of social work, medicine, clinical psychology, and nursing. Currently Jewish and non-Jewish chaplains are examining the issue of licensure, debating whether or not pursuing it would advance the profession.

The spirituality era of the chaplaincy field has served a unifying purpose, and the Jewish healthcare chaplaincy movement has joined in efforts to advocate for the expansion of the field. At the same time, Jewish healthcare chaplaincy has resisted a broader cultural pressure to move toward a universalist model of chaplaincy. Jewish chaplains have vocalized areas of discrepancy or discord between the prevailing model of CPE and Jewish approaches to caregiving, religious leadership, and life in general. Whether speaking for their own participation in the broader professional field or advocating for patients, they have been most vocal about Shabbat and holiday observance, kosher dietary laws, the absence of a central endorsing agency for religious functioning (a standard for ministry in Christian communities), and Jewish approach to religious thought, emphasizing a midrashic dialogical process as opposed to systematic theology.

An offshoot and example of this commitment to a multicultural and multi-faith approach to spiritual care was NAJC's development and support of programs to develop a professional field of spiritual care in Israel, in 2005.[16]

While the broader field of chaplaincy serves as a meeting ground between psychology and religion, Jewish healthcare chaplaincy adds another angle of viewing the diversity aspects through the lens of a minority religion. These themes are reflected in various characteristics of the field, as discussed next.

Characteristics of the Field of Jewish Healthcare Chaplaincy

Historically, Jewish chaplains have been rabbis. In 1993, NAJC decided "that lay people (in addition to rabbis or cantors) who have chaplaincy training, advanced Jewish education, and advanced secular education can become full professional members of the NAJC."[17] This change was intended to shape Jewish chaplaincy in a more authentic manner. The requirement that chaplains be clergy, which included cantors, was a reflection of Christian models of leadership. Though the profession of Jewish chaplaincy was new, it drew upon the centuries-old caregiving practice of *bikkur cholim*, and it was believed that it should not exclude the religious leadership of Orthodox women who could not be ordained as rabbis but nevertheless embodied religious leadership. Over time, women and men from across the Jewish religious spectrum have begun to pursue careers in chaplaincy without ordination, even when ordination was open to them. Chaplaincy is emerging as a new model of Jewish religious leadership, overlapping with but not completely coinciding with the rabbinate.

Jewish chaplains hold a variety of different kinds of positions. Initially they served solely as what is now referred to as "faith-specific chaplains." In such a paradigm, the vast majority of the patients served by these are Jewish. The chaplains tend to the patients' and their families' religious needs, such as ensuring the availability of kosher food and enabling Shabbat and holiday observance. They might be consulted by the interdisciplinary healthcare team about halakhic, cultural, and ethical issues regarding the care of Jewish patients. This approach to staffing reflects a multicultural approach to spirituality and emphasizes distinctiveness. In the 1990s and beginning of the twentieth century, the model of the "multi-faith chaplain" emerged; such a position could be held by a person from any religious background. These chaplains are assigned by clinical unit or service line, visiting all of the patients on those units regardless of religious identity, even including those who do not identify religiously. This approach is based on the belief that spiritual care during times of crisis can take place in a meaningful way, human to human, across religious and cultural boundaries. Some Jewish chaplains are supervisors of CPE, working in either Jewish or religiously diverse contexts. Some Jewish chaplains are also employed as directors of their healthcare pastoral care departments, overseeing the administrative functioning.

Professional Jewish chaplains in all of these roles integrate psychological theory and counseling methods into their practice. Whereas traditional understandings of the rabbinic role have included teacher, halakhic advisor, decision maker, and officiant, the Jewish healthcare chaplain seeks to provide a supportive role that may also bring connection or resonance with Judaism and Jewish tradition and community. The chaplain provides an opportunity for those cared for to narrate their story of illness and hospitalization, as well as emotional response and sense of meaning. The chaplain strives to help patients access their own spiritual resources, whether they come from traditional religious sources or newer, creative, and sometimes secular places. Sometimes a chaplain and patient will have a shared experience of prayer or another religious experience; however, this is a matter of assessment. Chaplains are also trained to be psychologically self-aware of their experience while caregiving. As one report of a CPE program describes, the chaplain interns would ask, "When the particular need of this patient becomes obvious to me, how do I react to it? Do I want to run away from it, or do I want to sidestep it, or do I want to meet it squarely and attempt to minister to it?"[18]

When rabbis (or other Jewish leaders) choose to work in a healthcare setting, they place themselves professionally in an organizational context significantly different from the synagogue or other Jewish institutions. Each hospital determines the exact place of its chaplains or department and to whom they report within the organizational structure. With the structure and culture of healthcare, chaplains are often considered an auxiliary and voluntary service, where the primary purpose is medical, surgical, or psychiatric care. Chaplains acquire both medical and organizational vocabularies, using terms such as "intern," "resident," and "assessment." Chaplains are members of the healthcare interdisciplinary team, joining physicians, nurses, social workers, psychologists, psychiatrists, and child life specialists in determining goals of care. Whereas a congregational rabbi might oversee the provision of assisting with direct services, such as housing for a homeless person, a chaplain would refer this to a social worker (and knowing when and how to refer to other members of the team is considered a competency area). In the healthcare settings and their classification of professional specialists, chaplains focus their work primarily on the provision of religious services, spiritual care, and emotional support.

Jewish chaplains can potentially serve patients in all clinical areas of healthcare settings. Depending on the healthcare setting and their specific job description, they can work with people throughout their life course. The combination of humanism and of religious (and cultural) distinctiveness is a unique feature of the field. Being in service is a characteristic of the helping professions, although caring for people from diverse religious and cultural backgrounds is not necessarily a typical part of that service.

In 1993, Jewish hospital chaplain and CPE supervisor Phyllis Toback raised the issue of caregiving across religious boundaries, offering the case example of a Jewish chaplain's response to a request for a Christian emergency baptism.[19] Her reflection piece sparked a lively conversation in which some Jewish leaders responded that although healthcare chaplaincy in North America was an "interfaith ministry" in which "the [Jewish] chaplain must counsel them [non-Jews] and pray with them in a religious language that *they* understand,"[20] Jewish law prohibited Jewish chaplains from performing Christian sacraments. These policymakers knew that their ruling conflicted with a prevailing American ethos of minimizing distinctions between clergy: "We intentionally run counter to a distinct trend in North American culture. There is a tendency, due perhaps to the popular culture of secular Christianity, to view all clergy as interchangeable to some degree."[21]

This story reveals that over forty years after the field had begun to diversify religiously, practitioners continued—and continue today—to struggle to balance the universalism of counseling and the particularism of their specific religions. Jews in the field walk a tightrope between a commitment to caregiving on a human level, person to person, that can transcend religion, culture, race, ethnicity, gender, and all other identity differences, and a commitment to providing for the distinctive needs of diverse populations.

Jewish healthcare chaplaincy is also a meeting place for Jews from across the Jewish spectrum. As with multi-faith chaplaincy, these encounters can be meaningful and even exhilarating. In multi-faith chaplaincy, when patients, families, or staff ask Jewish chaplains to engage in an activity that is contrary to his or her religious practice, the chaplain must navigate a patient-centered approach to caregiving and concern for his or her own religious and spiritual well-being. Issues that have raised such tension have included requests to recite *b'rit milah* blessings at a medical circumcision not conducted according to *halakhah* and to officiate at a cremation. A Jewish approach to healthcare chaplaincy is well poised to navigate the space between caregiver and care recipient with its commitment to respecting difference.

The essence of the Jewish healthcare chaplaincy field is that it is Jewish at its core, not merely an association of chaplains who happen to be Jewish. Yet Jewish chaplains debate what makes their profession Jewish. Is it the provision of Jewish religious services (e.g., the *Mi Shebeirakh* prayer for healing, the *viddui* deathbed confession, kosher food)? Is it the theoretical paradigms that inform the practice and accompanying Jewish language? Does the environment, the identity of the institution, contribute? Considering that professional chaplaincy employs a relational caregiving model in which the healing relationship is uniquely characterized by the specific caregiver and care recipient, how do the identities of the patient and chaplain make the chaplaincy care "Jewish"?

Bethamie Horowitz's social-psychological study of Jewish identity is helpful for conceptualizing the Jewishness of Jewish healthcare chaplaincy. Horowitz moves away from sociodemographic paradigms for understanding Jewish identity that correlate strength of identity with "activity levels of Jewish individuals in terms of ritual practice, cultural and educational involvement and institutional affiliations, philanthropic giving, and friendship networks."[22] Horowitz finds this essentialist approach static, as it is based on fixed notions of normative Jewish practice and does not account for historical context, changes in identity over the life span, and the diversification of the Jewish community. Horowitz incorporated a psychological lens into her study that allowed her to look at subjective meaning making. She was particularly interested in two questions: "How are American Jews Jewish?" and "In what ways, if any do they connect to Jewishness and Judaism?"[23]

These questions for probing and understanding Jewish identity are especially apropos to two activities that are specific to healthcare chaplains, which generally are not employed by rabbis outside of healthcare institutions, even rabbis in other settings or roles in which they draw on psychology and training in counseling: spiritual assessment and theological reflection.

While hospitals routinely ask about a patient's religious identity and record it in the medical record, professionally trained chaplains use spiritual assessment tools to understand a patient's or other recipient of care's subjective spiritual experience. Researchers and practitioners of spiritual care frequently distinguish between religiosity and spirituality and between religious services and spiritual care. Applying Horowitz's approach to understanding to the work of the Jewish healthcare chaplain, one might ask: How are the various components of the spiritual care provided Jewish? And how do the caregiver and care recipient connect the encounter with Judaism? Additionally, one can examine how other aspects of caregiving (e.g., the environment, language, and paradigms for caregiving) echo or resonate with aspects of Judaism.

Jewish chaplains have voiced protest against early models of spiritual assessment. While the tools are meant to be useful for assessing the spiritual condition regardless of religion or culture, Jews found that they reflected a Christian approach to spirituality, limiting their ability to accurately reflect a Jewish experience. Because they used such categories as providence, grace, forgiveness, and relationship with God—concepts not absent in Judaism but not central either—Jewish chaplains felt inauthentic using them. In 1994, Rabbis Marion Shulevitz and Mychal Springer published the first articulation of a Jewish approach to spiritual assessment.[24] Another tool draws on a statement by twentieth-century theologian Mordecai Kaplan. As described by theologian Neil Gillman:

> Kaplan used to teach that there are three possible ways of identifying with a religious community: by behaving, by believing, or by belonging. Kaplan himself insisted that the primary form of *Jewish* identification is belonging—that intuitive sense of kinship that binds a Jew to every other Jew in history and in the contemporary world.[25]

Basing a spiritual assessment model on this Jewish approach to identity allows for a profile to be taken of the patients' identities—how they subjectively construct their Jewishness. Their Judaism can manifest primarily as a form of peoplehood (belonging) and manifest in ethnic association (i.e., Zionism), or communal affiliation, even in secular organizations such as the Jewish War Veterans or Hadassah. The behaving category makes space for understanding Jewish identity through either a traditional observance of *mitzvot* or through action, such as social justice activism. Believing can capture a spirituality based in religious belief, one's relationship with God, or activities of the intellect that are not necessarily based in religion, such as scholarship or worldviews. This paradigm can be used like a Venn diagram to examine Horowitz's question about how one connects to Judaism.

A profile of a person's behaving, believing, and belonging can be constructed and then each area can be examined for how it interacts with the other areas and the person's attitudes and affective response to the Judaism. This final step helps the chaplain formulate future goals of care. Spiritual assessment in and of itself can be a form of spiritual caregiving, as it allows a person to articulate his or her sense of meaning.

A chaplain will help a patient engage in theological reflection, a process by which a person draws from his or her spiritual resources for guidance with the current situation. Again, Horowitz's constructivist approach to Jewish identity provides insight relevant to this process:

> The image of Jewishness implicit here is not an unchanging "given"; rather, Jewishness is seen as constituted by the individual living in a particular web of relationships within a particular cultural context. The individual does not simply inherit Jewishness as a whole self-contained package; rather s/he engages with and potentially incorporates elements of Jewishness into the self through a process that anthropologists have termed the reinvention of ethnicity. This approach to the study of Jewish identity emphasizes the diverse ways of being Jewish, rather than better or worse levels of Jewishness.[26]

Not only do chaplains create a framework for care recipients to engage in this process for coping with their current situation (illness, hospitalization, medical treatment, surgery, caregiving, dying, and bereavement), they engage in theological reflection for guidance in their practice of spiritual caregiving. They reflect on their own spiritual resources to provide insight into human nature during times of crisis and models of healing and resiliency.

Conclusion

Jewish healthcare chaplaincy has emerged as a profession in its own right. Stemming from the rabbinate and still largely comprising clergy, it distinguishes itself with its own specialized knowledge, education, credentialing, professional associations and institutions, publications, and work environments. Jewish healthcare chaplains meet Jews and those with connections to Judaism and the Jewish community in new places and in ways they would not be cared for otherwise.

Wendy Cadge, a sociologist of religion, has described the general field of healthcare chaplaincy as a "profession in process" or "a professional group with many segments in transition."[27] The same can be said of the profession of Jewish healthcare chaplaincy, as it, too, engages in the continued work of strengthening and integrating the professional standards and practices its leadership has formulated. Additionally, the Jewish healthcare chaplaincy movement is in transition in contributing its vision to the broader field of chaplaincy. It has the potential not only to address concerns of the Jewish community, but to advocate and shape a philosophical stance toward caregiving and diversity that benefits the broader field and American society. Alongside other movements that advocate for the similarities throughout the entire field of chaplaincy, Jewish healthcare chaplaincy is poised to strengthen the field by providing language and approaches that help us understand the uniqueness of each individual served.

Jewish Pastoral Care

Rabbi Mychal B. Springer

When I began my pastoral care training twenty-one years ago, my biggest fear was that I would be expected—by patients, families, supervisors, Judaism—to pray with people. This expectation scared me because I did not have a faith that supported petitionary prayer. While I had grown up with a palpable sense of God's presence, my own life experiences and the challenges of becoming an academically rigorous Conservative rabbi had left me with a sense of God in eclipse. I did not want to represent to others that I thought God would be listening and responding. And I did not want to disabuse people of the efficacy of prayer if they felt its power in their lives. At the heart of the matter, I did not believe I had a right to be visiting patients and families as a rabbi without that faith. So I was stuck.

Eventually, I had to grapple with my fears head-on. That is one of the blessings of pastoral work: the very things we fear are the ones that can become our most important teachers. I found myself serving on a unit for women with ovarian cancer, and one of my patients, M., told me that she wanted to be able to pray but that she did not know how. Did God send her to me? My theology did not support that, and yet, that is how it felt. So my fear of praying came face-to-face with a real, live person who needed my help praying. I shared with her that I did not know how to pray either, and then the two of us committed to working together to figure out what prayer could actually be for us.

As I searched for an authentic way for me to pray, I gravitated toward Yehuda Amichai's poem "*El Maleh Rakhamim*" (God Full of Mercy). He plays with the traditional prayer and turns it on its head, writing:

Rabbi Mychal B. Springer holds the Helen Fried Kirshblum Goldstein Chair in Professional and Pastoral Skills and is director of the Center for Pastoral Education at the Jewish Theological Seminary in New York, New York.

> *El Maleh Rachamim* / God-Full-of-Mercy
> *Ilmaleh ha-El maleh rachamim* / If God was not full of mercy
> *Hayu ha-rachamim ba'olam v'lo rak bo* / Mercy would be in the world, / Not just in Him.[1]

This poem gives permission for anger and irony. By starting with the traditional formulation, Amichai conveys that the traditional beliefs and imagery are still alive, yet they need not be embraced without protest. It was that protest that spoke to me so fully as I encountered woman after woman who was dying of cancer. And the fact that it was ovarian cancer linked me to this poem in profound ways, as I wrestled with the womblessness of these women. The link between *rechem* (womb) and *rachamim* (mercy) felt particularly poignant as M. and I searched to experience God's mercy in the absence of her *rechem*.

Ultimately, M. and I decided to pray by addressing God. For M., "Dear God" was the way in. For me, evoking God through a variety of traditional names, including *HaRachaman*, the Merciful One, helped me to focus on the aspects of God that I needed to connect with the most. In order to pray with M., I had to let go of any sense of knowing how God worked. I had to allow myself to begin with the desire to feel God's presence, even as that took me into territory beyond what my brain could understand. I discovered, in praying with M., that there was a rich quality to that prayer space, that there was a palpable change, that at times I could sense God's presence, even though I could not tell you how. It was this experience of praying, the opening of the heart in a moment of vulnerability, that was the beginning of my becoming unstuck, of coming to believe that the experiences of being with others helped me tap into a relationship with God that went beyond rational explanations and began to restore me to faith.

One way in which the Rabbis conceptualized the human obligation to provide care for one another is grounded in the idea that people are commanded to emulate God's ways:

> The Holy Blessed One visits the ill, as it says, "And God visited him [Abraham] in Elonei Mamreih" (Genesis 18:1), so you too shall visit the ill."[2]

The Rabbis determined that God attends to the sick by looking at the story of Abraham when he is recovering from his circumcision. In keeping with the customary usage of the words *vayeira eilav* ("and God visited him"), the verse should continue with a verbal declaration from God.[3] But our verse is the exception, and these words are not followed by any verbal declaration at all. In looking to understand why this verse is different, the Rabbis extrapolated that the point of this visit was *bikkur cholim*, the visiting of the sick. Rashi, the twelfth-century commentator, drawing on the Midrash, interpolates that God asked after his *sha'al mah sh'lomo* (well-being).[4] Israel Kestenbaum writes that the absence of that verbal declaration comes to teach us that God's method was to *be with* Abraham.[5] There was no content that needed to be revealed, because the relationship itself, in the midst of Abraham's suffering, was the focus. Kestenbaum sees the loving gift of the relationship itself to be the source of the healing. As we look at foundational concepts of spiritual care, this insight about God's method of caring for the sick elevates the importance of presence, attunement, and drawing near over content. In striving to emulate God in caring for others, people must strive to become as fully present as possible.

This emphasis on being is echoed powerfully in the penitential liturgy of Yom Kippur and is present in the daily liturgy during *Tachanun*. In the prayer of supplication *Avinu Malkeinu*, "Our Father, Our King," we pray for God's mercy and grace:

> Avinu Malkeinu, have mercy on us, answer us, for our deeds are insufficient; deal with us charitably and lovingly, and redeem us.[6]

Our deeds are insufficient. In the face of all of Judaism's emphasis on *mitzvot*, of acting according to God's will, there is a fundamental assertion that our deeds fall short. If the measure is our deeds, then we cannot earn God's love. Literally, the prayer says *ein banu ma'asim* (we have no deeds). God's relationship with us is determined by God's *chesed*, God's love for us. Despite the importance of taking responsibility for our acts, ultimately God's love is a promise, is unwavering. This love is the basis of God's relationship with us and must be the basis of our relationship with others. In being present to the other, our orientation must be to be loving echoes, embodiments, of God's love.

The psalms cry out with the suffering of those who crave the healing presence of God. Psalm 27, for example, depicts a yearning to be close to God:

> *One thing do I ask of the Lord,*
> *it is this that I seek—*
> *that I dwell in the house of the Lord,*
> *all the days of my life,*
> *to behold the Lord's sweetness*
> *and to gaze on His palace.*[7]

The image of being close to God is of being physically in God's space, the Temple. The opposite image is of experiencing God's hidden face, God's inaccessibility. The psalmist dreads this experience of God-turned-away and pleads:

> *Do not hide Your face from me,*
> *do not turn Your servant away in wrath.*[8]

There is a pronounced physicality to the understanding of divine presence and absence. The physicality adds power to the cry, the beseeching. The image of the distance and the desperation to draw near takes center stage in the psalm. The dynamic of reading the psalm is that the voice that cries out demands to be heard. The psalmist grapples with anger, the possibility that the withdrawal is due to God's anger, and the fear and anger that the psalmist has about feeling abandoned. The lament itself is seen as faithful. Only through the lament is healing possible. As the anguish is witnessed, then the psalmist is able to experience God's face shining on him or her.[9]

The physicality of divine presence and absence translates strikingly into the realm of spiritual care. To begin with, the laws regarding *bikkur cholim* (visiting the sick) involve the obligation to be present with the person who is sick.[10] The physical showing up, which has no measure (the more the better), echoes the psalmist's plea to draw near. The laws about attending to the sick person's physical needs, drawn from the *aggadah* (Rabbinic story) about Rabbi Akiba who swept the floor when his student was sick, demonstrate that the realm of the spiritual must include an awareness of the larger context in which the suffering person dwells.[11] Spiritual care must include an awareness of who is shunned in our society and the ways in which people who are perceived as not being whole continue to be devalued. Based in the assertion in Genesis that we are all created *b'tzelem Elohim* (in the divine image; Genesis 1:27), spiritual care begins with truly seeing the divine image in all of humanity. This acknowledgment of the sacredness of humanity must be grounded in attuned relationships with particular individuals. By offering our presence to another, we value that person; we bear witness to his or her story and reality. By turning our face toward the other, we alleviate his or her suffering.

But the physicality of wanting to draw near also reminds us of the pain of God being beyond reach in ways that cannot readily be repaired. The destruction of the First and Second Temples in Jerusalem echoes the expulsion from the Garden of Eden and also the experience of being sent into slavery in Egypt. While the theme of exile as punishment for sins certainly exists in the tradition, the promise of return is just as firmly in place. Exile provides us with a chance to examine our ways and become reoriented on a path of right living, even as we have to grieve the losses that are involved.

Beyond the destruction of the Temples, the language of exile captures a truth about human experience that resonates apart from the specific historical events. The human condition itself is a condition of exile, of alienation. Inside of religious narratives we live with the hope of return, in its largest sense. Michael Fishbane sees "movements from disorientation and chaos to orientation and cosmos at a sacred center" as the central narrative of the Bible.[12] This narrative captures human experience on a profound level. Lurianic mysticism, which emerged in the sixteenth century in response to the Jewish expulsion from Spain, understands exile as "a metaphysical symbol for all that is wrong, out of joint, imperfect, or unredeemed in creation."[13] While biblical prophets warn that the destruction will be the result of the people's sins, once the destruction of the Second Temple happens we begin to see a non-retributive justice approach to Israel's sufferings. The Talmud teaches that each time God's people have gone into exile, *Shekhinah* (God's presence) went with us. And that when we will be redeemed, *Shekhinah* will be redeemed with us.[14] This teaching affirms that in the face of great suffering, presence in its fullest sense is the source of comfort. (From a gender perspective, it is noteworthy that the *Shekhinah* is God's feminine aspect.) But the passage goes even further in looking at the theological dynamics involved. Here we see that our longing for return and redemption is shared by God. An aspect of God joins us in our brokenness.

A line from the *hoshanot* liturgy (prayers of supplication for salvation offered during Sukkot, the holiday of booths) echoes this idea and can help us to understand the dynamics more fully. These prayers have their origins in the circumambulation of the altar in the Temple period. In the prayer "Save Yourself and us!" which is recited daily throughout the holiday, we chant:

> *As You saved the chorus who sang out "God saved!"*
> *And You who gave birth to them were saved with them, help us now.*[15]
> *As You freed them, declaring: "I will bring you out," which our sages interpreted:*
> *"I went out with you,"* hosha na! *Help us now....*
> *As You accompanied the people You sent into Babylon,*
> *Journeying into exile with them, help us now.*[16]

In the first couplet, we see that God saved the people and was somehow also saved with them. The Savior is in need of salvation. There is something about the process of human beings being saved that contributes to God's restoration. We could say that this hints at the limitation of God's power. Or we could say that the human experience is intimately bound up with the divine experience. If we return to the idea that we have to emulate God, we might almost see this as a variation that understands that God's experience in the world, as it were, is only possible in relationship with human beings. So when people are saved, God is also saved. This idea is further substantiated in the second couplet, where God is the one who brings the people out of Egypt, and yet God is also brought out of Egypt (*hotzeiti etkhem*) in the process. Finally, in the third couplet, God sends the people into exile and God goes, too. In the Hebrew the verb is *shulachti* (I was sent), conveying that God was sent into exile along with the people, not just that God chose to accompany them.

The interconnectedness of human experience and divine experience conveys great love. Somehow, human and divine stories depend on one another. So it is not too much of a stretch to say that when we attend to another person, we attend to God. When we help restore another person to a sense of cosmos, we help restore the Holy One to cosmos. This is what is meant when Lurianic mysticism teaches that the sparks of the *Shekhinah* are scattered throughout the world and in our exile we must gather up the sparks, through religious acts, so that God and the world can be restored to wholeness.[17] In this way, the healing of spiritual care is linked to redemption not just of the individual, but of humanity, the Divine, and the cosmos itself.

By accompanying us into exile, God is functioning in a healing way. The aspect of God that is broken, in need of redemption from exile, is the aspect of God that is most available to us when we ourselves are in exile. In the depths of our suffering, it is not the transcendent aspect of God that offers the greatest comfort. Back to the imagery of Psalm 27, the glory of being in God's Temple is not an option. Our only hope is to experience God's face shining on us. And the face we yearn to see has to be with us in our exile. The face cannot be at a remove, seemingly unaffected by the trauma of our overturned lives. By understanding that God is sent into exile with us, the Rabbis underscored that God's healing power is tied up in God being with us. And therefore, in order to emulate God, we must have access to our own brokenness as well. In order to offer spiritual care to others, we must make space for our own experiences of exile and know that we can only participate in their coming out of their Egypt when we know that our own experience of coming out of Egypt is bound up in their story as well.

Estelle Frankel quotes Rabbi Menachem Mendel of Kotzk's saying, "Nothing is more whole than a broken heart."[18] She offers her interpretation of what this means:

> If we can find a way to hold and embrace our pain gently, recognizing that brokenness is simply part of the human condition—in a sense, nothing special—then we may begin to feel empathically connected to all other beings. This is the broken heart that makes us whole.[19]

The God/*Shekhinah* who models going into Egypt with us shows us that we cannot remain separate from the suffering or we become irrelevant. Spiritual healing begins with joining with the other, even as we maintain our separate identities. In order for caregivers to be attuned to the other's wholeness, they must embrace their own stories of exile and return, their own disorientation, brokenness, and experiences of reorientation. Only then can there be genuine ability and willingness to enter into the disorientation of exile in order to journey with another, with the hope of participating in some aspect of return.

One very dramatic way in which the reality of brokenness and the need for healing is highlighted inside of Jewish tradition and practice is through the marking of Tisha B'Av, the Fast of the Ninth of Av, which commemorates the destruction of both Temples in Jerusalem and the expulsion from Spain. By including this day in the liturgical calendar, the Rabbis emphasized that the experience of suffering must be grappled with regularly, that brokenness is central to our communal experience and our understanding of our relationship with God. The restrictions of the fast day convey that Tisha B'Av is both a day of atonement and a day of mourning.[20] As a day of atonement, it reminds us that we have to grapple with the responsibility we bear for how we function in this world. Spiritual caregivers need to be equipped to help people reflect on their lives and sort through the ways in which they have gone astray, which is the first step of turning in *t'shuvah* (repentance) and seeking forgiveness. As a day of mourning, Tisha B'Av helps us to recognize that the human need to tell the story of our losses is key to our being able to move toward wholeness.

The book of Lamentations is read in the synagogue on Tisha B'Av. The book tells the story of the destruction of the Temple in vivid language and draws the reader/listener into the story as a witness. Kathleen M. O'Connor reflects on the ways that the book of Lamentations orients us in spiritual care.[21] She speaks about the function of the lament. The lament is the crying out for "the Absent One, the God who hides behind the clouds."[22] Precisely because God is not available, the lament can be fully articulated without being minimized. O'Connor gleans a theology of witness from the book of Lamentations:

> Lamentations can shred the heart and spawn despair, but, paradoxically, by mirroring pain it can also comfort the afflicted and open the way toward healing. It can affirm the dignity of those

who suffer, release their tears, and overcome their experience of abandonment.[23]

The witness plays a key role in helping the sufferer heal. In the face of overwhelming suffering, it is the crying out itself and being heard by the witness that provide the possibility of redemption, that make hope possible: "Although lamenting the truth in even a partial way can take generations, there is no way forward without bringing suffering to voice."[24] Spiritual care rests on being able to hear the other into speech. This process can feel overwhelming to the caregiver, who needs to grapple with his or her own pain in order to see the pain of others most fully.[25] By confronting our despair, we come to renewed life and the establishment of a more robust community.[26]

A middle-aged Jewish woman, Stephanie, whose husband is dying, met with me not long ago. She wanted me to give her guidance about how the Jewish tradition could help her travel through the period of his dying. She began by seeking information. This is often how pastoral contact with clergy begins. The temptation is to answer the question, to be polite. But if we return to the idea that the essence of *bikkur cholim* (attending to the sick) and, by extension, attending to those who love them is being with them, then we need to invite the one we are caring for to move away from the content, to make room for a fuller connection. I invited Stephanie to put the resource question on hold for a moment, assuring her that we would return to it. I did not want her to think that I was not mindful of her expressed need, but I needed to help her learn how she could draw on me as a resource in a fuller sense than she had expected.

As we began to talk, she told me about her relationship with her husband and some of what his illness had been like for her and their family. She conveyed that she knew his time on earth was very limited, and she had a sense that others had gone through this before her, so she wanted to benefit from the wisdom of others. Her impulse came from wanting to overcome the isolation of going through a profoundly disorienting experience. Although she could not avoid the disorientation in its largest sense, she had enough positive experiences inside of Jewish community to know that our tradition could ease the suffering by holding her up as she went through it. She proclaimed herself a reader in search of material to read, and I did give her references to a couple of books. (We are, after all, the people of the book.) I also told her about some communal resources, such as the Jewish Healing Center, which offers spiritual counseling and support groups. But our time together went beyond these resources.

I recognized that Stephanie felt inadequate in the face of having to travel this road. She wanted to know how experts would advise her to do it, since she felt she did not have internal resources sufficient for the task. After listening to her describe how she had navigated her husband's illness so far, it was clear to me that she was a highly competent woman who had already risen to many challenges, yet the final stages of preparing for her husband's death had left her feeling self-doubt. The problem with my giving her even great answers would have been that doing so would have exacerbated her greatest challenge—coming to believe that she has what she needs—or will find what she needs—to survive even this most devastating loss. So one strategy that I chose was to tell her that most ideas about what to do at this stage in life are really very simple, if she just lets herself think of them.

I gave her an example. She told me that her husband loves piano music but that he is too weak to play the piano anymore. I suggested that perhaps she could work with her husband to make a CD with his picks of piano pieces, with his favorite pianists for each piece. Once she got the idea, that she could look for ways to make his legacy concrete through his passions and his commitments, her creativity began to flow. This idea of legacy ties in with the afterlife. Judaism has a traditional belief in the afterlife, though there are diverse takes on this belief among Jewish thinkers throughout the centuries and in our own day. While some Jews believe in a literal afterlife, others focus on the ways in which the person lives on in this world through his or her legacy.

We then moved on to thinking about Stephanie's connection to aspects of the Jewish tradition that she could draw on. I asked her if there was anything in the *siddur* (prayer book) or any Jewish practice or teaching that is particularly significant to her. She responded that even though her husband was too sick to accompany her, she chose to go to synagogue on Yom Kippur. We talked about what drew her to be there, and she described the pull of the community and the familiar melodies. Given that she did not like going anywhere alone, this was the beginning of her accepting that as her husband declined and eventually died, she would need to function alone in the world. The synagogue provided a context in which she could begin to experience herself in new ways, with a sense of protection.

I wondered if there were any Yom Kippur prayers in particular that stood out for her. She responded that she has always loved the *piyyut* (liturgical poem) "As clay in the hand of the potter." *Mahzor Lev Shalem*, a High Holy Day prayer book, offers the heading "Human Vulnerability" for this prayer. Without even realizing it, Stephanie had called up the perfect religious resource for herself. The opening verses are as follows:

> As clay in the hand of the potter, who thickens or thins it
> at will, so are we in Your hand, Guardian of love;
> *Recall your covenant; do not heed the accuser.*
> As stone in the hand of the mason, who preserves or breaks it
> at will, so are we in Your hand, God of life and death;
> *Recall Your covenant; do not heed the accuser.*[27]

At this moment of her husband's complete vulnerability and her own tremendous vulnerability, she had gravitated to a prayer that depicts the human condition as being fundamentally one of vulnerability. Clay in the hand of the potter evokes the image of not being in control, of life as delicate, of God holding us, in the most tactile terms. When we began to discuss the meaning of her *piyyut*, Stephanie was amazed to discover how much wisdom her own heart possessed in its choice of liturgy. By bearing witness to Stephanie's internal reality, through her engagement with this text, Stephanie and I were able to connect in a deep way. That experience of presence led Stephanie to touch gingerly on a raw place—the looming prospect of becoming a widow, with all that that meant for her. A name she did not want. A life she did not want. The words of the refrain *lab'rit habet*, translated here as "recall Your covenant," literally mean "look to your covenant."[28] The plea for God to look—to see, to witness—enabled Stephanie to hold God accountable for seeing her reality, for not turning God's face away, for staying bound to her no matter what lay ahead. That was the eternal promise of the covenant.

In the end, Stephanie gave *me* guidance about how to journey with a dying husband. In order for me to connect with her in her competence and her self-doubt and her fear and her yearning to be held by

God, I needed to make room in my heart for the dreaded reality that someday—and who knows when—my husband and I will be separated by death. While the language of our conversation gave voice to her story, the texture of my presence was given form by my willingness and ability to experience myself as vulnerable alongside her. If I kept Stephanie at a distance, feeling secure in my own life, then I could not enter into the space of truly accompanying her. I must go into exile with her, in the sense of recognizing that we share a destiny as human beings and we are fundamentally connected in that destiny. Stephanie felt lifted up in the experience of being heard as she gave voice to her reality, better equipped to bear the suffering that she cannot avoid.

Jewish spiritual caregivers must have a love of *chiddush* (new insight) and the ways that Torah is made new through people's lived experience. They must be proficient in the *chavruta*, the partner-learning model of the *beit midrash* (the study house), which understands that passionate engagement leads to the uncovering of truth. The caregiver must also have an appreciation that *eilu v'eilu divrei Elohim chayim* ("these and these are the words of the ever-living God"),[29] which leads to a multiplicity of interpretive possibilities. A mandate for the spiritual caregiver is to listen with respect to the wisdom that each person derives in the process of wrestling with the reality of his or her life. Finally, competent spiritual caregivers must see themselves as God's partners, participating in the redemption of the world through *tikkun olam*, the human contributions to the repairing of the world.

At the end of Shabbat, when it is dark outside, traditionally Jews recite *Havdalah*, the ceremony that distinguishes between Shabbat and the rest of the week, the holy and the everyday. In the *Havdalah* ceremony we say, "Behold, God is my salvation. I will trust and not be afraid."[30] This verse, taken from Isaiah 12, asserts that trust will enable us to overcome fear. It is the fear of the dark, of the chaos of night. I love this verse because the assertion about trusting reminds us that we have reason to be afraid. The trusting is necessary precisely because the fear is real. Spiritual care offers us the place to explore the fears while we cultivate the relationships, human and divine, that strengthen our capacity to trust, the relationships that cultivate our hope in the transforming power of God and God's partners in our lives.

Pastoral Care in a Postmodern World

Promoting Spiritual Health across the Life Cycle

Rabbi Nancy Wiener, DMin,
and Barbara Breitman, DMin

As Rachel and Ethan approached a table full of friends at their wedding, they overheard a conversation that gave them a glimpse of their world from a different perspective.

"Can you believe it, a wedding where both sets of parents are still married and in love?"

"I know, and where all of the grandparents were under the *chuppah* with them?"

"Rach told me the whole family saw this wedding as another moment in their miraculous journey as Holocaust survivors."

"I found it amazing that all of their cousins knew enough Hebrew to sing the Seven Blessings."

"Yeah, unlike my family, everyone is Jewish."

Moving from table to table, Ethan and Rachel rejoiced with their guests, an unusually diverse group representing the rich and varied lives of their two families: *sheitl*-wearing women and their black-hatted husbands; single mothers with children

---

Rabbi Nancy Wiener, DMin, is clinical director of the Jacob and Hilda Blaustein Center for Pastoral Counseling and Dr. Paul and Trudy Steinberg Distinguished Professor of Human Relations at Hebrew Union College–Jewish Institute of Religion in New York, New York. Barbara Breitman, DMin, is assistant professor of pastoral counseling and director of training, Jewish Spiritual Direction Program at Reconstructionist Rabbinical College in Wyncote, Pennsylvania.

they had proudly adopted or birthed; gay and lesbian, straight, and transvariant friends and family. All were there under one roof, an unlikely scene for so many people, but it was their world and they loved it. For many of the guests, though, it was a bittersweet day. The joy they all shared with Rachel, Ethan, and their families was powerful. Yet, they were reminded of how their own lives differed from the traditional ideal represented by these marrying families: an ideal with which many, if not all, had been raised; an ideal some had aspired to fulfill, but been unable to reach; an ideal some had openly rejected; an ideal that had inspired others to forge creative alternatives.

Bill always knew he wanted to be a parent. From the time he was a young child, he loved helping his parents with his younger siblings. He'd always imagined he'd get established in his career, marry, and have children. His career followed his anticipated trajectory. However, none of his relationships had led to a long-term commitment. His forty-fifth birthday was just around the corner, and part of his life plan had been to have kids while he was young enough to keep up with them while they were little and to remain vibrant as they entered adulthood. While some of his family and friends encouraged him to lower his standards and marry, Bill knew he didn't want to enter a marriage just to have children. After years of hearing about orphans in Africa, Bill acted on his desire to have a child by fusing it with his commitment to *tikkun olam* (repair of the world). He contacted an international adoption agency, and ten months later, Bill welcomed his three-year-old son to a new home. Bill beamed the day of his son's naming, knowing he had a chance to fulfill his own dream, bringing another Jew into the covenant, the community, his family.

As Sasha prepared to enter the room filled with family and friends, she was acutely aware of the absence of her beloved grandfather and her best friend from childhood. And she was overwhelmed by the energy and excitement she felt in the room as everyone took their seats and looked through the booklets they found there. Together they were going to offer prayers

> of wonder and prayers of thanks, blessings of completion and blessings for life, health, joy, and peace. Some of the blessings and prayers had been said by Jews around the world for centuries. Others were brand-new. All helped them acknowledge and celebrate the profound change in identity and status that Sasha and all of them were experiencing now that Sasha's transgender transitioning was complete.

Like so many American Jews today, Sasha, Bill, Rachel, and Ethan gathered with their communities, comprising Jews and non-Jews, to celebrate significant life transitions in ways that affirmed their Jewish identities. Given the myriad possible options available to them, it is significant that they chose Jewish ritual forms and idioms to sanctify their lives. But they did so in ways that simultaneously preserved and diverged from the ways Jews have marked their life transitions through the ages. Every time we gather to ritually mark a life transition, we acknowledge a moment in a transformative process that has already begun yet will continue to unfold. Every life-cycle transition signifies a shift in relationships not only for the primary individuals experiencing the transition but for parents, siblings, extended families, friends, coworkers, and community as well. Each will experience losses and gains.

Pastoral caregivers have long recognized and supported kin as they reorient themselves to changes wrought by a transition that evokes complex or conflicted emotions. The opportunities and challenges for postmodern caregivers are greater: not only do we need to counsel the central players and to craft rituals that affirm life choices and changes of status and identity not previously imagined, but we need to help members of our communities embrace an expanding diversity of families and life choices.

The pace of social transformation has escalated in the past fifty years:

> A child born at the turn of the twentieth century and a child born at the turn of the new millennium might go through nearly identical physiological stages of maturation and somewhat similar psychological changes, but theories of individual development would not adequately explain the differences in the lives of those two individuals and their respective beliefs and behaviors.[1]

Pastoral counseling "is the professional specialty that focuses most specifically on existential issues."[2] Throughout life, people seek answers to existential questions of meaning and identity. As pastoral caregivers, we can accompany people as circumstances and transitions prompt them to reevaluate who they are, who they want to be, and how they want to live. We can support people through the challenges of mortality and vulnerability, through times of consolation or desolation, joy or sorrow. We can draw on and offer both the wisdom and doubts of our religious traditions and communities so that those seeking meaning and purpose in our increasingly complex world might find ethical grounding and vision.

We are living in a postmodern Jewish reality:

> Choices have multiplied, and they are no longer predefined.... The life cycle is not an anthropological given that can never change. Our contemporary situation makes us aware of how flexible the life cycle really is or, at least, how flexible it has become.[3]

Many long-held assumptions, perceived "givens," and well-worn templates no longer speak to who we are. In the modern era, we Jews asked how we could fully participate in the dominant culture and retain a connection to our traditional and communal narratives. In the postmodern era, we need to ask new and different questions: How do we open our eyes, minds, hearts, and communities to acknowledge and encompass the true diversity of the postmodern Jewish lives people are actually living? How do we promote emotional and spiritual health in a world where identity remains fluid, multiple, into adulthood and even into older age; and in which dimensions of self, conventionally considered to be givens (e.g., gender, sexual orientation, and religious affiliation) can be more fluid than stable over a lifetime? As the life cycle changes in response to postmodernity, how do Jewish pastoral caregivers and communities meet people's needs? How can the personal questions created by the fluidity of postmodern lives become communal questions and shape new communal imperatives?

The World Health Organization (WHO) defines a healthy city or community as

> one that is continually creating and improving those physical and social environments and expanding those community resources

> that enable people to mutually support each other in performing all the functions of life and in developing to their maximum potential.[4]

As WHO suggests, to be a community that promotes health, we need to respond creatively to our rapidly changing world, so that our members can engage in all aspects of life, celebrate those lives, support each other, and reach their maximum potential.

Premodern Jewish "Givens"

In many ways, premodern Jewish communities *perceived* themselves as meeting WHO's criteria for a healthy community. For centuries, Jews approached their lives as a set of givens. These givens defined the parameters of their relationships and their life expectations. First, the natural world, as explained in Genesis, was a set of binaries: light and dark, male and female, good and evil, and so on. While variety was recognized, that which defied categorization was deemed anomalous, and attempts were made to make these anomalies conform to existing categories.[5]

Second, premodern communities shaped their lives based on the assumption that God and the Jewish people had a unique relationship, a covenant, which brought with it love and responsibilities. In order to maintain the human end of the relationship, each Jew was required to fulfill the commandments God had given to the people at Mount Sinai. Each individual was required to learn the laws that pertained to all Jews, as well as those that were sex-specific or age-specific, in order to fulfill them. Being a Jew informed every aspect of one's life.

With these and other givens, the road map for the ideal Jewish life becomes a predictable and stable set of expectations. When a male is born, a father brings his eight-day-old son into the covenant. At circumcision, the son's life path is projected as a series of blessings the community hopes to enjoy with him in the future: study of Torah (leading to a life guided by Torah), acts of loving-kindness, and marriage. In contrast, a daughter does not need to be brought into the covenant; she is covenanted through her father.[6] The socialization of children over the age of three occurs in sex-segregated environments, so that children can learn and prepare for the gender-bound expectations and responsibilities of adulthood. Girls learn the tasks of running a home and caring for children alongside the generations of women in their families. At age three (or five[7]), a boy begins his study of Torah. (Interestingly, this enables his father to fulfill his own obligation to make sure that this happens.)

From then on, male children study Jewish texts and then trades, alongside the men of their community. At thirteen, the young man becomes a responsible Jewish adult, and his father recites the *shep'tarani*, a blessing that frees him from responsibility for his son's actions. No parallel public coming-of-age ceremony is celebrated for young women. With marriage, the man becomes responsible for his wife and takes on the obligation to be "fruitful and multiply."[8]

In this construction of a Jewish world, each life transition in a male's life is the focus of a public ritual and celebration, emphasizing the significance of the male's membership in and responsibility for the continuation of the Jewish people. Moreover, each transition becomes linked to a specific chronological moment.[9] A child's birth signals the beginning of a new life cycle, and significantly, no other life-cycle transition for the parent is communally marked until death.

For millennia, Jews around the globe held additional noteworthy customs and teachings as truths or givens: Jews should marry only Jews; Jews share a common ancestral history, a set of common beliefs, as well as remarkably similar customs and traditions; Jews have a bond with each other that transcends time and space; Jews have an abiding sense of mutual responsibility; Jews have an ongoing relationship with God and the Land of Israel. And, even though some acknowledge that Jews live around the globe, many Jews imagined that their own local customs were normative for all Jews.

Governed by givens, these premodern Jewish communities believed they were providing each community member the support necessary to live out a life of meaning and purpose through covenant with God. Jewish ritual was the primary, and in many cases only, means for a Jew to feel supported by a community through life's transitions. Rabbis provided legal guidance as needed.

Modernity's Challenges to a World of Givens

Over the past two centuries, liberal Jews have challenged many of the long-held Jewish "givens." In response to Enlightenment ideas, which brought women's capacities and place in society into European intellectual discourse, they rejected the notion that only a male's religious life transitions were worthy of communal celebration. They revisited the Jewish life cycle with the goal of promoting parity for males and females. At the beginning of the nineteenth century, German Reformers created a new, egalitarian confirmation ceremony, for boys *and* girls who completed their religious school education. By mid-century, the Reformers utilized an additional approach to reach their goal of gender parity: they reworked and reinterpreted existing rituals. Beginning with Jewish marriage laws and ceremonies, they raised the status of women, by creating a *ketubah* that made no references to dowry, bride-price, or virginity and a ceremony in which both bride and groom articulate their mutual obligations and commitments. If the marriage did not work, husband *or wife* could initiate a *get* (Jewish divorce). No longer was divorce dependent solely on the husband's initiation and consent.

While the first girl celebrated a bat mitzvah in the 1920s, it was not until the 1960s that bat mitzvah became an anticipated life-cycle celebration for some girls. However, its form remained in flux. In some communities, the ceremonies were either identical to or similar to the bar mitzvah ceremonies of their male peers. In others, the role the girl took in the worship service was radically different. Beginning in the 1970s, creative ceremonies of welcome and naming, some of which incorporated ways of affirming entry into the *b'rit* (covenant), were created for girls. As with bat mitzvah, one single form did not emerge, and unlike circumcision, its timing was not fixed. The urgency that family and community experienced around being present at circumcision did not transfer to naming or *b'rit* ceremonies for girls.

Nevertheless, each of these changes contributed to Jewish communities' affirming females as having agency in their own lives. Their intimate relationships as well as their relationships with God and community became independent from those of their parents and their husbands. The life transitions long defined as central to a Jewish life were no longer exclusively tied to males. Even so, with the exception of confirmation, celebrations of life-cycle transitions over the course of a Jew's lifetime remained distinctively tied to the male-centric conception of the Jewish life cycle. While ceremonies were created or modified, there was no apparent awareness that people experiencing these new transitions needed pastoral support or time for reflection.

Challenging the Next Set of Givens: The Impact of Modern Feminism

From the 1970s through the 1990s, Jewish feminists claimed the authority to draw from exsiting Jewish symbols and rituals, transform old ones, and create new ones to publicly name and sanctify hitherto unrecognized transitions in the lives of girls and women—from menarche to menopause, from *simchat bat* (baby naming and entering the covenant) to *simchat chochmah* (becoming an elder). Though there was never any unified movement or standardization of ritual form, there was a common goal: to make it possible for girls and women to sanctify their lives and life-cycle transitions in a Jewish context and in a Jewish idiom. These new public rituals and celebrations made visible, in profound ways, Jewish females' membership in and responsibility for the continuity of the Jewish people. Jewish women were beginning to create new visions of theology and community.

By challenging gender-bound roles and redefining family, feminism also added new dimensions to the life cycle, often breaking the links between traditional developmental milestones and chronological ages. For example, adult *b'nei mitzvah*, originally introduced to enable women who had been unable to celebrate in adolescence a chance to take their place as adults in religious communities, has become a celebratory option for adult Jews of all genders and ages.[10] The full inclusion of women's spiritual expression shaped and transformed modern Jewish culture for women and men. We might say, "Culture itself, then, is a 'Thou,' with whom a person, an 'I,' may enter into a mutually formative relatedness."[11]

For millennia, Jewish communities coerced into conformity those whose lives and loves did not follow the trajectory deemed normative. The feminist revolution and the modern gay liberation movement not only opened our eyes to the true diversity that exists in our midst, but also opened up social spaces in which people could celebrate and sanctify lives that had been hidden from public view. Gay and lesbian Jews began to publicly affirm their Jewish gay and lesbian identities and to live lives enriched by the history and experience of both cultures.

In private, at gay and lesbian synagogues or a growing number of inclusive Jewish communities and synagogues, lesbian and gay Jews began to ritually mark and celebrate significant life transitions. Some mirrored more traditional events such as ceremonies of commitment, while others had no Jewish precedent, such as coming-out rituals to honor not only the lesbian or gay Jew, but also parents and family members.[12]

Even with these major changes, Jewish communities, influenced by the feminist and gay and lesbian movements, still retained some key traditional Jewish understandings. Jews live their lives in a matrix of ever-evolving relationships with self, family, community, and God. Meaning and purpose are derived from participation in community. Each person is inherently relational, not autonomous. In Hebrew, Jews are known as the children of their parents. Jews make daily reference to both their ancestors and the generations to come. No matter where they are in their life cycle, whether or not they have children, they understand themselves to be a link in the chain that extends backward and forward. As Buber expressed it, "In the beginning is the relation,"[13] and "We live in the currents of universal reciprocity."[14]

Some twentieth-century rabbis responded to the growing culture of psychotherapy by offering supportive counseling focused on life-cycle transitions. Recognizing that those participating in a ritual often experience changes in identity and shifts in relationships, giving rise to existential and religious questions, these rabbis reached out to congregants to help them negotiate such passages. They also made themselves available to individuals and families who were grappling with religious issues and questions not tied to the life cycle.

Postmodern Jewish Life and Pastoral Responses

Postmodernity brings new perspectives and realities that clergy and pastoral caregivers must recognize and honor in order to offer effective care. No longer are identity crises confined to adolescence, as Erikson asserted in the 1950s.[15] In an ever more complex postmodern society,

> identity formation turns out to be a flexible and, most likely, a lifelong process. As the experience of transitional periods in life has multiplied—with changes of profession, new trainings,

> second and third marriages, and so forth—the need to rework and reestablish one's identity has ... become an enduring task never to be quite completed.[16]

A world of fixity has been replaced by one of fluidity. A world of binaries has been replaced by one of diversity and multiplicity.

That said, it takes a long time for our inner landscapes to reshape themselves to align with external realities. As the experience of some of those who attended Rachel and Ethan's wedding attested, notions of a normative Jewish life cycle and the "givens" to which they were tied are still embedded in many of our psyches and communities. When individuals or groups name and sanctify hitherto unnamed (or even unimagined) life-cycle transitions, it has a doubly profound impact. It promotes their own health and well-being, while challenging and stretching conventional notions of normalcy and health. The rapid changes in recent decades have left some Jews seeking pastoral care because their understanding of themselves as Jews and of Jewish values and traditions has been shaken. In contrast, there are other Jews who feel (or fear) that their lived experiences are still rendered invisible or even pathological by those who adhere to traditional norms.

When feminism challenged the gender binary—the division of all human beings into male and female with distinct and separate rights, roles, and attributes—it forever changed understandings of personal identity, family life, workplace, law, culture, and religion. Feminism ushered in deep transformations that are now part of the warp and woof of postmodern society. Now, it is transgender and gender-nonconforming Jews who are making their voices heard. As they emerge from almost total invisibility, they are seeking to bring their "whole, true selves" into the Jewish community.[17] Like the rabbi who supported Sasha (above) by creating a ritual for gender transitioning, pastoral caregivers are increasingly being called on not only to support a transitioning person, but also to support extended family through the process of a loved one's gender change. Moreover, we cannot achieve full equality for transgender and gender-nonconforming Jews until we tackle the obstacles that the gender-bound Hebrew language creates for them. How can we call someone to the Torah for an *aliyah* when "son of" or "daughter of" is not an apt label?

As pastoral caregivers, we need to confront our own inner landscapes and question the enduring nature of our own givens. To be able to serve others, we must first engage in serious soul-searching so that we can each articulate our own understandings of Jewish teachings and values. We need to continue to study broadly, including but not limited to those texts and traditions that had been relegated to the margins for generations, but which have particular relevance for our contemporary circumstances. For example, the Talmud actually speaks of four, not two, natal sex possibilities: male, female, male with some female genitalia, female with some male genitalia. While the Rabbis' concern was figuring out which gender-bound laws pertained to Jews of ambiguous genitalia at different stages of life, they did not question their bona fides as Jews, their inherent holiness and uniqueness, or their membership in the community. Knowledge of this Rabbinic material enriches the quality and depth of the compassionate care we can offer all Jews—those once marginalized, those who struggle to understand themselves as the composition of their communities changes before their eyes, and all those in between.

While the late modern era ushered in the acceptance of a sexual-orientation binary—gay/straight or homosexual/heterosexual—in this postmodern era a growing number of Jews openly identify as bisexual. Experiencing sexual attraction for and being comfortable with sexual intimacy with both males and females, their primary relationships may shift between men and women over the course of their lives. As pastoral caregivers, many of us have already been called upon to counsel bisexual Jews (and their family and friends) through a coming-out and acceptance process and then to accompany them through future life-cycle junctions. A growing number of pastoral caregivers will be called upon to counsel someone prior to an opposite-sex marriage, then through a divorce, and eventually in preparation for a same-sex marriage.

While ethnic, cultural, and racial diversity have been a part of the Jewish experience throughout our history, contemporary forces of intermarriage, conversion, and adoption have recently expanded the scope of that diversity. Medieval Jewish travelogues and commentaries on our holy texts remind us of the racial and cultural diversity that has been a reality of Jewish life since the first Diaspora. Yet the 2011

UJA-Federation of New York Jewish Community Study was the first contemporary study to ask about race. It found that approximately 12 percent of—or eighty-seven thousand—New York Jewish households are "bi- or multi-racial or nonwhite." (Many respondents self-identified as both Jewish and black, Hispanic, or Asian, or as biracial, and some white Jewish respondents identified their households as bi- or multiracial.) In addition, 13 percent identified themselves as Sephardic (Spanish or Portuguese descent) or Mizrahi (North African, Middle Eastern, or Asian descent). These results showed that in the city with the largest Jewish population in the world, an impressive 25 percent of Jews—over four hundred thousand—are living in racially and ethnically diverse households.[18] Be'chol Lashon,[19] an advocacy and service organization that promotes inclusivity, estimates that 20 percent of the six million Jews in the United States are racially and ethnically diverse, including African-American, Latino/Hispanic, Asian, Native American, Sephardic, Mizrahi, and mixed-race individuals.

As Jews who do not trace their heritage to Europe are increasingly making themselves seen and heard, they are challenging the centrality and pervasiveness of the Ashkenazi Jewish narrative in North American Jewish communities. They also heighten awareness of how the bipolar nature of racial discourse in the United States, which frames racial differences as the binary of white and black, completely fails to capture the true hues of Jews and the rich diversity of our communities. As pastoral caregivers, we need to expand our knowledge about the multicultural dimensions of Jewish ritual, liturgy, practice, song, and celebration, so that we can develop some fluency with the rich diversity that already exists. No matter our own ethnic or cultural backgrounds, we need to become far more familiar with not only other Jewish cultures and the range of Judaisms, but also the many non-Jewish cultural identities of those we serve.

If we are to support the health and well-being of the families in our midst, we need to offer creative ways of incorporating elements of non-Jewish cultural forms into life-cycle celebrations. For example, a young adult of Japanese-Jewish descent may choose to wear a kimono at her Jewish wedding to highlight two fundamental aspects of her identity. The complexity of what will be entailed to truly become multiculturally literate Jewish pastoral caregivers is beyond the limited bounds of this chapter. But it is undeniable that this is what is being asked of us as postmodern Jewish professionals. Our counseling can help people accept changes in customs that have been emotionally cathected for generations. We can guide them through the unfamiliar waters, and we can support them and counsel them as they explore the losses and reflect on new possibilities that change entails.

American society in general has become more accepting of diverse choices for family formation and re-formation. The divorce rate continues to hover around 50 percent, and remarriage and blended families have become commonplace. As the vignette about Bill's adoption decision underscores, the taboos against single parenthood have notably subsided, and as a result, single people of varied gender identities and sexual orientations are adopting or birthing children through advanced reproductive technologies. In addition, many more couples are deciding not to have children (contrary to the long-held Jewish given) but, instead, to create life cycles and lifestyles that revolve around adult milestones and achievements. How couples and families sequence work and childrearing is more variable than in the past. No gender-based assumptions can be made about who will be the primary provider for a family or who might be primarily responsible for child care. People are weaving idiosyncratic life-cycle tapestries.

In an open and diverse society, religious identity, once seen as fixed, has become fluid. As a result of experimentation and study, there is growing fluidity of affiliation within individual religions and among different religious traditions. The American Jewish Committee's 2009 study *Religious Switching among American Jews* describes significant rates of interdenominational switching: "33 percent of those raised as Orthodox still follow that orientation; 45 percent of the Conservative remain Conservative; 69 percent of the Reform remain Reform; and 63 percent of Other remain Other."[20] Other research also points to increasing rates of nondenominational affiliation, especially among Jewish young adults.[21]

Many other factors contribute to the postmodern experience of plural and fluid identity. Prolonged life expectancy has increased both the number of stages and the developmental tasks and transitions of the postmodern life cycle. A new stage, lasting from the late teens to the mid- to late twenties, sometimes called "emerging adulthood," is now recognized as a discrete time of life. During this life stage, primarily middle-class emerging adults seek to find their way in an increasingly complex economy and culture by engaging in prolonged explorations in terms of life partners and careers.

At the upper end of the life cycle, for many elders there is now a "Third Age" between mid-adult maturity and final dependence and death. This Third Age is seen as an era of personal fulfillment, after the obligations of full-time paid work and child-rearing have ended: a time when healthy elders are seeking opportunities for ongoing learning and working, new projects, spiritual growth, and making contributions of their wisdom and experience. Pastoral caregivers can acknowledge these significant new life stages and accompany those experiencing them as they search for meaning and purpose. We can help people mark and celebrate the transitions that emerge as hallmarks of these stages by creating new rituals reflecting Jewish values and teachings. This has already begun for the "Third Age" with new rituals for, among others, spiritual eldering and retirement.

In our postmodern society, "the constant flux of roles and situations generates 'plural selves' and 'plural identities.'"[22] Contemporary Jews, seeking to define and express their Jewish identity while affirming other identities, often turn to pastoral caregivers for help. While once Jews spoke of themselves as having a set of common beliefs, a common ancestral history, a bond with other Jews that transcends time and space, and an ongoing relationship with God and the Land of Israel, in postmodernity these are not the ways that some contemporary Jews understand themselves. As pastoral caregivers, we can sensitively accompany all Jews or those who seek to be Jews, honoring people's multifaceted identities: from the single Jewish man who feels a cultural connection to Jews and Judaism, but neither believes in God nor is observant nor has a personal relationship to Israel; to the third-generation African-American Jewish mother who brings jazz and gospel idioms to her daughter's bat mitzvah ceremony; to the *sheitl*-wearing woman affirming her maternal ties by embracing her transgender child at her Shabbat table; to the rabbinic student who is a Jew-by-choice still retaining close, loving ties to his Methodist family of origin; to the daughter of divorced Ashkenazi parents who moves back and forth between her father's house and the home her lesbian mother shares with her Mizrahi partner. By enabling all Jews to find their unique voices and create lives of meaning and integrity, we will enrich their lives and the life of our Jewish communities as well.

As pastoral caregivers, we need to think systemically and work to educate ourselves and our communities about diversity. If we embrace and nurture the full potential of those who seek our support, but return them to communities that cannot respond in kind, then we have not fully done our job. Pastoral caregivers need to get involved in communal change as well: working on task forces, sponsoring educational panels in synagogues and Jewish agencies, engaging in anti-racism and diversity work in the organizations in which we serve. We need to be voices for change and embody the changes we envision.

For us pastoral caregivers, these are the realities; these are the backdrops and contexts of contemporary Jewish life. The containers that framed Jewish lives and transmitted meaning from one generation to the next have exploded for some of us, fractured for others, or begun to fray around the edges for yet others. The questions Jews are asking are new. Their desire to find answers to existential questions of meaning, purpose, community, and identity persist. While today we fall short of the WHO definition of a healthy community, we can knowledgeably work to create new paths toward that goal.

A Final Thought

Theology informs our practice as pastoral caregivers. God's self-description "*Eh'yeh asher Eh'yeh*" (Exodus 3:14), which defies easy translation, asserts that God will be what God will be or that God is what God was, is, and will be. Made in God's image, we are ever in process, ever becoming. In Judaism, God has many names, aspects, qualities: "Creator," "Healer," Compassionate One," "Wisdom," "Presence," and myriad others. So have we! Like God, our identity is relational and never entirely unitary or stable. Jewish tradition often ascribes plural words in Hebrew to speak of God, *Adonai* and *Elohim* being the best known. Yet how often do we limit ourselves and others by focusing on a singular or single aspect of identity? How will Jewish pastoral care change if we embrace our own plural identities and the multifactored selves of those to whom we offer care?

Seminary-Based Jewish Pastoral Education

Rabbi Nancy Wiener, DMin, Rabbi Julie Schwartz, and Michele F. Prince, LCSW, MAJCS

Over the past few decades, Jewish seminaries around the country and around the world have expanded their course offerings and created programs and centers dedicated to pastoral education. To aid us in this endeavor, we have turned outward to learn from our Christian colleagues who gave birth to the field of pastoral education, and inward to understand more fully what is distinctive about a Jewish pastoral approach, how pastoral training enhances the lives of our seminaries, our students, the countless Jews and Jewish communities they will serve, and those beyond the Jewish community whose lives they will touch, and finally, which best practices contribute to effective seminary-based Jewish pastoral education.

In our work at Hebrew Union College–Jewish Institute of Religion's (HUC–JIR's) three stateside campuses, we have shared a passion for the field and a commitment to advancing it. Individually and jointly, we have forged paths in Jewish pastoral education that have been adapted and replicated by other Jewish seminaries. Our Cincinnati campus was the first Jewish seminary in the country to become an accredited clinical pastoral education (CPE) center. The New York campus's Jacob and

---

Rabbi Nancy Wiener, DMin, is clinical director of the Jacob and Hilda Blaustein Center for Pastoral Counseling and Dr. Paul and Trudy Steinberg Distinguished Professor of Human Relations at Hebrew Union College–Jewish Institute of Religion in New York, New York. Rabbi Julie Schwartz is director of pastoral care and clinical pastoral education at Hebrew Union College–Jewish Institute of Religion in Cincinnati, Ohio. Michele F. Prince, LCSW, MAJCS, is executive director of OUR HOUSE Grief Support Center and former director of the Kalsman Institute on Judaism and Health, Hebrew Union College–Jewish Institute of Religion in Los Angeles, California.

Hilda Blaustein Center for Pastoral Counseling was the first endowed center at a Jewish seminary dedicated to pastoral education for rabbinic and cantorial students that integrated classwork, fieldwork, mentoring, and supervision. The opening of the Kalsman Institute on Judaism and Health at our Los Angeles campus made us the first Jewish seminary to establish an institute dedicated to the broader issues of Judaism and health, bringing people from diverse fields together to discuss the current and future directions of Judaism, health, and healing and, most recently, gathering Jewish pastoral educators together to share best practices and to explore the future of the field.

Over the years, at each of our campuses, we have designed and introduced courses and collaborated with faculty and administration to make pastoral education a centerpiece of Jewish seminary-based clergy training. We have worked with colleagues as they engage in providing a pastoral presence in their work in healthcare facilities, in congregations, on college campuses, at day schools and religious schools, at camps, and in countless other contexts. And, all the while, we have cherished the time we have spent with our pastoral education colleagues who work in diverse settings, as we have all sought to establish the field of Jewish pastoral education and to create educational modalities that remain true to Jewish teachings and values and prepare students for the joys and the challenges that await them.

A Bit of History

For countless generations, "rabbi" was primarily understood by its literal meaning, "teacher." Rabbis were people respected for their learning, who taught and offered legal and ritual guidance to others. They studied sacred texts and legal reasoning in yeshivas, institutions of Jewish higher learning. Jewish communities consistently had a single response to the question "How do we best prepare a rabbi to serve the Jewish community?": through formal study and living in the community. Knowledge of how to fulfill God's commandments was at the heart of rabbinic education. As for the interpersonal, rabbis learned the laws that pertained to all realms of life and then depended on sacred text, folklore, and custom, their own life experiences, and the examples of other rabbis to guide them as they interacted with individuals, families, and communities navigating the waters of their lives.

While the structure of life-cycle rituals provided some support, rabbis received no formal training to respond in a caring or interpersonally supportive manner at times of transition or uncertainty.

Beginning approximately 150 years ago, European and American Jewish seminaries asked this same question, "How do we best prepare a rabbi to serve the Jewish people?" The answer at the vast majority of seminaries remained the same: through rigorous academic Jewish study. A few liberal seminaries in Europe and HUC in the United States began to apply modern scholarship to the study of traditional Jewish texts.[1] To best serve the growing Jewish community, HUC developed a unique curriculum for the late nineteenth century, reflecting a bifurcated identity: academic institution of Jewish higher learning cum professional school, replete with courses, workshops, and symposia focused on the nonacademic skills of the rabbinate, such as homiletics, diction, and pedagogy.[2] HUC recognized that in addition to academics, American rabbis needed to gain practical skills, grounded in Jewish values, teachings, and beliefs. Some instructors taught classic texts but led students to consider contemporary application.[3] HUC created a new field for rabbinic education and dubbed it "practical rabbinics."[4]

Over the course of the twentieth century, other Jewish seminaries adopted this fundamental change of identity. By the middle of the twentieth century, as psychology became part of the academic and cultural mainstream, Reform and Conservative Jewish seminaries began to offer courses in pastoral psychology. Even after many Jewish seminaries had added pastoral courses (required at some, optional at others) to their curricula, many academics and administrators at Jewish seminaries continued to see the professional aspects of the program as adjuncts to the all-important institution of higher learning at the heart of the seminary.

Understanding Seminary-Based Jewish Pastoral Education in the Context of the Pastoral

In recent decades, we have modified the question that guided Jewish seminaries for so long. Now we are asking two related, but different, questions: "How do we prepare students for the broad jump from acquiring specific knowledge and building discrete skills to learning from one disparate setting to another?" and "How do we prepare individuals for the diverse tasks and roles of Jewish clergy in a self-reflective, spiritually informed, and healthy manner?"

These new questions recognize the diverse roles and expectations that currently exist for Jewish clergy: teacher, preacher, pastoral caregiver, worship service leader, spiritual guide, spokesperson for the Jewish community in interfaith settings, and social activist, to name only the most obvious. We can find some valuable insights and guidance in answering these two key questions from the biblical depictions of a pastor/shepherd. From Psalms we learn that a biblical shepherd/pastor had many roles and needed to exercise a variety of skills.[5] To be a biblical pastor, one had to treat each sheep differently, providing each the space or distance it needs from him or her and the others in the flock to be comfortable; lead all members of the flock to where they can find nourishment; bring the group together when danger is at hand; keep each individual member of the flock in sight, taking note of changes in behavior and environment; and offer extra protection to the young or weak, until they are able to appropriately care for themselves. As we think of these images, we can find resonances with a skilled contemporary clergyperson who leads people toward the holiness they are pursuing, comforts, guides, encourages, strengthens the weak, refreshes, restores, and protects.[6] A well-trained pastoral caregiver offers all of these skills and sensitivities to individuals, families, and communities in a professional, intentional way.

These new questions also recognize that the personal life of the Jewish clergyperson is as much of a litmus test for seminary education as the clergyperson's ability to respond to the lives of those he or she serves. As a shepherd knew that she could not succeed in providing these essentials to her flock if she did not provide herself with the basics to sustain herself throughout the day—adequate water, food, rest, and shade, to name a few—our newest Jewish clergypeople are learning that caring for the self is not antithetical to caring for others. It is a necessary component for the care of others to be done effectively.

Pastoral education is often erroneously equated with training that focuses specifically on healthcare chaplains. While such training constitutes a significant subset of the field, best known through the nationally accredited, largely hospital-based programs under the auspices of the Association for Clinical Pastoral Education,[7] pastoral education is far more. Pastoral education focuses on helping the learner develop a way of being in the world with integrity. It combines intellectual knowledge with self-awareness, attunement, and responsiveness to others and a deep grounding in a faith or spiritual tradition, accompanied by reflective practice. It emphasizes the centrality of being present, so that one can be engaged fully and intentionally. It focuses on care of the soul (the meaning of the Greek word *psyche*). While many Jewish clergy receive some of their pastoral education in a healthcare setting, the majority of it takes place under the auspices of seminaries.

Our Christian colleagues introduced us to the notion that pastoral education is practical theology; it is that aspect of seminary education that encourages students to explore the nexus between their lived experiences and their beliefs.[8] To revisit and perhaps expand HUC-JIR's now nearly century-and-a-half-old insight, Jewish clergy need to study both rabbinics and practical rabbinics. To effectively recognize and meet varied needs, including pastoral, of contemporary Jews, a well-designed Jewish seminary education encourages students to explore the nexus between their lived experiences and the wide range of topics from rabbinics to history to theology to Midrash to liturgy to Bible (to name a few) that they study while in seminary. They learn not only about our tradition, but their relationship to it as it is expressed through their interpersonal relationships, their relationship with God, their own spiritual practices, and their professional experiences. They discern for themselves, with the guidance of teachers, supervisors, and mentors, how all of these pieces fit together. The primary goal of seminary-based Jewish pastoral education is, thus, integration of all aspects of learning so that Jewish clergypeople can best bring all that they are to all that they do. No small task. But, undeniably, an essential one.

Jewish Pastoral Education as Integration

How do we prepare students for the broad jump from acquiring specific knowledge and building discrete skills to learning from one disparate setting to another? And, how do we prepare individuals for the diverse tasks and roles of Jewish clergy in a self-reflective, spiritually informed, and healthy manner? The Jewish pastoral education response to both questions is the same: integration.

The primary goal of pastoral education is integrative. The goals of pastoral education are skill-based and self-knowledge-based. On the skill side, pastoral education helps students develop better listening skills. Students learn how to listen on different levels: emotional, psychological, developmental, spiritual, and theological. They learn to assess the needs of others, both spoken and unspoken. They learn to assess their own abilities and to contract with others to clarify what they can/will and cannot/will not offer. They learn to respond in conversation, in silence, through prayer, through study, through presence. They learn to see the links among their intellectual interests and knowledge, their spiritual longings and forms of religious and spiritual expression, their own history and psychological makeup, and the interactions that they have with others. They learn to see others in the context of families and communities, seeking to know people through their significant relationships and their unique ways of being in and experiencing the world. On the self-knowledge side, they learn to identify and express their own emotions more effectively; they learn to identify their own needs and to seek ways to have them met appropriately; they learn about self-care and its relationship to providing effective care for others; they learn about personal and professional boundaries. They learn that wherever they are and whatever activity or role in which they are engaged professionally, they always have the possibility of offering a pastoral stance.

Imagine a Venn diagram of Jewish clergy in diverse settings, highlighting the different skills and attributes they need to draw on, often over the course of a single day. From the classroom to graveside to the boardroom to the bimah to you-name-it, inhabiting the shared space, at the heart of the diagram, are interpersonal skills. If the rabbi cannot connect with the students in the classroom, cannot read their body language and be attuned to their emotional responses to his presence in the room, and cannot effectively convey delight in the material, then the interaction will be flat. If the rabbi intones the prayers at a funeral in a competent, yet monotonous manner, if she offers a eulogy that does not capture some of the spirit of the individual who has died and the realities of the immediate mourners in the days following the death, then she has helped the mourners complete the tasks associated with a funeral and burial, but has not helped them feel accompanied in the loss, understood at this particular moment.

And yet, in a survey of alumni conducted by HUC-JIR (New York) in the late 1990s,[9] we heard that the area our alumni felt least prepared for and least competent in was the interpersonal and the pastoral. At ordination, they felt ill-equipped to enter a hospital room or a house of mourning and have a meaningful conversation, to understand what was being communicated verbally and nonverbally at a board meeting, to establish boundaries with congregants or make time for themselves and their families. While HUC-JIR's history of including practical rabbinics courses and fieldwork bespoke its commitment to experiential learning, we had not adequately created a curriculum that promoted the type of integration that was necessary. And we had never really created the supportive scaffolding that could make these field experiences part of an ongoing reflective practice that would provide the connective tissue between it, classroom learning, and the spiritual life of the student.

The 1990s was a decade in which the Jewish mainstream embraced health and healing in new ways. The first national conferences on Judaism and healing were held. More Jewish clergy engaged in CPE training than ever before. Jewish chaplains asserted their sense of having a collective identity by creating the National Association of Jewish Chaplains. A growing number of Jews started exploring the fields of spiritual direction and spiritual practice, fields that to that point had been dominated by Christians. And individuals connected with seminaries who had either had a significant personal experience with illness or who had benefited from CPE training began to take a serious look at the ways in which our Jewish professionals could be schooled differently to understand themselves as Jewish pastoral caregivers, promoting healing and wholeness for others and themselves.

The first efforts at HUC-JIR, which have been replicated at other seminaries, worked with the bifurcated model of Jewish seminary education: academic graduate program and professional school. Those of us who oversaw fieldwork programs and/or taught professional development (i.e., practical rabbinics) courses[10] began to look at them with a different eye, hoping to enhance them so that they could be more integrative.

Supervision for fieldwork had always existed as an option for students. Faculty advisors were available if the student sought guidance, but ongoing reflection and supervision were not part of the fieldwork program. Borrowing from our own positive experiences in CPE, we began to create more intentional and focused supervision programs on all of HUC-JIR's stateside campuses.[11] We recognized that meaningful interpersonal relationships and experiences are not confined to healthcare facilities. They take place in every possible setting and in every imaginable circumstance.

Accordingly, we introduced new supervisory, reflective opportunities, either focused on students in a particular year or as nonmandatory supplement to the fieldwork program, providing individual and/or group opportunities. As these programs have evolved, they have come to include both individual and group supervision at HUC-JIR, with students preparing verbatims to present on incidents that they have encountered at committee meetings, in classrooms, in one-on-one counseling, in response to a sermon, at a youth group event, and so on. Now, at each site where a student has a fieldwork placement, a member of the clergy or professional staff receives training as a mentor from HUC-JIR. Our students are coming to appreciate the value of reflecting on each experience so that they can grow professionally, personally, and spiritually.

Next, we looked for ways to encourage students to participate in CPE. We recognized the impact that it had on our own professional and spiritual formation and wanted to make it possible for future generations of rabbis and cantors to do the same. Since feedback from our alumni indicated that they felt least equipped to work with families confronted with serious illness and death and that many were extremely apprehensive when they first needed to make hospital visits, we focused on making CPE accessible to more students. In New York, we accomplished this by seeking funding to cover CPE tuition. With a CPE supervisor-in-training working as an administrator, Cincinnati embarked on the process of becoming a CPE center. As a liberal seminary, responsive to demographic changes in the Jewish community, we also valued the interfaith approach offered in most CPE programs. The number of students getting CPE training increased on all of our campuses during the 1990s. By 2010, the vast majority of HUC-JIR rabbinic students completed a unit of CPE prior to ordination.

Cognizant of the fact that not every student would choose to do CPE and that some students might want a less intensive first pastoral experience, all of HUC's stateside campuses began to introduce pastoral counseling courses with fieldwork components. By the early 1990s, both New York and Los Angeles offered an elective on hospital chaplaincy, which fused classwork and required hours in healthcare settings providing care. With both courses, students received some on-site supervision and time to reflect in class and in one-on-one meetings with the instructor. In order to provide the broadest range of counseling opportunities to our students, we forged partnerships with Jewish federations, social service agencies, and synagogues, enabling students to learn alongside seasoned mental health professionals. In the 2000s, many of these relationships have resulted in our being able to offer pastoral internships, alongside congregational and organizational internships each year.

Moreover, we took to heart our responsibility as pastoral educators to model the truth that the formation of relationships serves as the hub around which all other clergy work revolves. No texts can be taught, no prayer can be shared, no ritual can transform unless the relationship between rabbi and congregant, patient, student, co-worker, co-clergy, et al., is already formed or is in the process of forming. Once a conduit is opened or a potential Buberian I-Thou relationship has formed, then the rabbi or cantor and the individual can move together and approach the tasks and challenges that lie ahead attuned to each other. We made ourselves available as supervisors, teachers, and sounding boards for our students, modeling the multiplicity of relationships that they would likely have with a single congregant over time.

As we looked at our existing courses, we recognized that while we appreciated the nexus between our education in rabbinics and the pastoral work that we did, we had not made this as explicit a part of our teaching as it could be. So we brought theology and rabbinics more explicitly into our pastoral courses, and we consciously sought to create assignments that would help students see this as a natural part of their learning. We also developed more electives to complement courses offered in other fields with a pastoral perspective. So, for example, as students learned about life-cycle liturgy, they could take an elective on counseling for the life cycle.

All of these innovations had profound effects on our students during their tenure at the school and for our alumni as they began their work as ordained clergy. Reports from senior rabbis and congregations by the early 2000s indicated a growing sense that new ordinees were more comfortable and competent in counseling situations. But the real integration we seek is only possible when a Jewish seminary experiences a cultural shift. Fortunately for us, at HUC-JIR, and at other Jewish seminaries, such systemic shifts are in process.

A Cultural Shift, a Curricular Shift

All three of us, and many of our Jewish pastoral education colleagues, have participated in a conversation like the following:

> A rabbinic student enters the office of the pastoral educator at his seminary and says, "I'm never going to serve in a congregation or work in a healthcare setting. Neither one has any appeal for me. I'm planning to either teach in an academic setting or work for a Jewish institution. I want to be a rabbi because it will enable me to offer a perspective that's different from those of the other professionals in those settings."
>
> The pastoral educator nods. The student continues, "So, you see, I shouldn't have to serve a student pulpit. I don't need to have that practice because I'm never going to use it. And I shouldn't have to spend time in a hospital, doing pastoral stuff, because it's not relevant to what I want to do."
>
> The pastoral educator gently responds, "You will never serve a congregation? Really, never, ever, ever? You're never, ever going to walk into the room of someone who is sick or dying who will welcome you as a rabbi? Will you sign a contract today with those stipulations, promising that if you do ever serve a congregation or visit someone in a hospital who is in need of a rabbi's visit, then you owe me a million dollars?"
>
> By this time the student is smiling, and he enters into a serious conversation about our human inability to predict the future and how he feels about recognizing something that is

> out of his control. The student and the pastoral educator continue with a discussion about the ways that a rabbi is a rabbi in all settings and that the skills gained from congregational and pastoral work will be invaluable as a professor, an administrator, or any other professional setting in which the title "rabbi" will be recognized.

This student is not alone in his assumption that it is more efficient and logical to specifically train rabbinic students for a particular type of rabbinate. Many in our communities reason: a rabbi does not really have to focus on pedagogy if there will always be an educator to fill that role; a cantor does not really have to learn pastoral care if most of the cantor's time will not be spent in the hospital. This line of thinking leads them to the conclusion that all rabbinic and cantorial students can simply select the critical skills for each area connected with their current long-range plans and hope these will be enough to carry them through a career. Yet, as Jewish seminary faculty and administrators, we would never dream of suggesting that since a rabbinic student's career goal is focused on day school education, we need not ensure that he has a graduate-level grounding in rabbinic text! The concept that one begins as a specialist and ends as a generalist would be laughable from a medical or most any other professional school model, and so it is for Jewish clergy as well.

It is not surprising that students begin their rabbinic and cantorial training with the sense that some skills are more important than others. Each one has a different picture of the rabbi or cantor whom he or she wants to become. Their inspiration to become Jewish clergy emanates from a sacred commitment to our faith, our traditions, and our texts. They live out this love through sharing it with the world—congregants, students, Jews, and non-Jews. They live out this love by demonstrating the lasting value and meaning that they find in Judaism and planting seeds for its perpetuation. For countless decades, many rabbinic and cantorial students devoted years of their life to study at seminary and believed that after having ingested enough rabbinics or enough sacred text and music, they would be ready to serve as rabbis and cantors. Yet, the primary struggles that new clergy face are not related to the lack of critical knowledge or scholarship.

Clergy approximately six months into their initial positions were queried about their experiences in making the transition from ivory tower to the trenches. That data revealed that "the ability to build, maintain, and repair interpersonal relationships was the crucial foundational skill needed."[12] These new practitioners recognized that the "vast majority of difficulties they encountered were in human interactions."[13] And even seasoned clergy reflect:

> It has become clear to me that counseling/chaplaincy is essential for anyone being ordained or invested. At the very least, it gives the rabbi or cantor vital insights into their own gifts and limitations when working with congregants. Ideally it combines personal growth, academic study, and clinical experience so that Jewish clergy are prepared to meet the challenges of congregational work.[14]

An Integrated Approach to Clergy Education: Today's Realities and Visions

Starting in the late 1990s, under the guidance of then-provost Dr. Norman Cohen, HUC-JIR began rebuilding its curriculum from the ground up. Faculty on all three stateside campuses discussed educational philosophy, goals, and mission for a liberal Jewish seminary. Then, faculty in each discipline had cross-campus discussions about their existing curricula and goals, as a springboard to identifying specific learning goals for each discipline. Eventually, faculty from different disciplines discussed the courses they offered concurrently or in successive semesters to see how they either complemented each other or could serve as building blocks toward a shared end.

For the first time, we were discussing three interrelated strands toward which classes in all disciplines could contribute: academic, professional, and personal/spiritual. We identified three main ways of assessing a student's growth: knowledge (information and comprehension), skills (analysis, application, performance, and synthesis), and personal characteristics (internalization of material, love of the material, and spiritual connection with the material).

While HUC-JIR engaged in this process beginning in the late 1990s, other Jewish seminaries have adopted the same holistic approach to assess and develop programs. Our seminaries seek to prepare Jewish clergy who can lead with integrity. For this to be possible, all of the varied dimensions of seminary education must become integrated into the fiber of their beings.[15] Like a page of Talmud, their response to any situation will naturally be grounded in our texts and traditions, sensitive to the multiplicity of relationships that define their lives, attuned to the idiosyncrasies of the moment and the situation, met with a willingness to be as fully present as possible to those with whom they are relating, and considered creatively and purposefully in light of ever-changing circumstances.

Another way to picture rabbinic and cantorial education is as a second Venn diagram. Each different subject studied—Bible, Mishnah, Talmud, Midrash, codes, history, philosophy and theology, liturgy and ritual, Hebrew, Aramaic, Jewish education, pastoral care, homiletics, social justice, and so on—is a circle in the diagram. Many students could go through their years at seminary finding some links among the fields and trusting that in time other meaningful connections will become clear. All of this, they assume, will be fodder for future teaching, sermons, eulogies, and wedding addresses and will be building blocks for further study throughout their rabbinates and cantorates. While we hope that, in fact, their assumptions prove true, as pastoral educators, as members of cutting-edge seminary faculties, we are taking a more holistic approach. We are concerned about how students take this knowledge and move it from their head to their hearts and from their hearts into their own lives and into their actions and interpersonal interactions.

To address this concern and turn it into a concrete educational goal, we were fortunate to be working at a seminary with a provost and some colleagues at each of our campuses dedicated to this issue as well. We recognized that in addition to the cross-campus faculty conversations based on discipline, in order to achieve the movement from knowledge to actions and interactions that we sought, we needed to learn more about some of the meta-messages that run through different courses. In this way, no discipline's courses, including pastoral courses, would continue to be perceived as standing apart from others, but all could be understood as sharing vital understandings and approaches with each other. A few examples can serve as important illustrations.

In the introductory Bible courses, students spend time learning about how to analyze biblical texts. They spend hours parsing words and consulting concordances to deepen their appreciation for the ways that context and syntax can help clarify a word or phrase's meaning. As they pore over these texts and resources, they probably do not take the time to consider how the same attention to detail, the same appreciation for context and syntax, will make them better listeners, better pastoral caregivers. The Bible instructor may create an assignment that involves utilizing a text in a sermon. Or she may spend time talking with students about the different syntax and tone that the different prophets used to communicate with the Israelites in different contexts. The instructor of pastoral care can then reference this understanding and help students reflect on how they choose different vocabulary, syntax, and tone depending on who their audience is and what the context will be. They might consider how the way that individuals address them, as soon-to-be clergy, is different from the way their friends or family do. Conversely, in order to appreciate the difficulty individuals may have turning to another for help and support, they may spend class time looking at biblical stories where one person explicitly seeks another's assistance.

In all text courses, not just Bible, students learn to listen to and comprehend language, metaphors, and imagery that reference realities that often lie far beyond their personal experiences. While they may not expect to find it in a pastoral care course, we, as pastoral educators, can lead our students to appreciate the many ways they can approach the people in their lives with the same reverence and care that they approach holy texts. They can listen closely to see if the person sitting with them is emphasizing certain words or phrases, is using them in normative ways, is struggling to find ways to express something. These skills, so important to students as they come to appreciate the varied associations and creative uses of language that the rabbis of earlier generations made to make meaning out of traumatic or unfamiliar situations, can open a student up to hear the attempts of someone that they are sitting with to do the same in their lives. The approaches of different philosophers and theologians to tackling life's enduring questions can help them clarify their own theological assumptions and listen closely as others share theirs with them.

Through the study of history our students are exposed to the power of myth, the distinctions between history and memory. In pastoral care courses, they learn to listen to the guiding myths with which an individual, family system, or congregation operates. Just as they learn about the subjectivity of any historical account or the power of myth and memory, even when not historically demonstrable, we can encourage students to listen to the memories people share with them and the meanings that they ascribe to them, valuing their importance, even if the facts/history are fuzzy. When students study medieval codes or Talmud or responsa literature, they will learn about the methodology at the heart of the halakhic process, and they will learn to apply that process to contemporary issues. As they gain greater reflective skills through fieldwork supervision, pastoral education, and reflection groups, students demonstrate a growing interest in interpersonal ethics and boundaries as well as medical ethical issues.

The study of Midrash helps us to appreciate the ways that the stories we tell raise new questions for us as circumstances change. New events and new experiences engender new questions and lead us to retell our stories in new ways. Once our students appreciate the midrashic process, they can consider how they can create midrash that can promote healing and wholeness in their communities. And they can listen to the stories, the personal narratives that others share with them, and appreciate the movement from chaos to coherence that might come with time as the new or unexpected variable gets integrated into someone's life story.[16]

Ideally, a supportive infrastructure to facilitate students' professional and spiritual formation will permeate the seminary environment in an intentional and varied way. Beyond the classroom, we can reinforce the idea that we are a community of learners, a community of individuals all growing personally, intellectually, professionally, and spiritually. Faculty members can be trained to facilitate small reflection groups, comprising faculty and students, to discuss meta-issues related to being a contemporary Jewish leader, such as how to define sacred text; what our relationship is to Israel (the people, the state, *k'lal Yisrael*); what religious practices hold the most meaning for us and which ones we struggle with most; and how our unique understandings of our relationship with God influence the way we live our lives. At the seminary, we can build deeper, more personal bonds between students and faculty, sharing our joys and struggles, beliefs and doubts, as together we engage in the process of living as Jewish professionals with integrity.

Whether it is Jewish genetic diseases or voting patterns of American Jews or changing Jewish demographics, our lives individually and collectively are tied to a whole host of issues. Through community-wide forums attended by faculty and students from all of our programs, we can see how a single issue raises halakhic, theological, ethical, social-action, educational, communal, and pastoral issues. As we learn together and discuss these issues, we can help our students appreciate that thoughtful and effective responses as clergy require them to consider each issue from all of these perspectives. At the heart of this process is creating a community in which each individual is honored and heard, where the best of pastoral skills and reflective practice are brought to bear.

We can build time for students and faculty to nurture their own spiritual lives through worship, spiritual direction, and personal practice. We can organize retreats, set aside space for meditation or yoga, and create worship opportunities that enable all of the members of our communities to develop rich spiritual lives.

In addition, cantorial and rabbinic students have opportunities for reflection through the supervision related to their fieldwork. They learn how to own their uncertainties and turn to peers and seasoned professionals for support and guidance.

> Recently, a student serving a small congregation brought a verbatim to her small-group supervision. A newcomer to the community, a Jew of color, is finding it hard to feel like she belongs. As the student rabbi listens to the woman's story, she hears the woman's pain and frustration. She notes the choking back of tears and the wistful longing the woman's phrasing conveys. The woman has come to the synagogue to feel at home, but instead she feels like an outsider. The student listens attentively, expresses her concern, offers her own welcome to the woman, and introduces her to some members.
>
> In retrospect, the student thinks of the biblical injunction to remember the stranger, for we were strangers, and her own

> experiences of feeling like an outsider. She recalls the discussions from various classes about the meaning of "Diaspora" (*galut*) and longing. As the woman shares memories of her experiences at her former congregation, words from Psalms and Lamentations come to mind. And in supervision, the student rabbi shares all of this with Jewish peers and with a member of the clergy, who can help her explore the many dimensions of this interaction, knowing that they will accompany her as she goes on a journey with her congregant. No single class would have allowed her to do this, no secular training in counseling. An integrated Jewish seminary curriculum can.

We participate in a remarkable transformational process with our students while they are in seminary: from fear upon being exposed to a new field or entering a new situation to comfort to confidence to creativity. The fusion of classroom (didactic) learning, hands-on experience, and reflection work their peculiar magic and help student rabbis and student cantors become more comfortable, competent Jewish leaders.

> Katie, a third-year rabbinic student, arrived for her first day at the hospital. Her supervisor, a seasoned rabbi, informed her that she would be covering a few units, among them the neonatal intensive care unit (NICU)/maternity. Together with other seminary students, Katie and her supervisor entered the unit. All of the students' eyes scanned the scene: nurses checking charts and monitors, parents sitting next to tiny incubators connected to tubes and machines or with tiny swaddled neonates in knitted caps on their laps. Overwhelmed by all of the new sights and sounds and smells, they moved forward through the unit, keeping pace with the supervisor.
>
> Just outside the NICU, on the way to maternity, the supervisor pointed to something hanging on the wall and said, "Here's where you find the kit to respond to fetal demise." The supervisor noticed that all of the color drained from many of their faces, including Katie's. Katie's mind began to race: hospitals were to cure or heal; pregnancy and birth were causes for joy, not pain; the words "fetal" and "demise" were not meant to go together.

The group followed the supervisor into a nearby conference room. There, the supervisor and the unit's head nurse provided a didactic about fetal demise, discussing not only the contents of the kit, but the multiple levels of care that the team offered. Katie's first night on call, she was paged. When she arrived at maternity, she was informed that there had been a fetal demise. In the middle of the night, she called her supervisor, distraught. She knew what she was expected to do but felt incapable of doing it. How could she be there for this family when she was so upset herself? She had paid close attention during the didactic, but none of it seemed to be at her disposal now when she needed it. Her supervisor spent time with her on the phone and talked her through a number of issues, encouraging her to see what she could do, rather than focusing on what she believed she could not do.

The next morning, she reported to her peer group of seminarians about the experience. She shared with them, step-by-step, what she had done and how she had felt. She also reflected on how she was currently feeling and what she had begun to learn about herself in urgent situations in which she is called on to be there for others. She was not the only student who had to use the kit while on call. Together, as a group, the students shared the variety of ways that they had responded and what they had learned. Each student, in his or her own idiosyncratic way, came to relate to the kit and the circumstances in which they use it in new ways. All began to use it as a tool that they could modify in ways that made it their own and that could render it useful and meaningful in diverse circumstances. And simultaneously, each, at his or her own pace, began to grapple with the larger existential and spiritual questions that accompany individuals at a moment when what was longed for as a moment celebrating life becomes a time to mark a death. Nothing that they had known before about themselves or the world could be taken for granted. All gained new understandings and competencies that had meaning and applications far beyond the specifics of fetal demise.

Katie used what she had learned when a child died in a freak accident just days before his bar mitzvah. Another member of her group looked back on her experience of initial fear and getting beyond it when she got her first call to accompany a family to the morgue. And yet another group member looked at the information that he was handed about how the congregation he had just come to serve had celebrated Rosh Hashanah, studied it carefully, so he knew it well, went through his first High Holy Days with the congregation, and then considered how he would modify things so that the next year they could be more meaningful for the community he had begun to know.

How do we prepare students for the broad jump from the acquisition of specific knowledge and the building of discrete skills to the application of learning from one disparate setting to another? And how do we prepare individuals for the diverse tasks and roles of Jewish clergy in a self-reflective, spiritually informed, and healthy manner? The answer: integration.

Integrity, peace, and wholeness are concepts that are semantically linked in Hebrew. At the liturgical height of a Jewish service, when the Torah is out of the ark, we sing of the Torah that "its ways are ways are ways of pleasantness and all its paths are peace [*shalom*]." We identify Aaron and his descendants as "pursuers of peace [*shalom*]." Unblemished stones used to build the Temple in Jerusalem are described as being whole or having integrity (*shaleim*). Jacob, with his leg wounded following his night with the angel, is described as whole (*shaleim*). His integrity (*sh'leimut*), his wholeness, is not diminished even when his physical state is altered. If we can help our students find a sense of *sh'leimut* in themselves, then they will be able to sense it and/or promote it in others. If we help them appreciate the ways that their *sh'leimut* is tied to their integrating all that they know—cognitively, emotionally, and spiritually—then we believe that they can help others do the same.

Jewish seminary education for clergy is becoming a tapestry that emerges from the intertwined strands of academic graduate school, professional graduate school, and nurturing environment for focused spiritual formation and reflective practice. This combination, when successful, produces clergy who can appreciate themselves and others in the context of past, present, and future; who can connect with others, the world, God, and themselves in ways that are rich, varied, and meaningful; and who can make useful associations among the many fields of Jewish seminary education to respond in creative and appropriate ways to the disparate settings and circumstances in which they operate.

At the core of this integrative process toward which pastoral education and contemporary Jewish seminary education aspire is one idea: to be human is to be in relationship. Pastoral education underscores this connective tissue that binds all of the different types of learning that occur at seminary. The Jewish piece of this pastoral message is this: To be a Jew is to be in relationship with self, others, the world, the Jewish people, Jewish teachings and culture, and God. It is to be engaged in and working on all of these relationships simultaneously. By extension, then, pastoral education focuses on helping future Jewish professionals appreciate the relationship between their effectiveness in all spheres to their developing an integrated sense of self, a sense of wholeness, a sense of integrity. As we seek *shalom* in the world, we can devote ourselves to helping ourselves; as we help others, we find a sense of *sh'leimut*.

Judaism and Caregiving

Rabbi Stephanie Dickstein, LMSW

"Rabbi, please make a *Mi Shebeirakh* [prayer for healing] for my mother." This is a common request, and as a young pulpit rabbi, I gave the common response: "How is your mother doing?" It was not until much later that I realized I should have been asking a different or, at least, additional question. I have learned to respond, "How are you doing?"

Most people who live with illness, the decline of aging, or disability do not do so in isolation. They have family members and friends who travel the road with them. At some point, one or more individuals in that group cross the line from caring to caregiving. These are the individuals whose daily life is directly and regularly affected as they deal with the multitude of logistics and hands-on aspects of care.

Caregiving is not a new phenomenon. Archeologists suggest that the careful burial of deformed teens and adults means that these individuals were cared for despite their lifelong disabilities.[1] Our ancestors have long cared for those who could not function independently. The vast majority of healthcare took place in the home and was provided by family members or others connected to the household. There were also professionals who could be consulted for specific medical services and institutions of last resort. The role of caregiver has long been legislated in Jewish law in terms of obligations and expectations of family members and, to a lesser degree, the community. However, it is only within the past few decades that we have come to understand and discuss the emotional and spiritual experiences of the caregiver as something separate from that of the care recipient.

Rabbi Stephanie Dickstein, LMSW, is spiritual care coordinator for the Shira Ruskay Center of the Jewish Board of Family and Children's Services in New York, New York.

Jewish Teachings about Obligations between Family Members

Halakhah (Jewish law) on caregiving derives from interpretation of the fundamental commandment "Honor your father and mother" (Exodus 20:12) and its corollary to revere your mother and father (Leviticus 19:3). The vast literature on this topic from Talmudic times until today testifies to the clarity of this *mitzvah* in the abstract and the complexity in the way it is lived in each relationship and at each stage of life. One is obligated to treat a parent with honor to the greatest extent possible. This may ultimately absolve the child of giving the parent hands-on physical care. Parents are exhorted to prepare for their own future needs and to behave in ways that facilitate their children honoring them. There are extensive writings on the legal and ethical obligations of adult Jewish children to care for their aging parents.[2]

There is an assumption of parental care for children, but it is time limited. Parents are obligated to teach their minor children physical and spiritual survival skills and to facilitate their marriage. There is no requirement to give adult children financial support. Parents of disabled children should maximize the level of independence of those children while ensuring their safety and health.[3] They should also arrange for ongoing care beyond the parents' lifetime.

The mutual, yet differing, obligations of husband and wife to each other are outlined in the *ketubah* and expanded on in writings about the marriage contract. A husband's obligation to support his wife includes the requirement that he pay for her medical treatment, while the husband is entitled to receive personal care from his wife. These expectations of care assume that love, loyalty, and shared history will facilitate the ongoing care of an ill spouse. However, *halakhah* recognizes that when the relationship no longer offers meaningful marital companionship, ending the marriage may be an option.

Halakhah does not consider other familial relationships to have the same level of obligation for caregiving as parent/child or husband/wife. Grandchildren have some level of obligation to revere their grandparents both as ancestors and because they are elderly. If the middle generation is unavailable to care for grandparents, grandchildren should assume that responsibility to the extent possible.[4]

There is extensive Jewish narrative literature about sibling relations, which can be both troubling and redemptive. There is much less discussion of the legal obligations of siblings to each other. Biblically, the terms "brother," "neighbor," and "friend" are used interchangeably. At the very least, siblings are first on the list of those beyond parent and child that one should help financially and in other ways. All adult siblings have the same level of responsibility to their parents. This is important to note, as dissension among siblings can cause stress for caregivers of aging parents.[5]

Dimensions of Contemporary Caregiving

To provide meaningful spiritual care it is necessary to understand the many dimensions of caregiving today as well as for the near future. Individuals become caregivers in different ways. Sometimes there is a sudden event, such as an injury that changes lives in an instant. More often, the recognition that one is a caregiver comes slowly. An initial diagnosis of a chronic or life-threatening illness puts the patient's support system into a whirl of medical and information management. It may not be until further along in the illness that one or more people begin to self-identify as caregivers. This is often the case for children of aging parents. The point at which a person finally self-identifies is significant because caregivers generally do not reach out for help for themselves until then.

Advances in medical technology have created an explosion in the number of people who will need care for an extended period of time. Americans are living longer and healthier lives, but many are surviving into extreme old age, with dementias and frailty. Others survive life-threatening illnesses or injuries and are living longer with chronic illnesses or physical and emotional disabilities that impact on their ability to care for themselves.

In 2009, more than 65 million people, 29 percent of the U.S. population, provided unpaid care for a chronically ill, disabled, or aged family member or friend for an average of twenty hours per week.[6] Changes in technology and the location of services have led to caregivers providing more complex medical interventions than in the past. Most care recipients live in their own home. Almost a third live in their caregiver's home, while only a small percentage reside in nursing homes and assisted living.[7]

While aging baby boomers have brought new attention to both the elderly and their caregivers, individuals of all ages are in need of and are providing care. There is a normative expectation of becoming a caregiver for an aging parent or spouse, and these caregivers have some advantages. They usually have a network of contemporaries to offer peer support as well as communal agencies and institutions oriented toward common needs of the elderly. More isolated, however, are caregivers "out of time." These include teens and young adults with chronically ill parents, who face developmental challenges from being tied to concerns at home when they should be seeking independence and creating their own families. There are also a growing number of elderly parents with ongoing responsibility for developmentally or mentally disabled adult children or who take part in caring for adult children or grandchildren with life-threatening illnesses.

Changes in family structures and mobility have implications for work with caregivers. For example, the prevalence of divorce implies that children will be caring for elderly parents separately, possibly with the added dimension of negotiating with stepparents and siblings. The delay in having children means that more families are dealing with child care, aging parents, and grandparents at the same time. Most in the largest group of caregivers, ages forty-five to sixty-five, are also employed, balancing work and family.[8] Geographical mobility of Americans of all ages means that family members may not live close by when someone requires care. Long-distance caregiving is a significant issue, as are questions of moving a frail person and the burden of hands-on care falling primarily on one member of a family. Non–family members, such as friends and neighbors, can also be primary caregivers when the care recipient is emotionally estranged, lives physically distant, or has outlived immediate family. However, non-family caregivers may be disenfranchised by medical providers or have their efforts questioned by people in their own circles.

Gender plays a significant role in caregiving. As presented above, the Jewish legal discussion seemed to treat men and women equally. However, *halakhah* assumes that a married woman's primary responsibility is to her husband, not to her parents. Sons have the primary obligation to provide hands-on care for their parents. In contemporary society, women provide over 60 percent of all care.[9] The stereotype of daughters and daughters-in-law doing the majority of care is accurate. Sons are more likely to deal with financial matters. Traditionally, women were socialized to view caregiving as a natural role. Many of the tasks of day-to-day caregiving require skills that women already have.

Nevertheless, it is important to note that approximately 40 percent of care is provided by men. This includes the daily care done by elderly husbands and unmarried adult sons. For older men, caregiving may require not only a change in identity but also learning how to do household tasks that had not been their domain previously. Male caregivers are at higher risk of isolation and are less likely to ask for help or to talk about their experiences in settings that offer support. It will be interesting to observe whether and how the men socialized in this more egalitarian culture deal with the demands when they become caregivers in the future. Additionally, both gender and class affect other aspects of caregiving such as communication with medical professionals and health aides.

This chapter focuses on providing spiritual care, which would be necessary and beneficial in the best of all possible worlds. However, we do not live in that world, so any discussion of Jewish support for caregivers must mention the obligation to advocate for policies that could ultimately ease the stresses faced by caregivers. These include greater public education and awareness, more financial relief, better communication, coordination, and collaboration with healthcare professionals, and heightened recognition and support for family caregivers in policy initiatives.[10]

Spiritual Issues for Caregivers

There are many ways to conceptualize the spiritual issues for caregivers. A pioneering book on these spiritual issues is *That You May Live Long: Caring for our Aging Parents, Caring for Ourselves*, edited by Richard Address and Hara Person. This collection of essays includes Jewish teachings and personal reflections. It takes the reader on a journey from family relations and aging to acceptance of death.

In her groundbreaking publications and lectures on the spirituality of aging, Dayle Freidman outlines ten core Jewish values and dilemmas in caregiving. Among her teachings are *shalom bayit* (harmonious family relations), legacy, the primacy of saving a life yet accepting that there is a time to die, God's role, compassion, and the healing of body and soul. She delineates the tension between doing the right thing and not being able to do everything.[11]

My book, *With Sweetness from the Rock: A Jewish Spiritual Companion for Caregivers*,[12] was inspired by my work offering spiritual support to caregivers, as well as listening to the recently bereaved share their stories of the blessings and curses of caregiving. Within each of the seven Jewish themes that structure the readings, there is an ebb and flow from the challenges of the caregiving experience to its benefits and the gifts of the spirit. The image of waves in the ocean is apt because caregiving seldom happens in a predefined path. Joy and despair, success and failure, a step forward and a step back can all happen within one hour. Unpredictability and lack of control are major factors in the journey of the caregiver.

The first theme is *b'rit* (covenant). By definition, caregiving involves partnership. The caregiver and the care recipient are the primary figures in the relationship, but the covenant extends to other family members, friends, and a wide variety of professionals. The physical or mental decline/disability of one partner creates the need for a covenant of caregiving, but the ability of both partners to interact with each other and with others is a key spiritual resource. Isolation, whether through withdrawal or abandonment, that can accompany long-term illness is among the most devastating of spiritual challenges.

The theme of *mikvah* (a ritual pool of natural water) represents purification and renewal. This becomes necessary because caregiving may bring one into contact with distressing bodily excretions and wounds. Cognitive or emotional decline can drag us into dark places of the mind and soul. The biblical concept of *tumah* (ritual impurity) exists in relation to contact with real or symbolic death. Fear of death or longing for the relief of death is often the dark secret of caregivers. When we come into contact with that which drains us of life, we need to find some space and a way to renew ourselves. Tears, the wordless expression of distress, can also provide relief.

The season of *t'shuvah*, encompassing assessment, confession, repentance, and return, that culminates in Yom Kippur offers structure for another spiritual challenge. No caregiver is perfect; everyone involved will make mistakes. How do we forgive ourselves and others?

How do we evaluate what can improve if we do not allow time for self-assessment? If we can acknowledge that we are only human and honestly examine our helpful and hurtful deeds with a goal of doing better, we can return to the tasks and the relationship with a more open heart.

Time is another significant theme in caregiving. There is both too little and too much of it. For caregivers, time can lose meaning as day and night become irrelevant. Shabbat is the reminder that there is "evening and morning," with distinct moments, including those for rest, reflection, and pleasure. For those who are observant, Shabbat and the holidays offer some respite from the ordinary routines of illness. Conversely, they can add more stress when it is too difficult to mark the holiday as it had been or medical treatments require "breaking" Shabbat.

Despair and anger are integral parts of caregiving. There is rage at the illness, at the inadequacy and inhumanity of the healthcare system, and at those who have disappointed and abandoned the caregiver. There can be anger with God in the face of suffering and despair at the accumulation of physical and emotional losses. Tisha B'Av is the fast day on which Jews recall the destruction of the Holy Temples. It is a day when we imagine alienation from God. It is preceded by three weeks filled with rituals of despair at the impending destruction. But Tisha B'Av is followed by seven weeks of comfort, during which we take a liturgical and celebratory journey of healing from trauma.

Light in the midst of darkness is a universal symbol of hope that is so important for caregivers. There are many times when Jews light candles. The two Shabbat candles represent the thought and deed that connect us to the weekly and eternal cycles of time, while the braided candles of Havdalah remind us that we are intimately tied with others and dependent on each other to create light. The Chanukah lights commemorate survival and the miracles that surround us. The *yahrzeit* candle holds the pain of loss and the comfort of memory even as it demonstrates that love is stronger than death.

Finally, there is the theme of *shalom*, peace and wholeness. Caregiving can be heartbreaking, but paradoxically a broken heart has the potential of making one more open to loved ones, to the community, to God, and to one's own soul. Jewish liturgy is structured so that our prayers conclude with an expression of gratitude and a request for peace. Gratitude from others and the appreciation that the caregiver can express to others strengthen connections. Learning to recognize blessings and to be thankful for small gifts and accomplishments can begin to heal the shattered heart.

Providing Spiritual Care

How do we engage a caregiver in order to offer spiritual support? Those who are caring for someone who is ill and dependent have very real needs for concrete services and information. The spiritual care provider must be a resource for connecting caregivers to places where they can get these services. This does not mean that we must personally be able to call the best doctor and eldercare lawyer or fill out forms for transportation. We should be aware of general resources in the community so that we can make and follow up on appropriate referrals. Certainly some of what we recognize as spiritual suffering can be eased by dealing with concrete needs such as proper pain control, a competent home health aide, or funds to help a distant loved one visit. It is also true that there are significant issues with our healthcare system and serious gaps in the services available to those facing long-term caregiving situations. However, we should not underestimate the way in which responding to spiritual distress and offering spiritual resources can enable a caregiver to function more effectively and to find sustaining meaning.

Just as each caregiving partnership is unique, so, too, is the way that spiritual resources are offered and will be received. What is helpful to one individual may be perceived as useless by another. It is critical to remember that spiritual support is found in the relationship between the provider and the caregiver and in the meaning making that they explore together.

Spiritual support can be provided by a variety of professionals as well as trained volunteers and community members. Clergy have expertise in the provision of spiritual care as well as being teachers of traditional religious wisdom and law. Certified chaplains who serve in hospitals and other institutions may be either clergy or trained laypeople. Mental health professionals, social workers, and nurses are increasingly being educated to include the consideration of spirituality in their therapeutic work.

Creating a spiritually supportive environment that recognizes caregivers is a first step. In a communal institution such as a synagogue, acknowledging that caregivers are among the members can happen in many ways. Caregivers can be mentioned when prayers are offered for those who are ill. Newsletters and websites make a statement by listing concrete resources and spiritual teachings. Training *bikkur cholim* volunteers to visit the sick should include inquiring about the state of the caregiver as well as the patient. Healing services allow for the identification of those involved in long-distance caregiving as well as those who are local. An ongoing series of Jewish family life educational programs that combine psychosocial content with Jewish values and teachings sends two important messages. The first is that spiritual content is part of all life-cycle issues. The second is that caregiving, with its stresses and rewards, is a normal human experience and that this family is not experiencing something that puts them on the margins of the community. The visible partnership between the synagogue, community center or school, and the Jewish Family Service normalizes the benefit of psychosocial support.

The medical system is beginning to recognize that cost-effective healthcare depends on treating the whole patient in the context of his or her family, support system, and home. Ideally, professional chaplains are part of multidisciplinary teams that understand that each professional provides essential and interconnected services. Spiritual assessment tools and treatments that are offered to patients can also be helpful in work with caregivers.

Entering into a relationship in which a professional can share some part of the journey is essential for providing spiritual support. In some cases, such as congregational clergy and their members, a relationship may already exist based on other encounters and ongoing participation in communal activities. Some members or their spouses/partners will reach out when their emotional or spiritual distress becomes too intense to bear alone. With serious acute illness, the clergy will probably be involved quite early, but they need to remember that the journey of the caregiver is separate from that of the ill family member. The growing pattern will be that of a gradual increase in caregiving responsibilities from occasional to all-consuming. Clergy need to be alert to changes in participation by their members, which may indicate that caregiving is requiring more time and energy or causing more distress.

Informal networks may be useful as part of an initial assessment of need for outreach on the part of clergy, even as privacy and confidentiality will have to be part of the consideration. The complex relationship between rabbis and lay leaders adds another layer to the delicacy to reaching out and offering spiritual support. Congregational clergy generally have experience with a type of crisis intervention. Following a death, the rabbi's spiritual authority comes from knowledge of *halakhah* and how ritual can be used to guide the family through the initial days and weeks. Providing spiritual support for caregivers requires a different set of skills. It requires the ability to offer a supportive presence over time in the face of uncertainty and informed by an understanding of the spiritual themes identified above.

Spiritual care can also be provided by a professional who enters the relationship for the explicit purpose of offering service to the patient and/or the caregiver. This is most common for institutionally based or community chaplains or spiritual care providers in social service agencies. Here, the illness/disability and the caregiver's role are already identified as the cause of the initial encounter. While some will immediately share intimate issues with a clergyperson, most need time to assess how much they can trust the spiritual care provider. Some will expect the rabbi to function in the role of religious authority who can tell them what to do or answer the question "why," rather than as someone who can accompany them through the ebb and flow and help them figure out how.

Those who do not usually define themselves as religious/observant or spiritual may have reservations about how much a rabbi or Judaism can really speak to their needs, even as they seek something profound to offer them meaning and guidance in the midst of chaos. Some observant Jews, who are connected to a synagogue, may seek out spiritual support from a professional other than their own rabbi. They may want to feel free to explore resources beyond what might be considered acceptable, or they simply may not want to share their intimate struggles with someone they see in daily situations. Program-based spiritual relationships tend to be short-term and focused around the story told by the caregiver or observed in the immediate present of the home or hospital room.

Resources and Tools of the Spiritual Care Provider

What are the resources and tools of the Jewish spiritual care provider? Fundamental to all the work is an open heart and skilled listening. It is the ability to create, even for a few moments, a safe space in which the caregiver can share his or her story, what is spiritually meaningful and what is causing distress at this time. The spiritual care provider is not God or God's official spokesperson, but does offer the possibility of divine presence in the room and the situation. Although the caregiver may begin the conversation by asking what Judaism has to say about the situation, the spiritual care provider's first response is to explore more about where the question is coming from. The spiritual care provider's goal is to understand the experience of the caregiver in the present and the extent of his or her Jewish and spiritual awareness in order to build a spiritual remedy.

There is a wide range of Jewish spiritual resources, many of which are elucidated elsewhere in this book and in the literature of Jewish healing. Some well-known resources from Jewish practice include prayer, alone or with a community; the study of sacred texts; and Shabbat and holiday celebrations, rituals, and the exploration and application of the themes of the holidays to one's personal situation. Music, chanting, creative arts, meditation, natural settings, healing touch, physical activity, and relaxation are also very much within Jewish tradition.

One use of these resources is to offer the caregiver sacred language and a way to describe his or her situation and give voice to feelings. Various kinds of text study are a primary tool for this. In an article in *The Outstretched Arm*, I describe how a collection of eighteen verses from Psalms can serve both a diagnostic and a treatment function.[13] While each of the verses can be interpreted in many ways, they give voice to a range of spiritual and emotional thoughts. The caregiver is asked to choose one or two of these verses that most strongly express his or her feelings at this moment. This can become the focus of conversation for the meeting. The caregiver can take the collection home and do the exercise every few days, making note of how the choice of verse and its interpretation changes each time. Of course, reading psalms has a long history as a spiritual resource in times of trouble, but for many contemporary Jews it is not obvious how these ancient words of praise for God speak to them. The spiritual care provider can teach the caregiver to see that indeed these poems and prayers do offer language and describe a journey of mixed emotions, doubt, and hope that characterizes the path of the caregiver.

Studying biblical narratives or Talmudic stories that involve illness, difficulty, family conflict, or caregiving can help caregivers reflect on their own situation while reminding them about the different interpretations of the same story. This opens up the possibility of new readings of the caregiver's own narrative.

Prayer is another resource with many aspects. It can be comforting to many caregivers to have a rabbi recite traditional prayers of healing on behalf of their loved one, and for them as well, perhaps adding words that come from the knowledge gained in the relationship. For those who are familiar with Jewish liturgy, the spiritual care provider can suggest ways in which the caregiver can offer those prayers focusing on phrases and readings that address the deep concerns of the moment. Additionally, caregivers can be empowered to create and recite personal prayers from their heart.

For many caregivers, the stress of constantly being on and responsible is overwhelming. The spiritual care provider can explore which of the resources named above might assist the caregiver in relaxing for even a few moments. By discussing chants, teaching a *niggun* (melody) or verses for brief meditation, reciting a *b'rakhah* (blessing) to bring awareness to eating, or talking about the importance of physical exercise and walking outside, the spiritual care provider can educate the caregiver about benefits of activities that provide physical relaxation while teaching Jewish values of the connection between body and soul and the obligation to care for our own health. Given the increased risks to the health of caregivers, this is an essential element.

Jewish life is lived most fully in community. Caregiving can result in a decrease in communal involvement and even isolation. One of the roles of a spiritual care provider may be to try to facilitate reconnection with community. This may involve arranging for volunteers to visit or for respite care so the caregiver can go out for a while. Sometimes bringing in others cannot be the first step in reducing isolation. Perhaps the caregiver is ashamed because of the state of the home or is embarrassed by the frailty or behavior of the care recipient. Former friends, distressed by the decline of their contemporary, may find it too frightening to visit. Maybe they need support as well. While I do not see technology as a panacea for isolation or a replacement for human contact, it can be of great benefit to caregivers as well as to those who are ill. Online communities can provide support, social and intellectual stimulation, and a visual connection with loved ones who are physically distant.

Support groups for caregivers can be an invaluable setting for spiritual care. These groups offer community, lessen isolation, and allow for a sharing of experience and hard-won expertise. All of the themes and resources discussed above can be part of the work of a group. When a caregiver is able to connect to the right group, measurable improvement in the emotional and spiritual health of that person is usually the result. However, there are numerous systematic and individual impediments to participation in these groups. Lack of time and the uncertainty of a caregiver's life top the list. Other issues include lack of respite care, transportation, the variety of caregiving relationships and situations (e.g., spouse versus adult child, long distance versus in-home, chronic versus terminal), and cultural and personal levels of comfort with privacy and sharing. Nevertheless, given the support that groups can offer caregivers, they remain a significant spiritual resource to explore.

The Spiritual Gifts of Caregiving

This chapter has considered caregiving in the context of Jewish family obligations. It has focused on the need for spiritual support because the stresses of caregiving can be so challenging to the physical, emotional, and spiritual health of caregivers. It has offered tools and resources for providing spiritual care that responds to suffering. Scattered throughout has been the idea that caregiving has benefits for the caregiver as well as for the care recipient. Helping the caregiver to recognize, celebrate, and find comfort in this sacred work is a core task of the spiritual care provider. These gifts include surviving a difficult trial, discovering that one has the strength and ability to make a difference, finding a caring community, reconciling with people and with the past to create a legacy of compassion and healing, and understanding that hope, gratitude, and joy can exist even in dire circumstances. The Talmud teaches that deeds of loving-kindness are equal to all of the other commandments.[14] May those who offer support for caregivers be privileged to guide them to experience the gifts of their loving acts.

The Jewish Professional as Personal Caregiver

Rabbi Stephen B. Roberts, MBA, BCC

Hillel says:
If I am not for myself, who will be for me?
And, if I am only for myself alone, then what am I?
And, if not now, then when?

—*Pirkei Avot* 1:14

I live in New York, yet over the last twenty-four months I have spent almost twelve of them in South Florida. Aging family. My father has been hospitalized numerous times and not expected to survive on multiple occasions. I have repeatedly flown into South Florida to be with my family while having a plane reservation back to New York. Then, repeatedly, I have had to cancel the return flight, staying days and weeks beyond what I had expected.

My ninety-four-year-old mother-in-law struggled more and more living on her own until she crossed a major dementia line. When that occurred, I was yet again back in South Florida within twelve hours to help coordinate the situation. We had to move her back to New York within four days.

I spent countless days upon days dealing with nursing home and Medicaid applications, helped my family to arrange home hospice for my father, worked with my mother to arrange home care for my father, and relieved my mother, who was personally at the point of exhaustion, to take care of my father so she could get her own strength back.

The ability to provide love back to my parents and in-laws by being with them as they age has been spiritually moving and meaningful. Yet, it has been physically and emotionally exhausting at times.

Rabbi Stephen B. Roberts, MBA, BCC, is president and chief executive officer of Clergy for a Healthy America in New York, New York.

As working Jewish professionals, we give day in and day out to others. It is our love and our lives. There are more financially rewarding paths. However, spiritually and emotionally, our path rewards us beyond dollars and cents. It is why we get up daily, say *Modeh ani l'fanekha*, and then go out and help make the world a better place. Yet, we need to ask, "How do I manage my life when I am not only a working Jewish professional but also a personal caregiver?" This chapter hopes to allow you to wrestle with this question and find answers for you and your own family.

Jewish Professional as Personal Caregiver

All of us, as working Jewish professionals, will most likely find ourselves at some point in our careers also as personal caregivers. Some of these situations are short-term, some a few months or years, and some lifetimes. Each situation is unique.

Long-Term Caregiving

Caring for aging family members is one of the most likely situations we may find ourselves in. Family is defined not just by blood but also by marriage and choice. In our mobile society, it is common that those we love who need our help are not around the corner but rather halfway across the country. Often in today's world, where we now have children when we are in our thirties, forties, and fifties, we have family responsibilities at home and at the same time need to help those who are aging. How do we balance work responsibilities, financial concerns, and family life with the need to take care of others? How do we seek support from the Jewish community that we work within when we are unsure of how long and how often we will need the support, such as time off from work, repeated unexpected trips out of town, loss of concentration at work when present, and multiple phone conversations and e-mails during the day that are not "work related"?

Caring for children with special needs is another common situation many of us find ourselves in. The range of needs is wide. Yet, for many, the caregiving role will continue for years, decades, and even lifetimes.

Medium- and Short-Term Caregiving

It is now fairly common for people to live into their eighties and nineties. Thus, our parents and others of their generation with whom we are close may go through the dying process while we are in the middle of our career, requiring us to find ways to deal with end-of-life care. Often people will spend weeks or months in hospice. When loved ones have a major illness or require surgery, we may find ourselves facing caregiving issues of varying and often uncertain duration.

Hillel's Insight: A Model for Jewish Professionals as Caregivers

Our Lives Prior to Personal Caregiving

As Jewish professionals, our lives often focus and revolve around the second line from *Pirkei Avot* 1:14: "And, if I am only for myself alone, then what am I?"

We are educators, cantors, teachers, rabbis, administrators, social workers, and so much more. We give of our *n'shamah* (soul) on a daily basis to help build a stronger Jewish community. We create innovative lesson plans to touch students—at all ages—and struggle when we miss the mark; we visit the sick so that they know that both the larger Jewish community and also God/Higher Power/Creator has not forgotten them in times of illness and need; we work with those struggling with a range of issues—financial, emotional, physical, and spiritual; we listen to our community as they come to us asking for help—help with dues as they find themselves under/unemployed, help with their children as they approach school for the first time or bat/bar mitzvah, help with integrating family members who have major mental illness into the Jewish community, help redesigning our buildings so that those with disabilities feel truly welcome and invited.

Giving of ourselves and our knowledge freely, we sit through and fully participate in a variety of meetings: board meetings, case-planning meetings, parent-teacher meetings, meetings on how meetings should be run. At these meetings we are expected to give and give and give. We help others to fill up spiritually and emotionally.

We lead services—struggling to make them spiritual and meaningful—for a wide range of age groups and needs. We lead/guide groups:

support groups, bereavement groups, spirituality groups, Torah and Talmud groups, and so much more. And when we lead, we give fully of our body, mind, and spirit. When we are done, we are often physically exhausted but spiritually full.

Our lives revolve around giving. A key in our giving is that not only do we receive much in the giving but also, as we "mature" in our jobs, *we find the essential balance of both giving and "renewing."*

Renewing allows us to stay focused on the second line of Hillel's quote. Ways we renew may include taking off a day during the week for ourselves (many of us "work" professionally on Shabbat and Sundays, so it is often a day when most other people are working); regularly taking off weeks or a full month for vacations and *torah lishmah* (study); exercising; reading for pleasure; working on a hobby; setting aside mealtime for family that is not to be interrupted by our "work"; joining and participating in a group of like-minded professionals with whom we spend time to help keep us thinking in new and regenerative ways.

Yes, renewing is self-care. Only we can take care of our own *n'shamah* so that we can continue to give so freely and passionately and professionally to others. This ongoing renewal process is often the core of our ability to give and give and give to so many others. But this "renewing" is mostly done so that we can continue to give to others. It is really about balance to allow us to serve the larger Jewish community.

Our Lives Adding Caregiving

When we suddenly find ourselves in the role of personal caregiver, our own range of personal needs becomes very different, and the demands on our time increase, sometimes in small ways but often dramatically. Our struggle is to feel comfortable—no, that is not the right word—rather, our struggle is to fully integrate into the core of our beliefs Hillel's first and third teachings: "If I am not for myself, who will be for me?" and "And, if not now, then when?"

I often ask myself and engage with others the question *"Why did Hillel start the quote asking about 'self' first?"* In the role of caregivers, we need to look at this important question.

I hypothesize that the answer is very straightforward. Hillel addressed the hardest struggle first, the struggle of keeping the focus on ourselves and our needs, particularly when our lives suddenly become stressful, unpredictable, and full of added demands on our time, mind, body, *n'shamah*. It is a difficult struggle, one that is hard to live by when we have so many pressing issues being addressed to us by the larger community. We often think/feel/believe that if we do not do/act for others, then God's work will not be done and we will have missed the mark.

Hillel, one of the greatest teachers ever, teaches us otherwise. Especially at times such as when we are personal caregivers.

The answer to Hillel's question of "If I am not for myself, who will be for me?" is *no one*. And the answer to his question of "And if not now, when?" is *never*.

This is a lovingly honest answer. One that I implore you, the reader, to hear.

We must stand up and take care of ourselves when we move into the role of personal caregiver. If not, we will wither and die—spiritually, emotionally, and maybe even physically. No one else can or will stand up for us. And we must do it immediately, or as close to this as possible, when we shift into that role and continue to stay focused on ourselves over time.

I fully support that Hillel's teaching should be our mantra when we become caregivers. We must put our needs first, our personal and caregiving needs, before those of the larger community. And I fully acknowledge that this is so much easier said than done. Which is exactly why Hillel taught in the order that he did.

Tachlis—The Practical Issues We Face as Caregivers

When we become caregivers, we face new demands on our body, mind, and *n'eshamah*. We now must drive to multiple appointments, sometimes in distant cities; listen intently to words from other professionals that we are unfamiliar with and which thus often have no meaning when we first hear them; clean up the person we are taking care of; arrange schedules of both our family and those helping in the caregiving process; shop in new places and for new types of items; fill out endless unfamiliar paperwork—insurance forms, federal forms, nursing home applications, and so on—and when "rejected" have to file appeals and follow-ups; listen with "half an ear" when we are supposed to be sleeping; comfort a range of family members and friends who are struggling with the situation; answer multiple e-mails and phone calls; deal with the hurt when family and close friends suddenly "disappear" at the time we need them most.

Further, the time we had in our schedule that we often used for "renewal" is gone. No more exercise on a regular basis, no reading for pleasure, no attending professional meetings and working with colleagues, no time for hobbies, and the list goes on and on. *No more time off.*

One of the biggest risks that these new demands place on us is that we will suffer "compassion fatigue." The next few sections look at compassion fatigue, what it is, and ways to prevent it.

Compassion Fatigue

What is compassion fatigue? Any person who is a "helping professional," who provides assistance or aid to others, is at risk for compassion fatigue.

> In simple-to-understand language it is the "cost of caring" of [repeatedly giving to those suffering and in need] *that shows itself as spiritual, physical and/or emotional fatigue and exhaustion.* It comes about as a result of caregiving that causes a decrease in the caregiver's ability to experience joy or to feel and care for and about others.[1]

As Jewish professionals, we are often called upon to support individuals, families, and communities after a death, when families are confronted with illness, when congregants have been the victim of a violent crime, when there is violence in the schools, when communities hurt because of cultural or religious conflicts. In the best of circumstances, we are at risk for compassion fatigue. When the added stress of being a caregiver is added, our risk increases substantially.

Research and field findings have led to some specific suggestions to help prevent compassion fatigue. A significant issue involved with compassion fatigue is isolation:

> One of the ways trauma seems to affect us all, caregivers included, is to leave us with a sense of disconnected isolation. A common

> thread we have found with sufferers of compassion fatigue symptoms has been the progressive loss in their sense of connections and community. Many caregivers become increasingly isolated as their symptoms of CF [compassion fatigue] increase. Fear of being perceived as weak, impaired, or incompetent by peers and clients, along with time constraints and loss of interest, have all been cited by caregivers suffering from compassion fatigue as reasons for diminished intimate and collegial connection.[2]

It is crucial for us to understand the potential for isolation when we become personal caregivers as Jewish professionals. Our time is suddenly focused within on those we are taking care of. Suddenly we have no time for the activities we engaged in with the larger community that renew our *n'shamah*. Unless we work very hard at preventing this from occurring, we become isolated. Often we are aware of this occurring but feel we have no choice. We think we can set things aside for "awhile" with no real consequences. When we do not practice "If I am not for myself," it can easily lead to compassion fatigue.

Signs of Compassion Fatigue

What are the warning signs that you are on the way to having compassion fatigue? How do you know when you are in trouble and need to make changes in your life, especially when you are giving the same amount to the Jewish community and now also acting as a personal caregiver? Warning signs include the following:

- Lowered frustration and tolerance and increased irritability
- Outbursts of anger or rage
- Extreme fatigue
- Frequent headaches
- Depression
- Decreased feelings of joy and happiness, in general
- Decreased enjoyment of vocation or career
- Inability to maintain balance of empathy and objectivity
- Increased substance use or abuse
- Change in eating habits

- Chronic tardiness when this had not been an issue previously
- Increased absenteeism or tardiness (these last two bullet points should not be confused with being repeatedly late or missing time due to running someone around to appointments, etc.)
- Losing hope
- Lowered self-esteem
- Diminished sense of purpose
- Hypertension
- Blaming self or others
- Workaholism
- Hypervigilance
- Sleep disturbances

How do you know if you are experiencing compassion fatigue? How do you recognize compassion fatigue within yourself? It has many symptoms, including the following:

- Increase in interpersonal conflicts and/or staff conflicts
- Difficulty concentrating
- Loss of hope—hopelessness
- Lack of energy and enthusiasm
- Lack of interest or participation in meaningful or enjoyable activities
- Loss of purpose in life
- Decreased functioning in nonprofessional situations
- Anger at God/Higher Power and/or loss of faith in God/Higher Power
- Questioning religious beliefs
- Isolation or withdrawing from others and/or loneliness
- Dread of working with certain congregants or clients
- Silencing and/or minimizing congregants'/clients' stories
- Feeling lack of skill with certain congregants regarding issues about which you had previously felt confident

- Increased transference/countertransference issues with certain congregants
- Depression and/or constant sadness
- Mood swings
- Rigidity, perfectionism, and/or obsession about details
- Difficulty separating work life from personal life
- Nightmares
- Mental images of congregants'/clients' traumas
- Recurring and/or intrusive thoughts or images
- Elevated or exaggerated "startle" response
- Thoughts of self-harm or harm to others
- Questioning the meaning of life
- Decreased interest in intimacy and sex

What should you do if you are experiencing some of the warning signs leading to compassion fatigue? Hillel has us ask, "If I am not for myself, who will be for me?" The lovingly honest answer is "No one." Thus, saying "It [compassion fatigue] will go away on its own" is not a recommended course of action. To say it will go away on its own is not being there for yourself.

Rather, follow the various practical strategies listed in the next section of this chapter. Given all that you are going through as both a caregiver and Jewish professional, it is not easy. Actually, it is quite hard. The consequences of not addressing the issue, though, can be professionally and personally devastating. All that you love and care for is at risk by doing nothing—your relationship with your loved ones, your job, and, yes, even your life.

As a very first step, I encourage reaching out and discussing your situation with a colleague, preferably one with additional training in the field of mental health (e.g., a social worker, a rabbi who is a pastoral counselor, a school psychologist).

Addressing Compassion Fatigue

The hardest step of all is asking for specific support from those you work with/for. You give and give and give to others. When you find yourself as a personal caregiver, now is the time to ask back. It is one of the hardest things we can do. However, it is the key in "being for myself."

This is not easy for a variety of reasons. We are just not used to stepping up and asking for our needs to be met. We might fear for our job if we ask for support. We fear looking "weak" and ineffective. And so much more.

Here are some tools that are effective ways to address compassion fatigue.

Supervision

- Find a supervisor you are comfortable with, such as a social worker or spiritual guide.
- You may need to meet with two or three people before you find the right person. It is more important that you find the right person than to go with the first person you meet.
- Meet with your supervisor on a regularly scheduled basis at least twice a month. As a personal caregiver, more is better, not less. This might be the only time in your busy schedule where the focus is on you and your needs. This is a key part of "If I am not for myself, who will be for me?"
- Practice self-supervision such as positive self-talk, working on changing or reframing your perceptions and thoughts.
- Seek short- or long-term assistance from a professional with an expertise in compassion fatigue and the ability to resolve the personal and professional issues of compassion fatigue.

Connectedness

- Attend a peer support group (e.g., clergy, teacher, executive director). Help create one if there is not one already available. Yes, with all the demands now placed upon you involved in personal caregiving, the idea of attending a new regular "meeting" may seem illogical on its face. However, this is practicing "being for myself."

- Participate in a peer study group. Again, help create one if there is not one already available.
- Attend your denomination's regional and annual gatherings. Find colleagues to share your experiences with one-on-one.
- Intentionally build in time to your calendar for your family. In particular, set aside one night or day a week for just your spouse. Put it in your calendar as a meeting. Eat a meal together. If you have children, ask family, friends, and congregants to watch them so you have private time.
- Intentionally build time into your calendar to spend with your children. With all the demands of caregiving, this must be scheduled time or it will not happen. This should also be a nonbusy time in which you can communicate. It does not need to be a long period of time, but it should be a regular time so your child can count on it. It could be walking the dog in the morning, taking them to school or picking them up, or washing the dinner dishes together.

Self-Focus

- Follow the example of the Creator in most sacred texts: take a weekly day off. While a whole day off may now be impossible due to the additional demands on your time, taking time off regularly is critical not only to your "surviving" as a caregiver, but also to your continued "flourishing" during this time.
- Religiously schedule *daily* time for practicing your spiritual tools, such as prayer, meditation, and reading of sacred texts. This need only be five or ten minutes.
- Practice stress reduction and find ways to laugh.
- Remind yourself on a regular basis that your best is all you can do.
- Be intentional about maintaining a balance between your work and your personal life.

- Become a nonanxious presence.
- Be intentional, as opposed to reactive, with people, places, things, and situations.
- Take vacations—religiously. Retreats of various kinds are helpful also.

Some individuals find writing in a journal helpful. For those who are more verbal, talk into a tape recorder—there are even some that that have a computer program that will automatically transcribe for you. Perhaps you fancy yourself a poet or writer of fiction. Go ahead. Explore your artistic side by drawing, painting, or sculpting. Maybe knitting, crocheting, or quilting is more your speed. Explore or renew activities you enjoy. Find a way to go on an outing to thc theater, a music performance, or a museum.

I hear the voices in your head laughing as you read this. They are saying, "Who is he kidding? He has no experience with what I am living with. There is just *no* time for any of this." Wrong! From my years as a hospital chaplain, I knew people who were at a hospital every day with their loved ones. Some of them, with some strong suggestions from the staff, incorporated as part of their routine, when their loved one was tired in the afternoon, leaving for ninety minutes to go to a museum close by or just to get out and walk and get coffee.

If you are more of a sports enthusiast, you may engage in bike riding or running a marathon or triathlon (please consult your physician or other primary care provider first, especially if you have been sedentary). Perhaps you are more of the observer and you find it relaxing to watch tennis matches, baseball, soccer, football, basketball, or ice skating.

Try to listen to relaxing music, sing, or read for pure enjoyment. It does not have to be for a long time. It should be intentional and should feel like "my" time.

Take time to be with your friends and family. You may want to schedule a regular time to meet with some of your colleagues (e.g., teachers, social workers, rabbis, cantors, executive directors) to discuss life as well as your vocation. As in any profession, there are some things only insiders understand.

Take a vacation from work! Spend time away from both your house of worship and, if you have another vocation, your other job.

Have a date night if you are married or have a partner. Try to take even a brief mini-vacation once every three months. Delegate to others you trust. People tend to appreciate the opportunity to participate and contribute in your absence.

Physical Self-Care

One of the first things to "go" when we become caregivers is physical self-care. We are "just too busy." However, all we really need is thirty minutes five days a week for aerobic exercising. One suggestion is to spread it out with three brief ten-minute walks.

How often have you heard the suggestion to "park at the far end of the parking lot"? Now would be the time to do this. Get in the habit of using the time when you are walking in the lot to say a short prayer. Combine the physical with the spiritual.

Also, you know the expression "take a deep breath." Well, it really is helpful to inhale and exhale slowly several times a day. Try closing your eyes and raising your arms while breathing in and lowering them breathing out. It is really quite relaxing!

Obtain routine annual physical exams. If you have a chronic disease such as asthma, heart disease, diabetes, and so on, make sure you keep your appointments and try to have an extra month of medication on hand. Do not wait until you have symptoms to go to the doctor, but if you do, then go right away.

Nutrition

Healthy eating is a great way to provide self-care, especially when you are under so much additional stress. This can be extremely difficult. Snacking is often a way we temporarily relieve the stress we are feeling. And if the snacks are high in calories, our weight can go up dramatically in a short period of time.

- Change the snacks in the house from processed to fresh fruit and fresh vegetables. Almost all supermarkets now sell fresh fruit and vegetables already cut up. Change the ice cream in the freezer to one that is lower in calories.
- If you eat out, consider placing half your meal in a container to take home before you start eating.

- Eat only when you are hungry, and try to stop eating about three hours before bedtime.
- Drink lots of water. Most adults need about sixty-four ounces of water a day, or eight eight-ounce glasses. Try drinking water instead of coffee, tea, sodas, or juices.
- Add breads and cereal that are high in fiber. Keep things like refined sugar, processed white flour, and white-flour products to a minimum.
- Avoid late-night binges.
- Limit your intake of caffeine, which is found in chocolate, coffee, and soft drinks. Consider drinking caffeine-free herbal tea.
- Try not to "self-medicate." If you drink, limit your intake of alcohol to one glass a day. If you smoke or chew tobacco, stop! You may need help to discontinue. Avoid the use of illegal substances.

In conclusion, we are reminded that the answer to Hillel's question of "If I am not for myself, who will be for me?" is *no one*. And the answer to his question of "And if not now, when?" is *never*. Now let us go forth and be for ourselves, today and every day.

Part III

Jewish Approaches to Coping with Challenge

Tradition, Texts, and Our Search for Meaning

Rabbi Richard Address, DMin

Teach us to count our days rightly, that we may obtain a wise heart.

—Psalm 90:12

A man sits across from me one afternoon. He is in his early seventies, retired, and restive. He has been married for decades and has been active in his community and his synagogue. He is aware, for the first time, that something is missing in his life. For years he worked, raised a family, and maintained a life that revolved around a busy daily routine. Now, for the first time, the foundations upon which he relied have gone. His children are now grown. He has been retired from his career. He sits across from me and asks, "I have so much to give, Rabbi, but my life seems to be lacking a purpose. How can I find that sense of meaning?"

This man is not alone. He is in relative good health and active. He enjoys a rich social life and married life. Yet, like so many of his contemporaries, he has reached a stage that has him looking inward. Aware, perhaps, that his own clock of mortality is ticking, he has begun a journey of discovery—perhaps of his true self. And he is not alone! The generation behind him is in close pursuit, as the first wave of baby boomers is now turning sixty-five. The revolution that is modern longevity assures us there will be new opportunities for personal growth and a search for what it means to grow old; and grow old we must, for despite the desire and fantasy of many boomers that their own aging can be delayed and death denied, the reality of mortality is common to us all.

Rabbi Richard Address, DMin, is senior rabbi at M'kor Shalom in Cherry Hill, New Jersey.

There are a wealth of texts from Jewish tradition that speak to our aging journey. Chapter 12 of Ecclesiastes presents a rather dim and depressing view. Yet, other texts celebrate the gathering of wisdom as we age and the need to respect the old. Moses lives to the mythical 120 and is said to have died "with eyes undimmed and vigor unabated" (Deuteronomy 34:7). Physical strength in biblical times seemed to have been as personal as it is now. Joshua celebrates the fact that at eighty-five he is "as strong this day as I was the day that Moses sent me; as my strength was then, so is my strength now" (Joshua 14:11). Yet, Barzillai, in 2 Samuel, laments his decline as he turns eighty: "I am this day eighty years old: and can I discern between good and evil? Can your servant taste what I eat or drink? Can I hear anymore the voice of singing men and singing women? Why then should your servant be a further burden to my lord the king?" (2 Samuel 19:36).

The idea that length of days does not necessarily equal physical strength, vitality, or even wisdom is an often overlooked insight from the body of our tradition. How we age *is* personal and very reflective of how we have lived our life. An insight into this can be gleaned from the Wisdom of Solomon: "It is not the length of life that makes for an honorable old age ... but rather it is wisdom which constitutes a person's silvery brow and a spotless life the true ripeness of age" (Wisdom of Solomon 4:8–9).

There is a moment in our lives when we, like the person in my office, come to sense a need to step back and evaluate what we wish to stand for as our life evolves. We ask what our legacy can be. We search for a sense of meaning that rests outside of ourself. It is at this moment that we begin to acquire true wisdom. Not everyone can do this. There are so many extenuating circumstances in modern life that conspire to restrict a person's ability to reflect and renew. Yet, each of us, in our own way, approaches this precipice. Some will have the courage and luxury of time and means to leap. Others will be unable. Yet, that desire for something of meaning is, I feel, always present. Judaism, in its richness of values and texts, can provide the means to support that next journey. We are not of a system that promises a defeat of death. We are a community and a tradition that celebrates the living of life, no matter what the circumstances of that life may be. For us, the acquisition of wisdom is the embrace of meaning. Irvin

Yalom was correct when he reminded us that we are "meaning-seeking creatures."[1] A challenge for us will be how to seek guidance for our search for meaning from within the rich tapestry of Jewish tradition.

The celebration of wisdom is really a celebration of an ability to appreciate and value the experience that life has provided to us. As many of us have come to know, "book knowledge" does not necessarily equate to wisdom. No, in our own individual search for a sense of personal meaning as we grow older, we gradually come to understand the value of living life and the importance of trying to learn from our own experiences. This appreciation has even been transformed into ritual.

A recent development in this area has been the slow use of a ritual called *simchat chochmah*. This is a ritual that has emerged out of the Jewish feminist movement, which is said either in public or in private and often around a significant birthday. It is a prayer or prayers that give thanks for having lived and, as a result, acquired a certain life experience that has allowed the individual to gain perspective and a sense of self. One such prayer reads as follows:

> River of light and truth, You have sustained me these many years and brought me to this place in my life's journey. Let me look out with wisdom, from the high ground of my years and experiences, over the terrain of my life. Let me gaze out toward the past and the future with a heightened sense of Your presence as my Guide. Let me see that growth is not reserved for any one season, and that love and fulfillment are not the exclusive provinces of the young.
>
> As today I celebrate my life's continued unfolding, I am awestruck by the wonder of my being. And so I pray that kindness and compassion may be on my lips, that strength and courage may be with me in my comings and my goings, and that I may continue to learn from and to teach those dear to me.
>
> O God my Creator, as You are the first and the last, may my life ever be a song of praise to You.

Baruch atah Adonai, Eloheinu Melech ha'olam, shenatan meichochmato l'vasar vadam.
We praise You, Eternal God, Sovereign of the universe. You give of Your wisdom to flesh and blood. Amen.[2]

The acquisition of wisdom begins with the understanding that we are part of something beyond our own self. It is an acknowledgment that begins to stir somewhere in our own soul, that we are a vital link in that chain of *l'dor vador*, from generation to generation. Part of Judaism's gift to us is the fundamental belief that these moments that allow us to gather wisdom, and thus meaning, are never bound by time or age. I believe that one of the messages of the tradition of the yearly repetition of Torah reading is the lesson that every year we live we have the opportunity to see the texts in a different light. We are not the same person we were a year ago, and so we will bring new experiences and insights to the text that were not there a year ago. It is a rather empowering symbol: no matter what our age, the opportunity for our spiritual growth is always present. The celebration of the Torah, our *simchat Torah,* also is symbolic of an understanding that time continues to move. We change and evolve and become aware that as we age, one of our own fears is that we will run out of our own time.

The texts of Torah can be instructive in shaping a guide for our spiritual growth as we age. The foundation for this spiritual path is what I call a theology of relationships. It is based on a simple belief that as we grow older and become more aware of our own mortality, the power of personal relationships becomes increasingly important. This is rooted in the very first texts of Genesis. The creation stories of Genesis 1 and 2 underscore the fact that our fundamental relationship rests with God. What this means is that we become aware that we search for a sense of meaning and purpose in the context outside of our own person. To believe only in our own self is to court a sense of personal idolatry. The texts seem to call to us to understand that we are part of a larger reality—a universe, nature, and history—and that this time of life can be about finding our own place in that generational chain. The image of being created *b'ztelem Elohim*, in the image of God, sends a message to us that there is something eternal, something transcendent that rests in us. It is that uniqueness that we seek to find as we age. Being created "in the image and likeness of God" means giving each of us the permission to seek our own unique relationship with the world.

Martin Buber echoes this search in a famous passage:

> Every person born into this world represents something new, something that never existed before, something original and unique. It is the duty of every person in Israel to know and consider that he is unique in the world in his particular character and that there has never been anyone like him in the world, for if there has been someone like him, there would have been no need for him to be in the world. Every single man is a new thing in the world, and is called upon to fulfill his particularity in the world.[3]

We are given the challenge of searching for our own true self in relationship with how we perceive God, and the importance of this search is enhanced by a simple phrase found in Genesis. It is there, in the context of trying to find a companion for Adam, that the text reminds us that it is not good for us to be *l'vado*, "alone" (Genesis 2:18). This simple, yet powerful word carries with it the key to the theology of relationships that I feel is the foundation for our own search for our own unique self. For this word carries with it not a sense of needing private time. This word carries with it, I feel, the existential aloneness that we all fear. It is the aloneness that some feel in the depth of a soul, a sense of being *kareit*, or cut off, from one's own self. It is the aloneness that some feel when many surround them, yet they feel isolated, cut off, and alone. It is a sense of isolation that is reflected in the next chapter of Genesis.

Genesis 3 is the myth of Eden. It is the chapter that introduces us to the reality of our own mortality. The myth of the tree of life allows us to confront the fact that eventually each of us will enter the ultimate aloneness of our own death. This is the *l'vado* that drives us to find out our own sense of meaning. It is the reality of our mortality that propels us to seek relationships and build community. We do not wish to be alone, for this triggers, in a deep and profound way, that we all must face our own mortality. What is one of the great fears of many of us as we age and face the prospects of declining health and dependency? It is not only a desire to not live in pain and suffering, but also to not be alone in those final days. That is why Genesis 3 remains for me *the* most powerful of our Torah texts, for not only does it remind us that our time on earth is bound, but it also raises the real question of our life. God roams the garden, seeking his creations, and asks *the* question: *Ayekah? Where are you?* (Genesis 3:9).

This is *the* question. Why? Because it is the question that follows us throughout our life. God is constantly asking us where we are. That question is really three equally radical requests. These are the questions that become so powerful for each of us as we grow older and confront our mortality. These "why" questions form the basis of life; they flow from God's *Ayekah?*:

- Why was I born?
- Why must I die?
- Why—for what purpose—am I alive?

I suggest that at some moment in each of our lives, and it varies from person to person, we come face-to-face with these questions. This is the moment when we can begin to acquire true wisdom, and it is in the search for these answers that we find our own uniqueness. The answers to these questions lie beyond the material world. The answers to these questions are subjective, personal, and rooted in our own personal and family history. Not everyone will wish to enter the search for these answers, yet I suggest that everyone, at some moment in life, comes to ask them. The ability to seek the answers requires some risk and it is to another text that we can turn for an approach to understanding that challenge.

In Genesis 12, Avram is called to go to a place that he does not know. The Torah portion *Lekh L'kha* (go forth) can be seen as symbolic of a vital aspect of our own search for meaning as we age. Avram is asked to "go forth from your native land, your father's house, to the land that I will show you" (Genesis 12:1). Avram takes up this charge, relocates his family, and does so out of a sense of faith. This is not a call to radically uproot one's family, although some do that. It is, however, a call that there may come a time in our lives that we need to listen to this "call" to go forth and take a risk so we may live.

There are moments of transition that present themselves to us in our own aging process. Children graduate from high school and college. They leave the home and start out on their own. Even those who move back for a temporary respite return as different people from when they initially left. For many baby boomers, even those who must delay retirement due to changes in the economy, this transitional stage of life raises interesting questions. Given the revolution in life spans and the miracles of medical technology, many boomers who find themselves in their fifties and sixties can reasonably expect to live not years, but decades. It is in this context that those "why" questions come into play as never before. For many, this is a time that they can contemplate going forth into a phase of life about which they do not know. This is a time of great transition, and it requires a certain leap of faith, as evidenced by Avram, to move forward. What this does tell us is that Judaism says that our future is ours to create. Yes, it can be anxiety-provoking to risk changing one's career or lifestyle, to pursue a dream or passion. Yet, this text reminds us that to find that sense of meaning and uniqueness, it may be necessary at some time in our life to "go forth."

This is not easy. Many of us find ourselves bound by so many circumstances that going forth may not be an option. Many baby boomers find themselves caught in the middle of a variety of needs. They may be caring for adult children, grandchildren, and older parents. They may be, at the same time, continuing to work out of either need or choice. They are present not in a sandwich generation but what I refer to as a "club sandwich" generation: involved in a multigenerational bind of caregiving and concern. This reality, for many, controls and restricts how much going forth may be possible at any given time. What Genesis 12 may also be saying, however, is that these situations are never permanent. Life changes and these circumstances change, and when they do, and the *mitzvot* have been fulfilled, the texts remind us that it is never too late to go forth.

I think we can see this in the events that precede Genesis 12. In the final verses of chapter 11, we are told that Terach, Avram's father, has died (Genesis 11:31–32). Immediately, Avram hears the call to go forth. It is almost as if the texts are saying that one may be ready to hear that *lekh l'kha* call only after other intervening circumstances have been removed. It is only after a major life-changing event (e.g., death, divorce, job offer) that we see the opening to go forth and pursue the next stage of life. The challenge in all of this is the ability to be open to that call, to not fear to take the risk of moving forward in life as these moments of transition become real and available. Many opt to take the risk. Many opt to stay in the known, preferring the status quo of comfort. There may be no right or wrong. It is, however, important to know that as we contemplate our own futures and our own search for meaning, Judaism supports our taking those risks. Each of us is given the chance, we hope many times, to transition into another phase of life. To change who we are and what we call ourselves is daunting and filled with awe. Yet, for some, it becomes a matter of life itself.

The personal moments of transition help give richness and texture to life. The circumstances for these moments of transition can be as varied as the stars in the sky. Change is always a challenge. To risk those changes requires faith in one's self and in an ultimate truth. Going forth into the future often requires us to wrestle with our most basic of fears. Such is the lesson of Jacob in Genesis 32. Jacob is about to reunite with his brother Esau, the brother from whom he took the birthright blessing. They have not seen each other in years. The family history and parental involvement in the brother's relationship raise fears in Jacob. So, he finds himself on the evening before he is to meet Esau by the river Jabbok, and he, like Adam, is *l'vado*, alone.

How often when we have had to make life-changing decision do we find ourselves "alone"? Just as Jacob then wrestles with a mystical and mythical "man" (Genesis 32:25), so, too, we wrestle with our own internal voices and feelings and fears. Change is never easy. Jacob emerges from his night of wrestling changed. He is called by another name, Israel, because he struggled through the night to come to a decision. Likewise, as we go forth in life and transition into new phases, we often wrestle with decisions about a future that we may not be totally sure of. Yet, we move forward into life and, in many ways, change who we are, what we are called, and how we call ourselves. Judaism supports this growth, this change, our movement and transitions. There are no guarantees that these transitions will all be good and will be for us a blessing. Judaism does teach us, I think, that transitions and changes are a part of our life and those who fail to wrestle and move forward can find themselves bound in life by regret, living in a land of "what if," which is not a healthy place to reside.

Let us also recognize that some of these decisions about our aging are very difficult. There are moments when people will become dependent on others, frail and unable to function independently. This is a powerful fear for us all. Many families wrestle with heart-wrenching decisions about how to support loved ones who can no longer support themselves. They wrestle over if and when and how to cede care of that loved one to a nursing home or to place that loved one in a care community. Not all of these decisions about transitions are made while one is healthy and independent.

Judaism reminds us, however, that no matter what the context of the decision, the result must be based on a sense of the sacred. Judaism instructs us that our decisions must be based in and embraced by a sense of *k'dushah*, "holiness."

We learn this from an understanding of Leviticus 19, a chapter that places all of life in a context of the sacred. The chapter is a powerful summary of Jewish life and how we are called upon to act, from ritual laws to family dynamics, to medical ethics, to laws of the marketplace and the ethical treatment of people less fortunate than we are. In every section the text reminds us that we are to follow these admonitions because "*Ani Adonai*," "I am God": "You shall be holy because I, the Eternal, am holy" (Leviticus 19:2).

In making decisions about our own life, we are guided by Jewish tradition to seek the sacred. This chapter underscores our relationship with God. We come to see our lives as a reflection of what is holy and sacred. This helps us in our own search for what our answers to those "why" questions can be. Our search for our unique place in creation needs to be informed by a sense of the sacred. This is the direction toward which we move in our life transitions. This is the direction that helps sustain us and provide for us a sense of our own unique purpose. This turning to meaning is enhanced by the importance of our relationships as we grow and age.

I think there is a very good reason that many of us find a need to "give back," in some way, to our community as we get older. It is not only that many people may have more time. I think that there is a psycho-spiritual motivation that is based on the desire for our lives to count for something beyond our work identity. It is part of this desire to leave a legacy. The "give-back" syndrome is based on creating strong and personal relationships with people and causes outside of our own self-interest. It is a means through which we can find a sense of definition to our own life. Jewish tradition refers to these acts as *mitzvot*, and it is in doing these *mitzvot* that we often encounter a sense of a spiritual presence. All of this is, I feel, a part of our own turning to meaning that is part of the possibility of our own aging.

There is another text that I feel can be an important coda to these series of textual guidelines for our own aging. It is the majestic section from Deuteronomy 29–30 that calls on us to realize that life will be a series of choices and that we are commanded to "choose life." This famous phrase, *u'vacharta bachayim*, carries with it an important message in so many ways. The full verse of Deuteronomy 30:19 reads, "I call heaven and earth to witness against you this day. I have put before you life and death, blessing and curse. Choose life so that you and your offspring will live." The secret of that choice, as the next verse states, is to live a life of holiness by following the statutes and judgments that Moses has laid out (Deuteronomy 30:20). Verse 19 teaches us that what we choose and how we make choices impacts not only us, but also our children and following generations. We do not make choices alone, and what we choose impacts others. No matter what our age!

Making choices that reflect a value of life can be a challenge for us as we grow older. Many of us will face difficult choices as we age. Despite our desire for a long and healthy, pain-free life, the natural aging process will eventually win out. As brilliant as medical technology has been in pushing back the reality of mortality, we all have the same end. One of the greatest challenges for many of us will be how to make difficult choices in periods when we need extended care or end-of-life care. How can those choices be "for life"?

Here is where Judaism offers us another gift. It is a religious-ethical system that sees no one answer to these questions. Rather, it understands that each person brings to the issue his or her own self, and thus, context is of great importance. Each person is unique. Each case is unique. Judaism offers humane guidelines even in decision making at life's end. The greatest value is the dignity and sanctity of human life and the preservation of that life in dignity and in sanctity. That is the *k'dushah* factor that operates in these choices. That is why we know from Jewish tradition that the use of drugs to relieve the pain of a dying patient is a *mitzvah*, even if those dosages shorten a life that is ebbing. That is why the Jewish community supports institutions like hospice. Choosing life is really about choosing a path of holiness, no matter what our circumstance may be. This is not always easy. In fact, in many instances, these choices are the hardest that we will face, and it is important to remember that there is no one *right* path for everyone.

Each of us must face these moments and make choices that reflect our own beliefs, our own history, and our own fears. Each of us can choose to receive the blessing of life in our own way.

This text in Deuteronomy also points out something that we all learn as we experience life. That life lesson is that we control very little of life. So much of what happens to us is random. How we choose to respond to these random acts of life really helps determine who we are and, in many ways, what our legacy will be. Looking back on our life path, we can pick out several moments when a random act occurred that led to a choice that changed our life. These moments of meaning have been both good and bad, a blessing and, at times, a curse. How we chose to act as a result has helped shape who we are now and who we will be in the future. That is why the instruction to make choices that reflect blessing and life is so powerful. That is why we are reminded that those choices impact not only us, but also those who are around us now and those who will follow us in life.

Jewish tradition can provide a pathway that helps guide us on our own search for meaning and purpose as we age. It is a tradition that urges us to "go forth" and seek our own unique self, to have that search focused on making choices that reflect what is holy in our own life, knowing that these choices will affect those who come after us. It is a tradition that supports the necessity, at times, even to change how we see our self. It is a tradition that teaches that in the face of the ultimate reality of mortality, we can find meaning and purpose in the relationships that we create and nurture throughout our life.

There are numerous books, websites, and programs that tout the secrets to finding one's unique self. I am convinced that this all does come down to a few basics. Part of this is random and all of it takes work. Every once in a while we are fortunate enough to witness this or experience it. The basic issue, I suggest, still remains our desire to not be *l'vado*, but to be with other human beings.

Joseph and Betty have been married over seven decades. I spent part of an afternoon with them. It was a visit to discuss caregiving options as Betty was in hospice care. The reality that death would sever this marriage was intensely present. The most powerful moment in that visit was when this husband and wife held each other, embraced, kissed, and said how much they loved each other. In the face of the ultimate reality, it was still love and the power of this relationship that remained the focus of their lives. Jewish tradition and our texts can serve as a wonderful guide for our journey; yet, it will still be how we translate those texts and that tradition into our life with people and our relationship with God that will define our unique path of life.

Bad Things Happen
On Suffering

Rabbi Rachel Adler, PhD

We are made for suffering just as we are made for joy. What we see, what we hear, what we feel through our skin, our limbs, our internal organs, what we experience through lives intertwined with the lives of others can either hurt us or delight us. The same delicate nerve retia send impulses to our brains both of pain and of pleasure. Perhaps we could not have been created without reactivity to both pleasure and pain. Perhaps the two experiences are somehow interdependent; our capacity for joy is deepened by our encounters with suffering, and our capacity to endure suffering is enhanced by previous experiences of joy, love, beauty, justice—positive values that do not die.

The psychologist Viktor Frankl argues that what human beings require for survival, even more than adequate food, shelter, and basic necessities, is meaning.[1] We inhabit not only physical space but also a *nomos*, a universe of meaning that contains our values and beliefs, our ethics and our hopes, embodied in sayings, stories, metaphors, poetry, and song. If our *nomos* is shattered, we may be overcome by anomie, an agonizing state of existential meaninglessness.[2]

The cultural critic Elaine Scarry writes about physical pain and its effects on the universe of the sufferer.[3] Intolerable pain, says Scarry, unmakes the universe, expunging thought and feeling, self and world, "all that gives rise to and is in turn made possible by language."[4] In severe torment, the sufferer is utterly isolated, unable to experience relatedness, unable to defend her values from a torturer's insistence that she betray them, or to give or withhold consent to a medical

Rabbi Rachel Adler, PhD, is professor of Jewish religious thought and feminist studies at Hebrew Union College–Jewish Institute of Religion in Los Angeles, California.

procedure, unable to attend to her surroundings, unable to speak—for language is displaced by gasps, moans, and screams. In contrast, Scarry observes, "To be present when the person in pain rediscovers speech is almost to be present at the birth or rebirth of language."[5]

I want to argue that some of Scarry's ideas are also germane to sufferings from emotional and spiritual pain. There is more than one way to unmake the little world that is a person or even the larger world that is a people. There is more than one kind of pain that can leave us tormented and bereft. And to be present when the sufferer re-achieves relational speech is to be present at the rebirth of redemption. That is the point when the sufferer begins to reconstitute a shared *nomos* with others, speaking to be heard by others and by God, often, as I have suggested elsewhere, in the form of lament.[6]

Lament is a nonlinear, chaotic genre in which questioning, reproach, self-blame, repeated vignettes of horrors, moments of hopefulness, and moments of bitterness gush out, limited only by poetic or musical form. Lament is a cross-cultural phenomenon. There are traditions of lament in countries from the Mediterranean to Africa, from China to Ireland spanning more than three millennia.[7] Often the lament genre was associated with women as performers or leaders, although participants in many cultures, including ancient Israel and Jewish Babylonia, might also be men.[8]

The Protestant Bible scholar Walter Brueggeman has suggested that lament is a form of protest that "shifts the calculus and redresses the distribution of power between the two parties, so that the petitionary party is taken seriously and the God who is addressed is newly engaged in the crisis in a way that puts God at risk."[9] This power shift is possible because God is a God of justice and not a cosmic bully. According to Brueggeman, the lamenter refuses to present a compliant false self to God while repressing her genuine feelings. Donning a mask of submissiveness would render the relationship manipulative and insincere. Instead, the lamenter confronts God with the immediacy of suffering in a way that renders retribution unjustifiable. We see this in Lamentations where the female voice, Daughter Zion, keeps crying out, "See my torment," "Look about and see," "See, *Adonai*, my distress," "See, *Adonai*, and behold those to whom You have done this" (Lamentations 1:9, 1:12, 1:20, 2:20). God must witness human misery, the wreckage of lives and peace, the full impact of violence and injustice.

The lamenter in Ezekiel 16:23 wails, "*Vai, vai*!" ("Woe, woe!"), but it is equally human to wail, "Why, why?" Why do some good people die young? Why are some haunted by loss and misfortune while others thrive? There are many Talmudic passages on these questions, and frankly, none of the answers is very satisfying. Why do we keep on asking? We ask because of our dread of chaos. The anthropologist Clifford Geertz defines chaos as "a tumult of events which lack not just interpretations but *interpretability*."[10] Most of us demand that our lives make sense. To argue that what happens to us is utterly random is to argue that life is totally absurd. Few of us want to make that argument because it leads to nihilism. If what happens to us is utterly random, why bother worrying about the quality of the decisions we make? Why bother making *any* decisions? Humankind has a poor tolerance for chaos, and absurdity is a kind of chaos.

The desire to avoid chaos, however, does not mean that we will accept just any theological answer to the question "Why do bad things happen?" We can list some garden-variety answers here, but theodicies commonly irritate more than they comfort.

Reason 1: Bad things happen because you as an individual or as a member of a community or nation deserved them. You are *guilty* and were punished. This is, in essence, Deuteronomy's answer. It is also the answer many sufferers give to explain their own suffering, a harsher judgment than others would have given them.

Occasionally the Deuteronomic answer is true: suffering is a consequence of our own behavior. If someone was an abusive parent, his children may spurn him and refuse to care for him in old age. Alternatively, suffering may be a consequence of the nation's behavior. If a nation allows large-scale pollution, its residents may get diseases that come from inhaling or ingesting pollution. The innocent will suffer along with the guilty in such a case. Children in the low-income areas where polluting projects are often located will have higher rates of asthma, for instance. Hence, it is certainly not always true that you personally deserved what you got. Sometimes consequences are communal.

***Reason* 2**: The bad happenings are *natural* consequences. If you live in Los Angeles and an earthquake shatters your Wedgwood china, it is because earthquakes are a natural consequence of the many faults in the tectonic plates under Los Angeles. You and your Wedgwood were in the wrong place at the wrong time. Rabbi Yosef in the Talmud says, "Once the destroyer is given permission to destroy, it does not differentiate between the righteous and the wicked."[11] That is, one can be caught up in mass catastrophes that do not distinguish between the deserving and the undeserving. This also applies to human-caused catastrophes such as war.

As scientists learn more, we can sometimes prevent certain natural consequences from occurring. Right now, if your brain cells get a certain kind of plaque on them, you will get dementia, but perhaps in ten or fifteen years it may be possible to prevent that. What about all the people who lived before the medical intervention? Their tragedy is that we did not yet know how to save them. But again, that is hardly their fault.

***Reason* 3**: You were a *victim* of human evil. Remember, God gives everyone the ability to choose their actions. Some choose actions that hurt others: murder, theft, profiteering, disseminating hatred, and lynching all are acts that the victims did not deserve but that happened because others exercised their free will to do evil. Victims pay the price for the freedom of choice God gives humanity.

***Reason* 4**: Some sages believed that there is some *randomness* in the universe, and we are responsible for taking precautions for our own safety. In the Talmud, Rabbi Yannai argues that before crossing a bridge, one should examine the bridge.[12] He goes on to say that a person should never put him or herself in a dangerous situation, reasoning, "I've been good, so God will make a miracle for me." There *are* miracles, as any physician can attest, but we do not know on what basis they are distributed. It is not on the basis of deserving, in any case.

The trouble with giving rational explanations is that they do not even begin to mitigate the pain and the rage that suffering and loss evoke in us. When we are suffering, even when we are crying out, "Why? Why?" few of us desire a rationale for our anguish. What we really want God to understand is that it hurts. That is the tragic gulf between Job and God in the whirlwind speeches (Job 38–41). God, eager to explain, says, "Look, let me give you a God's-eye view of how I manage a complex, intricate universe." But Job is probably thinking, "Excuse me, but I'm bleeding."

The philosopher Emanuel Levinas argues in his essay "Useless Suffering" that the whole notion of theodicy, of defending God's justice in the face of an apparent challenge, was made obsolete by the Holocaust, the ultimate indefensible enormity.[13] Moreover, Levinas contends, we should not employ anyone's suffering as instructive, or inspiring, or fascinating, or useful in any way. Anyone's suffering is useless suffering and an outrage. The only moral response we can make to suffering, Levinas says, is to do all we can to alleviate it. In fact, only in being present to the suffering of other people do we become completely human. It is upon us to relieve suffering wherever the ravaged face of the other lifts itself to ours, even when we ourselves are suffering. For Levinas, that is the bedrock and beginning of all philosophy.

Suffering is inherent in the human condition, but we can become hardened to our own torment or to the anguish of others. There are people who despair of help or of healing: the *muselmänner*, the "muslims" of the concentration camps who became indifferent to whether they lived or died; convicts held under inhumane conditions who retreat into madness; warehoused nursing home residents lacking basic attentions. Similarly, it is all too easy to block out the pains and needs of others. The bystanders who ignore the man who has fallen or become ill on the street, the torturers who inflict pain for state reasons or for no reason other than to break the prisoner, the thousands of viewers who witness war and devastation on television and eat their dinners unmoved—in other words, potentially all of us—can diminish our humanity, either because we have been unbearably damaged by our sufferings or because we shield ourselves against the impact of others' sufferings and refuse to assume responsibility for suffering others. Saints and martyrs are those who are open and receptive to all the experiences of the human condition, even to suffering, without anger, without despair, and without withdrawal, either from others or from God. The rest of us can leave ourselves open to compassion and to hope by the practice of lament and by a life of active caring. Our ease, our health, our mobility, our good fortune are temporary blessings, but the love and the compassion we have given and received continually sustain us.

Judaism and Disability

R'fuat Hanefesh—The Healing of Our Souls, Individual and Communal

Rabbi Lynne F. Landsberg
and Shelly Thomas Christensen, MA

On *Shabbat Zakhor* we read, "*Zakhor—remember* what Amalek did to you on your journey after you left Egypt—how, undeterred by fear of God, he surprised you on the march, when you were famished and weary and cut down all the stragglers in your rear" (Deuteronomy 25:17–18).

It is especially fitting that *Shabbat Zakhor* falls during or very close to the month of February, which the Jewish community has designated as Jewish Disability Awareness Month. The Hebrew word in Deuteronomy that we translate as "stragglers"—*hanecheshalim*—appears only once in the entirety of the Bible. To explain its meaning, the medieval commentator Ibn Ezra suggests that its Hebrew root (*chet-shin-lamed*) may have a meaning similar to a more common Hebrew root (*chet-lamed-shin*) that means "to be weak."[1] As such, he took *hanecheshalim* to mean "those who did not have power to walk." Similarly, Rashi understands it to mean "those who lack strength," though he adds that this is "on account of their sin."[2]

Who were "the stragglers"? They were people who were slow, weak, and feeble—the invalids. Perhaps in ancient times, these people were, in fact, considered *invalid* human beings and so the Israelites abandoned them, leaving them on their own to struggle at the rear of the Exodus.

Rabbi Lynne F. Landsberg is senior advisor on disability issues for the Religious Action Center of Reform Judaism in Washington, D.C. Shelly Thomas Christensen, MA, is program manager of the Jewish Community Inclusion Program for People with Disabilities at the Jewish Family and Children's Services in Minneapolis, Minnesota.

Modern Judaism does not connect disability with sin. However, the invalidation of people with disabilities remains a modern bias. Where are the "stragglers" today? Unfortunately, our society—including many Jewish communities—continues to leave them behind.

The 2010 U.S. Census reported that 56.7 million Americans have some sort of a disability, accounting for 18.7 percent of the population.[3] Without available statistics regarding the number of Jews with disabilities, there is no evidence that the percentage is very different. Jews with a spectrum of disabilities, including physical, sensory, cognitive or intellectual, psychological, and learning disorders, require much more than ramps and designated parking spaces in order to participate in Jewish life.

Jews with disabilities have been a segment of our community whom the Jewish world has traditionally ignored. A culture immersed in education and intellectual endeavors had little patience to accommodate and serve Jews with disabilities. Diaspora architecture that featured many stairs to enter the building and/or to ascend the bimah seemed to symbolize that Judaism recognized only those who could make the climb. Consequently, Jewish communities shut Jews out by not altering all physical barriers, by neglecting to provide sign-language interpreters or Braille prayer books, by failing to provide religious school accommodations to meet the needs of children with disabilities, by not teaching our youth to welcome peers with disabilities, and by not urging adults with disabilities to volunteer or join synagogue groups or committees or to use their talents in leadership positions or actual Jewish jobs. We shut these Jews out by maintaining attitudes of discomfort and disdain.

We Jews would never consciously do it, but are we unconsciously putting a stumbling block before the blind? Equal access to all things Jewish means more than a ramp.

Rabbis and synagogue leaders are often under the impression that they do not have congregants with disabilities who require special accommodations. And in one troubling way, they may be correct: Jews with disabilities are often *not* present within our synagogues, because they perceive they are not welcome.

In 1990, the Jewish community, especially the Reform movement, advocated with the American religious community to help Congress pass the Americans with Disabilities Act (ADA). The ADA is the civil rights bill for people with disabilities. However, more than two decades after the ADA was passed, Senator Tom Harkin, an original sponsor of the ADA wrote, "With the ADA, we have climbed the mountain and reached the top, but we still have not fully arrived at the Promised Land."[4]

The ADA requires all public facilities to be basically handicap accessible. Because of a potential violation of the separation of church and state, the ADA law exempts religious organizations. But, we Jews are hardly exempt from this obligation. Our prophet Isaiah tells us clearly that God's house should "be a house of prayer for all people" (Isaiah 56:7).

The ADA made outright employment discrimination illegal. Even though it is illegal, it still exists. We Jews must understand and admit that we, too, discriminate by not demanding that Jews with disabilities have equal access not only to our front doors, but to all things Jewish, including jobs.

It would be very hard for the Jewish community to discriminate against Jews with disabilities seeking jobs if the job seekers presented outstanding Jewish resumes. The only way that Jews with disabilities can build such resumes is by being offered a great Jewish education beginning at an early age and continuing through Jewish schools of higher learning.

In *Mishneh Torah*, Maimonides teaches, "Every member of the people of Israel is obligated to study Torah—regardless of whether one is rich or poor, physically able or with a physical disability."[5] Promoting inclusion of those with disabilities in Jewish studies educates and benefits all those in the classroom. Inclusion teaches through experience that we are, all of us, created in God's image. Even better, inclusion helps us understand how to see past the disability and acknowledge the Jewish soul first. The ADA provides a moral mandate to all religious communities to eliminate barriers to participation and improve access to buildings and to all programming.

A new day is upon us because of the advocacy of parents who dream of a Jewish education for their children and because of the insistence of people with disabilities to participate in all aspects of Jewish community life. As a people who believe that we are all created *b'tzelem Elohim* (in God's image; Genesis 1:27), we must see individuals as people first—people with gifts to share, friends to make, spiritual needs to be met, and lessons to teach.

Rabbi Bradley Shavit Artson, dean of the Ziegler School of Rabbinic Studies at American Jewish University, says:

> The Mishnah tells us "don't look at the flask, but at what it contains." In teaching ourselves to see the inner sparks that light a person's soul, rather than merely glancing at the casing that holds those precious assets of personality, aspiration, and caring, we can act like God in the wilderness, healing when we can, and transcending limits when we cannot.[6]

Synagogues and communal institutions must make conscious efforts to eliminate physical, communication, and attitudinal barriers that separate individuals with disabilities from our community. We must interpret "Do not separate yourself from the community"[7] as a reciprocal imperative. It is a directive to intentionally welcome people with disabilities and their families in meaningful fashion to the community that belongs to all of us. The ADA mandates access to public buildings, but it cannot mandate access to the human heart.

Today, post-ADA, a growing number of Jewish organizations are wrestling with how to be more inclusive of people with disabilities and their families in community life. More children with disabilities are attending Jewish day and supplemental schools as well as day and overnight camps. As new construction and renovations are undertaken, organizations seek ways to eliminate architectural barriers.

Increasing numbers of communities and organizations have participated in Jewish Disability Awareness Month since it began in February 2009. Raising awareness is the first step to understanding the desire by Jews with disabilities and their family members to belong to the Jewish community. The healing has begun.

Rabbi Lynne F. Landsberg

I have been told that in my former life, I was an effortless multitasker, a fast talker, and a quick thinker. I had speaking engagements across the country and composed my most powerful speeches in airplanes and taxis. In my former life, I was Rabbi Lynne Landsberg. And although I am still Rabbi Lynne Landsberg, the rest has changed.

One morning in January 1999, I was driving my then eight-year-old son, Jesse, to Sunday school when my Jeep skidded on a patch of black ice and wrapped around a tree. Thank God, Jesse emerged without serious physical injury.

For me, however, it was an altogether different story. That tree came through *my* window and left me with a traumatic brain injury.

After six weeks in a coma and four months in the hospital, I embarked on a life of intensive rehabilitation. I had to *re*-learn how to walk, talk, read, and perform regular daily activities. I continue to cope with memory loss.

I have slowly *re*-learned how to live. But the traumatic brain injury has left me with persistent physical and cognitive challenges. Now, I walk with a cane, require assistance with many minor tasks, and have continual problems with my memory. My speech therapist says I must speak *slowly* to be understood. For a New Yorker, that is the hardest part.

When I reentered the world, I was shocked at what I learned. *Before* my injury, I belonged to one minority that was cohesive, strong, articulate, and definitely heard—the American Jewish community. What I learned after my injury was that I became a member of a second minority that is daily the victim of discrimination. Ten times larger than the American Jewish community, this minority remains almost invisible and barely heard: Americans with disabilities. Discrimination permeates every aspect of life for this minority.

My own experience is relatively minor but still jarring. Every day, in commercial establishments, meetings, social situations, or events large and small, people look at my cane first. I sense their discomfort and ultimately feel dismissed.

Since my accident, I daily thank God for my rehabilitation. I thank God for my resilience. And I thank God for my religion.

Judaism at its core is a religion of resilience. All of Jewish literature, all of Jewish history, and all of Jewish liturgy move us through moments of tribulation to moments of celebration.

Judaism presupposes that we can master adversity, and it gives us the prescription for action that guides us on our way. All of Jewish learning enjoins us to turn our experience of slavery inside out, by commanding us, "*B'chol dor vador chayav adam lirot et atzmo k'ilu hu yatza miMitzrayim*"[8]: in every generation, to view ourselves as if we went forth from Egypt. This is a command to see ourselves as one with the oppressed and to pursue justice for everyone. We can and must recognize the suffering of others and actively support and foster their resilience.

I have identified three ways that the Jewish community supported and fostered my resilience from the day of my accident to today as I became a person with a disability.

First, throughout my coma and hospital stay, many prayers were offered on my behalf. God does not discriminate by healing those patients who garner the most prayers. Rather, prayer strengthens those who pray, thereby enabling them to reach out and offer help.

The *Mi Shebeirakh* and other prayers made me feel that the arms of the Jewish community were wrapped around me, holding me tightly and lovingly, keeping me in this world.

Second, the Jewish community helped me through my hospitalization by visiting—not just stopping in, but by being there physically and emotionally. This is the *mitzvah* of *bikkur cholim.*

The people who visited me did much more than drop by. While I was in a coma, they sat with me, held my hand, and told me stories. My room was often full, regardless of whether I was conscious or unconscious.

The many people who fulfilled the *mitzvah* of *bikkur cholim* had a powerful effect on me. Whereas prayer kept me here, each visit diminished my feelings of isolation and connected me momentarily to the world.

Third, in addition to prayers and visiting, Judaism commands people to provide practical support by lending their time and talent to others in times of need.

While I was in the hospital and even after I came home, the Caring Committee of our synagogue, Temple Micah of Washington, D.C., provided delicious Shabbat dinners for my family. Every Friday, the dinner would arrive with Shabbat essentials: a challah, candles, and wine for *Kiddush.*

The meals kept coming until I could prepare Shabbat dinner with substantial help from my nurse and my husband, Dennis. This was for me a crucial step forward. But it was just one of many sobering realizations that I would never be able to do the things I used to do in the same way I had done them before.

We Jews are taught to provide practical support. In his work *Torat HaAdam*, the thirteenth-century scholar Nachmanides instructs us to help the incapacitated person attend to his affairs of life.[9] While I doubt there were many Nachmanides scholars in my local Jewish community, people instinctively knew to help me in this way.

A substantial group of people provided meals and rides, ran errands, arranged playdates for Jesse, and went shopping for our family.

As prayer kept me here and visits reconnected me to the world, practical support helped put my life back in working order so I could begin thinking about being productive again. Becoming productive has been a lengthy process that began over a year after my hospital stay and continues to this day.

As I progress, I am impressed that the Jewish community continues to support my resilience. My body has recovered about as much as it ever will, while my mind and spirit continue to benefit from this help. As I've studied the *Mi Shebeirakh*, I have come to understand that my healing falls into two categories: *r'fuat hanefesh*, a healing of the *nefesh* (commonly translated as "soul"), and *r'fuat haguf*, "healing of the body." I think of *guf* as the outer self and *nefesh* as the thinking, feeling inner self, and I wonder, what does it mean to heal the all-encompassing soul?

For me the healing of the body has come far more quickly than my doctors had forecast. But my *r'fuat hanefesh* has been much slower.

I know that healing of the *nefesh* requires one to accept certain harsh realities. Continued healing is dependent on my emotional ability to mourn the old Lynne Landsberg and to embrace the slowly developing skills of the new Lynne Landsberg. No longer do I measure my successes by comparing them to my former achievements. It cannot be a matter of what I have lost, but what I have gained: an understanding of how much good is in each and every day and each and every person.

The three forms of help I had received during my hospitalization—prayer, visits, and practical support—have evolved. They continue to foster my resilience. Now that I am alert and can interact, I find that the Jewish community's voice of prayer has become a voice of encouragement. Every step of my reintegration has been backed by a cacophony of cheerleaders.

Encouragement is a form of functional facilitation. This does not mean simply saying, "Let me know if there is anything I can do for you." Although we have the best of intentions, saying that assigns the isolated person the task of asking for help—something that makes him or her feel inferior.

The encouragement I received was in response to a disability brought about by a sudden, traumatic injury. There are many different types of disabilities—some traumatic, some lifelong, and some that come with age. Regardless of the cause, encouragement helps to facilitate meaningful participation in life.

Functional facilitation means being specific about what, when, and why. If a person is blind, you might say, "I just read an editorial in the *Jewish Standard* that I think you'd find interesting. Could I drop by Sunday and read it to you? I'd love to hear your opinion." If a woman is elderly and unsteady, you might say, "I can be your steady arm at the Sisterhood luncheon on Wednesday. We'd love to have you join us." If a person is unable to drive, you might say, "I'd like you to come to temple with us this Friday night. You live in our neighborhood—we'll pick you up."

This may feel intrusive, especially when the person you are encouraging is only an acquaintance or even a stranger. But take it from one who knows, it is definitely not intrusive! I believe that encouragement is a holistic healing tool, an evolved form of prayer.

Bikkur cholim evolved as well. While I was in the hospital, those who fulfilled the *mitzvah* of *bikkur cholim* brought the world to me. Once I got home, my visitors brought me to the world.

Rabbi David Saperstein, director of the Religious Action Center and my former boss, phoned one day to say that he would drive my nurse and me to Baltimore to attend the annual conference of the Jewish Council for Public Affairs. At the conference, I became reacquainted with current events in the entire Jewish world and how we approach them. Because of experiences like these, I came to see *bikkur cholim* evolve into my "passport" into the big world outside my kitchen.

Practical support at first ordered my world so that I could think about becoming productive again. Like prayer and *bikkur cholim*, practical support evolved. On our way to the conference in Baltimore, David Saperstein made me gasp when he told me that he wanted me to return to the Religious Action Center as soon as I was ready. The possibility seemed inconceivable, yet the thought of my contributing again to the Jewish community as well as having the chance to think, learn, and become productive again was as irresistible as it was frightening.

The fact that the new Lynne Landsberg cannot speak publicly with the ease of the old is just one of a long list of deficiencies caused by my brain injury. I have learned that I cannot measure my successes by comparing them to my former achievements. Instead, I am now thrilled every time I can do something new.

The practical support of the Jewish community comes in the form of challenge. By repeatedly raising the bar, the Jewish community continues to encourage me to perform at my current best. This is exactly the way we people with disabilities want to be treated. We do not want things automatically simplified for us. We know what we cannot do. We prefer to concentrate on what we can do and keep improving on that. We need and want the bar to be continually raised.

As Jews, we must recognize that the extreme discrimination of Americans with disabilities occurs within our own Jewish world as well as in the public sphere. Those of us without disabilities need to understand that sometimes well-intentioned words and actions can be hope shattering or dismissive to people with disabilities. We have a responsibility as Jews to recognize people with disabilities as fully included human beings.

When I stopped attending Temple Micah because of my accident, I was a nationally known speaker for the Reform movement. I returned four months later, a congregant with a disability using a wheelchair. I felt warmly received when I returned, not only by the greeting and affection of members of the congregation. Especially poignant was the message that Temple Micah regarded me as a fully included member by virtue of the accessible parking space next to the accessible entrance, the elevator that opened a few feet from the sanctuary, the aisles wide enough so that my husband could choose a seat and have me sit in the wheelchair right next to him rather than my being relegated to the "handicapped section."

It behooves all of us to see that people with disabilities are counted in our *minyans* everywhere, by making sure that they can get into all of our Jewish buildings: to meet with us, to pray with us, to learn with us, and to teach us.

Isaiah tells us that God's house should "be a house of prayer for all people" (Isaiah 56:7). The Talmud teaches that a synagogue should be built with windows in the sanctuary.[10] This is so we can see who is outside and unable to join us. As Jews, we have to maintain "mental windows" everywhere so that we understand that those whom we refer to as "shut-ins" are not shut in. Please, ask yourself and every Jewish institution that you belong to or support in any way whether we are doing all that we can to ensure access in all aspects of Jewish community life.

The primary legacy of Rabbi Alexander Schindler, the renowned past president of the Union of American Hebrew Congregations, is outreach. Rabbi Schindler much preferred using the word "ingathering." Rabbi Schindler's view of this ingathering was all-embracing. Only now have we recognized why Rabbi Schindler, when referring to Moses's admonition "Would that all God's people were prophets" (Numbers 11:29), would add, "All God's people—including the hearing impaired and the wheelchair bound, and the disabled in body and spirit."[11] We have the opportunity now to heed Rabbi Schindler's call to embrace people with disabilities.

There is a saying in the disability community: "Before ramping buildings, you've got to ramp attitudes." If we want to make changes in this country in order to allow people with disabilities the rights they are due, we must begin by opening the eyes of Americans and helping them understand that they have to change their attitudes. Where better to start than at home?

Shelly Thomas Christensen

Our son Jacob is an honor student at the University of Minnesota. He works part-time in the same job he has had for ten years. He celebrated his bar mitzvah, attended religious school through confirmation, and went on a Birthright trip to Israel. When Jacob was seven, he was misdiagnosed with attention deficit hyperactivity disorder (ADHD). At the age of fifteen, he was diagnosed correctly with Asperger syndrome.

Rabbi Landsberg's essay on *Parashat Zakhor* reminded me that I had a vault of memories that illuminate the journey through my own wilderness of raising Jacob. Like many parents of children with disabilities, my husband and I traveled lonely and isolated roads. While it is difficult to recall this emotionally complicated journey, time has helped me find peace. Remembering is our way of making meaning and forgiving ourselves. As parents of children with disabilities, we can eventually make it to our own safe haven, our own Promised Land, where we can reflect on how impactful the journey has been and how we have been able to heal our weary souls.

If we fail to make meaning of this unplanned journey, we cannot have hope. Like the Israelites who lost hope many times on their journey in the wilderness, parents of children with disabilities struggle with the unknown and fear for the worst. Like the Israelites, we rail at God in anger because we have lost our hope.

I dreamed about our children long before they were born. In my dream, they were healthy and happy Jewish children who grew up attending religious school, celebrating *b'nei mitzvah*, going to camp and college, and living a better life than my husband and me. They would be independent and successful adults and raise the next generation of Jewish children. Those were my hopes and dreams.

Our sons, Aaron, Jacob, and Zachary, were raised in a supportive and extended Jewish family of *bubbes*, *zaydes*, aunts, uncles, and cousins. We joined a wonderful Reform congregation, Bet Shalom in Minnetonka, Minnesota. We felt that we had found a good place for the kids to go to religious school. We liked the congregational vision statement: "Family of Friends."

But even friends do not disclose everything about themselves. How ironic that during one of the most difficult events of my life, I never told anyone at our synagogue that Jacob had been diagnosed with ADHD. I feared that disclosing information about Jacob's disability would label him and take away his chances to get a Jewish education.

When parents learn that their child has a disability, they begin a journey that takes them down a road that was not in the master plan for their child or their family. Whether the diagnosis comes at birth, later in childhood, or as the result of an injury or accident, the feelings can be devastating. It does not seem to matter what the diagnosis is. Parenting a child with a disability means that life has taken an inexplicable and devastating turn. Life becomes filled with strong emotions, difficult choices, interactions with many different professionals and specialists, and an ongoing need for information, services, and emotional support. Hopes and dreams dissipate in the face of the diagnosis.

There are unspoken rules about raising Jewish kids. I believed that Jewish children should be excellent students, well-behaved, popular, well-rounded and accomplished in academics and social enterprises, and active in the Jewish community. They should be a credit to their parents and their religion.

My reality was a contradiction of the rules. My child had difficulty holding a pencil. He constantly spoke out of turn, ran around the classroom at random, refused to do his homework, and spent hours playing Sonic the Hedgehog on his Nintendo. I saw this as an indictment of my failed Jewish parenting skills.

As parents we do not even know what we do not even know.

Urgency drives us into panic mode. Every minute that ticks by without action is a minute wasted. Our child's life depends on us to navigate a terrain that is a true wilderness. Finding information about the disability, trying to imagine the future, trusting our child to people we do not know such as medical and special education providers, worrying about finances and insurance, and keeping up to speed with other life responsibilities compound this enormous life change.

I did not want anyone to see how out of control I felt. I prayed every time Jacob went to religious school that no one would notice the signs of Jacob's disability. It was all I could do to keep up with his public school and medical needs. I did not think I could manage issues at his religious school too.

In anger I asked God, "Why me? Why my child?" I waited, expecting God to come up with some holy excuse for making my son different.

I never shared my deepest feelings about how I felt betrayed by God. When you have to blame someone for something you do not understand, God is a good target. I felt powerless to control my son's life, and in that weakness I never turned to my Jewish community for any kind of help or support. I was so afraid of being exposed as an incompetent mother that I did not want to be vulnerable, even if it might have helped to express my anger and confusion. It would have been healing to hear, "God didn't single you or Jacob out for this. Maybe God is hurting too."

I lost myself during those years. I threw myself into taking charge of Jacob's life. A timid and shy person by nature, I developed a voice with sharp edges that demanded attention for my child *now*. I became a "warrior mother." I acted tough in order to wrest control from teachers and special educators who seemed more intent on being in charge than in helping Jacob. I was so focused on making things right for Jacob that I did not even hear my own cries for help. I was angry and driven by a relentless need to fix everything now.

A new normal finally emerged as the phone calls from school, the doctor appointments, and prescription refills filled our daily lives. I took time to study our legal rights under the Individuals with Disabilities Education Act. But knowing the laws was not enough. I needed to begin healing from the inside. The first step was to understand the very nature of parenting a child with a disability.

I enrolled in graduate school and earned a degree in developmental disabilities to find my own answers. I realized that parents react in similar ways to the diagnosis regardless of what that is. We grieve, we panic, we become overwhelmed, and we do not want to be vulnerable in a world of acronyms, paperwork, and professionals telling us what we "should" do. We feel that we must give up control over significant portions of our children's lives.

Once I watched Jacob as he slept peacefully after a long day of holding his behaviors together in school. I wondered how he felt about being different. I realized then that I was mistakenly seeing only Jacob's disability. I had not been paying attention to his wonderful personality, his quick sense of humor, his kindness, his sweet soul. I saw in that moment the truth. Jacob, like each of us, was created *b'tzelem Elohim*, in God's image. God seemed to answer my anguished outcries in this moment. I stopped and noticed the peace I felt, the gift of clarity and understanding that had eluded me. In God's silence, I heard God's voice reminding me that this beautiful boy was the sum of all his attributes.

I gave myself a gift then. Peace of heart, mind, and soul. Standing at the door of Jacob's room and seeing that spark of the Divine in all that he was.

After that, my question to God changed. I stopped asking, "Why?" and started asking, "What can we do?" God answered my questions by providing the insight to make meaning of this journey, to understand its complexity and its hope. The answers came in becoming vulnerable and open to the community.

In my Jewish community, I met other struggling parents. It was comforting to know that there were others who were beginning to find their way back to the Jewish community. We were vulnerable and nervous about exposing our children, because we did not know if we would be turned away or welcomed in.

Instead of hiding out, dropping my kids off for religious school, and being as absent from the synagogue as I possibly could, another loss turned me around. When my dad died, I wanted to honor his memory and began attending services with my family to say *Kaddish*. This one step into the synagogue became my lifeline to the community. My comfort level increased, and I was no longer fearful of what would happen if I disclosed information about my son's disability. Isolation was replaced with good partners who worked with Jacob and my husband and me to ensure that his education was meeting his needs. I learned then how important it is to tell our stories, share our information, and ask for help. No one does this alone.

These days I look back at who I was and honor that self for being a loving parent who navigated an isolating and unknown wilderness until I was able to let others join me on this journey. I forgave myself for all the times I lost my temper, afraid and helpless, and all the times I put everyone's needs ahead of my own. I did the best that I could.

I began to celebrate the joys of being a parent. I celebrated all of the accomplishments, the *b'nei mitzvah*, the confirmations, and the graduations.

It took the peaceful sleep of a sweet child for me to recognize that God was there on this journey with me. In one heartbreaking moment, I gave up the anger and found the tranquility in my soul to raise my son with grace and with clarity. The healing of my weary soul at last began.

What You Can Do

We, members of Jewish institutions, must urge our leaders, who learned the word *hineini* (here I am) years ago in Hebrew school, to relearn the word. We can all learn to understand its many implications by living them.

Hineini is spoken verbally and nonverbally through words and through actions. Both physical and emotional accessibility add substantially to the healing power of the Jewish community. Even when we can no longer effect another's physical healing, we can certainly aid spiritual healing by making prayer, music, study—all of Torah—easily accessible.

We must break down the physical, communicative, and attitudinal barriers wherever they are, and we must come together as a greater Jewish community to say in unison, "*Hineini*—here we are to help people heal by accommodating their disabilities and urging them to lead full Jewish lives."

- Educate your community to understand fully that people want to feel that they belong. Jewish life is all about belonging to a community.
- Ensure that people with disabilities are included in all aspects of congregational life.
- Pinpoint members of your community with various appropriate skills (e.g., someone with a degree in special education, an ADA architect). Ask them to work with and teach community staff and lay leaders, sensitizing them to disability issues.
- Invite people with disabilities, parents, siblings, and other family members to tell their stories.
- Acknowledge the feelings people with disabilities and family members have toward God.
- As Jewish professionals, do not try to have all the answers or try to "fix" a situation. Be a partner and collaborate with parents. They know their child best.
- Promote inclusion by using accessibility symbols on your website, bulletin, weekly e-mails, invitations, and programs.

- Include an accommodation statement on all materials, and include contact information so people can make their requests for accommodations.
- Use person-first language ("person with a disability") in all modes of communication.
- Conduct an accessibility audit: assess your organization's physical spaces and programs so you can adapt them to be fully accessible.
- Once recognized, alter the inaccessible. For example, provide a ramp to the bimah or a floor-level reading desk for access to the Torah. Provide mezuzot, prayer books, water fountains, light switches, and brochures within reach of all.
- Have your leadership take a wheelchair tour of the entire facility.
- Offer printed materials in accessible formats (large print, Braille, audio, and American Sign Language versions).
- Do not do things *for* people with disabilities. Do things *with* people with disabilities. As the disability rights community says, "Nothing about us without us."
- Recognize Jewish Disability Awareness Month (February) and continue the practices all year long.
- Start an inclusion committee of lay leaders and professional staff to lead your organization's inclusion initiative, oversee your audit, gather suggestions, and more. Make sure to include as members people with disabilities.
- Include people with disabilities in leadership roles, committees, and programs.
- Our texts have wonderful examples of inclusive practices. Study and share the texts.

❖

Judaism and Resiliency

Rabbi Shira Stern, DMin, BCC

Accessing the power of human resilience in the face of illness or trauma is the key to survival and healing; how we use both our inner and external resources ultimately determines our spiritual health. Helping our patients, clients, residents, and inmates find the individual and common keys to claim these tools should be our main focus if we are to accompany them on their journeys.

Judaism at its core provides both models of resilient behavior as well as effective rituals from which we can glean tools to find our own resilience. As we hone our own skills in growing spiritual resilience, we can then model and teach what we have learned to those most in need of *hizuk* (strength).

The important question is, "How can our own spirituality contribute to a resilient worldview, and by extension, how can we use these resources to provide a practical construct for those whom we serve?"

Definition of Resilience

Some people are born resilient; they always land on their feet despite any and all obstacles in their path. They manage their bad news, disappointments, and disasters with remarkable aplomb. But what about the rest of us, who are scared and confused and helpless when plans go awry? Is there a way for us to experience trauma or stress or difficulties and respond to them in a healing fashion? Can we learn something from the lives of others that will inform *our* behavior, so that we survive our bad breaks more readily? And is there a way to do more than survive—actually to thrive—in life?

It is difficult to define resilience, because it is much more than simply the "power or ability to return to the original form, position, etc.,

---

Rabbi Shira Stern, DMin, BCC, is founding director of the Center for Pastoral Care and Counseling in Marlboro, New Jersey.

after being bent, compressed, or stretched; [in other words, the definition of] elasticity."[1] Human beings cannot be unaffected by trauma; we are not as malleable as stress balls, and, contrary to the dictionary definition, we also never revert to our "original form." We bear the scars, both internal and external, of trauma and misfortune. And, sadly, we do not always have "the ability to recover readily from illness, depression, adversity, or the like."[2] We are certainly not always characterized by "buoyancy."[3] We carry with us the memories of the day or moment or, sometimes, the prolonged agony of a loved one hanging on to life.

I found great resonance in Carole Radziwill's memoir entitled *What Remains: A Memoir of Fate, Friendship, and Love.* Having lost three loved ones within a three-week period—her husband at thirty-six, his first cousin, and her best friend—she had come to realize that the key to resiliency was reestablishing balance after your world implodes.[4]

Resilience can also include surviving the predictable vicissitudes of an ordinary life; one marked by anticipated losses and joys.

Therapeutic Examples

At ninety-two, Eugenia (Jean) Kaye describes her recent medical intervention during an ad first aired during the 2012 Summer Olympics in London. Jean is a woman "of a certain age," who publicly thanks her team of surgeons and nurses at a New York City hospital.

In a heavy German-Jewish accent, Mrs. Kaye wants us to know that she received extraordinary attention for a risky cardiac procedure that has given her a new lease on life. She reports being more energetic and is looking forward to dancing at her great-grandson's bar mitzvah. Then she stops for a moment to calculate, "If I'm ninety-two now ... *oy*, he's seven ... okay we'll see. But I get my inspiration from a lady who lives in my complex who's 103! And she's the head of the welcoming committee. So who knows?"

What makes a person resilient? Why do some manage to find a way to negotiate the more difficult challenges in life when others, with much better prognoses, succumb early?

Resiliency can be divided into three major categories: (1) a state of survival, which ensures that the person or the community continues to exist on some level in this world; (2) a state of thriving, a result that allows the person or community to build on the traumatic experience and transform that trauma into something meaningful; and (3) a state of inspiration, by which a person or community can become a model replicable by others.

I have encountered a number of inspiring people whose stories have taught me how to negotiate the future when the present implodes around you. I would like to share three stories of such people (whose names and situations have been changed to protect their privacy). Perhaps they will provide a coping mechanism that can be adapted within a variety of workplaces.

Lorraine S.

The first time I met Lorraine S., she told me what it felt like to watch the two military officers walk up to her front door, to tell her what she absolutely did not want to hear. She started screaming before they had pressed her doorbell and refused to let them come through the door. The long and painful process between the death notification and her son's funeral some two months later would send most of us over the edge, but over time, Lorraine found ways to serve her son's unit that allowed her to feel that she was maintaining a connection with him.

She came to my practice two years after her son died in Afghanistan, having survived the initial loss and the immediate aftermath. She wanted to work on how to grieve for Steven, always keeping his memory alive while moving toward living her life once again. She has managed to hold those two very contradictory feelings inside her while, at the same time, she has learned to embrace activities that honor what Steven might have become had he been able to celebrate his twenty-first birthday. She works to support and prepare other military families for what to expect when their loved ones are deployed, and she continues to reach out to the many others in Steven's unit who continued their tours of duty after Steven died. That does not mean she does not have her moments of what she calls "Steven time"—mornings that she spends crying for him, looking at his pictures, and fingering the clothes that still hang in his closet. Her priest continues to send her daily devotions, which she reads each morning as she drinks her coffee, but healing for her also comes from the friends and family who still are willing to talk about Steven.

Lorraine models three important lessons for us:

1. Grief is not a straight line: you are awful, you get better, you are good, it is done. Grief sometimes catches you completely off guard: some little trigger sets you off and you suddenly feel the way you felt months ago. You might even articulate that you have suffered a setback, but in reality, you have allowed yourself to feel the loss again acutely because you are better equipped to deal with it now that some time has passed. Lorraine has taught me this lesson often, and her resiliency lies not in her feeling good at any point in time, but in her feeling bad, experiencing it, and finding her way back to an even keel. Even if it takes time.
2. If you stop feeling the pain, you also stop feeling the joy—joy in remembering the first step, the first tooth, the first "I love you" hug.
3. Grieving requires time, and every person moves through the grieving period at their own pace. Rushing the experience only means that it will take longer to run its course.

The most important thing Lorraine has taught me is that resilience often comes disguised as something else. Have you ever put on your "game face" on days when you are feeling particularly low? And when someone tells you that "you look wonderful today," does it often coincide with moments when you really just want to jump back into bed and pull the covers over your head? The small steps that you take when the larger ones seem too difficult are the very steps that move you forward, even when you cannot recognize the progress.

Naomi B.

My second story is about Naomi B., who is a sixty-eight-year-old survivor of cancer—over eight years and several life-threatening complications along the way from initial diagnosis. I remember the first time we spoke about her fears of dying, when she was still recuperating from her first surgery and septicemia had set in. She felt intense despair because she was not ready to go, and she was overwhelmed by the thought that she would not see her grandchildren grow up.

For several years, she waited for the other shoe to drop, because the cancer would recur in different parts of her body. After the third surgery, she told me that were she to have another recurrence, she would not allow any more medical interventions. Now she says, "Maybe. We will see."

What has Naomi taught me? Naomi has taught me that gratitude factors hugely in her recovery, and she expresses that gratitude to everyone who has helped her along the way. From the friends who drove her for chemo and radiation treatments, to family who "dropped in" to stock her kitchen and bring her food that might whet her appetite, to doctors and nurses who have been responsive to her fears and questions, she has always said "thank you." Her illness has paralleled turning toward a spiritual life she never had, and as she slowly reengaged in the world, Naomi has moved from the safety of her apartment to traveling across the globe to fulfill what became a personal affirmation of spiritual gratitude. She does not wear her battle with illness on her sleeve, although she still participates in both group and individual support. She does not want to be defined either by her illness or by her survival; instead, she chooses to be known as a voracious reader with a keen scientific mind and a curiosity and appreciation of the world around her.

One of her most poignant moments occurred as she recuperated from yet another operation by watching the Beijing Olympics, which she never thought that she would live to see. And, yes, she watched those in London this summer with a sense of awe, still grateful but ready to look forward to something in the future.

Her medical team marvels at her physical ability to regain health after each subsequent bout of the disease, but I think that she gives us a glimpse of her secret as she keeps her eye on the prize: physical survival is not the only goal. In the past eight years, she has worked hard to repair and strengthen relationships that were important to her and to let go of ones that were hurtful and debilitating. A relatively shy person, she has pushed herself out the door to find new ways to connect with neighbors and friends that she might otherwise have ignored. And if you ask her whether she is better off now than she was nine years ago, she answers with a resounding "yes." Despite the pain and the indignities of surgery and subsequent medical care, despite having lost friends to the same disease, despite aging almost a decade, "Yes," she says.

Resilience lies not in some achievable goal, but in being able to pick yourself up when it is the hardest thing in the world to do, over and over and over again. In tiny steps. In small increments. And, sometimes, in accepting that one can go two steps backward and not lose everything.

Eric and Ellen

Finally, meet Eric, who as a child was physically abused by his parents, so much so that when his older brother died, he and a remaining sister were removed from the house and adopted by another family. Though both children had found a "safe haven," they never forgot the beatings or the sexual abuse. Never forgot the emotional betrayal.

One would assume in this situation that two children, two years apart, experiencing the same injuries and receiving the same mitigating care, would find the same measure of healing. But in this case, Eric grew up, went to college, married, and started a family. His most important focus was to create a healthy, happy, and loving environment for his children, providing them with the unconditional love that he never had himself. His sister Ellen did not fare so well. She struggled for years with depression and risky behavior, and she died shortly before her thirty-sixth birthday.

Lorraine, Naomi, and Eric: each individual survived, but not in similar fashion.

Lorraine feels deeply connected to her "boys and girls"—recognizing that the hole in her heart will never be fully filled, but healed enough to see some light in the darkness. And Naomi now has the unfamiliar task of figuring out what the rest of her life will look like.

Eric found ways to heal some of the hurt from childhood and made a thoughtful choice to parent his own children very differently. Instead of inflicting pain, he *chose* to end the cycle of violence in his family tree. His resiliency does not ensure that he never questions his behavior; sometimes minor events trigger a painful memory that causes him enough distress to talk about it in sessions. His resilience lies in the ability to feel his own frailty, when he cannot ignore the demons or shoo them away. Eventually he recalibrates and finds his way back to wholeness again.

And Ellen did not have enough resiliency to negotiate her complicated life. In reality, sometimes people do not succeed, but not from want of trying.

Therapeutic Responses

Accessing the tools to find our own resilience in the face of illness or trauma is the key to our survival and healing. The question is, how do we harness both our inner and external resources? How do we model it for our partners, our children, our friends, and even our parents?

One answer comes from the psychiatrist Viktor Frankl, survivor of Theresienstadt, Dachau, and Auschwitz, who suggests that his key to survival was focusing on the image of his beloved wife:

> My mind clung to my wife's image, imagining it with an uncanny acuteness. I heard her answering me, saw her smile, her frank and encouraging look. Real or not, her look was then more luminous than the sun which was beginning to rise.[5]

In his book, which we know as *Man's Search for Meaning*, but which translates from the German as *Saying Yes to Life in Spite of Everything: A Psychologist Experiences the Concentration Camp*, Frankl comes to realize that "even in the most absurd, painful and dehumanized situation, life has potential meaning and that therefore even suffering is meaningful."[6] The world is a better place because Viktor loved Tilly and because he was able to sustain her presence despite the nightmare in which he lived.

As a therapist, however, would I tell my client Naomi or Eric or Lorraine that their suffering is meaningful and therefore should make their lives bearable? I would agree that love—which can present itself in many different forms—is crucial; it certainly is for me. But for those who have not experienced unconditional love or who are in such despair that they are drowning in their own sadness or cannot see anyone beyond themselves, such an answer would be an affront. It would also be fairly ineffective: either you feel the love that grounds you, or can articulate what it is, or you cannot. Like intimacy, talking about it and engaging in it are just not the same thing.

A second response to how we find the key to resiliency is affirming the power of connection so that we never feel alone. Relating to others and forming community are essential ingredients, but they do not always work on their own. Often my clients talk to me of feeling alone even when they are surrounded by people. They describe what I call "empty arms" syndrome: the act of reaching for a beloved resulting in hugging the air; it just reinforces their loneliness.

Spiritual Responses

For me, a third response resonates more strongly, because it requires that I leave the world of thoughts as a method of ensuring survival and makes me access life on a larger plane, the world of the spirit.

I usually begin with a prayer, because the ritual of saying it helps me focus—like putting on sneakers to work out, or putting on a helmet to bike ride, or lighting a *yahrzeit* candle on the anniversary of my father's death. Sometimes, it is a sentence or two: "God, just help me do this." Or maybe: "Help me find the right words." At other times, I recite the prayer that I learned from my teacher Rabbi Sheldon Zimmerman, "A Prayer for Prayer":

> *In your openness, I find healing.*
> *In the promise of Your love, I am soothed.*
> *In Your wholeness, I too can become whole again.*
>
> *Please listen to my call—*
> *help me find the words*
> *help me find the strength within*
> *help me shape my mouth, my voice, my heart*
> *so that I can direct my spirit and find You in prayer*
> *In words only my heart can speak*
> *In songs only my soul can sing*
> *Lifting my eyes and heart to You.*[7]

I use on myself the same spiritual assessment tool that I developed when I was a full-time chaplain working in acute care hospitals. It has become a spiritual thermometer that gauges how I feel on any given day.

After the focusing prayer, I hum to myself the following song, taken from our Shabbat liturgy. Even if you are not musically inclined or if your relatives have banned you from participating in any and all singing activities, I find that the reverberations in my throat from chanting actually help me concentrate more efficiently.

> *Kol han'shamah t'hallel Yah, Halleluyah!* My whole soul praises God, Halleluyah!

In this song, the word for "soul," *n'shamah*, also means "breath." My very breath praises God. My whole being praises You. Like a mantra, I repeat the line several times until, even when I am feeling really down, I begin to believe it myself: *Kol han'shamah t'hallel Yah, Halleluyah*! I then take each Hebrew letter of the word *n'shamah* and begin a simple four-part checklist:[8]

<table>
<tr><td colspan="12">*N*ame That Emotion: What am I feeling?</td></tr>
<tr><td colspan="4">Abandonment</td><td colspan="4">Anticipation</td><td colspan="4">Courage</td></tr>
<tr><td colspan="4">Isolation</td><td colspan="4">Hope</td><td colspan="4">Gratitude</td></tr>
<tr><td colspan="4">Joy</td><td colspan="4">Love</td><td colspan="4">Sadness</td></tr>
<tr><td colspan="4">Depression</td><td colspan="4">Despair</td><td colspan="4">Forgiveness</td></tr>
<tr><td colspan="12">*S*how the Support: What keeps me going?</td></tr>
<tr><td colspan="4">My internal resources</td><td colspan="4">strong/weak</td><td colspan="4">present/not present</td></tr>
<tr><td colspan="4">Family resources</td><td colspan="4">strong/weak</td><td colspan="4">present/not present</td></tr>
<tr><td colspan="4">Friend resources</td><td colspan="4">strong/weak</td><td colspan="4">present/not present</td></tr>
<tr><td colspan="4">Community resources</td><td colspan="4">strong/weak</td><td colspan="4">present/not present</td></tr>
<tr><td colspan="12">*M*ake It Happen: Do something</td></tr>
<tr><td colspan="4">Life review</td><td colspan="4">Spontaneous prayer</td><td colspan="4">*Viddui*
(end-of-life prayer)</td></tr>
<tr><td colspan="4">*Mi Shebeirakh*
(healing prayer)</td><td colspan="4">Social joining</td><td colspan="4">Therapeutic presence</td></tr>
<tr><td colspan="12">*H*eighten the Healing: Enhance the senses</td></tr>
<tr><td colspan="3">Music</td><td colspan="3">Scent</td><td colspan="3">Quiet</td><td colspan="3">Light</td></tr>
</table>

Name that emotion. *Show* the support. *Make* it happen. *Heighten* the healing. Find one's *n'shamah*, find one's breath, find one's natural cadence.

It is critical that we as caregivers, clergy, chaplains, and leaders in the community understand that these exercises are not just for those we serve. It is imperative that we, too, understand our own spiritual structure and reinforce it on a regular basis. In my own search for resiliency, I have learned these lessons from unexpected sources. In reading through how the Army addresses the issue of spiritual resiliency, I found this image of "breathing cadences," which resonated deeply for me:

> When we run during physical training, we often sing familiar cadences to keep pace. Those cadences or "Jodie calls" not only keep us in step, but they also help facilitate our breathing as we run. The Army's current operational tempo has called us all to join in a long distance run of heart and soul that requires discipline, perseverance, and deep breathing to finish successfully. Wayne Cordeiro does a great job in his book *Leading on Empty* of describing the need for a spiritual leader to maintain a "life cadence" that includes daily, weekly and monthly spiritual practices that maintain the pace and depth of their spiritual lives. Are you "in step with the spirit" as you run this long race of leadership? Do you count off a "life cadence" that helps you maintain the pace of leadership in this midst of the high velocity challenge in which God's called you to serve? Your answers to those questions are gauges to the reality of your resilience. Each of us possesses the potential to establish those "cadences" so that we continue to receive the inspiration to bounce back and push further ahead in our spiritual missions.[9]

Each morning, the daily liturgy provides us with the words to articulate our gratitude that our soul, our breath, has been returned to us to enable us to survive.

Sometimes I find myself weak and scared, and lonely, and depressed. At other times, even after a long day during which I felt I only put out fires and did not accomplish what I intended to do, I feel good. At the very least, I have addressed the issues that are important to me, or, as Viktor Frankl said, "Man is *not* fully conditioned and determined but rather determines himself whether he gives into conditions or stands up to them."[10]

It is not easy to stand up to difficult conditions or tragedy or trauma. And most of us have felt like we are hanging on to this life by a thread, whether it is for a moment or some protracted time. Resilience is not the constant bright light that shines our way ahead, but in getting up each day to rekindle the tiny flame. Rabbi Steven Kushner points out that *the* original eternal light was not eternal at all; it required the Israelites to renew the oil and the wick *each and every day*. The same thing is required of our own light: day after day, whether we anticipate great joy or we dread what is about to happen, we wake up and reignite the flame. Sometimes that is about all the energy that we can muster. Sometimes it is the starting point for a great move forward.

It is what our ancestors Adam and Eve learn to do after they have been thrown out of paradise. Rekindling the flame is what Naomi does each time she reaches inside and is able to articulate gratitude for her remissions, or what Lorraine feels when she checks her e-mail at two in the morning and sees a note from a soldier on the front thanking her for her emotional and spiritual support.

Spiritual Texts

Within Jewish textual resources, I have isolated three examples: (1) Isaac, for whom simply surviving his father Abraham's test of faith is his sole focus; (2) Joseph, who endures his brothers' jealousy and spiteful behavior; and (3) Miriam, who witnesses overwhelming oppression and abject cruelty and still retains the ability to lead the Israelites in songs of gratitude, shoring up their personal and collective resources. Each has become a Jewish role model for finding resilience, but each provides a different level of success in Judaism: Isaac survives, Joseph thrives, and Miriam inspires. Each aspect reflects another example of resilience—all necessary for the community of Israel to flourish.

Isaac

In Genesis 22, we hear little from Isaac as he and his father prepare to journey to Mount Moriah, as commanded by God to determine

Abraham's commitment. The boy is silent when his father wakes him early to begin the trip, remains quiet as they saddle the donkeys and load up the supplies, and is still mute when the two leave the servants behind to climb the mountain. Only once does he ask the predictable and obvious question about the absence of a sacrificial animal, as Abraham has brought all the necessary accoutrements for making a sacrifice.

Perhaps Isaac is silent to avoid confrontation with his father, as are many children whose parents are negligent or driven in their work. Or perhaps he has already acquiesced to the reality of his own demise, as suggested by Rabbinic commentators.[11] We know that Isaac survives the traumatic event, but he is virtually unheard from until his father dies and he and Ishmael are tasked with burying him. He survives first his wife's barrenness, then the fighting siblings, and, finally, the ultimate treachery when Jacob steals both the birthright and the first-born's blessing. Isaac's most important contribution to the world is siring his boys and, for Judaism, especially for siring Jacob, our third patriarch.

Life happens *to* him—he seems not to be in control of any event other than fulfilling the requisite rituals of marrying, blessing, and burying one's dead. Isaac is the prime example of our patients/clients/residents who cannot articulate their own pain enough to ensure healing from grief. His resiliency saves him when he loses both parents—his father, when Abraham bound his son, and his mother Sarah, when she realized what might have happened on her husband's secret business trip—and it enables him to survive the grieving period.

Joseph

In the story of Joseph and his brothers (Genesis 37–45), Joseph begins life as a doted-upon son of his father's favorite wife and is yet another example in the Torah of a parent favoring one child over all others. His mission in life seems to be flaunting their father's favoritism to his brothers and using his dream life to predict the future.

He knows his parents love him beyond measure, and maybe that is why he is able to endure being thrown in a pit to die at the hand of his brothers, being sold into slavery, and then having to endure imprisonment for a transgression that he did not commit.

We know that Joseph rises to power by interpreting Pharoah's two dreams and becomes the second in command only to the royal king because of his keen and accurate understanding of Pharoah's nightly visions. He saves the people of Egypt and, by extension, all those who flocked to that country when drought prevailed in the region, including his band of brothers, who came in search of food.

Joseph does much more than survive; he *thrives*. His story is the ultimate riches-to-rags-to-riches-to-rags-to-riches tale. He experiences trauma, then uses the lessons learned to inform his next step. To quote Nietzsche, "What does not kill us makes us *stronger*."[12]

Miriam

Our final proof text for resiliency is the prophetess Miriam, whose life story and whose function in the triumvirate of Moses, Aaron, and Miriam is to inspire and sustain the Jewish people through her passion. She is, according to a term used in clinical pastoral education, the ultimate "Living Human Document,"[13] defined as "both the people who receive care as well as a study of ourselves, the givers of care."[14]

In a remarkable blending of two separate texts from Numbers, we learn a critical lesson about the healing power of God's presence. In the first, we read:

> On the day the Tabernacle, the Tent of the Testimony, was set up, the cloud covered it. From evening till morning the cloud above the Tabernacle looked like fire.... Whenever the cloud lifted from above the Tent, the Israelites set out; wherever the cloud settled, the Israelites encamped. (Numbers 9:15–19)

Just three chapters later, Aaron and Miriam are overheard gossiping about Moses, and God is incensed. Immediately, Miriam is afflicted with leprosy all over her body. In a panic, Aaron begs Moses to act, and he prays for her healing. God requires she be sent away from the encampment for seven days:

> So Miriam was confined outside the camp for seven days, and the people did not move on till she was brought back. After that, the people left Hazeroth and encamped in the Desert of Paran (Numbers 12:15–16).

Although Miriam initially incurred God's wrath for her slip of the tongue, the message connecting these two texts is that neither the children of Israel nor God abandoned her when she was cast out of the camp, for neither the pillar of fire by night nor the cloud by day moved until Miriam emerged, cured, from her tent. The living human document has learned to receive God's care so that she might convey that message to the people.

Why was Miriam punished and not Aaron? Both Miriam and Aaron gossip about Moses. Why punish the one and not the other? We know that Aaron was responsible for the priestly duties, while Miriam was the prophetess who could get the *erev rav*—the mixed masses of Israelites and others—dancing in gratitude to God after the splitting of the Reed Sea. It was Miriam's ability to find water in the desert that sustained the Israelites as long as she lived. Miriam was the inspiration for a people uncertain of what the future would hold, and she was instrumental in keeping the people focused. Perhaps Moses spoke intimately with God, but Miriam was able to connect with humanity on a much larger scale. God needed to make a point with Miriam to avoid any more rebellion from anyone else against Moses.

How is Miriam resilient beyond surviving leprosy? Miriam is said to have encouraged her parents to reunite as a couple after they had split for fear of bringing a baby boy into the world. It was Miriam who watched over Moses as he floated down the river and who engineered his adoption by Pharoah's daughter. Her entire life is a study in resilient behavior: despite dangers she might have faced, she always kept her focus on what would benefit the Israelites.

From Isaac we learn to help promote stasis and to use the rituals and practices available to us to help us negotiate life's more difficult moments. From Joseph we learn to pay attention to our inner life and to reflect on how we can use our strengths to overcome challenges. From Miriam we learn to hear the still small voice of God that lives within each of us, if we but pay attention, and to encourage ourselves to recognize God's presence, even when it does not appear as a cloud or a pillar of fire.

Conclusions

Judaism provides us with more than ritual; it provides us with replicable models. While I have shared three, there are many more whose life work was the continuation of the Jews in history. We have many choices, but the survivor, the thriver, and the inspiration can inform the way that we and, by extension, our clients/patients/residents function in the world. As a community, we have survived two Temples destroyed, expulsion, the Crusades, the Spanish Inquisition, the pogroms, the Holocaust, and modern-day anti-Semitism and anti-Zionism. As individuals, we still need exemplars to help us navigate life's more difficult complications, and we need look no further than the Torah texts.

Whether you call it spiritual connection or resilience, our survival relies on the continual act of taking our internal pulse and determining how we are going to approach the day—knowing that every bump in the road or tragic turn of events will have its impact on us and leave us scarred; knowing that when we loosen our grip on the stress ball, we will not bounce back as quickly or as perfectly, but we can eventually find a familiar, if somewhat changed, shape again.

Our spiritual leaders exhort us to be better: better Jews, better people, better parents, better children, better selves. But it is more important to provide those whom we serve with the wherewithal to change and renew and become as resilient as they can be. It is in asking the right questions and providing the appropriate model that we will lead people into returning to their own true selves.

Doing *Kaddish* to Turn Mourning into Dancing

Rabbi Anne Brener, LCSW

The *Kaddish* is a Jewish liturgical composition used to punctuate turning points by praising the name of God. The prayer has various forms, depending on when it is used. While it is most frequently used at the end of sections of a prayer service or to close a session of study, the most familiar form of the *Kaddish* is the *Kaddish Yatom*, or the Mourner's *Kaddish*.

The Mourner's *Kaddish* is one of Judaism's primary tools of mourning. Traditionally, it is recited by the mourner three times a day for a prescribed period of time in the presence of a *minyan* (prayer group) comprising a minimum of ten people (historically they were male) who have reached the age of majority, thirteen years, and have been called to the Torah. Those surrounding the mourner in prayer affirm the mourner's words of *Kaddish* by saying, "Amen," at various points in the prayer.[1]

As seen by Jewish mystics, the Mourner's *Kaddish* is a prolonged exercise in purgation, cleaning, and purification, understood to be a tool for cleansing the soul of the deceased.[2] It can also be seen as a way to polish the world, after the rupture of death, to make the world once again a fitting vessel for holiness. Saying *Kaddish* can strip away the details of the stories that bind the mourner to what is past. It can open them up to an as yet uncharted experience of holiness.[3]

Several months after the deaths of my mother and sister when I was twenty-four, I left my hometown of New Orleans. When people confronted the wisdom of my flight, I whimpered, "I have to get away. Every tree, every street corner has a memory. It's excruciating." Today

---

Rabbi Anne Brener, LCSW, is professor of ritual and human development at the Academy of Jewish Religion in Los Angeles, California.

when I return to New Orleans, people ask me what it is like to be back. I reply, "Every tree, every street corner has a memory. It's exquisite."

Those polar opposite snapshots, which include magnolia trees in full bloom and corners where I disembarked the streetcar every school day, illustrate the affirmation that change and healing are possible. This possibility is implied in one of the blessings frequently given to mourners: "May his/her memory be for a blessing." These words are often intoned when the memories and experience of suffering are strong. They offer the hope that the difficult images of illness and death that have taken up residence in the memory of the bereaved will soon recede and be replaced by thoughts of happier times. They express the hope, as well, that the challenges and heartbreak that are, sadly, often present in close relationships will find a path to healing and, even after a death, can be replaced by forgiveness, compassion, and peace. The change in my own perception of my hometown illustrates that transformation. I credit this conversion to the work of "doing *Kaddish*." Somehow, through the mysterious combination of ritual, emotional expression, community support, and time, my very painful memories became blessings.

Doing and Saying *Kaddish*

The rituals of grief can be containers for the "grief work" about which psychotherapists speak today. This chapter explores the *Kaddish* as such a ritual, providing a potent tool for that labor of bereavement and thus becoming a metaphor for "grief work." Reflecting on the healing that can take place on the wings of the *Kaddish*, I hope to reveal the prayer's power to heal. The chapter is titled "Doing *Kaddish*," as opposed to "Saying *Kaddish*," to honor the variety of ways in which people mourn, whether or not they avail themselves of the traditionally crafted Jewish rituals. I want to acknowledge that while there are many valid ways of grieving, *doing Kaddish* connotes the grief work that takes place during the time that one would traditionally be *saying Kaddish*,[4] whether or not Judaism's prescribed mourning practices are observed. Using the phrase "doing *Kaddish*" is a way to welcome into the circle the age-old *Kaddish* experiences of women, who were traditionally excluded from saying the prayer, and to make room for mourners who may not have access to or who do not choose to follow the traditional Jewish practices. "Doing *Kaddish*" is not offered in place of saying *Kaddish* but as a way of deconstructing the prayer, its meaning, and the process for healing that the prayer presents. "Doing *Kaddish*" affirms the spectrum of mourning practices, which could include the ritual recitation of *Kaddish* in a traditional *minyan* or spending time in nature contemplating change. It could apply to work done with a therapist in the privacy of an office and everything in between from which a bereaved person derives comfort. I believe that all of these can bring healing and that all of them are holy. All of these ways of "doing *Kaddish*" can assist the mourner to turn "mourning into dancing" (Psalm 30:12).[5]

The Dance of Mourning

"You have turned my mourning into dancing" (Psalm 30:12) is said to have been penned by David in anticipation of the dedication of the Temple. The phrase reveals his intention that the Temple be a place of transformation and healing. Furthermore, the words attributed to David's son, Solomon, encouraging, "anyone ... in distress ... [to] come [to the Temple] and pray,"[6] also indicate that Jewish ritual has at its core, dating back to the practices of ancient times, the intention of healing. The rituals of antiquity, performed in the Temple, are the ancestors of the ritual practices that Jews observe today.

King David's phrase "mourning into dancing" intimates a vision of transformation that can be misleading. Taken literally, the pledge of "mourning into dancing" promises the substitution of joy for pain. In the agony of grief, this may be what is yearned for: an immediate salve for wounds—fast relief—instant and sudden transformation. However, seeing "mourning" and "dancing" as still photographs—one of contracted grief and the other of expansive celebration—encourages those who suffer to hold their breath and ask, with great impatience, "How quickly can I replace the first image of myself with the second? How can I get back to who I was before the rupture of loss?"

Not so fast. "Mourning into dancing" is a deceptive phrase. Once we have been initiated by grief, we can never be who we were before. Seeing mourning or dancing as frozen postures is a one-dimensional reading of both of these words. This superficial understanding can promote a cruel and false hope of instant healing. Such a goal may deny mourners the opportunity for the deeper self-examination for which mourning calls and deny them access to the meaningful healing and transformation that will allow them to come to peace with the severe decree: the promise that was fulfilled to me by my work of "doing *Kaddish*."

This reading of the phrase "mourning into dancing" literally encourages the conception of mourning in static terms. This misconception is perhaps rooted in Western culture's fear of the dark. Contemporary Christian theologian Matthew Fox tells us of the culture's need not for enlightenment, which so many seek, but for "endarkenment."[7] He supports the search for the patinaed wisdom that comes from lingering in the darkness and experiencing what of value might emerge. But in Western culture, loss and its terrifying spaces of yearning, depression, anger, and anxiety are often met with the belief that any one of them will engulf the mourner, swallowing him or her up forever. Grief is understood as a kind of disease. It is to be avoided.

It is hard not to think of mourning in terms of this horror. As has been frequently discussed,[8] Western culture, frozen in its denial of death and wedded to its rejection of darkness,[9] provides very little that prepares those who confront change to see the universe of loss as having more than one dimension. As Ernest Becker, in his Pulitzer Prize–winning book *The Denial of Death*, tells us:

> The idea of death, the fear of it, haunts the human animal like nothing else; it is a mainspring of human activity—activity designed largely to avoid the fatality of death, to overcome it by denying in some way that it is the final destiny for man.[10]

Or as political commentator Melinda Henneberger said in a critique of American Pollyannaism:

> Real optimism, real faith, is the opposite of a Hallmark-card denial of death and other inconvenient facts of life. It's the opposite of play dumb, keep moving, and for God's sake keep the body bags off camera.[11]

The attitude of which Henneberger speaks permits human beings the charade of denial and robs them of the opportunity to contemplate the reality of human finitude.[12] It shortchanges them by further denying them the very thing they seek. For while the phrase "mourning into dancing" actually falls short in its promise of fast and superficial relief, it in fact makes a much richer promise. It can transform the understanding not only of suffering and loss, but also of the dance of life and the enriching possibilities that are presented when we linger to explore the dark wilderness, mindful of the words of the morning liturgy that remind us that God created both dark and light:

> *Yotzer or uvorei choshekh oseh shalom uvorei et hakol*
> *Creator of light and Creator of darkness*
> *Maker of peace and Creator of all*[13]

Mourning, as a dance itself, is a life-affirming process that ironically can end up delivering in the long run what is sought in the short run. For by performing the dance of mourning—giving full expression to each of the steps—it is possible to discover a new exuberance for celebrating life.[14] It is possible to come to terms with what it means to be human or, as poetically described by Adrienne Rich, "to remember your name."[15]

The phrase "mourning into dancing" suggests a process: something in flux, something that changes. In fact, the most important word in the phrase may not be the obvious ones that describe the starting point or the destination. It may be "into," that little word in the middle. It is the shortest one and is seldom capitalized, but it holds the key to our understanding of healing. "Into" connects the mourning and the dancing and denotes the path on which transformation takes place. The word "into" is itself a dance—a small dance that leads over time to the big dance: the energetic rearrangement of the mourner's view of the universe, which allows him or her to replace the contracted pain of loss with energetic and hopeful movement into the future.

But that is the English rendition of the phrase. In the original Hebrew, *hafakhta misp'di l'machol li* describes the process, with the word *hafakh* implying a more revolutionary transformation, a process or ritual for turning things around. This Hebrew word, *hafakh*, rendered in English as "turned into," literally means "to transform" or "to overturn."[16] This short Hebrew phrase describes the mourner's transformative journey from what kabbalists call *mochin d'katnut*, the contracted mind of narrow vision, to *mochin d'gadlut*, the expanded mind, which is capable of seeing a much bigger picture.[17] This journey is the journey of healing. When we are in the state of *katnut*, we are likely to view the challenge that is faced from the narrow perspective of our own experience. This makes sense. When life kicks you in the belly, the immediate response is to put your hands on your abdomen and bellow, "Why me?" But despite the uniqueness of each existential confrontation, each challenge an individual meets is also a face of the human condition. In the state of *gadlut*, the narcissistic worldview of the one who suffers is loosened. We may feel a connection with others who have been similarly challenged. We may view the experience through a broader lens, one that takes into account all of humanity. The mourners' dance becomes a shared experience.

As stated above, "mourning into dancing" suggests a pictorial definition of ritual. It describes the way in which ritual provides a process for transforming experience. The Hebrew employs the word *machol* for "dance," as opposed to the word *rakad* or any of the many other words that appear in the Bible and are translated with only the one word "dance" in English, conflating all the possibilities for movement that exist within the variety of Hebrew words. *Rakad* is more of a recreational dance, while *machol* is associated with ritual; *machol* contrasts with the image conjured by the English rendering of "dance." *Machol* is specifically used for dances performed in a circle,[18] such as the word describing the celebratory dance performed as the Israelites marched through the Sea of Reeds:

> Then Miriam the prophetess ... took a timbrel in her hand, and all the women went after her in *dance* with timbrels. (Exodus 15:20)

Often associated with praising God, these dances were ritual dances, performed in community, often by groups of women.[19] *Machol*'s Hebrew root emphasizes the circularity of the dance by connecting it to words such as "writhing" or "twisting," as in the circular motions made by women giving birth.[20] This window on what in English is simply "dancing" is appropriate to describe the often painful ritual journey toward rebirth that is required when we mourn. We can only imagine the role of dance in our ancient rituals of healing.[21] For now, the *Kaddish* is the tool for the journey. However when we recite the *Kaddish*, shuckling forward and back, swaying side to side, it, too can be seen as a dance of healing.

The Mourners' Blessing

> *Hamakom y'nacheim etkhem b'tokh sh'ar aveilei Zion v'Yerushalayim.*
>
> *May you find a Holy Place of Comfort [God] in the midst of others who remain who mourn Zion and Jerusalem.*

In addition to the *Kaddish*, there is a special blessing formulated to comfort mourners: "May you find a place of comfort." This prayer is traditionally recited at the end of a funeral. Comforters form two lines facing inward and intone these words as the mourners walk through the double line away from the gravesite, to the house of *shiva*, where they will recite the *Kaddish* surrounded by those who have come to nourish them with food and comfort.[22] I believe that the "others who remain who mourn Zion and Jerusalem" describes those who have been schooled by the challenges of loss and have learned compassion and kindness. This constitutes a holy community. The name of God, which the blessing invokes on behalf of mourners, is *HaMakom*, which literally means "The Place." When the *Kaddish* is said, according to traditional directives, it is the *minyan* itself that becomes "the place" of healing. Within the *minyan*, the wounds of grief are attended to through the balm of the words of the *Kaddish*. Dare I assert that "*HaMakom Y'nacheim*," the "Place of Comfort" in which the mourner says *Kaddish*, is a representation of God on earth, through the presence of (to paraphrase the last part of the blessing) others who have been schooled in grief and its rituals of healing.

Continuing the Conversation

Everyone dies in the middle of a conversation. After a loss, people often feel that there will never be an opportunity to express what remains unsaid, what perhaps could not be said during the lifetime of the deceased. But the Jewish rituals surrounding the *Kaddish* provide tools to perform what are perhaps the two hardest tasks that humans are called to do: to heal relationships even after a death and to transform the relationship from a physical to a spiritual connection. I base this understanding of these transformative possibilities on the mystical belief that a mourner's works of *Kaddish* or acts of goodness performed in the name of the deceased affect the souls of those who have died.[23] I believe that this view of the power of human words and deeds creates a metaphor that makes it possible for us to have a sense that, even after a death, we remain in dynamic relationship with those who have died.[24] This encourages the bereaved to use the Jewish mourning rituals to facilitate the continued conversation and its attendant healing. These practices provide different degrees of focus and support for mourners over time and extend for the rest of their lives. They make it possible for the conversation to continue until the mourner, too, passes beyond the curtain that separates life and death.

But to continue the conversation the mourner must have a voice. We are told that "we serve round things in a house of mourning because a mourner, like the egg and the lentil, has no mouth."[25] It is during the week after the death, beginning with intoning the *Kaddish* at the funeral and then in the house of *shiva*, that the community helps the mourner to find his or her mouth. The great Jewish scholar Abraham Joshua Heschel quoted a Hasidic teaching: "There are three ascending levels of mourning: with tears ... silence ... and song."[26] Rabbi Samson Raphael Hirsch points out that the word *almanah*, or "widow," comes from the Hebrew root *a-l-m*, which means "to be dumb" and refers to the fact that a widow has "lost her mouthpiece and defender in the loss of her husband."[27]

More and more today I see mourners pressured to find that voice prematurely. While many may find comfort in speaking at the funeral of one who has died, I have concerns that the current practice of having mourners speak at the funeral may shift their attention from the appropriate grief work to concern with writing and performance. The first words that a mourner should be expected to say are the formulaic words of the *Kaddish*, which come near the end of the funeral service. Forcing the mourner to literally "come to terms" with the loss at such an early stage, by speaking at the funeral, interrupts the natural flow of emotions, which Heschel describes. I wonder if mourners would, indeed, be better served by observing a period of silence in which they can marinate in the chaotic emotions of grief before making a statement about the deceased that will become set in stone. Setting words in stone is something that tradition reserves for a later ritual: the unveiling.

Finding the Mouth through the *Kaddish*

The journey of grief is indeed about the challenge of literally "coming to terms" with the physical loss of one who has been a central presence (either physically or emotionally) in the life of the mourner. But it is more than that. Mourning is a spiritual journey as well, one that challenges the basic assumptions of a bereaved person regarding the nature of the universe and his or her role in it. For many, grief can provoke an existential and spiritual crisis. They may feel that the God that they may have prayed to in the past has delivered a crushing blow. In anger or bewilderment, the mourner may withdraw from God or at least from the image of God that may have sustained him or her in the past. So the mourner may find that he or she is bereft, not only of the one who has been lost, but often also of the bedrock in the universe—God.

Jewish ritual anticipates this spiritual alienation.[28] Evidence of this is found in the fact that mourners are exempt from many *mitzvot* in the early stages of grief. And mourners are confronted with the message that grief will initiate a spiritual challenge in the very first ritual that they are expected to perform. According to *halakhah* (Jewish law), upon hearing of the death of someone close, mourners are bidden to tear their garment and immediately recite "*Barukh Dayan HaEmet*" (in praise of "God, the True Judge").[29] In one act, the mourner is challenged to trust God's truth despite the ruptured feelings. This formulaic blessing, in effect, catapults the mourner onto a spiritual journey, which begins with the initial moment of brokenness caused by the news of the death and continues through the emotional work of grieving. This is likely to be a time when we are least inclined to praise God! The journey concludes when the mourner comes to a resolution of grief, which is signified by the ability to praise God. This can often take a long time. In my book *Mourning & Mitzvah*, which guides mourners through the rituals of mourning across the entire mourners' path, eight chapters take place between the tearing of the cloth to the moment when the mourner can say, "Praise God." Almost half the book is dedicated to repairing this rupture, and that is the ideal goal of doing *Kaddish*: bringing the mourner to a sense of peace, wherein he or she can again praise God, the True Judge.[30]

A death creates a rupture. To those who grieve, it feels as if the very world in which they live has been shattered. Holiness seems to have exited from the world. The world feels flat and as though its Divine Animating Spark, or as God is referred to in the *Kaddish*, "the Great Name/the *Sh'mei Rabba*," has departed. Saying *Kaddish* allows the mourner to breathe the *Sh'mei Rabba* back into the world. Surrounded by comforters, the mourner stands peering into that chasm and becomes a conduit through which God's Great Name can reenter the world.

There is a legend that the words of the *Kaddish* are the words that would be said by those who have died to describe what they have learned about the ultimate purpose of life: to make God present in the world.[31] As the mourner says *Kaddish*, that role is being fulfilled. It is ironic, poetic justice that this practice occurs at a time when a person may be the most alienated from God.

The Jewish mystical tradition maps the created world as consisting of four successive worlds that emanate from God or from the etheric *Ein Sof* (a name for Divinity that means "without end"). Each world manifests with increasingly concrete dimensions. The worlds extend down the ladder of abstraction from the highest world, the world of *Atzilut*, the world of the spirit, to the world of *Assiyah*, the physical world in which the actions of human bodies take place. The world of intellect (*B'riah*) and the world of emotions (*Y'tzirah*) are the intermediate steps between the two. Human beings, we are told, live simultaneously in all four of these worlds. When a death occurs, each of these worlds feels the rupture. Mourners say *Kaddish* from each of them, fulfilling each world's unique task of grief work. The *Kaddish* can facilitate that work.

Those who stand for *Kaddish* do so, quite literally, in the world of *Assiyah*. Their feet are on the ground, and they are surrounded, one would hope, with people who bring comfort. From this place on solid earth, the *Kaddish* can propel the mourner all the way back up the ladder, through all the worlds, to the highest point in the world of *Atzilut*, almost to the *Ein Sof* itself.

The words of the *Kaddish* can be understood as petitioning for holiness to be returned to each of the worlds. In saying *Kaddish* from each of the four worlds, those who grieve heal themselves. They heal the deceased. They heal the world. And they heal the Name of God. We will walk through each world and then explore the tasks of grief in each of them, as we see how the *Kaddish* can be used to bring healings.

But the work of doing *Kaddish* is not for the mourner alone.

Comforters gather around the mourner in the house of *shiva*. They say "amen" while the mourner recites the *Kaddish*, helping him or her find the voice needed to continue the conversation. These "amens" of the comforters play an important role in the healing process, as will be shown below. These "amens" nourish the souls of the mourners, while the dishes they bring to feed the mourners nourish their bodies. They play a crucial role that makes it possible for the mourners to do their work. They make it possible for the *Kaddish* to be like a magic tool for transforming silence into words. It takes us through all four worlds: *Assiyah*, the physical world; *Y'tzirah*, the emotional world; *B'riah*, the intellectual world; and *Atzilut*, the spiritual world. In each world, the *Kaddish* empowers us to conjure healing in ways beyond our understanding.

The Magic of *Kaddish*

The *Kaddish* is said in a language that's unfamiliar. We do not say it in English. We do not even say it in Hebrew. The *Kaddish* is written in Aramaic, a language that very few people today speak. Perhaps that is purposeful in that it tells us that the act of doing the *Kaddish* is in some ways more important than understanding what the *Kaddish* says, at least at the beginning of the grief process. Aramaic is the same language of another word that is as mysterious and magical as the *Kaddish*: *Abracadabra*.

Abracadabra is actually an Aramaic word that means "I create as I speak." And this is what the *Kaddish* does: *Abracadabra*, the *Kaddish* is spoken and a bridge to healing is created. In the early stages of grief, in the world of *Assiyah*, that bridge connects mourners to community at a time they may feel most lost and alone.

In this physical world, when mourners first begin to say the *Kaddish*, they often feel as if the words are being mouthed from deep inside a thick balloon. Numb, uncertain, there is no sense that things can change, that healing is a possibility. But healing comes from a place of mystery, a place we do not know yet, cannot possibly know, because nothing in life has prepared the mourner for facing the gaping hole that a death brings. A death of someone central to a life shatters all assumptions about how the world works. The mourner becomes unmoored. However if mourners are open to the possibility that there is something that they do not know and say the *Kaddish* with this uncertainty and with questions and curiosity, then the *Kaddish* can take them to someplace that is not yet imaginable. As the mourners begin, the words of the *Kaddish* may be nothing more than black letters on a white page, and it may seem like a miracle to get from the beginning to the end. But those black letters can be a lifeguard's rope extended from the tradition to save the mourner's life. And that miracle can be a sign that other miracles will come.

As mourners say the *Kaddish*, that balloon in which they feel trapped begins to rise, like a hot-air balloon. The *Kaddish* slowly takes those who mourn to the place of mystery where miracles happen and transformation is possible. While the mourners ascend, those below, who say "amen" to the *Kaddish*, metaphorically hold the tethers that keep the balloon connected to the ground. Those "amens" say to the mourner, "Go. Let the *Kaddish* take you to that mysterious place, where the unimaginable can happen, where healing is possible. Say the *Kaddish* with every emotion, with every question. Say it with tears. Say it with rage. And as you do that, we are here, tethering you to your life, tethering you to your community. We promise, with our 'amens': We are here. We will help you through this." In their "amens," the mourners hear these unspoken words of comfort and support as the air balloon lifts off to take them to the mysterious place where they come face-to-face with the void.

And then, *abracadabra*, the balloon ascends to the emotional world, *Y'tzirah*. Here the *Kaddish* becomes a wireless connection between the worlds. Mourners speak and their words create a vehicle for continuing the conversation with the one who is lost. On the wings of the *Kaddish*, mourners discover that the part of them that lives in that conversation is still alive. They can still say the things they need to share. The person mourned is once more present, as the mourner engages in the most excruciating task of being human: transforming the physical connection with one who has died to a spiritual connection. All the unsaid words, unfinished issues, and raw emotions are transmitted, as the *Kaddish* becomes a vehicle for communication.

And then, *abracadabra*, the balloon rises higher, to the world of *B'riah*, the world of intellect. The words of the *Kaddish* themselves come into focus. Up until the mourner entered this world, the words and their meaning were less important than the role they played: an anchor in the physical world, a line of communication in the emotional world. Here, mourners look at the words of the *Kaddish*. They read its translation and try to grasp the meaning. They can be taken aback, even repelled. The words of the *Kaddish*, "Magnify and sanctify the Great Name," may challenge them. They ask the most confrontational questions: "Why would I want to magnify the name of such a God? What kind of God would cause such pain? Why do good people suffer? What does it mean to be human and to live on a planet where living things must die?" With these questions in *B'riah*, the world of the intellect, mourners face their shattered faith and their understanding of the God that they may feel has betrayed them. The *Kaddish* becomes a kind of crowbar, in Bob Dylan's words, "knock-knock-knockin' on heaven's door,"[32] in an effort to wrest an answer from the Great Mystery to the inscrutable existential questions.

Then, *abracadabra*, and seemingly out of nowhere, the words hit a sweet spot and the balloon rises higher, as if through an opening in the sky, to a place where a much bigger universe can be seen than the universe in which the mourner lived before the loss. This births a new kind of spirituality and a new understanding of God. The questions posed in the world of *B'riah* were not answered. But it seems to matter less. As mourners take comfort in this new vision, they recognize that they have not only *not* lost God, they have also not fully lost the person they mourn. The words of the *El Malei Rachamim*, the prayer said at burial, are realized, and we feel the combined presence of God and the one we mourn, fulfilling the prayer's hope that the deceased will "rest under the wings of the *Shekhinah* [God's Presence]." A process that began on the side of awe that is filled with fear and horror has been transformed into the awe of radical amazement and wonder.[33] *Abracadabra*, the mourner has spoken the *Kaddish* and created a new universe for a home. This universe can hold the paradoxes of horror and wonder in one heart at the same time: life can be beautiful even in the midst of pain. The facts remain, but the mourner is different, and his or her understanding of the Great Name is different.

With this mysterious insight, the balloon returns the mourner to earth, into the loving arms of those faithful community members, "the *aveli Zion v'Yerushalyim.*" They are the ones who remained on the ground, continuing to say, "Amen," and holding the tether, which made it safe for the mourner to make this profound journey. The mourner returns, carrying the *reshimu*, the residue of mystery. Touched by grace, infused with wonder, the mourner is impelled to heed the *Kaddish*'s instructions to walk that mystery onto the earth. "*Abracadabra*," despite the wounds, the *Kaddish* has been spoken and has created access to wholeness once again. Through the work of "doing *Kaddish*," the mourner has become one of the members of the community of comfort, one of the *aveilei Zion v'Yerushalyim* who says "amen," described in the Mourners' Blessing: memory has become a blessing, and mourning is turned into dancing.

Creativity and Healing in a Jewish Context

Judith Margolis

I am a scientist by necessity, and not by vocation. I am really by nature an artist.... And of this there lies an irrefutable proof: which is that in all the countries into which psychoanalysis has penetrated it has been better understood and applied by writers and artists than by doctors.

—SIGMUND FREUD[1]

Any reaction to stimulus may be causally explained; but the creative act, which is the absolute antithesis of mere reaction, will forever elude the human understanding.

—CARL JUNG[2]

What provides solace in such difficult times?... "Life is not defined by science but by Mystery"—the Mystery, never solved, that lies "at the heart of the will to live."

—RACHEL NAOMI REMEN[3]

I have long been absorbed with what I call "creative response to infirmity"—how the practice of art-making allows one to remain fully alive in the face of illness, injury, bereavement, and even death. I could say that the artworks I will describe, or, more accurately, the process by which they came about, have saved my life. I claim no absolutes about cure, which was or was not forthcoming. I refer instead to a sense of healing—a trajectory from brokenness to wholeness—that manifest when I made art about, for example, my mother's final illness, a daughter's life-threatening cancer, and my beloved husband's death.

Judith Margolis is an artist and writer, and art editor for *Nashim: A Journal of Jewish Women's Studies & Gender Issues* in Jerusalem, Israel.

Like a two-way mirror, the complex human urge to create is illuminated by understanding individual works of art. At the same time, creative process, with its focus on metaphor and symbolism, transforms the artist. I often work in collage, mindful that bringing together a variety of unrelated images to form something wholly new resembles the process by which humans dream. I begin by rooting through my own unfinished or failed paintings and drawings, discarded printed media, scraps from old children's books, and other such detritus. Some are "found" images (literally, I pick things up from the street) or photographs that I have taken or sketches that I have made of objects and scenes that catch my eye unexpectedly. I try out different combinations of these materials, painting over and adding to the images, exploring their expressive potential until some juxtaposition seems to "work," or make sense. Repurposing something that I "happened upon" in a way that completes an idea and takes my art to a new place calls up the tension between what appears to be random chance and destiny.

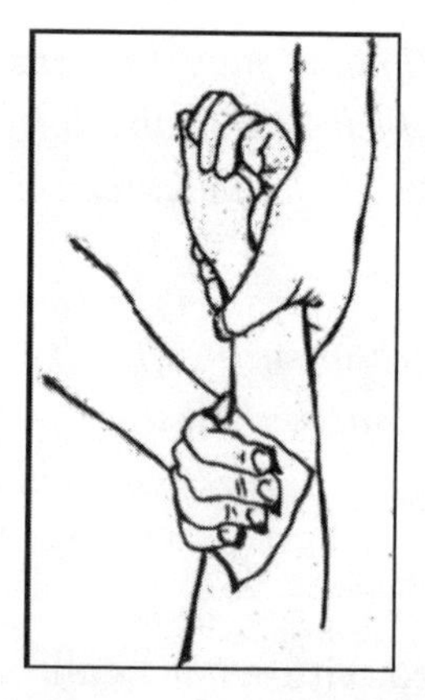

Figure 1. Judith Margolis, *Applying Pressure to the Wound,* ink on paper, 3 × 6 in. (2003).

I appropriated "applying pressure to the wound" (see figure 1) from a crumpled first-aid pamphlet that I chanced upon while strolling on a city street. I was especially taken by the text accompanying that image instructing us to "attend immediately to the wound and proceed." We have all been wounded in some way, I thought. The simple imperative reminded me how, beyond the crushing burdens that life delivers—the grief, financial worries, dysfunctional family harm—making art can be a way to "apply pressure to the wound," so to speak, in order to proceed and to continue to live and create.

What follows in this chapter are examples of my artwork accompanied by brief stories that track and contextualize my development as an artist. Integral to this illustrated text is the burgeoning ideation about how creativity manifests healing. My consciousness as an artist began when I was very young. Even as a child I knew how to draw. I was nine when my fourth grade teacher asked us to make drawings of our "grown-up" selves. The other children in my class drew childishly rendered cowboys, pilots, and ballerinas. I was developing early, and not only artistically. I had just learned how to make things look three-dimensional by using shading, and so I drew my "grown up" self as a full-figured woman whose breasts cast shadows across her chest. When the teacher confiscated the drawing and sent me to the principal's office, I began to suspect that drawing *breasts* was a *bad* mistake. A parallel subterranean knowledge suggested that my own developing female body was shameful. Thus I learned something that both nourished and disturbed me all my life as an artist. I understand about things by drawing them. And drawing what is "real" to me often makes other people uncomfortable.

Much of the art discussed here was inspired by or came about in the course of intense personal involvement with Jewish ritual. When I was in my early thirties I started to view Jewish tradition through my artist's eye. I combined, for example, an interest in Jungian interpretation of fairy tales with an unmistakable Jewish *tam* (taste), so that the resulting drawings retold the story of Sleeping Beauty with myself and my *bubbes* (grandmothers) and *tantes* (aunties) cast as the Twelve Fairy Godmothers (see figure 2).[4]

Figure 2. Judith Margolis, *Twelve Fairy Godmothers Pose for Their Picture*, pencil on paper, 18 × 24 in. (1990). Collection: Meredith Tax.

Bikkur Cholim (Visiting the Sick)

The *mitzvah* of *bikkur cholim* (visiting the sick) dovetailed nicely with seeking models for these stories that I was illustrating. I frequented an old-age home, where I encountered Elinor, whose room smelled like urine and whose eyes were cloudy with cataracts. She had no other visitors, but Elinor could speak, and while I drew her, she told me the same story over and over, about running freely with her little sister on the deck of their father's barge on the Erie Canal. I asked Elinor to draw a picture of this, and with great concentration, she drew the boat and herself and her sister, their sailor dresses, and straw hats. At the same time, I drew her (see figure 3), noting with my own pen the deep wrinkles in her face and her knobby arthritic fingers gripping the pencil. All the while, she told me again and again about the carefree happy time that was all that was left of her life's story.[5]

Figure 3. Judith Margolis, *Elinor*, ink and pencil on paper, 18 × 24 in. (1990).

I have often been curious about the fierce incentive I felt to expose myself to the confluence of sadness, repulsion, curiosity, and empathy that Elinor's circumstance elicited. Without knowing it would, I now understand that it helped prepare me to face my own mother's illness and death.

Kaddish

We had gathered to celebrate my mother's birthday, while she slumbered in the dim room. Some unexpected interior logic convinced me that birthday parties and vacations are not the only occasions worth memorializing or documenting. Without quite knowing why, I started taking snapshots of her silent form, framing as if they were already in a painting the light on her face, the snowy sheets with their blue shadowed slopes, the geometric technological configuration of life-support machinery. I did not expect to use the photos or even show them to anyone, but they were showing me what *I had* to see.

Over the next few years, while my mother went back and forth between hospital and home, I drew and took photographs; the medical apparatus surrounding her, her exhausted face tethered to an oxygen tube, my father tenderly feeding her, scooping cereal off her chin—these images recorded my fear and fascination with the unfolding drama of death. And thus I assumed my true calling, presaged in fourth grade, as an artist who looks at and records what she sees, right up to when I drew my mother, dead in her bed, five years later (see figure 4).

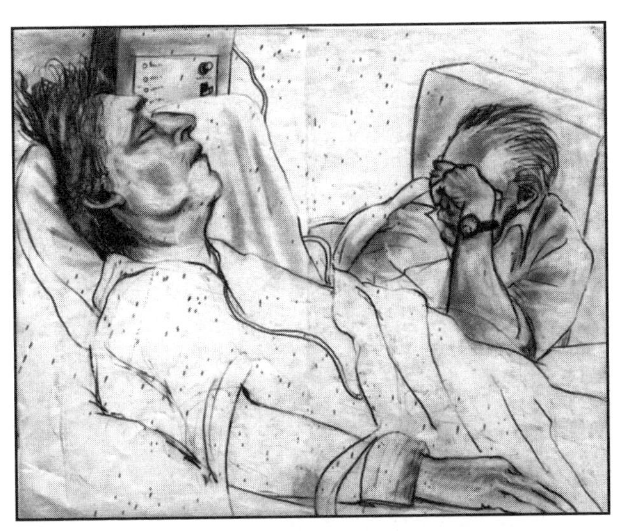

Figure 4. Judith Margolis, *Life Support/Waiting,* pencil on paper, 18 × 24 in. (1986).

My mother chose cremation and having her ashes scattered, so although the week of *shiva* in the warm circle of my community was comforting, there was no funeral or grave. All during the *Kaddish* year after my mother's death, I pored over the sketchbooks, photographs, and journal entries that I had kept during her illness, and from them

I produced a series of paintings called *Life Support.* Although these paintings are among my best work, exhibited in several shows and critically praised, I found that people shied away from engaging with them. "Too depressing," they said. My mother, who had often complained that I should make more "cheerful" art, very well might have felt the same.

It is very odd to deeply mourn a person you did not get along with. During that *Kaddish* year I mulled over what had not been resolved between us during her life. As I painted, compassion seeped from my hands and sprouted up in my heart. Could it be that the souls of our loved ones become purified through our favorable memories of them? I began to see my mother as a person, separate from my relationship to her. I remembered her visiting relatives in old-age homes and how she included people in family get-togethers if she knew they would be alone. The recollection of our mutual rejection was now cloaked in a radiant veil of appreciation for my mother's charity work and generous hospitality. In the painting, she dozes in front of the television surrounded by machines and a bluish vapor that, to me, mimicked the emotional storm that death had stirred up. To depict the tender emotions of my parents' impending separation after fifty-three years of marriage, I painted her with subtle gradations of acid/sweet color.

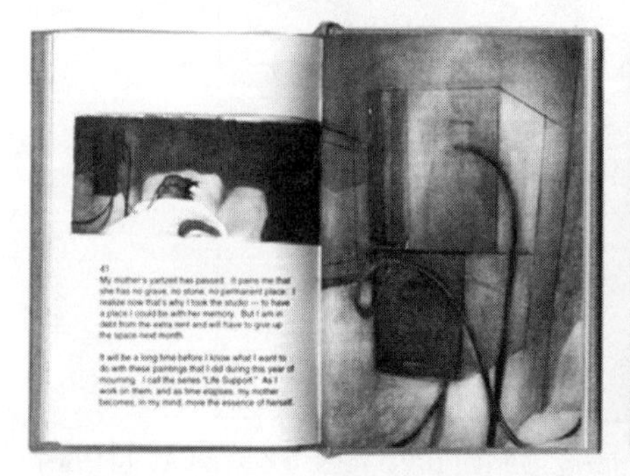

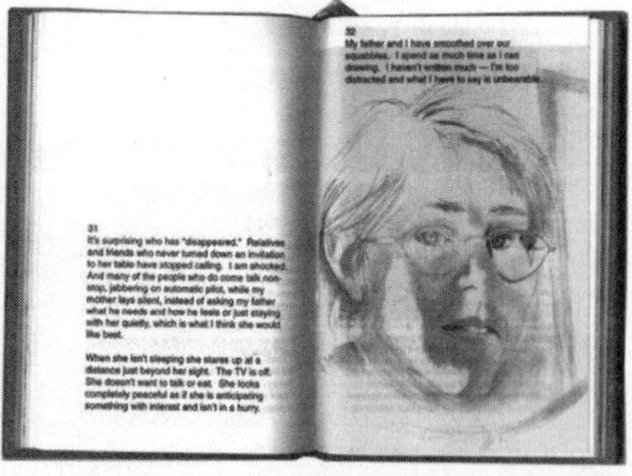

Figure 5. Judith Margolis, *Life Support, Invitation to Prayer,* limited-edition hand-bound book (Jerusalem: Bright Idea Books, 2000).

The journal entries, paintings, and drawings were infused with conflicted sorrow and guilt over family tensions and differences over the way that we mourned. But they also highlighted the courageous way that my mother and father faced infirmity and their own passing. I saw precious lessons of petition and praise embedded in every twist and turn. The idea of making a book with this rich material began percolating over the following years. An invitation to submit work for an exhibit of original contemporary Judaica at Hebrew Union College–Jewish Institute of Religion in New York[6] encouraged me to finally integrate the edited texts and sketches with the *Kaddish* paintings into a book called *Life Support, Invitation to Prayer* (see figure 5). These are some of the words that decorate the endpapers of the book:

Prayer for the ransoming of time
Prayer to stay centered
Prayer to be cared for
Prayer to accept care
Prayer to accept not being in control
Prayer for making deals
Prayer for help in the struggle with faith
Prayer on beginning whatever will happen next
Prayer to create prayer when I never prayed before
Prayer against depression
Prayer against despair
Prayer to escape one's failure
Prayer for a sense of worthiness
Prayer for shelter
Prayer for strength
Prayer for protection against painful truth
Prayer to look at the moon
Prayer for the fragrant forgiving air of evening
Prayer to write a poem
Prayer to set aside judgment at how others mourn
Prayer to do the "right thing"
Prayer to prepare dinner
Prayer to be generous
Prayer to forgive my sadness and fatigue
Prayer to value my life
Prayer against guilt

Prayer against my ineptitude
I am hurting and frightened and doing the best I can
Prayer for attending to the dying
Prayer of gratitude on this ordinary day
Prayer for some relief
Prayer for forgetfulness
Prayer for when I am afraid to move
Prayer for patience
Prayer for laughter
Prayer for energy
Prayer for courage
Prayer to learn to listen
Prayer to accept the decisions of others
Prayer to be forgiving
Prayer for clarity
Prayer to pay attention
Prayer for acceptance
Prayer for the good friend who helps me
Prayer upon waking in the night to crushing fears
Prayer to direct thoughts
Prayer to move past procrastination
Prayer to keep faith
Prayer to forgive oneself for being crazy
Prayer to forgive oneself for being selfish
Prayer to forgive oneself for being angry
Prayer to forgive oneself for being bored
Prayer to forgive oneself for being sad
Prayer to forgive oneself for being confused
Prayer in a difficult time
Prayer for guidance
Prayer against mistakes
Prayer to be good to myself
Prayer to let go[7]

I commissioned a master bookbinder to make a limited edition of twelve small books. Sewn into the spine of each is a silky ribbon to which I affixed a small silver *yad* (hand) (see figure 6), to represent the outstretched hand of God, my own petition in prayer, and, of course, my mother's hand, lost to the harsh illness that killed her.

33
I am at once mesmerized and horrified at seeing my father giving her the most devoted care, cleaning with Handi-Wipes the wife that he once stroked in passion. He is a model of goodness.

34
My good friend, Julie, came with me to visit them last night. Mom was completely quiet, asking only for water, each time with a heart-rending cry. Responding to Julie's warm interest and the question, "How did you and Carrie meet?" Dad told in great detail about their early life and dug out the photographs of his 30's-era art-deco apartment. As he spoke, he kept looking over to where my mother was lying, staring up with a faint smile on her face. We don't know if she was listening. It seemed she was. I kissed her on the forehead when I left and told her, "I love you." She frowned slightly when I said, "I'll see you Thursday," and I wonder if we will see each other again. I noticed as I left the room that the little toe on her left foot is completely black.

Figure 6. From Margolis, *Life Support, Invitation to Prayer.*

Transforming Experience

Some years after all this, I felt the damp chill of proximity to an unthinkable outcome when my college-aged daughter became very ill. I left Israel to spend five months with her while she went through chemotherapy for a cancer that, thank God, turned out to be curable.

I sat with her while chemo/poison dripped into her veins, and the notion of reincarnation and what awaits those who leave this world asserted itself into my musings. I was sensible of the notion that she had been and remained exactly who she was from the moment that she looked placidly at me her first moment of life. Seeing her so ill, I experienced waves of huge love and responsibility for her recovery alternated with conjecture about what a crapshoot it is—who gets sick, who survives. Slowly over time, another image and the phrase "waiting to be born" started to materialize in my mind. Glue stick, a small box of pan paints, and a few crayons sufficed as an ad hoc "studio," and I was able to work at night, making collages, while she slept.

When I returned home, I continued to work on a large collage in which time and space are *afuk* (reversed). In it, a baby floats in moonlit darkness, head down, while hands stretch up on either side of the starry expanse, like a heavenly midwife in attendance (see figure 7). Skeletons waiting their turn to live (or die) approach a crumbling stone staircase. Assorted images surround the birthing baby, including, in one corner, *Applying Pressure to the Wound*, described at the beginning of this chapter. I always shudder to hear about remissions becoming relapses. "Thank God, my daughter survived," I thought. "I got through that encounter with death. Now I can relax!" I was wrong.

Figure 7. Judith Margolis, *Waiting to Be Born*, mixed-media collage, paint, ink, and pastel on paper, 19 × 26 in. (2003).

K'riah

Two years later, after a shockingly brief illness, my beloved husband David Margolis, *z"l*, breathed his last. And I lost my friend/lover/soul mate of thirty-five years. It is traditional at Jewish funerals for the mourner's garment to be torn (*k'riah*), symbolizing the irreparable destruction that death wields. I *hated* that rip to my blouse at the funeral, the beginning of *rupture* to my life. Yet the ritual inspired something: I could not throw his shirts away, and an impulse took root, and then an insistent imperative, to *tear* up every one of his favorite colorful garments and sew the scraps together. Not only his shirts but many cloth fragments of the life that we had shared: his wedding tie; fabric from my wedding dress; our daughter's crib "blankie"; even a bit of the curtains from our first shared bedroom. These became what I call the *K'riah Quilt*, which is still in progress, and is all hand-sewn (see figure 8). With countless tiny stitches I reassembled what was torn apart, each piece charged with memory and meaning. It tells a story of how my life was once colorful and beautiful, and that it could be so again.

Figure 8. *Left,* Judith Margolis, *K'riah Quilt,* (detail) hand-sewn fabric (work in progress); *right,* Judith Margolis, *All Alone at Night She Dreams,* watercolor on paper, 6 × 4.5 in. (2006).

I also started to make small drawings and paintings of a woman sleeping alone under a patchwork quilt (see figure 8, *All Alone at Night She Dreams*). It was not until a few years later, when both the sewn and painted work were exhibited together,[8] that I recognized the connection between the images that I was painting and myself sewing the real quilt.

Most important was an ink drawing called *Learning to Live Alone with Only the Moon for Company*, which I did while traveling on a train (see figure 9). This is how it came about.

Figure 9. Judith Margolis, *Learning to Live Alone with Only the Moon for Company,* ball-point pen on cardboard, 8 × 8.5 in. (2005). This image was featured in Shulamit Reinharz, Ruth Weisberg, Judith Margolis, Dinah Zeltser, and Beth Ames-Swartz, "*Nish'ma*: Let Us Hear," *Sh'ma: A Journal of Jewish Responsibility* 36, no. 629 (2006): 11.

The Passover that we did not know would be his last, my husband and I made the seder together alone, just the two of us. That year, the telling of the story of the Exodus from Egypt was more inspired than ever before. Our table seemed to glow as we discussed the going out from Egypt, ate the delicious foods, and sang the traditional songs until three in the morning.

Afterward, as we walked in the brightness of the full moon and fragrant night air, I was so grateful to share my life with him, and I thought that, forevermore, a full moon would remind me that everything could be perfect. David became acutely ill at Shavuot, and a month and a half after that, by the full moon of Tammuz, he was gone.

All through that terrible time, experiencing such obliterative grief, I so wanted to talk with him! I wondered where he was and if I would ever feel his presence again. I found it painful to be in my home, to see the things that he had touched. It hurt to breathe. I could not bear to be in my studio, and I feared that I might never draw again. As if I was "running away from home," I set out on an open-ended trip to see friends and family in America.

One night, during a long train ride, I found an empty matzah box inexplicably discarded in the crevice of my seat. It reminded me of that last seder that David and I had made together. I had no art supplies and I wanted to draw. I tore a piece of cardboard from that box and on the back used a ball-point pen to blacken out the night, leaving a blank circle for the moon and little specks of no ink for the stars. I put in curtains fluttering, as if stirred by a breeze or spirit, and beneath the window I drew a solitary figure alone in bed.

My darling husband was gone. I was desolate to be apart from him. But, still, that amazing full moon returned each month to remind me of how perfect things can be.

In the next months I made many such drawings. It was the only thing that I felt like drawing. Like the Exodus out of *Mitzrayim* (Egypt), whose root means "narrow," it told of a passage through a painful and difficult place. Like the Passover story, which is told over and over, it had to be drawn and redrawn. Abraham Joshua Heschel wrote, "To apprehend the depth of religious faith we will try to ascertain not so much what the person is able to express as that which he is unable to express, the insights that no language can declare."[9] Making art is an opportunity to express what no language can declare.

I want to tell about another drawing that I started way before David got sick. It was of a kneeling woman without a head. I had found the image in a wastepaper basket after one of my drawing classes. A student had torn it up and discarded it in frustration, and I had saved the piece, moved by the muteness of the headless figure. I had glued it onto a large sheet of paper and pinned it up my studio, not sure how to proceed. Time went by and then David got sick and died, and I was not in the studio for a long time. I hardly understood why I should live, much less continue to make art.

But there was something about this figure. I felt better in its presence. Looking at the image felt like medicine. One day, after about a year, I went to the studio, which felt like another planet, and scrawled on the drawing, "How things grow," in awkward painted script (see figure 10).

Figure 10. Judith Margolis, *How Things Grow*, acrylic paint and pencil on paper, 24 × 30 in. (2006).

More time passed. I left the country and returned. One day I approached the drawing and painted in roots, or was it veins and blood? It was about something being alive. After a while, the blank space next to the figure started to make sense. After David died, his absence was a huge presence, an unending sequence of meaninglessness. In this drawing I honored that empty space, not drawing it, nothing so definite. Just rubbing around it with my finger with soft gray graphite, alone in the studio, with just the soft sound of my finger on the page. And finally the piece was finished, the lesson learned.

And so, I believe, there is something that happens, if we let it, despite one's intentions, that moves in the direction of healing, of life. And this happened for me after David died. Without thinking that I was making art—I was certain that I was not being very productive—I remember spending most of my time grieving and being sad, not seeing any point to anything. But evidently I was doing something. Because now I have all these drawings and paintings, the quilt, essays that I have written. All made during that time when I did not think that I was doing anything.

Although I am a trained artist, I believe much can be accomplished by creative invention that is simple and unskilled. For example, when I found my husband's harmonica in his desk after he died, although I did not know how to play, I noticed that moving the harmonica along my lips and simply breathing in and out made a quiet melody that felt as if I was extending his breath and making "music" for him. I especially like doing this at night, while walking on the street, like a walking meditation, allowing the "song" to loop around and repeat. The breath and the music and the measured steps keep me company. It requires no skill and is inexplicably comforting.

There is a complex alchemy of emotion, perception, and intellect essential to the making of art, which is about more than applying one's craft. It is not just willingness to do the art, but a felt imperative to proceed, instinctively or intentionally, facing fear, and saying the unspeakable, in a way that can fill up an empty heart with meaning.

The Healing Power of the Creative Process

The impulse to do creative work appears to have its own forceful intention of accomplishment. How else to explain the determination to create, despite pain and incapacity, that artists exhibit along with their art? Listening to other artists talk about their creative process, I have come to appreciate even more the way that art unleashes healing power. These examples are culled from a fraction of the many intimate conversations that I have had with many artists over the years who did creative work despite pain and incapacity:

- Shirley Faktor is an artist who suffers from a spinal injury and for whom pain has become an uneasy partner to her disciplined work in the studio. About her large-scale paintings that depict sensuous figures lounging in beds wrapped in comforters and sheets, she says, "In earlier years the bed was laden with comfort. But, now," she confesses, "I sleep less and [because of acute pain] I no longer find it a place of comfort. I cannot stand for long so I paint and I lie down. I paint and I lie down. Honestly, sometimes I wonder how the hell the work gets done. I swear, sometimes it seems like they paint themselves."[10]
- After a life of academic scholarship, Jeff Camhi, whose brilliant wife is fast disappearing into the rabbit hole of Alzheimer's, starts writing a personal-voice memoir for the first time. It surprises him how much he enjoys and is comforted by the creative writing in which he describes, among other topics, his wife, their long loving relationship, and his loneliness. But more, he exclaims, "Her world is diminishing, but mine is expanding." He is creating, he says, "a new self," and he feels exhilarated, despite his sorrow at his wife's decline. Is this a healing?[11]
- Miriam Lippel Blum is a Jewish educator who has self-identified as a "bionic woman," because she has had so many surgeries and "parts replaced," yet writes with, can you believe, *humor* about her struggle with the grievous complications of diabetes. Having suffered an amputation, macular degeneration, and more, she lives with daily self-administered dialysis and writes beautiful, funny, and poignant essays about life in the electric scooter lane. "I live as fully as I can," she declares, "and writing keeps me inventive and loving." When she admits that her life has already extended beyond what doctors predicted, she expresses triumph that she is "still around to make mischief."[12]
- Inspired by the biblical Jacob's encounter with the holy messenger, Chana Cromer, a visual artist with two broken hips, created sculptural canes to walk that have text and

images embedded so that the cane itself looks like a thigh bone. In the words of Rivka Miriam (poet), the art comes from "the point of fracture."[13]

- Albert J. Winn, an artist who describes himself as "living with HIV" (as opposed to dying of AIDS), made a mezuzah filled with blood to explore issues related to the "pariah status of certain illnesses," as explored by Susan Sontag in her landmark book *Illness as Metaphor*.[14] The artist's work brings attention to the inclination to avoid touching, or the "touching-recoiling" impulse, that people express around him when they are aware of his disease.[15]
- After surviving breast cancer, Susan Kaplow, a retired psychotherapist, began making art and was both gratified by the results of her disciplined effort and exceedingly comforted by certain Jewish customs and prayers. Astonished to hear a friend say she found "nothing" in Jewish tradition that was comforting, Kaplow wanted to inspire those facing serious illness to craft creative spiritual/healing responses to their own circumstance. To this end, she gathered examples describing inspiration and comfort that people did attain from Jewish tradition and designed these testimonials into a limited-edition book combining text with her own art.[16]
- "I'm not religious but my art is," says Robert Kirschbaum, an accomplished artist/printmaker whose minimalist images explore mystical numerology and the ancient Holy Temple. Raised in a secular environment, he nonetheless absorbed the fundamental idea that "Jews are a people whose experience has been shaped by exile and who long to return to our most sacred space." When personal hardships and post-9/11 issues weighed heavily on his creative spirit (his studio was near Ground Zero), the *Akeidah* (Binding of Isaac) and the symbol of the Temple as a sacred space served as potent metaphors for the universal aspiration for repair and redemption, allowing him, somehow, to resume his creative work. Of this experience he says, "Though I don't normally speak in such personal terms about my

art-making process, making these images did indeed serve to pull me out of a nearly ten-year morass of grief, anger, and depression."[17]

- Los Angeles artist Rebecca Newman describes the surprising-to-her force with which she willed herself to make art after surviving a stroke. The series of photographs called *Modah Ani* (the prayer of gratitude upon awakening) was taken from her hospital bed when she was still paralyzed on her entire left side. After a terrifying night, without tactile sensation or muscular strength, she awoke so grateful to be alive, and to see the dawn brightening her hospital window, that she managed to raise the hospital bed and use her drinking water pitcher to hold up the camera. During a very slow recovery, she continued to feel that she "had to" devise ways to make art, despite limited mobility and motor control. For example, she continued to make prints though she was only able to move enough to manipulate the settings adjustments on a scanner printer. Within these limits, she made a strikingly beautiful series of prints.[18]

In addition to the healing aspects of creative practice for the artist, being in the presence of art can be healing and beneficial to patients. An example is the positive response to *Faraway Places*, an installation of original artwork done on behalf of patients in the intensive care unit of Hadassah Hospital in Jerusalem.[19] At the public presentation ceremony for the project, Professor Shlomo Mor-Yosef, former director general of the hospital, wrote of how art's

> presence provides a healing environment for people suffering from disease and illness.... Hadassah is not alone in believing in art and beauty's special properties. Psychological research has shown that art has a way of bypassing our defenses and entering our inner being, that its nurturing qualities can help the healing process. "When you're in a hospital, it's high stress. When we are high stress, we go back to our primal need to be soothed," says Upali Nanda, Vice President and Director of Research for American Art Resources. Scientific studies, she says, show that art can aid in

> the recovery of patients, shorten hospital stays and help manage pain.[20]

The descriptions in this chapter of how my art and that of other artists came about demonstrate how creative and spiritual processes parallel each other. Both are admittedly difficult subjective states to evaluate, and both provide an arena in which we attempt to make sense of and find meaning in our experience. When God instructs Bezalel to assemble artists who have a "heart of wisdom" to create/decorate the *Mishkan* (Tabernacle), the biblical text seems to be addressing this ancient wellness paradigm. Perhaps the healing brought about by these most challenging and necessary of attitudes is nothing less than a notion of faith—that when we act creatively, and instinctively, despite hardship and infirmity, when we do what we love in order to speak our truth, therein lies healing.

Part IV

Judaism, Psychology, and Health

Judaism and Addiction

Rabbi Abraham J. Twerski, MD

I hesitate to write on this topic. I am not aware of an article on "Judaism and Arthritis" or "Judaism and Osteoporosis." I see addiction as a disease, not as a moral failure. To discuss Judaism and addiction implies that there is something unique about Jews vis-à-vis the disease of addiction, and this is a mistake.

But while there is no difference in the nature of the addictive disease as it affects Jews, there are special features in how Jews react or adapt to addictions.

The prototype of addictions is *alcoholism,* and even if we were not raised in a Yiddish-speaking environment, we are probably familiar with the phrase "*shikker is a goy.*" The denial that is characteristic of alcoholism in the general population is greatly intensified among Jews, and this holds true for addiction to drugs, gambling, and sex. Only food addiction has escaped the stigma of *shonde* (disgrace), and this may be because Jewish mothers have traditionally said, "*Ess, ess, mein kindt*" (eat, eat, my child).

In 1978, Jewish members of Alcoholics Anonymous (AA) were invited to join professionals and community leaders in the UJA-Federation of New York Task Force on Alcoholism. This led to the development of the organization Jewish Alcoholics, Chemically Dependent Persons, and Significant Others (JACS). Through its retreats, workshops, dialogues, and support programs, JACS has directly and indirectly assisted thousands of addicted Jews and their families to reach recovery.

The backbone of recovery from addiction is the 12-step anonymous fellowships. Most meetings are held in churches. It is a rare synagogue that has hosted an AA meeting. Many addicts resist going to 12-step meetings because they do not wish to hear that they must give

---

Rabbi Abraham J. Twerski, MD, is founder and medical director emeritus of Gateway Rehabilitation Center in Moon Township, Pennsylvania.

up the addiction, but they do not admit this. Rather, they rationalize why the 12-step program is not for them, and Jewish addicts may say that they cannot join a non-Jewish program that meets in churches.

The Causes of Addiction

After all the theorizing, we do not know the cause of addiction. Many people take a *l'chayim* and do not become addicted. Many people take an opiate painkiller or a tranquilizer and do not become addicted. Many people visit a casino occasionally and do not become addicted. All we can say is that for some unknown reason, some people are affected by a chemical or a behavior in a way that they feel compelled to continue it, it becomes progressive, and stopping the chemical or behavior has physical and/or emotional effects. What we do know: "what all addicts have in common is the incomprehensibility of their seemingly willful descent into oblivion."[1] In alcoholism there is a genetic factor. Whether this is true in other addictions is not clear.

Jewish ethical writings are replete with descriptions of how the *yetzer hara*, the evil inclination within a person, can lead one into self-destructive behavior. The Talmud says, "A person's *yetzer hara* renews itself every day and seeks to destroy him, and if it were not that God helps him, one could not resist it."[2] The 12-step program says, "We admitted we were powerless over alcohol [drugs, gambling, sex, food]," and only "a Power greater than ourselves could restore us to sanity."[3] If we substitute "addiction" for the *yetzer hara*, we can see that both have a similar pattern, and the recovery process of both is similar.

One significant factor in the Jewish community is that "enabling" is very common. To put it simply, an addict will not be motivated to relinquish the addiction until the distress incident to the addiction exceeds the pleasure derived from it. This is called the "rock-bottom" phenomenon. Rock-bottom is highly variable. What is rock-bottom for one person may be nothing for another person.

The Jewish family, whether because of strong emotional ties or to avoid public shame, is likely to "help" the addict by removing the negative consequences—for example, by getting a lawyer to dismiss drunk-driving charges or by paying off the gambler's debts. With all good intentions, such "benevolent" acts actually reinforce the addictive behavior, hence it is referred to as "enabling." The rabbi may naively be impressed by the addict's remorse as *t'shuvah* and accept his promise to desist from the addictive behavior, a promise that he cannot possibly keep.

The Jewish family is particularly prone to keeping secrets. Anything that could reflect on the family's reputation is concealed. If Washington is interested in avoiding "leaks," they should study the Jewish family's skill in concealing blemishes. This secrecy is an obstacle to recovery, since recovery depends heavily on the addict and family members attending 12-step meetings, which may be avoided for fear of exposure.

Because of the intense secrecy, there are no valid statistics on the incidence of addiction in the Jewish community. Those of us in the treatment field believe that the incidence is no less than in the general population, but we have no statistics to prove it. However, it is our opinion that all addictions have proliferated in the Jewish community.

Modern technology has eliminated many of the miseries that were prevalent just several decades ago, leading people to believe that it is possible to lead a life full of pleasure. Consequently, we have become the most hedonistic society in world history. This was formalized in the 1960s, when the youth culture adopted the dictum "If it feels good, do it." I believe that this attitude, which essentially dismisses all restraint on pleasure seeking, is largely responsible for the plethora of addictions plaguing modern society. In addition to alcohol, drugs, gambling, sex, and food, we also have addiction to shopping, to the Internet, to electronic games, and to pornography.

All the addictions have in common that they are all destructive, but the addict disregards this. In Proverbs 1:17, Solomon says that the bird that goes for the bait disregards the net that will trap it. This is characteristic of the addict.

The Role of Spirituality in Recovery

The 12-step program grew out of the Oxford Group, an evangelical Christian movement. Yet, if we were to devise a recovery program based on Torah ethics, it would be, word for word, the 12 steps of AA. I elaborated on this in *Self-Improvement? I'm Jewish!*[4]

The reason that the 12 steps are effective for all addictions is because they have nothing to do specifically with alcohol. They are a program for *character transformation*. This was succinctly stated by an alcoholic who celebrated his twenty-fifth anniversary of sobriety, who said, "The man *I once was* drank, and the man *I once was* will drink again." His sobriety was due to the character transformation that he underwent as a result of living according to the 12 steps.

The primary ingredient that brings about this character transformation is *spirituality*. It is important to distinguish spirituality from religion. Religious Jews are not immune to addiction. I have had as patients devout and Torah-learned Jews whose addiction was no different from that of nonreligious Jews or gentiles. The drug and alcohol epidemic has penetrated even into the yeshivot. Unfortunately, there are some people who are ritually religious but may lack the spirituality of religion.

In *Happiness and the Human Spirit*, I define the human spirit as comprising a number of abilities that are unique to the human being and that distinguish man from other living things.[5] In addition to greater intelligence, some of the more obvious uniquely human features are (1) the ability to learn from the history of past generations, (2) the ability to search for truth, (3) the ability to reflect on the purpose and goals of life, (4) the ability to have a self-awareness, (5) the ability to volitionally improve oneself, (6) the ability to have perspective, to contemplate the future, and to think about future consequences of one's actions, (7) the ability to be considerate of others and to be sensitive to their needs, (8) the ability to sacrifice one's comfort and possessions for the welfare of others, (9) the ability to empathize, (10) the ability to make moral and ethical choices in defiance of strong bodily drives and urges, (11) the ability to forgive, (12) the ability to aspire, (13) the ability to delay gratification, and (14) the ability to be creative. Spirituality, then, is simply implementing these uniquely human features.

That every human being has these abilities is undeniable. Hence, every human being has a *spirit*. If we neglect the spirit, we are neglecting an essential and integral part of our person, and we are incomplete.

The eminent psychiatrist Carl G. Jung expressed his concept of alcoholism this way: "[The patient's] craving for alcohol was the equivalent, on a low level, of the spiritual thirst of our being for wholeness...."[6] This is true of all addictions. Spirituality is necessary for wholeness, hence spirituality is the *sine qua non* for recovery from addiction. That Judaism requires wholeness is evident in the first few words of God to the patriarch Abraham, "I am God [*El Shaddai*]. Walk before me and *be complete*" (Genesis 17:1). Completeness and wholeness require spirituality. In my definition of spirituality, I make no reference to God. However, it is difficult to conceptualize spirituality without a belief in God.

An outgrowth of Alcoholics Anonymous was the concept of "codependency," which deals with the problems of the addict's significant others. The addict often blames a spouse or parents or others for the addiction, but the fact is that no one is responsible for the addiction. Nevertheless, family members must know their role in the addict's recovery. As was noted earlier, family attempts to "help" the addict may backfire. It is extremely important that family members of the addict attend codependency meetings, such as Al-Anon, Nar-Anon, Gam-Anon, S-Anon, or CoDa. If there is anything unique about addiction in Jews, it is that family members and others concerned are *extremely* codependent. The addict often refuses to go to 12-step meetings but eventually can be prevailed upon. It is much more difficult to get family members to the codependency meetings.

The Need for Purpose

One of the uniquely human traits that constitutes the human spirit is "the ability to reflect on the purpose and goals of our lives."[7] Note that implementation of this trait is not necessarily *finding* a goal or purpose. Rather, it is the *contemplation and search* for a goal and purpose that make one spiritual.

There is an anecdote of two vagrants who were arrested for loitering and brought before a judge. The judge asked the first vagrant, "What were you doing when the officer arrested you?" "Nothing," the vagrant answered. The judge then turned to the second vagrant, "And what were you doing when you were arrested?" The man pointed toward his buddy. "I was helping him," he said. It is obvious that if you are helping someone who is doing nothing, you are doing nothing yourself.

If the universe was not created and designed for a specific purpose, but just "happened" to come about as a result of a freak accident that converted primordial energy into matter, which over billions of years evolved into life on the planet Earth, then the world as a whole has no specific purpose and there can be no ultimate purpose to the existence of humankind. It is meaningless to speak of an ultimate purpose in a world that is without purpose.

A person may dismiss this, saying, "The idea of an ultimate purpose does not concern me. I want to be healthy, with my family well, and have enough for my needs and a few luxuries. That's all I care about. The theologians and philosophers can worry about ultimate purpose, not me." This person is deceiving himself. Even if he is not concerned about ultimate purpose *consciously*, it is a concern that exists in his *subconscious* mind.

I believe that low self-esteem is a crucial factor in all psychological problems. We cannot have self-esteem if we do not feel important and purposeful. We value items for primarily one of two reasons: they are either functional or aesthetic. For example, if we have a beautiful grandfather clock that does not work, we keep it because it is a handsome piece of furniture. On the other hand, if a can opener goes dull and cannot open cans, we discard it. It has no aesthetic value.

Not too many people are so attractive as to have aesthetic value. Even people who are attractive are likely to lose their beauty as they age. A lasting feeling of value requires that we feel we have a function, that is, a purpose on earth. Only then can we have self-esteem.

My father used to tell a story about a vassal whose master sentenced him to twenty-five years of hard labor. His wrists were shackled to a massive wheel set in the wall, and all his waking hours he had to turn this massive wheel. He would wonder, "What am I doing? Perhaps I am grinding grain, or perhaps I am bringing up water for irrigation." When the twenty-five-year sentence was finally over and he was released, he immediately ran to see to what the wheel was attached. When he saw that it was not attached to anything, he collapsed. Twenty-five years of backbreaking work, all for nothing! This was an intolerable thought.

True, during our working years, we may be so occupied with our daily tasks that we may not have conscious concern about an ultimate purpose, but the idea does exist in the subconscious and may erode our self-esteem. Finally, when we retire and are not distracted by daily work, the idea may strike us. The feeling that all one's life was essentially for naught is terribly depressing.

A person who believes that God created the world for a specific purpose, known only to God, and via revelation or through prophets instructed humans to live in a way that this purpose would be fulfilled, can have an ultimate purpose. Inasmuch as the concept of God involves attributes such as infinity, eternity, omniscience, and omnipresence, qualities with which humans have never had any sensory experience, it is a suprarational concept. All claims to prove the existence of God logically are subject to argument, and in the final analysis, belief in God requires a "leap of faith." Indeed, natural disasters such as tsunamis, earthquakes, tornadoes, hurricanes, and incurable diseases of both children and adults defy any logical explanation for why a benevolent God would allow these to occur. A believer must go beyond logic, and this is the "leap of faith." The person who has traversed this leap and has a firm conviction of God as the Creator of the universe can reason to an ultimate purpose in his or her existence.

This is why the 12-step program, emphasizing the crucial role of spirituality, has as the third step, "Made a decision to turn our will and our lives over to the care of God as we understood Him."[8] The Gaon of Vilna said that man's purpose in creation is to transform the physical self into a spiritual self.[9] Inasmuch as this is the philosophy of Torah Judaism, it is identical to the character transformation required for recovery from addiction.

Diamond Processing Plant

I grew up in a Hasidic home and am fairly well-versed in Torah literature. Yet, I must admit that my involvement in treatment of addiction strengthened my Judaism.

In our prayers, we say of Torah, *ki heim chayeinu* (for it is our life). We thereby express our belief that the Torah way of life is dear to us. However, when an alcoholic who is sincere in recovery leaves an AA meeting, he or she feels, "If I deviate from this program, I will surely die." This is not figurative, but very literal. The addict has learned, through bitter experience, that drinking is a life-or-death issue. I have learned to take the expression *ki heim chayeinu* literally.

I became involved with alcoholism treatment in 1965 when, as director of St. Francis Hospital in Pittsburgh, I inherited a detoxification unit of thirty beds with a revolving-door policy. Although AA had been around since 1937, it was still not "respectable." This was before Betty Ford, Jason Robards, Senator Harold Hughes, and other notable personalities disclosed that they were alcoholics. There were a few rehabilitation facilities in the country. Medical insurance was not paying for addiction treatment. Against all odds, with the support of the hospital and the community, I established a one-hundred-bed rehabilitation center, which survived for years only by the grace of God. Our treatment facility now operates in two states, with many outpatient clinics. On any one day our staff serves over fifteen hundred clients.

In 1990, I was contacted by the director of the Israeli Prisoner Rehabilitation Program. Eighty percent of prisoners were there because of drug-related crimes, and he did not have an effective treatment program. We opened a pilot project, Shaar Hatikva, to demonstrate to the government that treatment is more cost-effective than prison. Without treatment, 80 percent of drug-related ex-convicts were returned to prison within the first year. Of those who went through our treatment program, the recidivism rate dropped from 80 percent to 20 percent! In spite of its great success, the government withdrew funding, and the program closed in 2000.

Among the first residents of the Shaar Hatikva program was thirty-four-year-old Yair, who spent sixteen of his thirty-four years in prison. When I spoke to the group about the importance of self-esteem in recovery, Yair said, "How can I have self-esteem? When I get out of jail, no one will give me a job. When the social worker tells my family that I'm soon to be released, they go ballistic. I'm a burden and embarrassment to them. They'd rather I'd be dead."

I said, "Yair, have you ever seen a display of diamonds in a jeweler's window? They are beautiful, scintillating, and extremely valuable. Do you know what a raw diamond looks like when it comes out of the mine? Like a worthless, dirty piece of glass. It is sent to the processing plant and emerges as a beautiful diamond.

"No one can put beauty into a dirty piece of glass. The beauty was always there, but lying in the earth for centuries, it was covered with grime. The processing plant removes all the grime that was covering it, polishes it, and exposes the beauty.

"Yair," I said, "I know nothing about diamonds, but I know something about people. You have a beautiful diamond within you, a holy *n'shamah* instilled in you by God. For decades, this *n'shamah* has been covered with grime. We can remove the grime and expose the diamond within you."

Yair stayed in our program for three months, then eight months in a transitional facility. Upon discharge, he got a job and a small apartment.

One day, Annette, the director of the transitional facility, received a call from a family. Their elderly mother had died and left an apartment full of furniture, which they wished to donate to the facility. She thanked them, then called Yair. "We have a donation of furniture, but I have no way of getting it here," she said. Yair said, "No problem. I'll get a truck and bring it."

Two days later, Yair called Annette: "I'm at the apartment with a truck, but there's no point in my bringing the furniture. It's old and dilapidated." Annette said, "I don't want to disappoint the family. Bring it."

The facility is on the second floor of a building, and as Yair dragged an old sofa up the stairs, an envelope fell from the cushions, containing 5,000 shekels. Yair used to break into a house for 20 shekels, and here he had 5,000 shekels and was the only person who knew of its existence. He returned the money to the family, who donated it to the facility.

When Annette told me about this, I said to Yair, "Do you remember that I said you had a diamond within you? Many 'honest' people would have pocketed the money. Yet, with your history, you turned in the money. That's the diamond within you."

When I visited the facility, Annette showed me a bronze plaque that Yair affixed to the front door. It reads, "Diamond Processing Plant."

Other Addictions

As mentioned earlier, food addiction has escaped the stigma of *shonde*, and there cannot be much denial when a person is visibly overweight. However, bulimic patients may have normal weight, and they are generally not in denial to themselves the way the alcoholic is. They are very ashamed of their behavior, inducing vomiting, fasting, exercising, and using laxatives and diuretics, and their secrecy is so thick that parents of an adolescent girl may have no idea that their adolescent daughter is bulimic. If they do discover it, they may resist her getting treatment, chastising her to "quit this crazy behavior," totally unaware that she is unable to do so.

One addiction that often goes unrecognized is "addiction to people." A person may latch onto someone and demand their constant attention. They may impose themselves personally or make multiple phone calls. I have had calls from rabbis who cannot free themselves of someone who gives them no peace. When the rabbi leaves for vacation, they demand to have the rabbi's phone number. If they are refused, they are not beyond threatening suicide. Regrettably, there is no 12-step program for "people addiction."

The Internet has spawned more addictions. There are youngsters who are addicted to video games, neglecting their school work and losing sleep. There are people of all ages who spend many hours at the computer, skipping meals and staying up all hours of the night. There are some therapists who treat these addictions, but to the best of my knowledge, there is no support group like AA.

A particularly dangerous addiction is Internet pornography. Prior to the Internet, people were hesitant to go to the smut stores for fear someone would recognize them there. However, the Internet delivers the smut to the privacy of one's home or office or to a handheld smartphone. Many people who believe that watching porn is immoral are nevertheless unable to stop, and this addiction shows no immunity.

Women who discover that their husbands watch pornography feel betrayed, and it has ruined many marriages. They lose trust in their husbands. In addition, it is a "slippery slope," sometimes leading to acting out sexually. The website GuardYourEyes (www.guardyoureyes.com) has developed effective measures for people with pornography addictions. SA (Sexaholics Anonymous) and SLA (Sex & Love Anonymous) meetings are very helpful.

Compulsive gambling is not a new problem, but the incidence has increased greatly, due to the legalized gambling of the lotteries, poker on TV, and the proliferation of casinos. Jews are well represented in compulsive gambling, as I indicated in my book *Compulsive Gambling—More Than Dreidle*.[10] Religious Jews are far from immune to this problem.

Experts are referring to the increase in teenage gambling as "explosive." One research study revealed that 4 to 8 percent of adolescents have a serious gambling problem, with another 10 to 14 percent being at high risk of becoming compulsive gamblers.[11] In an alarming report from the American Psychological Association, it was found that problem gambling among adolescents is increasing at a much faster rate than among adults.[12] Another study showed that high school students who gamble are 2.5 times more likely as adults to become problem gamblers.[13] It is projected that teenage gambling will be an even greater youth problem than alcohol and drugs. Some examples:

- A seventeen-year-old male in New Jersey owed $4,000 to a bookie.
- A nineteen-year-old college student was panic-stricken because he had lost a semester's tuition money on sports betting at school and did not know how to tell his parents that he would have to come home.
- A sixteen-year-old girl says she just could not stop buying lottery tickets, and when she ran out of money she stole from her mother's purse. When asked how she purchased tickets at age sixteen, she said that older friends would buy them for her.

A recovered compulsive gambler shares his story:

> My *bubbe* was very religious. She could've been a rabbi. To prepare me for my bar mitzvah, she sent me to a rabbi to learn my haftarah, and she gave me money to give the rabbi for tuition. Many weeks I would keep the money and not go to the rabbi. At my bar mitzvah, I did not know the haftarah and my *bubbe* was very upset. I used to go to the track on Rosh Hashanah and Yom Kippur.[14]

I published this man's life story of addiction in my book *Compulsive Gambling*. Here is another story:

> For Justin Baum's twenty-first birthday, his friends took him to the Palms, where he played his first game of casino poker.
>
> After several return visits and time spent watching televised poker tournaments such as the World Series of Poker, Baum became skilled at reading his opponents and started winning—sometimes raking in pots worth thousands of dollars.
>
> But Baum didn't know when to stop. He fought off sleep with Red Bull and coffee during his longest gambling session, which lasted about seventy straight hours.
>
> "I always played until I was broke," he said. "I'd stay out for three days in a row and come home and sleep for three days."
>
> To feed his poker habit, Baum stole money from his parents and borrowed from friends, who were told that the money was for car payments or other needs. One day he left his job at a pharmaceutical plant to gamble and didn't return.[15]

Many parents are in denial. They refuse to think that the missing money is due to their adolescent child's stealing for gambling. As I pointed out, Jewish families are unaware of the nature of compulsive gambling, naively accepting worthless promises that "it won't happen again." They also tend to pay off the gambler's debts and hire attorneys to extricate him or her from the legal consequences of the gambling.

It is absolutely crucial that Jews shed their naiveté about all addictions and familiarize themselves with these conditions, which may occur in your spouse, children, parents, or siblings, though you may be oblivious of it. The earlier the problem is recognized, the better the chance of recovery and avoiding the often disastrous consequences.

All addictions share a commonality, which is the distorted logic of the addict. Unless we understand this, we can run around in circles while the condition progresses. For more information, I discuss the unique, logical-sounding but totally unrealistic thinking of the addict in my book *Addictive Thinking*.[16]

❖

Gratitude

Perspectives from Positive Psychology and Judaism

David Pelcovitz, PhD

The emerging field of positive psychology focuses on individual strengths and resilience, rather than psychological difficulties and psychopathology. By emphasizing how we can better understand and develop the underpinnings of happiness, resilience, and optimism, this field aims to maximize our ability to cultivate strengths in ourselves and others. In a seminal work in positive psychology, psychologists Christopher Peterson and Martin Seligman identify gratitude as among the most valuable character strengths.[1] This chapter will focus on recent psychological research on the benefits of gratitude, with an emphasis on how a better understanding of gratitude can enhance work in health setting. Approaches to enhance the mindful cultivation of gratitude will also be reviewed, as well as perspectives on gratitude contained in Jewish sources.

Recent research has viewed gratitude as both a disposition and an emotion.[2] As a disposition, gratitude is an approach toward life that is focused on what one has as opposed to what is lacking. Such an optimistic approach to life is characterized by an ability to focus on the positive in the present moment and an ability to appreciate nature, as well as one's family, friends, and community. As an emotion, gratitude is a feeling of appreciation one experiences after receiving help from others. Studies in positive psychology have consistently documented that whether viewed as an emotion or disposition, gratitude is consistently associated with higher levels of physical and emotional well-being.

David Pelcovitz, PhD, holds the Gwendolyn and Joseph Straus Chair in Psychology and Jewish Education and is a professor at the Azrieli Graduate School of Jewish Education and Administration of Yeshiva University in New York, New York.

In terms of associations between gratitude and psychological adjustment, grateful people are more likely than their less grateful counterparts to be happy, low in anxiety, agreeable, and open to the input of others.[3] Given the central role that thankfulness has in prayer as well as action in Jewish thought, it is of particular note that in a large-scale study of the role of religion in mental illness,[4] thankfulness in a religious context was found to have a unique role in protecting individuals from risk for both internalizing disorders such as depression, phobias, anxiety, and eating disorders and externalizing disorders such as substance abuse and antisocial behavior.

Gratitude and Physical Health

In addition to the psychological benefits of gratitude, a number of recent studies have found an association between gratitude and physical health. In one of the best known studies of the gratitude-health connection,[5] three groups were asked to make weekly entries into a journal. One group was told to count their blessings by listing five things that they were grateful for, the count-your-burdens group was asked to list five hassles that bothered them in the previous week, and the third group wrote about five events that took place in that week. The gratitude group reported fewer health complaints than the other two groups and exercised ninety minutes longer each week than did the participants in the count-your-burdens group.

There are a number of pathways that help explain the connection between gratitude and health. One likely source is the ability of gratitude to serve as a buffer against ongoing stress. In a longitudinal study of over one thousand older adults, researchers found that the physical impact of chronic stress caused by living in deteriorated neighborhoods was reduced in individuals who had high levels of gratitude to God.[6] Gratitude has also been found to impact on quality of sleep—another correlate of health. In this line of research, studies have documented a connection between having grateful thoughts just before falling asleep and feeling more rested the next day. In an investigation of 401 subjects recruited from a community sample,[7] those who scored high on measures of gratitude as a stable personality trait reported longer sleep duration, lower levels of daytime problems because of sleepiness, and a subjective sense of having slept well. The improved sleep appeared to be related to pre-sleep thoughts such as thinking about "enjoyable things I did during the last few days" just before falling asleep.

These findings are particularly relevant to work with chronically ill populations. Emmons and his colleagues randomly assigned patients with chronic neuromuscular disorders to a group that did a count-your-blessings exercise every evening just before falling asleep and a comparison group that completed daily experience rating forms every evening. Here, too, the patients assigned to the gratitude group reported getting more hours of sleep and feeling more rested during the next day than did the comparison group. Emmons notes that among the health benefits of improved sleep are lower levels of stress hormones and improved immune system functioning relative to those with impaired sleep. He concludes that "if you want to sleep more soundly, count blessings, not sheep."[8]

There is also evidence that gratitude is related to improved cardiovascular functioning. In experiments measuring heart-brain interactions, researchers found that when subjects focus on feelings of appreciation, the heart produces smooth rhythms that enhance communication between the heart and the brain. These changes are associated with a number of cardiovascular benefits such as lower blood pressure and heart rates[9] and are in sharp contrast to the unstable patterns evident when subjects focus on negative emotions such as anger or anxiety.

Gratitude and Coping with Difficulty

Those who receive high scores on scales that measure gratitude have been found to be more likely to have a sense of purpose in life as well as an ability to respond to life's challenges with an increased focus on personal and interpersonal growth.[10] For example, one of the more robust predictors of psychological recovery in those most directly impacted by the 9/11 attacks was the ability to let go of anger and focus on either helping others or cultivating enhanced feelings of gratitude for what they had.[11] Similarly, research on post-traumatic stress disorder (PTSD) in Vietnam War veterans suggests that low levels of gratitude might be a risk factor for PTSD and that when veterans with PTSD are able to cultivate feelings of gratitude, their trauma symptoms result in less impairment in their daily lives than PTSD patients with low levels of gratitude.[12]

In a study that illustrates how various approaches to dealing with life's challenges can affect coping with serious illness, University of Connecticut researchers found that after suffering a heart attack, how cardiac patients understood the underlying causes of their illness had a powerful impact on their long-term prognosis. Those who responded with anger—blaming others for their cardiac impairment—were more likely to have another heart attack in the next eight years than were those who responded with reordered priorities and an increased ability to focus on what was valuable in their life.[13]

A number of years ago I was involved in a study of how parents react to the stress of having a child with cancer. Almost immediately after the study began, my voice mail was inundated with messages from the research assistants conducting the interviews. They reported an almost universal complaint on the part of the parents of the ill children: "The questions being asked in the study only focus on the negative impact of our child's illness; why haven't you asked any questions about the positive changes that our family experienced as a result of the experience of dealing with a life-threatening illness in our child?" A series of questions was added investigating the positive aspects of their experience confronting one of the most harrowing experiences life can offer. Their answers resulted in the most valuable findings of the study.

The following example given by a mother of a child being treated for leukemia is a typical illustration of the study participants' view of positive family changes in response to coping with their child's illness:

> Before my child was diagnosed with acute lymphoblastic leukemia the most important priority in my life was perfecting my tennis serve. About six months after my child was diagnosed, my husband was spending the evening in the hospital with my son. As I was preparing to go to the hospital the next morning, my doorbell rang. My next-door neighbor was crying. There had been a storm during the evening, and her car had been completely destroyed when a tree that was between my house and hers was felled by the strong wind. I did my best to calm her down, calling her insurance adjuster and driving her to her job. Once she entered her office, I began laughing to myself. What would have happened

had the wind blown in the opposite direction and destroyed my car instead? Had my car been destroyed I would have calmly said to myself, "I better call a taxi," and eventually I would have found time to fix the car. Although six months earlier I would have had the same reaction as my neighbor, my scale of priorities had totally shifted. I know what's important in life. What's important is to be with my son and let my husband get some rest after his long night in the hospital. Material concerns mean very little to me now.

Gratitude and Values Education

From the viewpoint of parents and educators, a number of benefits result from teaching children to be thankful. As a purely practical matter, when children express gratitude, it makes it more likely that their benefactor will continue to act kindly toward them in the future. Perhaps more importantly, from the perspective of character education, the expression of gratitude also makes it more likely that the recipient will be generous to others.[14] Perhaps by focusing their attention on thankfulness for what they receive, we develop their ability to give.

Gratitude has also been associated with living life in an authentic manner, characterized by the ability to integrate one's beliefs and values regardless of external pressures.[15] Psychologists talk of the dangers of too much emphasis on "impression management"—educating children in a manner that places more emphasis on external impressions and material acquisition rather than on inner growth.[16] Children raised in a manner that lacks authenticity are at risk for developing superficial personalities that lack depth and empathy. Being raised in an atmosphere that prioritizes the impressions of others over an internalized sense of what is right inevitably leads to risk for unethical behavior when the child is alone and feels that nobody will ever find out.

When the acquisition of wealth and possessions is at the center of one's daily pursuits, risk for depression and social and academic difficulties often result. Research has documented that in adults materialism is correlated with low self-esteem, impaired social connections, and a lack of meaning and purpose in life.[17] Studies of children find similar difficulties when materialistic values dominate, with the added finding that such children are at increased risk for academic and family difficulties. Positive psychology research views gratitude as an antidote to the heavy costs of materialism, since, by its very nature, gratitude involves a focus on appreciating what one has been given by others rather than harboring feelings of envy and resentment for what others have.[18]

Perspective on Gratitude from Jewish Sources

Where does the name "Jew," *Yehudi*, come from?[19] Why are we not called "Hebrew" or "Israelite," as we were classified in early times? The reason, according to Rabbinic sources, is that the root of the name "Yehudah" is "to thank"—to express gratitude. Judah was the fourth son of Leah, and she felt a profound sense of gratitude when he was born. There was a tradition that Jacob was destined to have twelve sons who would constitute the twelve tribes of Israel. Since Jacob had four wives, it was assumed that each wife would be allocated three sons. When Leah gave birth to a fourth son, she was overwhelmed with a sense of thanksgiving: "She conceived again, and bore a son and declared, 'This time let me gratefully praise *Adonai*'; therefore she called his name Judah; then she stopped giving birth" (Genesis 29:35). Rashi comments, "I have taken more than my share, so I now need to give thanks."[20]

According to this perspective, a core component of Jewish identity is an underlying sense of gratitude to God, a continual recognition of being the recipient of heavenly blessings—the antithesis of a sense of entitlement. A Jew must acknowledge that he is a debtor who owes so much to his past—to his forebears and his progenitors; he is not a creditor to whom something is owed. This attribute of gratitude is reflected in his name and his identity, and it shapes his essential character: *Yehudi*.

Another indication of the enormous importance that Jewish thought places on our obligation to express gratitude is the following midrash: "In the future, all sacrifices will be abolished except for the thanksgiving offering. All prayers will be abolished except for prayers of gratitude."[21] Given the central role that sacrifices and prayer serve in Jewish life, this midrash is teaching us the central significance of gratitude. The need to express gratitude will remain even at a time that other spiritual duties and obligations will no longer be necessary.

Our Rabbis teach us that a key aspect of the experience of bringing the *korban todah* (thanksgiving offering) is the social component.

When bringing a thanksgiving sacrifice after being saved from a life-threatening event, people were required to bring forty loaves of bread in four different forms as well. One of each kind was given to the *kohein* (priest), leaving thirty-six loaves that had to be consumed that day and the following night. Sforno, a medieval classic commentator on the Torah, explains that this was to ensure that at the time that people expressed gratitude for their good fortune, they had no choice but to make this a social event. Included in this occasion was sharing their food while recounting to others the story of the lifesaving incident.[22]

An example of how far Jewish educators take this obligation is typified by the life of Holocaust survivor Rabbi Yisroel Zev Gustman, who was the head of Yeshiva Netzech Yisroel in Jerusalem. Rabbi Gustman insisted on carefully caring for the trees and bushes in his garden, even though his students frequently offered to help him perform these seemingly menial gardening chores. He explained that during the war, he hid from the Nazis in a forest where the shelter of the bushes and fruit of the trees repeatedly saved his life. He felt that caring for these trees and bushes was a necessary expression of gratitude to these instruments of his survival.

Ingratitude

Researchers have found that most individuals find feelings of indebtedness to be unpleasant. Many individuals are uncomfortable with feeling dependent on others. A favor creates an inherent sense of discomfort; it forces one to reciprocate and feel obliged. The recipient is now a debtor, he owes his benefactor and that makes him uncomfortable, so he tries to minimize and belittle the favor. Rabbi Shimshon Dovid Pincus points out that the Hebrew expression for "ingratitude," *kafui tov*, is related to the Hebrew word *kafa*, meaning "to be forced or pressured." For example, the Rabbis tell us that if an individual resists fulfilling an obligation in a religious court, the court is authorized to pressure him until he acquiesces. The term expressing this is *kofim oso*—they pressure or force him. Similarly, when the Jews were given the Torah at Sinai and were reluctant, at first, to accept, the Gemara says, "*Kafa aleihem*"—God tilted the mountain over them, threatening to annihilate them unless they agreed.[23] Based on this, Rabbi Pincus submits that, frequently, when a favor is done for a person, he feels obligated and even pressured to pay back the debt of gratitude that he owes to his benefactor. This creates a sense of imbalance, an uncomfortable feeling of dependence fueled by a sense of indebtedness and a need to reciprocate.[24]

Rabbi Yitzchak Hutner, reflecting the writings of the Maharal on the seriousness of ingratitude, writes of the seriousness of failing to be grateful:

> When a person receives a benefit from his fellow, a seed of Hesed [kindness] is planted in his world. If the nature of Hesed is functioning healthily and properly, this seed cannot but give rise to additional Hesed. But if the person is an ingrate, it is as if he uproots the sprouting of Hesed with his bare hands. Without a doubt, uprooting a planting of Hesed is even more antithetical to the essence of Hesed than is simply being uninvolved in matters of Hesed.... An ingrate damages and destroys the very attribute of Hesed.... One who is ungrateful to his fellow in this way; it is as if he is ungrateful to God, because his denial (*kefirah*) is a response not (just) to the particular act of Hesed that was done for him, but (also) to attribute of Hesed in the broadest sense.[25]

In light of this interpretation of ingratitude, it is not surprising to find the following statement made by the Maharal: "It is forbidden to do acts of *chesed* for one who will not respond with gratitude. For this reason, it didn't rain until man was created to pray for the rain."[26]

To the extent that ingratitude is viewed as heresy, the Maharal's position is understandable. We are not allowed to put an individual in a position where he or she is, in essence, ungrateful to God, and, at the same time, undermining one of the basic building blocks of humanity.

Habituation

The enemy of gratitude is habituation. The way the human brain works is that we quickly become accustomed to even the most spectacular of gifts.

I gave a paper at a beautiful resort in Hawaii. Surrounded by magnificent waterfalls, spectacular scenery, and unforgettable sunsets, I engaged one of the hotel staff in conversation. I asked him if it is possible to ever get used to working in such a remarkable setting. He answered, "To me this is just a job; I don't notice the beauty anymore. I drag my feet coming to work every Monday morning just like everybody else."

Related to this aspect of human nature is the unfortunate reality that we tend to be least grateful to those closest to us. Research on the psychology of gratitude has found that people tend to be more grateful for the unexpected. Human nature is such that we experience less gratitude for favors done for us by family and close friends than when somebody whom we are less close to does the same favor.[27]

The tendency toward habituation is also seen in the relationship between man and God. In the classic work *Duties of the Heart* (*Chovos HaLevavos*), Rabbeinu Bachya details the reasons for our ingratitude to God:

> Human beings ... grow up so accustomed to God's abounding favors that [these favors] seem routine and ordinary to them, as if they were innate, interminable, and inseparable from them for the rest of their lives. When their intelligence develops and their perception sharpens, they remain ignorant of God's favors. It does not occur to them that they have an obligation to express gratitude for them, because they realize neither the magnitude of the favor nor [the magnitude] of the One Who bestows it.[28]

Contrast this to the following incident that beautifully illustrates how, in the face of an extremely stressful chronic situation, individuals can show gratitude for even the most basic human experience: At a retreat for families of children with severe cognitive and physical limitations, I met with a family who had an eight-year-old daughter who was born with such profound brain damage that she was unable to speak or engage in even the most basic self-care functions. Her mother told me that for the first four years of her daughter's life she was unable to sit up, and the family was given little hope that this most basic of human activities would ever be possible. The child's parents heard of a program overseas that offered intensive physical therapy for their daughter's condition, having some limited success in working with these children. After years of visits to this program, their daughter was now able to sit up. The parents called over the counselor who was caring for their daughter at the retreat and with intense excitement showed me how this eight-year-old girl was now able to see the world from the perspective added by her newfound ability to sit. The girl flashed a million-dollar smile at her parents, who met the smile with tears of pride and gratitude.

The obvious lesson taught by these remarkable parents is that it is possible to have gratitude for even the most basic of gifts given to us on a daily basis. The challenge is finding a way, under normal circumstances, to continually remind ourselves, as Rabbeinu Bachya writes, of the "superabundance of Divine favors which [we] experience continuously."[29] Developing awareness of what to be grateful for even when life is going smoothly can require conscious effort and constant practice. Without practice, this trait will not flow naturally from humans' innate tendencies. The default setting is habituation.

Overcoming Habituation: Developing a Habit of Attention

Breathing is the most natural and reflexive continuous action of a person. The Sages, noting the similarity between the Hebrew word *n'shamah* (soul) and the Hebrew word *n'shimah* (breath), comment on the verse "Let all souls praise God" (Psalm 150:6) that we should praise and thank the Almighty for every breath.[30] This is the ultimate example of their awareness of continually working on the need to overcome the tendency toward habituation.

Psychologists tell us that the antidote to habituation is consciously being mindful of how fortunate our condition is and how it could have been otherwise. While not easy, we can develop a habit of awareness, a habit of attention.

Gregg Krech, an author and counselor who specializes in the psychology of gratitude,[31] walks us through a disastrous Monday morning that is destined for catastrophe from the moment the alarm clock fails to wake us, all the way through to a near-death experience driving to work. The series of mishaps culminates when faced with an angry tirade from the boss after arriving so late for work. It is only when things go wrong that our attention is grabbed. It takes such an "out of the ordinary" event to bring us to an awareness and appreciation of a "normal" day. Krech points out, "What would happen if we turn the story around and experience a day when the alarm goes off as intended and you arrive at work without unexpected traffic or accidents?" How do we cultivate an approach to life that pays attention to the expected?

Perhaps the most potent antidote to habituation, from a Jewish perspective, is the daily experience of prayer. One-third of the prayers in the daily service address the theme of gratitude. What can be a more powerful answer to the challenge posed by Krech than thanking God three times a day with words expressing gratitude for the "miracles that surround us every day"? Of course, this, too, is a challenge. It is difficult to concentrate on the meaning of words said during prayer, and many experience the need to emotionally connect to the meaning of these words as a continual challenge. However, as we discussed, there are multiple spiritual and emotional benefits that emerge from concentrating on connecting to prayer in a manner that cultivates a habit of attention to what we should be grateful for.

Recommendations from Positive Psychology Research on Cultivating Gratitude

Counting One's Blessings

As noted earlier, subjects who were asked to write about five things they were grateful for during the past week felt better about their lives as a whole, were more optimistic about the future, and felt physically better than did the comparison groups.

In a review of the research measuring the efficacy of this technique,[31] researchers summarize seven studies that found significant increases in feelings of well-being when people think about what they should be grateful for in this systematic manner. Of course, it is not necessary to write down what you are grateful for on a list. Going around the table during Friday night meals and asking family members to share what they are grateful for that week can reap similar benefits. This has the added advantage of increasing family members' knowledge of details about each other's life—a benefit that has independent advantages, according to research in family psychology.[33]

Direct Expression of Gratitude

Directly expressing thanks leads to even more dramatic benefits. In a study done by Seligman and his colleagues,[34] adults were given one week to write and then deliver a letter of gratitude in person to someone who had been especially kind to them but had never been properly thanked. Happiness levels of the individuals who carried out this exercise increased substantially for a month after they paid the visit to their benefactor.

A teacher was speaking to an eleventh-grade student who said that her love of learning came from a third-grade teacher whose enthusiasm for teaching continued to inspire the student even eight years later. The teacher asked, "Did you ever thank your third-grade teacher or even let her know of the way she changed your life?" When the student answered "no," she immediately asked her to go into a private area of the school office to write a note expressing her gratitude to the teacher. Both the student and the recipient of the note described the experience as deeply meaningful.

Developing a Grateful Personality

Research has found that overcoming the natural tendencies that serve as impediments to gratitude can help to cultivate a personality that is more likely to be grateful. The following characteristics serve as impediments to gratitude:

1. ***Self-preoccupation***: When we are self-preoccupied, little room is left for us to notice the needs of others. This calls for developing the muscle of empathy and awareness of the needs of others, which is one of the building blocks of gratitude.
2. ***Expectation***: Human nature is such that we tend to no longer be grateful or attentive to something that is expected and routine. What gets our attention is when our expectations are not met. A possible antidote is to develop the habit of paying attention to the lessons learned when our expectations are not met. When you are confronted with periods of illness instead of expected good health, once your health returns it is doubly important to try to hold on to the feelings of gratitude for good health.
3. ***Entitlement***: The feelings of entitlement that often accompany the many luxuries of day-to-day life in an affluent

society serve to block our awareness of how grateful we should be for the many gifts we regularly experience. When feelings of entitlement dominate, gratitude will, by definition, take a backseat. The antidote is to pay attention to the daily life of those less fortunate than we are. Periodic exposure to those living in poverty or with illness and disabilities can serve as an important antidote to entitlement.

Keeping a Journal

As noted earlier, systematically writing about what we are grateful for can have powerful benefits. There are many disciples of the early *baalei mussar* (moral teachers), such as Rabbi Yisroel Salanter, Rabbi Yitzchak Blazer, and others, who have transmitted to their students either orally or in their writings that these great *mussar* teachers had a practice of keeping what was called a *pinkus* (a notebook or diary) on their nightstand. They would record their experiences of the day and the lessons they learned from the previous day's activities before retiring for the night.

In other cultures as well, such as Japan, there is a similar practice called *naikan* (introspection). This is a way of life for many, marked by structured self-reflection that, in that culture, helps develop a sense of gratitude. Practitioners of *naikan* ask themselves the following three questions related to gratitude during their daily meditation: (1) What have I *received* from others? (2) What have I *given* to others? (3) What troubles and difficulties have I *caused* others? Whether in writing or thought, a daily *cheshbon hanefesh* (self-assessment) that includes reflection on our levels of gratitude and transcendence of self-involvement can be an important aspect of developing this trait.

Conclusion

The new discipline of positive psychology has signaled a paradigm shift in the mental health field. Instead of focusing on what is wrong with an individual, positive psychology systematically studies how to actively nurture strengths. At a practical level, this leads to empirical investigations into how to understand and promote positive emotions such as gratitude rather than a focus on mental illness. Positive psychologists are less interested in anger than in forgiveness; they are more likely to try to understand gratitude than cynicism. One of the founders of positive psychology, Dr. Martin Seligman, points out how when parents dream of how they want their child to be as an adult, their focus is not on raising a child who is not depressed or anxious but on a child who embraces life with joy and enthusiasm. This chapter has reviewed what recent research and practice have taught us about the benefits of overcoming habituation in order to cultivate feelings of gratitude. An integration of the wisdom of Jewish thinking on this value coupled with the emerging insights of this young field hopefully will enhance our ability to be helpful to those who turn to us in times of need.

Jewish Religious Coping and Trust in God

A Review of the Empirical Literature

David H. Rosmarin, PhD, Devora Greer Shabtai, Steven Pirutinsky, MS, and Kenneth I. Pargament, PhD

For more than a century, many leaders in psychology and related disciplines have theorized regarding the relationship between religion and mental health.[1] For the most part, it was widely asserted that religion exacerbates symptoms of mental disorders.[2] Over the past twenty years, however, a different approach to this subject matter has emerged, one grounded in empiricism. In fact, the recent proliferation of psychological research about religion and spirituality—over five thousand scientific studies to date—is nothing short of remarkable.[3]

Applying an empirical approach to the psychology of religion highlighted the shortcomings of previously held assumptions and led to a clearer understanding of the complex interactions between religion and mental health. In the general population, the overwhelming majority of empirical studies have indicated that greater basic religious observance (e.g., church attendance, Bible study) is modestly associated with better mental health and psychosocial functioning. Specifically, studies have found religiousness to be related to lower levels of depression and

---

David H. Rosmarin, PhD, is an instructor of psychiatry and an assistant psychologist at McLean Hospital / Harvard Medical School in Belmont, Massachusetts, and director of the Center for Anxiety in New York, New York. Devora Greer Shabtai is a psychology major at Stern College for Women, Yeshiva University, in New York, New York. Steven Pirutinsky, MS, is a doctoral student of counseling and clinical psychology at Teachers College, Columbia University, in New York, New York. Kenneth I. Pargament, PhD, is a professor of psychology at Bowling Green State University in Bowling Green, Ohio and Distinguished Scholar in the Institute for Spirituality & Health at the Texas Medical Center.

anxiety[4] and enhanced coping with life struggles.[5] However, research has also shown that religious life can have negative effects on mental health and functioning. A growing body of literature has documented that spiritual struggles—such as anger at God, existential/religious doubt, and interpersonal religious conflict—are robust predictors of general anxiety and affective symptoms.[6]

One significant limitation of this body of literature, however, is that very few of the empirical findings or related theory apply specifically to the Jewish community. While Jews represent only 2 to 3 percent of the population in the United States and 0.22 percent of the world population,[7] there are nevertheless over thirteen million Jews worldwide, six million of whom reside in North America.[8] Furthermore, meta-analytic findings suggest that Jews may have a marginally elevated risk for depression and anxiety compared to the general population,[9] creating a public health need for specific study within this population. However, two major obstacles have impeded progress in this area of investigation.

First, recent mental health research on religion has moved beyond simple assessments of religious involvement (e.g., belief in God, religious service attendance) to employ measures of proximal components of religiousness that are theoretically tied to mental health and functioning.[10] Examples include religious coping,[11] perceived closeness to God,[12] sanctification,[13] and religious/spiritual struggles.[14] While this development has greatly enhanced the empirical study of religion and mental health by explaining not just *whether* but *how* religion can be tied to psychological functioning, some measures of these constructs are inappropriate to use in a Jewish context due to predication on Christian doctrine and culture and utilization of Christian language (e.g., "church"). Across the various Jewish denominations, Judaism differs considerably from Christianity with regard to the emphasis placed on personal religious beliefs, personal connection to God, social justice, doctrinal practices, and religious motivations.[15] Specific scales and measures are therefore necessary to study Judaism and mental health, yet these have been unavailable until recently.

A second, and perhaps more important, barrier to the proliferation of research on Judaism and mental health is that few academicians have taken up the charge to launch programmatic research on this subject matter. Nevertheless, several well-designed studies have been conducted and are worth review. To this end, this chapter will discuss the two best-developed areas of empirical research on Judaism and mental health: (1) religious coping and (2) trust in God. For each area, we review research from both the general population and the Jewish community while discussing themes that have emerged from the findings to inform what about Judaism appears to be relevant to mental health. We then explore theoretical and conceptual foundations more broadly and discuss the unique contributions of both programs of study to the psychology of religion as a whole.

Religious Coping

Research on Religious Coping in the General Population

One of the most universal psychological functions of religious faith and practice is enhanced coping with suffering, pain, and other difficult life circumstances. Throughout time, individuals have looked to a Higher Power to provide comfort and support in times of distress.[16] It is therefore not surprising that religious coping—the process of drawing upon religious beliefs and practices to handle distress—is the most widely investigated construct in the psychology of religion today. The empirical study of religious coping has identified two distinct categories, involving (1) positive and (2) negative strategies.[17] Positive religious coping involves the adaptive and functional utilization of religious belief and practice to cope with life distress. Common examples include benevolent religious appraisals (e.g., perceiving one's circumstance as part of God's plan), active religious surrender (e.g., turning a difficult situation to God once one has done one's best), seeking spiritual support (e.g., speaking to clergy), and spiritual connection (e.g., building a stronger spiritual connection with God or others). By contrast, negative religious coping—or "spiritual struggles"—reflects signs of spiritual stress and strain within oneself, with others, and with God. Negative religious coping includes reappraisal of God's powers (e.g., reexamining one's faith and concluding that some things are beyond God's control), passive religious deferral (e.g., expecting God to solve all of one's problems without exertion of effort), and interpersonal religious discontent (e.g., arguments with members of one's religious community).[18]

As one might expect, positive religious coping can be a powerful aid for individuals undergoing difficult life events, while negative religious coping can exacerbate distress. Specifically, cross-sectional studies have linked positive religious coping to lower levels of emotional distress and psychosomatic symptoms[19] as well as better physical health outcomes.[20] Similarly, several studies—some of them conducted with national samples—have identified associations between negative religious coping and higher levels of anxiety and depression,[21] decreased self-esteem,[22] and even post-traumatic symptoms.[23] Meta-analytic findings suggest that these trends are significant across the extant literature on this subject matter.[24] More importantly, several prospective studies have found that positive and negative religious coping differentially predict better versus worse psychological adjustment over time, suggesting a possible causal relationship between these variables. For example, in a group of elderly, hospitalized patients assessed over a two-year period, positive religious coping predicted improvements predictive of changes in both mental and physical health, whereas negative methods of religious coping predicted declines in health and even illness-related mortality.[25] Similarly, high levels of positive religious coping and low levels of spiritual struggle have been associated with improvements in health over time among individuals with HIV[26] and patients undergoing kidney transplants,[27] and better adjustment to divorce.[28]

Jewish Religious Coping: An Empirical Approach

Before 2001, virtually all research on religious coping had focused exclusively on Christians, and only two studies were conducted within the Jewish community. In the first, Dubow and associates[29] investigated a sample of Jewish adolescents and found that Jewish ethnic identity served as a resource for coping with life stressors. The second study, conducted by Loewenthal and colleagues,[30] provided initial evidence that religious beliefs and spiritual support were related to positive affect among Jews who recently experienced a major life stressor. While these early reports provided the first empirical evidence of links between Judaism and mental health, the promise for further research on religious coping in a Jewish context remained bleak due to a lack of appropriate measurement tools. The most widely used scale of religious coping—the RCOPE[31]—contains many items designed for use with Christians. Moreover, this measure uses Christian language and does not assess for Jewish beliefs or ritual practices utilized in times of crisis. More centrally, the very nature of Jewish religious coping may differ from that of Christians, since Judaism—across all denominations—places unique emphasis on religious practice and community involvement.[32]

Thus, in order to foster systematic research on Jewish religious coping, Rosmarin and associates[33] developed the Jewish Religious Coping Scale (dubbed the JCOPE), a sixteen-item measure specifically designed to assess for positive and negative religious coping in a Jewish context. Initially, JCOPE candidate items (e.g., I talk to my rabbi; I look forward to Shabbat) were developed based upon previous research in the Jewish community, cited above, as well as interviews with rabbis and Jewish educators. Then, to develop and validate the measure, a two-part study was conducted. In study one, candidate items were subjected to a factor analysis to evaluate their psychometric structure. Consistent with research in the general population, candidate items broke into two factors representing positive and negative Jewish religious coping, respectively. Further, candidate items were found to correlate with an existing measure of Jewish beliefs and practices,[34] providing preliminary evidence of concurrent validity for the positive and negative JCOPE dimensions. In study two, items were subjected to a confirmatory factor analysis, and the sixteen-item scale was finalized. Further, it was observed that positive Jewish religious coping was associated with lower levels of anxiety, worry, and depression, and conversely, negative Jewish religious coping accompanied higher levels of these variables.

Following the development of the JCOPE, several subsequent studies have examined links between Jewish religious coping and health. Initially, Rosmarin, Pargament, and Flannelly[35] investigated the relationship between negative religious coping (spiritual struggles) and both physical and mental health in the Jewish community. Surprisingly, while spiritual struggles were associated with poorer physical/mental health in the sample overall, it was found among Orthodox Jews that individuals experiencing the highest levels of spiritual struggle experienced an *increase* in mental well-being, whereas non-Orthodox Jews' levels of mental health continued to decrease across the higher range of spiritual struggle (see figure 1).

Jewish Religious Coping Scale (JCOPE)

This questionnaire asks about different ways in which you might rely on religion to deal with stress. Choose the answer that best describes how often you do the following things when you have a stressful problem:

1: Never; 2: Hardly Ever; 3: Sometimes; 4: Most of the Time; 5: Always

When I have stressful problems:

1. I ask G-d to forgive me for things I did wrong.
2. I get mad at G-d.
3. I try to be an inspiration to others.
4. I try to see how G-d may be trying to teach me something.
5. I think about what Judaism has to say about how to handle the problem.
6. I do the best I can and know the rest is G-d's will.
7. I look forward to Shabbat.
8. I talk to my rabbi.
9. I look for a stronger connection with G-d.
10. I question whether G-d can really do anything.
11. I pray for the well-being of others.
12. I pray for G-d's love and care.
13. I wonder if G-d cares about me.
14. I try to do Mitzvot (good deeds).
15. I try to remember that my life is part of a larger spiritual force.
16. I question my religious beliefs, faith, and practices.

Scoring:

Positive Subscale items: 1, 3, 4, 5, 6, 7, 8, 9, 11, 12, 14, 15

Negative Subscale items: 2, 10, 13, 16

Source: David H. Rosmarin, Kenneth I. Pargament, Elizabeth J. Kramrei, and Kevin J. Flannelly, "Religious Coping Among Jews: Development and Initial Validation of the JCOPE," *Journal of Clinical Psychology* 65 (2009): 1–14.

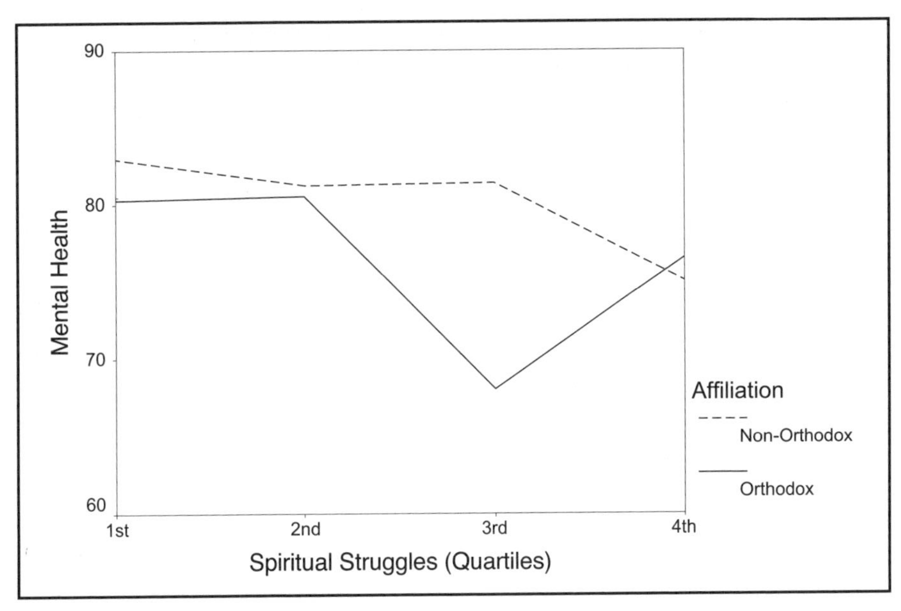

Figure 1. Spiritual struggle and mental health among Orthodox versus non-Orthodox Jews. (From David H. Rosmarin, Kenneth I. Pargament, and Kevin J. Flannelly, "Do Spiritual Struggles Predict Poorer Physical/Mental Health among Jews?" *International Journal for the Psychology of Religion* 19 [2009]: 253.)

While these findings have yet to be replicated, they may suggest that Orthodox Jews perceive spiritual struggle as an opportunity for spiritual growth—for example, to remain steadfast in ethical and religious conduct despite trying times and thereby demonstrate faith, as exemplified by the story of the *Akeidah* (Binding of Isaac; Genesis 22:1–19). By contrast, non-Orthodox Jews may be less deeply embedded in a system of spiritual and religious practices that help mitigate the impact of struggles and therefore may perceive them as negative and threatening regardless of their severity.

More recently, Pirutinsky, Rosmarin, and Holt[36] used the JCOPE to examine relationships between Jewish religious coping and obesity in a sample of 212 Jewish participants. Drawing from the maladaptive coping theory of obesity, which states that unhealthy eating is commonly used to regulate negative emotions, thereby leading to obesity, the authors proposed that positive and negative coping would moderate links between emotional functioning and obesity. That is, they posited that positive religious coping could replace unhealthy eating and thereby buffer against weight gain in the context of emotional distress.

Conversely, they hypothesized that negative religious coping could exacerbate emotional difficulties and thereby magnify any impact of negative emotions on obesity. Moderation analysis indicated that while negative coping had no effect on obesity, positive coping was a significant moderator. Specifically, poor emotional functioning predicted increased obesity among those with low, but not high, positive religious coping (see figure 2). This effect was large and remained significant even after controlling for several possible confounding factors. This study thus provides further support for the maladaptive coping hypothesis, suggesting that religious coping may provide an alternative strategy to maladaptive eating. Moreover, it supports the relevance of religious coping to a Jewish context by highlighting its potential role in buffering against a common health problem in the face of distress.

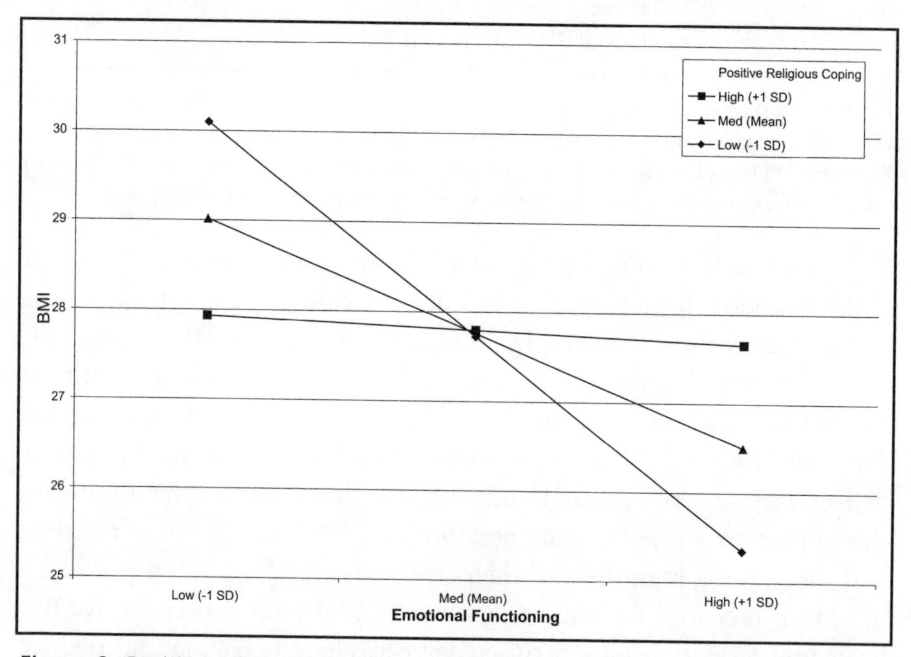

Figure 2. Positive religious coping, emotional functioning, and obesity among Jews. (From Steven Pirutinsky, David H. Rosmarin, and Cheryl Holt, "Religious Coping Moderates the Relationship between Emotional Functioning and Obesity," *Health Psychology* 31 [2012]: 396.)

A third study sought to broadly answer an important question in the negative religious coping (spiritual struggles) literature. As described by Pargament,[37] there are three potential ways in which negative religious coping may relate to depression: (1) negative coping may lead to symptoms of depression; (2) depression may lead to negative coping; or (3) there may be a complex interaction between these variables in which spiritual struggles are both a cause and effect of depression. To examine this matter empirically, Pirutinsky and colleagues[38] utilized structural-equation modeling to explore relationships between negative religious coping and depression in a community sample of eighty Jewish individuals over three time points. Findings suggested that a statistical model in which negative religious coping predicted *subsequent* depression was the best fit for the data, indicating that spiritual struggles appear to precede and perhaps even cause depression in the sample. This investigation was especially important, as most previous research on negative coping—in any population—has yet to examine potential causal models.

Jewish Religious Coping: Theoretical and Conceptual Themes

The empirical foundations of religious coping, in general, are multifaceted but boil down to a central theme: human beings commonly draw on spiritual resources in both positive and negative ways in the process of coping with life distress. The burgeoning study of Jewish religious coping, however, has added two important dimensions to this body of research. First, Jewish responses to trying times historically involve social action and charity, above all. From the American Jewish World Service to the Orthodox Union and beyond, Jews across the gamut of religious observance are known for their compassion and generosity in the face of distress. Perhaps as a result of this, it is commonly (mis)perceived that Jewish approaches to coping are primarily action-oriented and do not involve internal, spiritual processes. While research reports on the effects of Jewish religious coping on mental health remain sparse, each of these initial investigations suggests that religious coping is an important variable worthy of further consideration and research in the Jewish community. Thus, this research highlights the importance of *internal spiritual processes* when coping with life distress in the Jewish community.

Second, the studies by Pirutinsky reviewed above represent a shift for the psychology of religion by furthering theoretical models of *how* and *why* both positive and negative religious coping may relate to human psychological processes. The notion that religious coping can moderate behavioral responses (e.g., excessive food intake) to negative emotions, as opposed to simply exerting a direct effect on emotion, is also an important theoretical advancement worthy of further research. Moreover, the use of structural-equation modeling to examine potential causal models between religious coping and mental health is a considerable leap forward for this body of study, which typically involves cross-sectional or at best two-wave longitudinal study designs. Future directions for the study of Jewish religious coping on mental health remain myriad, however, as literally only a handful of published studies exist, as reviewed above. It is hoped that the coming years will see further research in this exciting and important area.

Trust in God

While the Jewish religious coping literature emerged from research on religious coping in the general population, a slightly larger body of studies—on the construct of trust in God—was born directly from Jewish religious thought. Trust in God (*bitachon*)—the notion that God plays an active role in daily affairs and directs worldly events in accordance with our best interests—has a uniquely significant place in traditional Jewish wisdom. While the tenets of trust in God are no longer believed in by all factions of the modern Jewish world,[39] they continue to constitute the root of Orthodox Jewish faith and remain a central theme throughout traditional Jewish religious literature. For example, the emphasis on increasing one's trust in God's benevolence is highlighted throughout the Torah—particularly in the book of Genesis—and the book of Psalms is replete with verses emphasizing the importance of trusting in God (e.g., Psalm 56:5, "In God I trust, I will not be afraid"). More relevant to this review, classic religious thought posits that trust in God represents an important framework to protect against anxiety and depression and to maintain equanimity and happiness.[40] Many Jewish thinkers over the ages thus have professed that trust in God can produce psychological benefits.

Research on Trust in God

In an initial attempt to empirically evaluate the claim that trust in God is psychologically adaptive, Rosmarin, Pargament, and Mahoney[41] developed a psychometric scale to measure trust in God and examined the relationship between scores on this measure and well-being and distress. The authors commenced their study by deriving candidate items for their scale from Jewish religious texts describing trust in God, as well as from suggestions from an international rabbinic panel (which miraculously reached unanimity). Subsequently, they administered scale items alongside well-utilized indices of psychological functioning to a large Jewish sample (N = 565). In a matter akin to positive versus negative religious coping, the authors found that trust in God was not a unitary construct that individuals were either high or low in, but instead consisted of two separate but related domains: *trust in God*, representing positive beliefs about God's power and love, and *mistrust in God*, characterized by the belief that God is impotent and/or malevolent. Although these domains were related (those high in trust tended to be low in mistrust and vice versa), they were independent in that some individuals were high in both trust and mistrust in God, and others were low in both. It was also observed that participants reported higher levels of trust in God, relative to mistrust in God, overall. In addition, consistent with classic Jewish thought and as hypothesized by the researchers, trust in God was associated with lower levels of anxiety and depression and greater happiness, whereas mistrust in God was associated with greater distress and lower levels of well-being.

Recognizing that trust/mistrust in God might be applicable beyond the Jewish world, as this construct is theoretically relevant to any monotheistic tradition, a subsequent study examined the relevance of trust in God to Jews, Protestants, and Catholics. Rosmarin, Krumrei, and Andersson[42] administered measures of general religious involvement, trust in God, and affective functioning to a community-based sample of 120 Christians and 234 Jews. While religious affiliation was found to be a poor predictor of symptoms, religious practices and trust in God were associated with lower levels of worry, trait anxiety, and depressive symptoms, whereas mistrust in God was associated with greater distress, among both Jews and Christians. Relationships were small but remained significant after controlling for significant covariates (e.g., age, gender). In a third investigation, Rosmarin, Pirutinsky, and Pargament[43] created a brief, six-item measure of trust/mistrust in God with the hope of further evaluating this model in psychiatric patient populations (Jewish or non-Jewish) (see table below), and results for this briefer measure were consistent with those in previous studies.

Brief Trust/Mistrust in God Scale

The following statements are concerned with your beliefs about God (Higher Power, Divine, Creator). Please indicate how strongly you generally believe in each statement:
Not at All; A Little; Somewhat; A Lot; Very Much

1. God loves me immensely.
2. God cares about my deepest concerns.
3. No matter how bad things may seem, God's kindness to me never ceases.
4. God ignores me.
5. God doesn't care about me.
6. God hates me.

Scoring:
Trust in God Subscale items: 1, 2, 3
Mistrust in God Subscale items: 4, 5, 6

Source: David H. Rosmarin, Steven Pirutinsky, and Kenneth I. Pargament, "A Brief Measure of Core Religious Beliefs for Use in Psychiatric Settings," *International Journal of Psychiatry in Medicine* 41 (2011): 259.

Intrigued by these initial findings and the notion that ancient Jewish wisdom can add to a modern understanding of psychopathology, Rosmarin and colleagues[44] sought to examine potential explanatory mechanisms by which trust/mistrust in God might impact human anxiety. Cognitive theory posits that core beliefs facilitate situation-specific cognitions or thoughts, which in turn create human affective states.[45] For example, the core belief "I am incompetent" may engender self-critical thoughts after making an innocent mistake and thereby lead to sadness and guilt (symptoms of depression). However, virtually all previous research on cognitive theory has focused on the "cognitive triad"—core beliefs about oneself, the world, and one's future—and neglected spiritual core beliefs, such as those involved in trust/mistrust in God. Modern cognitive theory has added that intolerance of uncertainty—the tendency to be greatly bothered by even a small possibility of a negative event occurring[46]—is a cognitive vulnerability (i.e., a latent structure of maladaptive core beliefs) for the development of pathological worry. Thus, in integrating trust in God with cognitive theory, a study published in the *Journal of Clinical Psychology* found that trust in God represents a set of core spiritual beliefs that allow one to better tolerate life's uncertainties and thereby decreases worry over time. Conversely, mistrust in God increases intolerance of uncertainty and consequently increases worry as well.[47]

Having established links between trust/mistrust in God and anxiety/depression across several studies and validated a cognitive model explaining these relationships, Rosmarin and colleagues[48] launched an ambitious project to develop and evaluate the efficacy of a treatment program to facilitate greater trust in God as an intervention for worry and stress in the Jewish community. It should be noted that numerous spiritually integrated treatments (SITs) have emerged from psychology of religion research in recent years.[49] Such approaches are similar to conventional psychotherapy in that they are healthcare interventions that seek to reduce symptoms and improve functioning, however spiritual/religious content is intentionally and purposefully utilized in the course of treatment delivery. While research on SITs is still in its early stages, over thirty clinical trials have been conducted including several randomized controlled studies,[50] and results from meta-analytic research have been encouraging.[51] However, no SITs had been evaluated within the Jewish community prior to this study.

Consulting once again with a team of Jewish religious leaders and educators, the researchers created a thirty-minute, self-directed, spiritually based treatment program dubbed "Increase Your Trust in God" designed to reduce stress and worry.[52] The program comprises Jewish religious stories, anecdotes, and spiritual activities including gratitude exercises and prayer. Once the program was finalized—a process that in and of itself took approximately twelve months—the researchers recruited and randomized a sample of 125 Jewish individuals to receive either the spiritually based program, progressive muscle relaxation (an established intervention for stress and worry), or no treatment at all. Participants in active treatment conditions completed their respective programs once each day for a period of two weeks. All participants completed self-report measures of spiritual and psychological functioning prior to, immediately after, and six to eight weeks following the study period. Over the course of treatment, participants receiving the spiritually based program reported large reductions in stress, worry, depression, and intolerance of uncertainty, as well as modest increases in positive religious coping and decreases in mistrust in God. Progressive muscle relaxation participants also reported treatment gains, but these were not statistically different from those observed among participants who received no treatment (see figure 3). Results thus provided initial support for the efficacy of an intervention for anxiety among Jews based on trust in God, further validating the relevance of this construct to psychological functioning in the modern day.

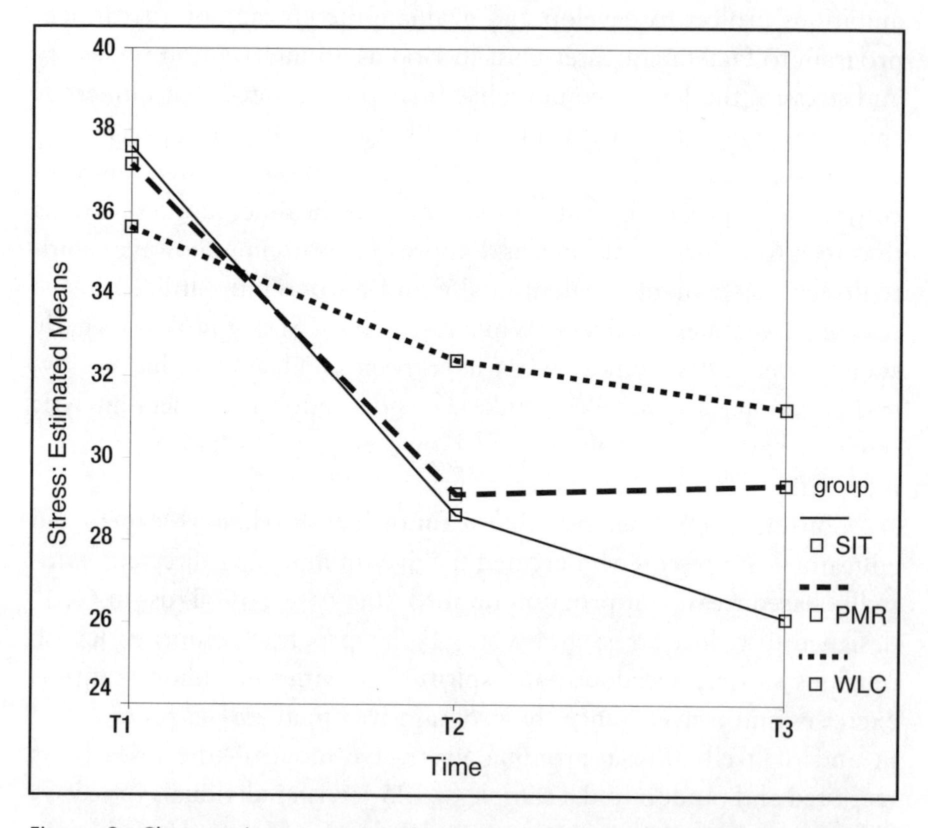

Figure 3. Changes in stress over the course of spiritually based treatment to increase trust in God. (From David H. Rosmarin, Kenneth I. Pargament, Steven Pirutinsky, and Annette Mahoney, "A Randomized Controlled Evaluation of a Spiritually-Integrated Treatment for Subclinical Anxiety in the Jewish Community, Delivered via the Internet," *Journal of Anxiety Disorders* 24 [2010]: 805.)

One final development in this area of study merits mention. To further build a conceptual basis for how trust in God may impact human emotion, Krumrei, Pirutinsky, and Rosmarin[53] recently evaluated the interrelationships among trust/mistrust in God, Jewish religious coping, and mental/physical health. Trust in God and positive religious coping were linked with lower levels of depressive symptoms, and mistrust in God and negative religious coping were linked with greater depressive symptoms. More importantly, support was found for an integrative cognitive-coping model in which the core beliefs of trust in God activate positive religious coping strategies during times of distress.

Trust in God: Theoretical and Conceptual Themes

It is known that religious beliefs (as opposed to practices or communal involvement) tend to play a more central role in Christian than in Jewish doctrine.[54] It is therefore ironic that while almost all psychology of religion research to date has been conducted with Christian communities, research on trust in God, which emerged squarely from Judaism, is one of the first organized programs of research on religious beliefs. It is also significant that this body of study has theoretically integrated religious beliefs into a mainstream psychological theory. Specifically, research on trust in God has provided important insight for the psychology of religion into the role of religious faith and belief in anxiety and affective disorders and the place of such beliefs within the cognitive model. It is now apparent that greater belief in a knowing, powerful, and benevolent God is associated with decreased need for certainty and predictability and with fewer appraisals of threat/danger throughout life.

Restated in terms of the cognitive model, trust in God is a set of positive core beliefs that engender situation-specific automatic cognitions, thereby influencing (reducing) the tendency to be anxious and worried. Conversely, mistrust in God, which involves the perception that God is not involved in daily affairs and/or is malevolent and cruel, appears to increase the need for certainty and may facilitate excessive vigilance and anxiety. Mistrust in God may therefore serve as a filter to highlight negative events and, in turn, exacerbate worry during times of uncertainty. Integrating positive and negative beliefs about God into the cognitive model is important because it facilitates the assessment of functional and maladaptive religious beliefs in the context of psychotherapy. Needless to say, spiritual themes are often ignored in psychosocial treatments,[55] and particularly in evidence-based approaches such as cognitive-behavioral therapy.[56] As such, this development is important in the provision of culturally and spiritually sensitive treatments.

It is also very significant that research on trust in God has facilitated the integration of *Jewish* spirituality into a clinical treatment program. As stated above, while research on spiritually integrated treatments is growing, we are unaware of any other investigations examining the efficacy of such programs within the Jewish community. This is unfortunate, as several important barriers to the dissemination of psychotherapy in the Jewish community exist. In the Orthodox community in particular, consultation and collaboration with religious leaders are often a pre- or co-requisite for religious Jews entering treatment,[57] and stigma is often present, posing a barrier to treatment seeking.[58] The utilization of Jewish spiritual beliefs and practices is therefore an important development from a public health standpoint.

Finally, research on trust/mistrust in God represents an exemplary model of integrating religious and social as well as clinical psychological perspectives within a program of empirical study. While interest in religion has grown within the field of psychology over the past twenty to thirty years, it is rare that psychology of religion researchers draw directly from religious sources in informing theoretical perspectives. It is therefore significant that the conceptualization and even operational definition of trust in God emerged from an eleventh-century Jewish religious text.[59] It is similarly unique to conduct empirical evaluations—using factor-analytic and other advanced statistical methodologies—to advance a psychological theory found in traditional religious thought. Furthermore, the consultation of community leaders and educators at key points throughout the program of research on trust in God has facilitated a rich synthesis of religion and psychology. An even greater advancement has been the application of religious theory to a practical, clinical paradigm by creating an effective mental health intervention within a scientific framework. In sum, from its origins in traditional religious thought, to initial empirical evaluation, to integration with a mainstream psychological paradigm (cognitive theory), to the implementation and testing of a clinical intervention, this program of research uniquely highlights the potential benefits of drawing from ancient spiritual wisdom to inform modern psychological thinking.

Concluding Remarks

From Sigmund Freud, Alfred Adler, and Erich Fromm to Aaron Beck, Albert Ellis, and Abraham Maslow, many of the most seminal figures in psychiatry and psychology have been Jewish. Moreover, Jews have been disproportionately over-represented among U.S. physicians (14.1 percent versus 1.9 percent of the general population)[60] and psychologists (39 percent of the most prominent psychologists of the twentieth century).[61] It is ironic, then, that theorists, researchers, and practitioners have historically neglected the interface between Judaism and mental health. Although the last twenty years has witnessed a dramatic upsurge of interest in the area of religion, spirituality, and mental health, empirically based knowledge about the mental health of Jews is still in short supply. This lack of information is problematic given the distinctiveness of Judaism and its adherents. Fortunately, there are signs of change—the research reviewed in this chapter points to the promise and potential of research and practice tailored to the Jewish community. There is, however, a great deal more work to do.

This work might be guided by several key questions: To what degree do mental health needs and resources vary across Jewish subgroups (e.g., Reform, Conservative, Orthodox)? How might these needs and resources vary among other Jewish individuals, such as males versus females or older versus younger individuals? What are the barriers that limit the receptivity among Jews, particularly the more Orthodox, to mental health services, and how might these barriers be addressed most effectively? How can we adapt evidence-based treatments and integrate them most effectively within Jewish communities? How can we encourage new researchers and practitioners to enter the field? Clearly, there is no shortage of interesting questions to push this vital area of study and practice forward. Hopefully these questions will fuel expansion of our knowledge of Judaism and mental health over the coming years.

Population Research on Judaism, Health, and Well-Being

Jeff Levin, PhD, MPH

Since the 1980s, researchers have systematically investigated the impact of religiousness, broadly defined, on numerous measures of physical and mental health and overall well-being.[1] One-off studies on this subject actually go back much further, to the nineteenth century,[2] but in recent years this research has expanded rapidly, by now totaling several thousand published empirical studies,[3] most with statistically significant results. Social, behavioral, and clinical findings suggest that selected religious behaviors, attitudes, beliefs, and experiences are associated with better health, fewer symptoms, less depression and anxiety, and higher scores on scales assessing life satisfaction, positive affect and happiness, and quality of life. Epidemiologic studies indicate that this general finding also is observed in lower population-wide rates of morbidity, mortality, and disability both overall and according to specific causes, such as heart disease, hypertension, cancer, and psychiatric disorders.[4]

This research, on the whole, is substantial and methodologically solid, although not without limitations; misinterpretation and overinterpretation of findings have been especially persistent. This issue has been examined and critiqued at length in many publications.[5] With respect to the subject of this chapter, a few limitations stand out.

First, the majority of published findings, population-based or otherwise, pertain to U.S. samples of Christians, with a smaller proportion

---

Jeff Levin, PhD, MPH, is University Professor of Epidemiology and Population Health and director of the Program on Religion and Population Health at the Institute for Studies of Religion at Baylor University in Waco, Texas.

addressing religion-health relationships among members of other faith traditions in North America or elsewhere. Published research on Jewish respondents, in Israel or the Diaspora, is relatively sparse. This is due in part to (a) the expense and difficulty involved in oversampling minority populations (e.g., Jews) in U.S. and global population-based health surveys, and (b) the sparsity of questions on health in social and religious surveys of Jews (e.g., the National Jewish Population Survey, the Israel Social Survey).

Second, even where Jews are included in study samples, there are too few for reliable conclusions to be drawn on how Jewish religiousness impacts on health. Moreover, the norms of religious assessment in such studies (e.g., "How often do you attend church services?") are not applicable to Jews. Confronted with a question about, for example, church attendance, how should a Jewish respondent answer: literally, and thus respond "never," resulting in a skewing of Jewish religiousness downward; or, rather, as if the question were written to apply to synagogue? But even if one were to take the latter approach, who is to say that the response categories would even make sense for Jews (i.e., "once a week" or "every Sunday" as normative)? Multiply this problem by all the religious questions in a survey and we can see why efforts to extrapolate population data to Jews and to the Jewish religion are thus contraindicated.

Third, the issue of religious affiliation or denomination, important for differentiating types of Christians, is differently contexted for Jews. The various Jewish movements are defined and identified on the basis of a variety of factors, not just halakhic (in terms of Jewish law), such as socioeconomic status, nativity, immigrant status, Jewish ethnicity, and religiously prescribed and proscribed behaviors—all factors that could impact on health—and, further, their configuration differs among the U.S., Israel, and non-U.S. Diaspora populations. Associated with these identities are respective norms regarding how Jewish religious observance is defined and what is considered proper or sufficient. This is a larger issue than can be discussed here, but, needless to say, the nuances of Jewish affiliation are not captured in survey questions like "What religion are you?: Protestant, Catholic, Jewish, other, none," any more than such a questions does justice to Protestants, others, and nones. This issue, alone, argues for programmatic research specifically on Jewish populations conducted by Jewish researchers who are familiar with Jewish life and the Jewish religion.

The present chapter focuses on population-based research, rather than smaller-scale clinical or behavioral studies. Additionally, the emphasis is on findings from larger social or epidemiologic population surveys that have investigated the impact of Jewish religious observance on physical health and morbidity, although some of these studies also examined selected indicators of mental health or well-being; these are covered here, too. For a more thorough overview of psychological studies of Judaism and mental health, the reader is referred to the previous chapter, "Jewish Religious Coping and Trust in God: A Review of the Empirical Literature," by Rosmarin and colleagues.

Overview of Research Findings

Research in the Jewish Diaspora

Among the earliest epidemiologic studies, a century ago, were a series of descriptive cumulations of population data comparing rates of morbidity and mortality among Jews and members of other religious categories.[6] By the standards of modern epidemiologic research, these comparisons may be a bit unsophisticated, but they provided the first empirical confirmation that Jews—whether construed of as a religious group, a tribe, an ethnicity, a "race," or something else (these studies were not always clear on this point)—had a distinctive pattern of health status in comparison with others.

Of the hundreds of such studies published from the nineteenth century through the 1980s, several clusters of findings pertained specifically to the Jewish people and/or practicing Jews: studies of cervical/uterine cancer morbidity and mortality, colitis and enteritis incidence, health-related sequelae of occupational exposures, and incidence and prevalence of psychiatric disorders.[7] In many studies, Jews were found to be at significantly heightened or diminished risk depending on the respective outcome. Other significant findings regarding Jewish populations were also found in studies of the epidemiology of cardiovascular disease, overall and site-specific cancer, and hypertension and stroke.[8]

Deciphering just what this means, what it says about Jews or about the Jewish religion, requires care. In describing results of epidemiologic studies like these, there are three caveats to keep in mind: such findings are presented on average, across a population, and *caeteris paribus*, or all things being equal (or controlling for effects of covariates, in methodological terms). These are population trends and do not imply, for example, that all Jews or no Jews experience this, that, or the other malady—just that the rate of experience may differ significantly from the rate among other population groups, for whatever reasons. Another consideration is that in some of these early studies we now recognize that it would be foolish to attribute to something intrinsically "spiritual" within Judaism an effect that is due instead to a demographic or biological characteristic of the Jewish people. A case in point: Travers's observation, in 1837, that he had "never seen a case of cancer of the penis in a Jew,"[9] and the many studies pointing to a strong protective effect of Jewish identity on cervical and uterine cancer incidence.[10] For years, this latter finding was believed to be a sequelae of circumcision, which in turn is a function of Jewish identity or observance to some extent, to be sure, but not an indicator of a health benefit accruing from something psychosocially consequent to Jewish spirituality. A current view is that there may, as well, be a genetic basis for the protected status of Jewish women. This issue is still debated,[11] but the take-home point is that neither explanation has much to do with any putative benefits of the inner spiritual life of Jews.

Only a few contemporary studies in the Jewish Diaspora have been published in the past twenty years, and these mostly emphasize mental health or well-being. Excluding the work of Rosmarin and colleagues, summarized in the previous chapter, these include studies of anxiety,[12] depression,[13] positive affect,[14] and life satisfaction,[15] but a consistently salutary effect was not observed. The only study that was national in scope, drew on a population-based sample, and looked at physical health was an analysis of data from the National Jewish Population Survey.[16] It concluded that "more 'distinctively Jewish' Jews, expressed in terms of subjective identification and traditional religious behavior, report better health, overall and after controls for potential confounders, including the presence of health limitations that might serve to constrain public religious participation."[17]

This research differs from earlier work reviewed above in that it tends to explore a putative health impact of Jewish religiousness, not simply health differences between Jews and those of other religious or ethnic identities. Still, there is not much to go by, not much research in either the United States or United Kingdom (and almost none elsewhere in the Diaspora), and for the most part, these are not population-based studies but are reliant on smaller, more localized, clinical samples.

Research in Israel

The situation in Israel is comparable in some ways. Most research on this topic also dates to the 1980s and explores aspects or dimensions of Jewish religious life as potential predictors or correlates of physical or mental health or overall well-being. As in the Diaspora, studies of physical health are rare. Evidence points to Orthodox Jews having lower overall mortality[18] and less morbidity due to myocardial infarction,[19] but not much more than that is known for certain.

With respect to mental health and well-being, a few psychological constructs have been well studied. Jewish religious observance has been found to exhibit a significantly protective effect against psychological distress[20] and to be associated with mental health or psychological well-being[21] and greater life satisfaction,[22] although some counter-evidence exists.[23] Non-findings were also observed for anxiety and depression,[24] but study subjects were medical students—a group perhaps highly "resistant" to any psychosocial resource that may prevent state-related stress disorders. Beyond that, these Israeli studies do not tell us much more than the Diaspora studies. There is some evidence for a positive religion-health link, but it is not consistent and is based predominantly on data unrepresentative of large Jewish populations.

Judaism and Health Studies: What We Need to Do Next

Taking both Israeli and Diaspora research into account, several limitations of this work are evident. These do not imply deficiencies in any respective study; on the whole, this work is outstanding and individual studies were excellently done, within the bounds of what was possible given existing sampling and data collection limitations. Through this work, a great deal has been learned. But as a literature overall, a few things limit our ability to draw firm conclusions as to a putative Judaism-health link. Each must be remedied for this area of research to advance.

First, there has been minimal reliance on population-based data. Again, this is not a criticism of studies based on smaller community-based, clinical, or recruited samples; they were appropriate choices given the study questions, the accessibility of Jewish respondents or subjects, and available research funding. But, the relative lack of population data limits our ability to infer population-wide risk or protective status to dimensions or expressions of Jewish religiousness for particular health outcomes. An idealized goal of this research is to enable conclusions about whether and how Jewish observance contributes to the health and well-being of Jews, in general, and not just those living in a particular community, belonging to a particular synagogue or Jewish federation, or identifying with one or another Jewish movement or denomination. To best achieve that goal, then *data from large-scale national probability samples* must be obtained.

Second, the health and well-being indicators used throughout these studies have been mostly single-item measures. There is nothing implicitly wrong with this—a single-item self-rating of global health is one of the strongest predictors of objective health status, longevity, selected biomarkers, mental health, and psychosocial outcomes such as well-being.[25] Still, more sophisticated health assessment, whether of physical or mental health, has not been the norm in these studies. We thus have minimal insight into the implications of Jewish observance for particular domains of health (e.g., subjective overall health, functional health or disability/activity status, chronic disease history, acute symptomatology, psychiatric diagnoses) or well-being (e.g., as elicited through indices assessing cognitive, affective, or somatic states). Studies of Judaism and health have largely not benefited from the state of the art of health assessment or well-being measurement. Investigators would gain from *more sophisticated measures of physical and mental health and general well-being*.

Third, unlike in the larger religion and health literature, studies of Judaism and health rarely stratify analyses "denominationally," or, in Jewish terms, by movement. There are a few reasons: Jewish respondents may not be asked about their particular Jewish religious affiliation or identity; even if they are, there may be too few Jews in certain categories to enable meaningful comparisons; or in analyses by non-Jewish investigators, there may be limited awareness that such variation exists or is meaningful. A few such comparative analyses of health have been undertaken, though, and their results have been interesting, as noted above.[26] Another complicating factor is that how Jewish religious identity is differentiated itself differs among North Americans (e.g., Reform, Conservative, Reconstructionist, modern Orthodox, *haredi* Orthodox, and other variants: Humanistic, Renewal, Traditional), Israelis (*hiloni*, *masorti*, *dati*, *haredi*), and Diaspora Jews (e.g., in the United Kingdom, where there are two distinct liberal movements). These categories are potentially salient indicators of the flavor of one's Jewish religious identity and thus help to shape responses to life challenges and, presumably, one's overall well-being. Accordingly, *stratification by intra-Jewish religious variation* is an important strategy, as it enables consideration of religious differences that distinguish among Jews ritually, in terms of belief, and to some extent socioeconomically and culturally.

Fourth, cursory measures of religiousness included in health surveys are not necessarily specific to or meaningful in the context of normative Jewish religious observance. Earlier, we gave the example of general population surveys inquiring about normative (weekly) church attendance as not being applicable to Jews. Just changing the wording, however, is not adequate. Would a single question assessing once-weekly attendance at shul (e.g., on Friday evening) really be the best marker of Jewish religious observance, much less the only one? For Jews, home rituals are also important, and moreover, the reason for and meaning of synagogue worship, plus *sui generis* factors like the composition of *minyanim* and which *siddur* (prayer book) is used, are nuances missed by "How often do you go to religious services?" Also, for Jews, issues of doctrinal orthodoxy do not necessarily loom as large as for Christians or members of other faith traditions. What best gauges Jewish religious observance is variation in what might be termed orthopraxy, rather than orthodoxy. The most successful efforts to assess Jewish religiousness therefore emphasize identifying and cumulating what Jewish respondents *do*, not simply what they think or believe. This is best done by Jewish investigators who can construct *measurement items and indices that assess constructs meaningful in a Jewish religious context.*

These suggestions make for a full plate and may be a lot to ask. Unless one has access to considerable funding and can mount an original national or global Jewish health survey, we must rely on secondary analysis of existing data, which may not check each of these boxes, or any. Fortunately, there is a way around this, for now. The present author's current research has found a way to address these issues inexpensively, enabling tentative conclusions to be drawn about the relationship between Jewish religious observance and health.

Ongoing Global Population Health Research

Since about 2011, the present author has developed a research program to address each of these issues, namely use of data sources (a) from large national or global population-based surveys, (b) containing more sophisticated health outcome measures, (c) enabling stratification by Jewish movement (in the United States and non-U.S. Diaspora) or by Jewish identity and observance (as in Israel), and (d) assessing Jewish religious observance in ways that make Jewish sense. This program of work has been guided methodologically by Kosmin's call for a "systematic comparative approach to national population surveys of Jews"[27] and by George and Landerman's endorsement of "replicated secondary data analysis"[28] as a strategy to investigate determinants of health and well-being while transcending the characteristics of particular study samples.

The challenge has been to identify data sources that contain sufficient numbers of Jewish respondents to enable reliable analyses of associations between Judaism and health or well-being. Several large-scale probability surveys were identified, mostly containing Israeli samples, as well as a few enabling Diaspora-wide analysis or U.S. estimates. Each survey is national or global in scope. These sources of data are the National Jewish Population Survey (NJPS),[29] the World Values Survey (WVS),[30] the Gallup World Poll (GWP),[31] the Survey of Health, Ageing and Retirement in Europe (SHARE),[32] the European Social Survey (ESS),[33] International Social Survey Programme (ISSP),[34] and the Israel Social Survey (ISS).[35] Details about these data sources, their samples, data collection procedures, and measurement issues can be found in the respective papers just cited.

An advantage of replicated secondary data analysis is the ability to examine a relationship between two sets of constructs or meta-constructs—for example, Jewish religious observance and health/well-being—in a way that varies the particular samples, time frames, locations, and measures. There is also a pragmatic reason for this strategy in the present case: most existing social and epidemiologic health surveys include only limited religious measures, most include measures of either physical or mental health but usually not both, and most samples are specific to just one Jewish national population (e.g., Israel or the United States). By conducting analyses with a pool of different data sources, we are better equipped to gauge an overall relationship between constructs that transcends the specifics on any one sample. Information about the samples utilized in the author's research at the time of this writing, is included in the table below. Additional analyses are planned, using data from the Israel National Health Survey and from several of the U.S. community surveys of Jewish populations that have been conducted over the past decade or so.

Current Program of Global Population Research Studies on Judaism and Health

Data Source	Year	N	Israel	U.S.	Non-U.S. Diaspora	Physical Health	Mental Health or Well-Being
NJPS	2000–01	4,484		X		X	
WVS	2001	1,023/859*	X	X	X		X
GWP	2006–10	4,073	X			X	X
SHARE	2005–06	1,287	X			X	X
ESS	2002–03	1,849	X			X	X
ISSP	2009–10	991	X				X
ISS	2009	6,056	X			X	X

*Israeli N = 1,023; total Diaspora N = 859

Analysis of U.S. data, taken from the 2000–2001 NJPS, found consistent associations between a variety of measures of Jewish religious observance and two health indicators—a self-rating of overall health and the absence of an activity-limiting health condition.[36] Summary scales of Jewish activities and Jewish observance and single items assessing synagogue membership, self-rated religiosity and Jewish observance, personal prayer outside of shul, and synagogue attendance each were associated with one or both health indicators in a salutary (health-promotive) direction. After adjusting for effects of age and other factors, the synagogue participation measures remained significantly associated with better health. This health impact of religious observance was primarily limited to Orthodox and Conservative Jews.

Data from the WVS enabled comparison of findings from Jewish respondents in Israel (data collected in 2001) and a Diaspora-wide sample of Jews aggregated from all other national samples over the survey's multiple rounds of data collection.[37] This atypical methodological approach is indicative of the decision making that may be required to enable national or global population-based findings on the health of Jews. Analysis revealed distinctive patterns of religion–well-being associations between Israeli and Diaspora Jews. Among Israelis, affirming the importance of God in one's life was modestly associated with greater life satisfaction (a cognitive measure of well-being), but not with happiness (a measure of positive affect). In the Diaspora, the same religious measure was associated with greater happiness, as was more frequent synagogue attendance, but neither was associated with life satisfaction.

Israel-only data came from five sources—the GWP, SHARE, ESS, ISSP, and ISS surveys—all studies undertaken in the 2000s.[38] Throughout these studies, significant impacts of various Jewish religious measures, notably frequent attendance at synagogue services, were found in relation to a variety of mental health outcomes—for example, less depression and psychological distress, greater positive well-being, more optimism, a better quality of life, and a higher level of happiness. Likewise, physical health effects of Jewish religious practice were also apparent in relation to subjective, functional, and symptomatic measures or indices of health status. A notable and consistent finding was that prayer was used as a coping response in the face of physical challenge.

In sum, this program of research has enabled documentation of religion-health and religion–mental-health linkages at the population level, in both Israel and the Jewish Diaspora, using multiple measures of Jewish religious observance, and across a diverse range of outcomes, including indicators of physical and mental health and overall well-being. From these analyses, three summary statements can be made: (a) Jewish observance, broadly defined, appears to exhibit a salutary impact on the lives of Jews; (b) the evidence in relation to dimensions of mental health and well-being is a bit stronger than the evidence for physical health effects; and (c) there is modest evidence of a gradient in these effects, such that the salience of a putative religious benefit seems to increase as one moves "rightward" from liberal to more traditional Jewish religious affiliation or identity. This brief summary is just a synopsis of the main results of these studies; the reader is referred to the full series of papers for greater detail on all of the findings from each study.

The "Why" Question

If research findings like these represent the "what" of a Judaism-health connection, then the next issue might be called the "how" or "why" question—that is, how do we make sense of these results? What do they mean? Are there explanations for an observable impact of Jewish religious participation on physical and mental health that is consistent with what we know about the determinants of population health? In a word, yes.

Alongside the accumulation of research findings on the "epidemiology of religion"[39] since the 1980s, a small literature has arisen that seeks to identify putative "mechanisms" or mediating factors that might explain or make sense of these findings. The operant task has been to outline those biobehavioral and psychosocial expressions, functions, and manifestations of religiousness that may be health-related. Several investigators have devoted a great deal of time to this question.[40] Among the possible answers to the why question are the following:

> For example, strong commitment to observing the tenets of religions may influence health through exposure to messages that promote and reinforce healthy behaviors, such as the avoidance of harmful substances (tobacco, alcohol, illicit drugs). Regular religious fellowship, such as through frequent participation in the life of a congregation, may influence health through enabling the receipt of social support from fellow congregants that can provide both tangible and emotional resources for preventing future health problems and addressing existing problems. Engaging in public and private religious worship, such as prayer, may engender

> positive emotions (related to contentment, forgiveness, love, gratitude, peace of mind) with potentially preventive or therapeutic benefits. Certain religious beliefs (such as a strong sense that God is securely in control) may be consonant with healthy beliefs or personality styles (a sense of self-efficacy) that are promotive of preventive health care practices. Finally, faith in God may lead to a hopeful, optimistic frame of mind that marshals positive expectations, which in turn can prevent or ameliorate psychological distress. In sum, expressions of personal and communal religiousness may serve to mobilize psychological, interpersonal, and congregational resources that result in better health care use, health practices, and health status.[41]

What is not to be missed here is that each of these mechanisms is naturalistic—that is, they do not posit anything of a "divine" or supernatural origin. Religion, as well as being a phenomenon involving beliefs and phenomena of a spiritual and possibly transcendent nature, also manifests in human life through behavior, attitudes, beliefs, values, experiences, and so on. Accordingly, social, behavioral, or epidemiologic researchers can investigate the impact of religiousness on human affairs, including one's health, just as they investigate any measurable phenomenon (e.g., income, marital happiness, criminal history) on health or any other phenomenon (e.g., blood pressure, voting behavior, beliefs about global warming). The influence of religiousness on health is thus potentially understandable in terms of the same sorts of psychosocial constructs—lifestyle behavior, social support, positive emotions, healthy beliefs, optimism—familiar to social, psychosocial, and behavioral epidemiologists, in general.

For practicing Jews, other mechanisms may suggest themselves. Could we imagine sequelae of characteristically *Jewish* religious observance that influence physical or mental health through behavioral, interpersonal, psychological, and even biological means? Some possibilities can be derived from Jewish religious distinctives regarding marital endogamy, dietary folkways, sexual norms, ritualized behavior, communal celebrations, tribal identity and bonding, love of God and Torah, high levels of education, socioeconomic status, belief in theodicy, normative responses to pain and suffering, differential propensity toward alcoholism, and mutual aid. Through these mediating or moderating forces, and perhaps others, Jewish religiousness may impact on human bodies and human populations through various means, involving reinforcement of genetic predispositions; physiological, psychophysiological, or pathophysiological responses; health-impacting personality styles; a hopeful (or pessimism-inducing) worldview; culture-bound psychological responses to stress or fear or challenge; and a greater (or lesser) likelihood of accessing material or medical resources.

But there is another possibility for a health impact of Jewish religious observance that is, by definition, outside of the capability of scientific study or observation to validate. If this point and indeed the discussion of the why question up to now seems guarded, cautious, and especially caveated, by epidemiologic convention, early Christian assessments were less circumspect in attributing health benefits accrued to Jews on account of our adherence to *mitzvot* (commandments) regarding health, diet, work, and the environment: "There can be little doubt that it is to his religion that the Jew owes his immunity from disease and his length of days."[42] By this, two propositions can be deduced: (a) Jewish observance itself benefits health naturalistically; and (b) as a result of Jewish observance, God blesses the Jewish people with health, as in Exodus 15:26:

> If you will heed *Adonai* your God diligently, doing what is upright in God's sight, giving ear to God's commandments, and keeping all God's laws, then I will not bring upon you any of the diseases that I brought upon the Egyptians, for I *Adonai* am your healer.

Saying that *mitzvot* are good for our health due to their psychosocial sequelae, as outlined above, is of course distinct from saying that the Jewish population's health status profile is such because God, working through supernatural means, chooses to grant health or healing as a blessing to individual Jewish people. As a practicing Jew, the present author will not rule this out. Our holy writings tell us explicitly of "the beneficence and omnipotence of God when it comes to a caring concern for the human condition,"[43] especially regarding health. This manifests in numerous references throughout Torah and the Rabbinic literature to God's promises of longevity, lowered disease risk, mental health and well-being, disease prevention, and even healing to those who are obedient to God and to the *mitzvot*.[44] Many of us take this on faith, gratefully, if not entirely understanding all the nuances. But, regardless—and here is a critical point often missed in the contentious academic discourse on religion and health—this is definitely *not* an issue that can ever be resolved by epidemiologic studies, of course. Or, in other words, "If one is looking to science, and to scientific methodology, to fully adjudicate this matter, then one is probably looking in the wrong place."[45] Still, belief in the possibility of "divine" action, of blessings of health and well-being meted out by a loving God, evokes images and emotions that resonate deeply within many religious Jews. As the science of mind-body medicine tells us, such beliefs by themselves, irrespective of their "reality," may be promotive of health, healing, and wellness.[46]

A clever take on this issue that finds a common ground between naturalistic and divine explanations for such findings comes from the Torah and the Mishnah. Fulfillment of a *mitzvah* leads to longevity,[47] we are told. Why? Because fulfillment of a *mitzvah* leads to an opportunity to fulfill other *mitzvot*;[48] thus longevity may not accrue as an explicitly natural outcome or effect of a particular *mitzvah* but, rather, as a means given by God to be able to perform *mitzvot*. God gives us more life so that we can maximize our days and continue to perform more *mitzvot*. There is enough here in this interpretation to make rabbis *and* epidemiologists smile.

A Research Agenda

Given the limited availability of large-scale population surveys of Jews, the author's series of studies will soon exhaust what is possible involving secondary analysis of such data. This is not to say that other investigators cannot fruitfully revisit these data sources with other religion-health/well-being associations in mind. The authors' analyses have been selective, focusing on broader overall relationships between exposures (religious measures) and outcomes (health indicators), adjusting for pertinent covariates, typical of the epidemiologic approach. More sophisticated, theory-based multifactorial models of interrelationships among Jewish religious measures, health indicators, and social and behavioral mediating variables could be posited and tested using these same data, in the style of social research. But unless a new global survey program is developed that includes an Israeli sample and until a U.S. population health survey is implemented (neither of which is on the horizon), then as this research program winds down, the population-based study of Judaism, health, and well-being is at a crossroads.

In order to advance this work, three next steps are identified—the first of which the author is pursuing as of this writing, the second of which is in a conceptual stage, and the third of which is presently a hypothetical.

First, *a continuation of the present research program* is planned. This line of work is self-limiting, as noted, as there are only so many probability surveys of national or global Jewish populations, and most of these already have been used. Two analyses in progress make use of data on religious correlates of psychiatric diagnoses from the Israel National Health Survey and data on Jewish observance and self-ratings of health from a selection of U.S. urban community studies. An analysis using a Diaspora-wide sample from the GWP is also being considered.

Second, the subject of Judaism and population health is not just about epidemiologic evidence of a salutary effect of being Jewishly religious; there is a communal dimension. Accordingly, at some point, *a comprehensive survey of U.S. congregations* ought to be mounted, in order to document what is being done within synagogues, across movements, and to identify and address health needs of congregants. Such an endeavor would be part program assessment (as in an expansion of the work described in the next chapter, "A Program Assessment of the Field of Judaism and Health: Program Review and Key Stakeholder Interviews," by Prince), part needs assessment (as in a combination of an epidemiologic study and a health services access and utilization survey), and part census of all the liturgical and religious activities—from healing services to meditation classes and more—that are going on in synagogues throughout the United States. Working closely with the various movements, the ideal here would be an electronic survey, with direct follow-up, sent to every identifiable Jewish congregation. The potential benefit of such a survey to the movements, the federations, Jewish professionals, the rabbinate, researchers, and ultimately the Jewish people is considerable.

Third, were such a congregational survey done, then a natural follow-up might be *a comprehensive national or global Jewish health survey and healthcare needs assessment*. This could be thought of as something like a Jewish version of the National Health Interview Survey or a U.S. version of the Israel National Health Survey. The challenge here, as for a congregational survey, would be to construct a sampling frame that does not leave out large numbers of the unaffiliated and *haredi* populations. These two segments of the Jewish people—the far-left and far-right wings, halakhically speaking—have long proved difficult to include in Jewish surveys for different reasons: the "who is a Jew" conundrum, for the former, and heightened insularity and distrust of outsiders, for some of the latter. These issues have complicated prior social surveys and are a source of the contention that still exists, in part, regarding accuracy of the National Jewish Population Survey.[49] An additional challenge is the considerable cost involved in mounting a national probability survey of health in the United States, much less globally. One possibility might be to partner with an existing survey outfit, such as Gallup, which has operations on the ground in most of the countries in the world. The cost would be in the millions of dollars, so such a project would need to be a major focus of Jewish philanthropy.

Regarding a national or global Jewish health survey, it is unknown whether the author, or anyone else, will ever be able to move forward with such an ambitious project, but the idea has been broached on several occasions.[50] The requisite funding, multidisciplinary coordination, and transdenominational cooperation would make this something of a "Manhattan project" for Judaism and health, which may not be feasible until at least a congregational survey is completed. But the opportunity to document the current physical and mental health status and overall well-being of the Jewish people and, simultaneously, to conduct a large-scale healthcare needs assessment, whether globally or just in the United States, is a worthy goal and merits serious consideration.

❖

Part V

Jewish Communal, Organizational, and Policy Perspectives

A Program Assessment of the Field of Judaism and Health

Program Review and Key Stakeholder Interviews

Michele F. Prince, LCSW, MAJCS

The Kalsman Institute on Judaism and Health is working to build a scholarly field around the connections between Judaism and health. As part of a larger research initiative called the Kalsman Institute Research Roundtable, the author and Adina Bodenstein[1] completed a formal assessment of the field of Judaism, health, and healing through a combination of program review and key stakeholder interviews.[2] This chapter examines the development of systematic and professionalized programming within the field of Judaism and health. The "overarching goal" of the Roundtable project and efforts to build the field of Judaism and health is "to better understand the health of the Jewish people and to improve the health and well-being in the Jewish community."[3]

Several confluent factors provide an opening for assessment and growth in the field. These include the proliferation of research studies on religion, spirituality, and health over the last twenty-five years and the emergence of the Jewish healing movement. These factors, along with a growing sense of communal obligation to enhance Jewish spirituality and well-being, present an opportunity for synergy and for meeting the needs of the Jewish community.[4]

Michele F. Prince, LCSW, MAJCS, is executive director of OUR HOUSE Grief Support Center and former director of the Kalsman Institute on Judaism and Health, Hebrew Union College–Jewish Institute of Religion in Los Angeles, California.

Provided here is a review and general appraisal of programs offered to the Jewish community through congregations, social service agencies, medical centers, educational centers, and other Jewish communal organizations. The field provides responses, services, and resources to those experiencing loss and illness and encourages healthy living through the engagement of spirituality and the pursuit of wellness as a sacred journey. Programs are provided by an interdisciplinary and multidenominational group of professionals and lay leadership. Both the individual and the community receive the benefits of the programming. Kalsman staff reviewed 226 programs and more than 20 healthcare centers and interviewed 30 stakeholders. The programmatic review and key stakeholder interviews unearthed strengths, weaknesses, opportunities, and challenges for the field of Judaism and health. The process revealed how programmatic offerings have both deepened and broadened in the past twenty-five years.

Programmatic efforts make an attempt to mine the Jewish tradition to improve health and well-being in the Jewish community. Jewish texts, rituals, and resiliency address the continuum of illness and wellness to draw on Judaism's rich and distinctively multifaceted resources in religion, spirituality, culture, and peoplehood. These explorations revealed that community is the backdrop in which we grapple with modern dilemmas while honoring Judaism's sacred texts and rituals. Many current Judaism and health programs are aimed at concepts of wellness, versus earlier work focused solely on responses to illness and loss. Stakeholder interviews also revealed that programs and organizations face financial, personnel, and outreach challenges.

Background

Jewish discourse around health and healing is not just a modern conversation, but part of a longstanding tradition of religious and scholarly writing pertaining to the intersection of the sacred and the physical, dating back to the Rabbinic era. Summarizing these discussions is not a simple matter of tracing a single historical trajectory; many distinct threads define this discourse. They include biblical, Rabbinic, and contemporary writing on myriad topics.[5] The Jewish canon, for example, has much to say about human anatomy and physiology[6] and about the etiology and determinants of illness and health, respectively.[7] Leading rabbinic sages, notably Maimonides, wrote about medical themes; he published extensively on both philosophical theology and medicine.[8] Modern Jewish religious bioethics is informed by a deep tradition of writing on the halakhic (Jewish law) dimensions of healthcare and healing.[9] Contemporary communal health services target specific populations, such as Holocaust survivors, elders in poverty, and patients, young and old, experiencing illness and loss.[10] Conversations continue about Jewish pastoral care and education[11] and focus on what has come to be known as the Jewish healing movement.

The contemporary Jewish healing movement emerged in the early 1990s. Professionals and lay leaders came to realize that as a consequence of modern life, many Jews no longer had easy or meaningful access to the spiritual and communal supports that had sustained previous generations of Jews through difficult times of illness and loss.[12] These Jewish leaders tried to provide institutional remedies for this issue. Communal agencies and organizations, grassroots groups, and synagogues developed and delivered health-related services and resources. These initiatives drew on wellsprings of Jewish thinking that spoke to the religious tradition as a resource for comfort and solace.[13] Such developments could not have come at a more opportune time, because Jewish religious leaders had begun to complain that in the healthcare field as in society, "the sacred is being supplanted by technology."[14]

Today's Jewish healing movement continuously evolves to encompass services and resources not only for those experiencing loss and illness but also for those who wish to foster wellness, through enhancing the engagement of spirituality and through framing the pursuit of well-being as a sacred journey. Judaism recognizes, inherently, the profound consonance and inseparability of "healing of soul, healing of body."[15]

The assessment developed by the Kalsman Institute establishes a baseline for programming available in Judaism and health as well as the opportunity for systematic program evaluation and development.[16]

Methodology

The program assessment was one phase of a larger research project led by the editors of this book and an advisory team. Kalsman staff designed the assessment to begin building a scholarly foundation for the field of Judaism and health, including promoting research, formalizing standards for evaluative research, and building an enduring professional community of scholars and practitioners to systematically research the connections between Judaism and health. This survey of the field of Judaism and health focused on providing a lay-of-the-land look at related programming in congregations, agencies, and healthcare centers. The assessment took a multi-modal research approach.

For the first step, a Kalsman Institute research advisory group identified key stakeholders involved in the many disciplines that populate work in health and healing, including clergy, physicians, and Jewish nonprofit professionals involved in social service organizations. In-depth interviews with key stakeholders explored personal and professional history, attitudes, and beliefs about their programs and institutions to extract themes, highlights, and goals to help further the field. Interviews took place from April to October of 2010.

The second step, in 2010, involved gathering information about programs and services available in the United States at the intersection of Judaism and health. Accordingly, the Kalsman Institute expanded the *2008 Jewish Healing Programs: Best Practices Sampler*, collected and published by Susan Rosenthal for the National Center for Jewish Healing.[17] Kalsman staff incorporated a large sample of all known current offerings in the field, including spiritual growth and support groups, educational programs for volunteers, conferences and retreats, and additional programmatic offerings. Staff reviewed 155 programs in agencies, organizations, hospitals, medical centers, and synagogues.

A third step, in 2012, involved reviewing an additional seventy-one programs prior to publication. These were programs submitted for consideration for a Los Angeles–based event called "Jewish Wisdom and Wellness: A Week of Learning," scheduled to take place in April 2013.[18] The Week of Learning is a festival-style, community-wide series of events, lectures, workshops, and experiential classes hosted by community organizations and synagogues throughout Southern California. The event was co-sponsored by the Kalsman Institute and Cedars-Sinai Medical Center and offered an opportunity to review the latest trends in programming concepts and areas of focus in Judaism and health.

Phase-one interviews elicited information regarding needs, problems, and the current state of the field. A copy of the interview questions is available, from the author, by request. Thirty key stakeholders were interviewed. A list of the personnel is included for this chapter.[19]

Program Review

Kalsman staff reviewed programs as a whole to obtain the "lay of the land" of the emerging field of Judaism and health. The staff reviewed each program individually and categorized it by answering such overview questions as "Where does it take place?" "What is involved?" "How is it structured?" and "Who is targeted?" in order to provide a basic map of the field of Judaism and health. Staff sorted results to discern patterns and trends.

Programs were divided by sponsoring agency, congregation, or organization and by geography, style, target, intent, and frequency. Healthcare staff, clergy synagogue leadership, and seniors, adults, and teens were targeted by the majority of programs. Notably absent were programs targeting men and young children. Many programs sorted into multiple categories, and the following classifications help illustrate the areas of focus and intent. Most programs convened around these topics:

- Successful aging
- Substance abuse
- Illness, in general or specific diseases
- Visitor support (*bikkur cholim*/visiting the sick), including caregiving support
- End-of-life and bereavement
- Jewish spiritual renewal or spiritual growth
- Jewish bioethics
- The healthcare system, education about insurance changes, and access to care

Newer areas of focus explored in 2011–12 included the following:

- Baby-boomer transitions
- Self-care and resiliency
- Support for underserved Jewish populations

Among the many program modalities used were the following:

- Educational courses and workshops
- Outreach and networking events
- Professional support meetings or courses
- Conferences or retreats
- Support groups

Staff reviewed other details, including program fee structures, inclusion of music or prayer, collaborating organizations, personnel or staff versus volunteers, and clinicians versus clergy. The program review and the interview components worked in conjunction.

Population

The program review revealed that programming in Judaism and health is available in great numbers in both the areas with the highest concentrations of Jewish individuals and the areas not as highly populated by Jewish individuals. According to the World Jewish Population Survey,[20] conducted in 2010, the U.S. metropolitan areas with the highest Jewish populations are as follows:

New York	2,007,850
Los Angeles	684,950
South Florida	485,850
San Francisco	345,700
Chicago	270,500

The first issue of *The Outstretched Arm*, a publication of the National Center for Jewish Healing, in 1991, said that a "handful of Jewish hospital chaplains, a few Jewish hospices, rabbinic visitation to hospitalized or home-bound patients, and the traditional practices of *bikur cholim*" defined the extent of organized spiritual care available for Jews in need at that time.[21] Over twenty years later, the offerings are more robust, diverse, and far-reaching.

Limitations

One limitation of this program assessment is that it is an accounting of a sample of programming and of the opinions of a sample of key stakeholders. A larger sampling of these leaders, including those from organizations not yet known to the Kalsman Institute, would be beneficial. No key stakeholders were interviewed from the Pacific Northwest region of the United States and those voices need to be added to the conversation. Interviews with line staff and lay leadership also would be useful. Another limitation is that recipients of services and resources were not interviewed here. Input from those interviews would be valuable.

The program assessment is thus not comprehensive of all programs and findings in the United States. It is also not a full evaluation of the programs explored in the program review. The assessment provides an important overview and covers volume and growth but does not offer a methodical review of content and financial strength, potential for growth, outreach and awareness, or replicability of each of these programs. This review also focuses primarily on offerings in the liberal Jewish community and largely does not assess programs and practices in the Orthodox communities. The addition of more Orthodox findings would enhance the exploration.

Despite significant growth in twenty-five years, this field continues to be in a building and sustaining stage of development,[22] and debate continues about the areas of focus under the umbrella of Judaism, health, healing, and medicine programming.

Exploratory Analysis of the Field: Key Findings

Thematic Findings

Strengths and Weaknesses: Stakeholders described the field's strengths and weaknesses as well as opportunities and challenges, as shown in figure 1. Strengths include a field of charismatic leaders and creative offerings that meet the needs of the Jewish community. The field is diverse and increasing its sense of identity. A passion for work at the intersection of Judaism and health translates into providers feeling pride and confidence in the diverse programs and services they provide. Overall, the intersection of Judaism and health is seen as an integral component of Jewish life and learning.

Weaknesses the field faces include the same challenges experienced by most nonprofit sectors: burnout, lack of sustainable funding, and lack of time for writing and research. Although charismatic leadership is a strength for the field, interviewees described the difficulty of replacing charismatic or founding rabbis and directors for continuity and long-term organizational strength. The leaders themselves, as well as line staff, are overworked and underpaid. The staff are in danger of burnout. Additionally, members of the field are not systematically involved in writing and research. A lack of methodical strategic evaluation results in a failure to ensure that the work and offerings remain relevant to and meet the needs of constituent populations. Key stakeholders fear that, without the ability to prove relevancy, both the constituents and potential funders will not share their sense of its inherent value.

	POSITIVE	NEGATIVE
INTERNAL FACTORS	STRENGTHS • Charismatic leadership • Multifaceted approaches • Collaborative • Interdisciplinary • Flexible • Holistic • Creative • Diverse • "It works. Period." • Resourceful • Egalitarian • Sustainable • Willing to touch the taboo • Judaism's long history of addressing questions of health, ethics, and healing • Meeting community needs	WEAKNESSES • Funding shortages • No professional training • People are overworked and underpaid • Chaos • Disorganized • "Quackery" • Lack of unified vision and theme • Too little research • "Calling this a field is premature" • The field is: —In its infancy —In its toddler stage —Dead • Lack of delivery of resources to rabbis • Lack of marketing/outreach and know-how • Inaccessable • Instability

EXTERNAL FACTORS	OPPORTUNITIES	CHALLENGES
	• An understanding that Judaism and health is an integral part of Judaism —Valued —Sense of identity is growing • Pastoral care is becoming increasingly important —Spiritual care is becoming more recognized within healthcare • Judaism and health as a theme • Growth of attention to self-care and resiliency	• No knowledge of the depth of wisdom around health that Judaism has to offer • Spirituality is not a fully accepted topic in Judaism • Pastoral counseling needs to become more central to rabbinic seminary education • Lack of funding and development strategies • Basic needs (e.g., food and housing) trump spiritual needs • Few young people are in the field

Figure 1. Stakeholder strengths, weaknesses, opportunities, and challenges.

Key Themes

Theme 1: Funding and Fundraising: Funding shortages are the most critical threat to the field of Judaism and health. Eighty-five percent of key stakeholders interviewed mentioned the need for assistance in strengthening the financial basis of their respective organizations. They described challenges in identifying donors and foundations, as well as a lack of structure to nurture and sustain relationships. Several key stakeholders said that they were good at grant writing but did not easily find compatible funders. Lack of time to put into the search for funding further complicates a lack of comprehensive fundraising skills and resources. A few stakeholders acknowledged a desire to explore more sustainable funding structures, fee-for-service or venture-philanthropy-oriented ideas, but they had not allocated time or energy to those development and strategic-planning efforts.

Theme 2: Emerging Leadership: Professionals in the field of Judaism and health want to attract and sustain a future generation of leadership. The needs of constituents to find meaning and to find services and resources at times of challenge will surely continue. Key stakeholder interviews indicated awareness that twenty- and thirtysomethings are not entering the field in high numbers. New jobs are scarce, and like other areas in Jewish communal life, there is a ceiling on growth.

According to Richard Siegel, director of the Hebrew Union College–Jewish Institute of Religion's School of Jewish Nonprofit Management, large numbers of senior management in the health and healing subsector, as in the field of Jewish nonprofit management as a whole, will soon retire, leaving skilled and experienced middle managers in high demand. Professionals need to strengthen administrative, fiduciary, and personnel management skills, as well as fundraising and organizational development skills.[23]

A recent study, *Generation of Change: How Leaders in Their Twenties and Thirties Are Reshaping American Jewish Life*,[24] suggested that there is no dearth of young committed Jewish professionals or lay leaders and that they are attuned to the diversity of Jewish needs and interests. The study divided Jewish nonprofits into categories of establishment versus non-establishment, and mainstream versus innovative. Stakeholders interviewed are asking themselves and one another, are Jewish health and healing services in organizations considered mainstream establishment organizations? Many personnel hold onto earlier self-images and organizational images as cutting-edge innovators.

Unlike limitations in programs and services offered through the Jewish healing centers and family service agencies, the Jewish seminaries are experiencing a difference of mood and continuing growth through the blossoming of pastoral education. Across denominations, the seminaries devote attention, funding, and personpower to improving and systematizing coursework and field internship experiences to ensure that current and future generations of Jewish leaders can help individuals and families in need. People expect Jewish clergy to bring sensitivity, experience, and expertise to their work with congregants and community members around issues of illness, loss, and wellness.

One of the key stakeholders interviewed, Rabbi Shira Stern, a pastoral counselor, stated that she believes that we need to make sure that learning comes not only from the "key players" but also from the next generation: "We need to be sure to grow this movement and not become so insulated that we forget why we're doing what we're doing."[25]

Theme 3: Collaborative Interdisciplinary Work: The collaborative and interdisciplinary nature of current work in Judaism and health, discovered through the program assessment, was and continues to be one of the field's key strengths. Bio-psycho-social-spiritual models of health and wellness take a broad, holistic approach to assessing and promoting health and addressing illness and pain. Institutions affiliated with Judaism and health utilize these models. The interdisciplinary nature of Judaism, health, and healing work reaches beyond the respective movement (denomination). It serves as an example of how the Jewish movements can come together to help individuals and families in need. One example is found at the Jewish seminary level, where interdenominational dialogue and collaboration are burgeoning in pastoral education.

Rabbis, educators, social workers, physicians, and psychiatrists come together to teach emerging Jewish leaders how to be present in the face of illness and loss—and to share learning among colleagues in the Reform, Reconstructionist, Conservative, Renewal, and modern Orthodox movements. In January 2012, seminary pastoral education faculty from across the movements gathered together for a conference focusing on the combination of fieldwork, classroom learning, and reflective supervision embraced by all the mainstream seminaries.[26]

This collaboration occurs outside the seminaries as well. Marjorie Sokoll, a Jewish Family Services leader, noted in her stakeholder interview that the transdenominational, egalitarian, and "honoring of all approaches" nature of the field is one of its key strengths. This allows for more acceptance of ideas, including, for example, more recent acceptance of the mind-body connection by the general lay Jewish community.

Perhaps because of this acceptance and acknowledgment of the potential for interdisciplinary collaboration, the most frequent request of the key stakeholders interviewed was a "system to enhance collaboration and connection." These leaders are looking for a systematic way to continue education, communication, and exchange.

The Kalsman Institute co-sponsored a Judaism and health conference with the Bay Area Jewish Healing Center (BAJHC) in 2003, which explicitly examined collaboration and the significance of cooperation as an organizational value, especially when it comes to healing concerns.[27] During a second collaborative conference between the two organizations, in 2009, the coordinators and faculty found striking the interdisciplinary mix of the attendees. Professionals from medicine, nursing, behavioral health, the rabbinate, chaplaincy, and the arts came together.[28] This combination of Jewish nonprofit professionals interested in health plus healthcare professionals interested in integrating their Jewish and clinical lives was not entirely surprising, based on the interdisciplinary and interdenominational nature of the team that planned the conference. The composition of attendees did give pause to the team members, who recognized that the conference was explicitly meeting an implicit goal of collaboration across disciplines. According to several conference participants, among the benefits of the combined disciplines was the opportunity to view problems and challenges through a new lens.

For example, Rabbi Naomi Kalish, 2012 president of the National Association of Jewish Chaplains, said in her key stakeholder interview that she sees that the composition of the field includes many types of organizations and groups, including chaplains, bereavement groups, healing centers, nonprofit organizations, educational centers, research teams, seminaries, and pastoral counseling centers.

Many of the professionals working at the intersection of Judaism and health come from the medical sector, where interdisciplinary medical rounds incorporate professionals from across healthcare fields coming together to exchange patient information in order to provide holistic care. This typically includes physicians, social workers, nurses, therapists, chaplains, and other allied care providers.

Theme 4: Destigmatizing the Taboo: Among the most important strengths that the Judaism and health field offers is that despite funding challenges and personnel limitations, programs meet the needs of the Jewish people. Many service providers in the field of Judaism and health touch areas of Jewish life, in particular, that often remain closeted. Aging, death, abuse, mental illness, and infertility are among the stigmatized issues in the contemporary Jewish community, even in the most sensitive and vibrant of groups. Rabbi Dayle Friedman, educator and author of *Jewish Visions for Aging: A Professional Guide for*

Fostering Wholeness (Jewish Lights), stated in her interview that one of the limitations of her well-known Hiddur program was that aging is still a stigmatized issue.[29]

Rabbi Anne Brener, social worker, author, and spiritual director, summarized a significant theme of the key stakeholder interviews. She said that many members of the Jewish community still shy away from seeking help needed at times of illness and loss. They themselves fail to reach out to those in need because of overburdened schedules, complicated reactions, and even fear of the unknown. Vibrant, well-trained, and staffed synagogue caring committees, for example, are in want of members to help.

This is a phenomenon especially worthy of further study. Many leaders of the Jewish community do take the opportunity to push for assistance in destigmatizing taboos related to health, illness, and healing, but these efforts are neither universally available nor broadly accepted.

Several communities have made an effort to offer services, provide community building and education, and have become focal points for Jewish individuals and families living with mental illness. One community conference, in 2002, which was designed to attack myths of mental illness, connected the suffering of individuals and their families to ancient Jewish sources.[30] At the time, attendees developed strategies to advocate for a parity law, which mandates equitable health insurance coverage of treatment for mental health alongside physical health conditions. Conferences, community education, and social activism have followed.

Infertility is another often hidden arena of Jewish life where young people are guided by traditional wishes, from bar/bat mitzvah age to the the day they will stand under the *chuppah* and set out to be "fruitful and multiply." Many Jews, men and women, hesitate to reach out to the community for assistance, and when they do, they find little of value.

One rabbi chose to speak about infertility during her Rosh Hashanah service, as both an antidote to difficult Torah texts read and studied on the holiday and an observed need in the community, but her sermon met with complaints. How could she, some of her congregants asked, talk about *that* from the bimah?[31]

Jewish seminary pastoral education continues to raise awareness of issues related to infertility and other family planning challenges. A

2009 conference and subsequent writing focused on miscarriage and neonatal death.[32]

Programmatic Findings

Select Agency Highlights. Many programs reviewed in this sample are located in Jewish Family Service agencies, and several focus on *bikkur cholim* training programs, or on training visitors of the ill. The Jewish Healing Program of Jewish Family and Children's Services (JFCS), Sarasota, Florida, developed a Continuum of Visiting Services program, dedicated to developing services for those who are isolated and experiencing life challenges. The Senior Services Department at JFCS trains volunteers who provide continuing telephone reassurance and visits through a friendly visitors program. *Bikkur cholim* para-chaplains are also trained, and they work to address the spiritual component of visits for people in their homes, nursing homes, or hospitals.

A doula services component of the program trains volunteers as companions for those who have a serious life-threatening illness. Those receiving services are able to move from one service to another on the continuum as their needs change.[33] The doula program is modeled after the innovative New York Shira Ruskay Center's Doula to Accompany and Comfort Program of volunteers who provide companionship and comfort for people whose life expectancy is eighteen months or less. (An end-of-life doula is like the traditional doula, who is a companion for women in childbirth, providing emotional, spiritual, and social support, and comfort and companionship.)

Another unique community program is the Rabbi/Social Worker Roundtable, developed by the J in JFS Committee of Jewish Family Services of Los Angeles (JFS/LA) to enhance relationships between JFS/LA clinical staff and congregational rabbis. The Roundtable fosters pastoral counseling consultation for the participating rabbis and exposes its social workers to the use of spiritual resources in counseling. Its goal is to encourage collaborative relationships in the areas of counseling referrals and program development.

Under the leadership of a JFS/LA coordinator, a group of six congregational rabbis and six JFS/LA social workers meet monthly, exploring issues of loss, addiction, abuse, marital counseling, bereavement, pet loss, and spiritual support, using presentations, case consultation, vignettes, and Jewish texts. The coordinator said that the program created a surprising level of bonding and meaningful collaborations among the participants.[34]

Just as Jewish aging is an area of scholarship, Jewish senior services are a focus of community programming. With a JFCS team outside of Boston, Malka Young, a licensed clinical social worker, developed award-winning senior social programming. A program called Kesher works closely with area synagogues and community volunteers to bring Jewish cultural and religious programming to seniors isolated in assisted-living facilities and nursing homes.

The Kesher program is now an expanded intergenerational program, Kesher 13, which includes a thirteen-hour experience for pre–*b'nei mitzvah* children and their parents. The children and parents participate in small-group activities, such as holiday programs and Shabbat services at assisted-living facilities, or become friendly visitors to one isolated elder in the community. The program is run through Healing Partners, JFS of Metrowest, Framingham, Massachusetts.[35]

Select Synagogue Programming Highlights. The expansion of the Jewish healing movement has greatly influenced synagogues, the traditional homes of community life. Congregational efforts include clergy pastoral counseling and *bikkur cholim* visitation. Increasingly, teams of members train to provide visits, contact, and assistance to individuals and families in need. Many congregations have committees that coordinate this work.

Few, however, model themselves after parish nursing programs in North American churches that offer staff nurses or social workers to provide community resources, referrals, counseling, and occasional crisis intervention. This model of professional coordination, common in church settings, is not widely embraced in the Jewish community.

More infrequently, congregations have committed to funding a social worker or coordinator who maintains the priorities of this work. An example is Congregation B'nai Jeshurun in New York City, which employs a social worker who gives private consultations to synagogue members. Temple Aliyah in Los Angeles embraces a social worker's case model by employing a staff member to contact synagogue members in times of death or crisis, followed by offering volunteer liaisons to aid families with bereavement resources, set up *shiva minyans*, and ensure food delivery.

Select congregations in the New York City area hire part-time social workers with assistance from the Jewish Board of Family and Children's Services and UJA-Federation. More recently, in 2011, a pilot program replicated this model in Los Angeles through Jewish Family Services and the Jewish Federation of Greater Los Angeles.

Additional synagogue points of inclusion through adult and youth education include a wide range of health and healing topics, such as Jewish bioethics, end-of-life care, and Jewish meditation. These are provided through classes, retreats, and workshops, as well as through sermons and supportive services. Congregations offer everything from yoga classes to lecture series to telephone-tree days (to touch base with members who no longer can easily leave home).

Several congregations focus their health and healing efforts on end-of-life matters. Initiatives emphasize volunteer training and adult education. Some communities concentrate on funeral and *shiva* practices and creating *chevra kadisha* groups (burial societies, responsible for ritual preparation), training congregants to do the ancient rituals of *taharah* (purification).

In 2004, Rodeph Sholom, a large congregation in New York City, tackled an ambitious project that aimed to change the synagogue's culture with respect to end-of-life issues. Through a planning committee and consultant, a focus group explored attitudes, expectations, and needs of congregants, as well as strategies for outreach and communication. Although the lay-clergy planning group was surprised by the challenges involved in engaging congregants in end-of-life issues and planning, the initiative eventually offered educational outreach, systems of congregant-to-congregant support and support groups, and a library of resources.[36] Efforts in 2010 included compilation of a significant set of materials that showcased the process, distributed to key stakeholders in the field.

Several congregations have initiated programs to help congregants meet the needs of the economic crisis. Stephen S. Wise Temple in Los Angeles, for example, began Kehillat Wise to encourage and empower congregants to help other congregants decrease mental, physical, and spiritual stressors during the current economic crisis. Through this program, congregation members are provided access to private, confidential sessions at sliding-fee scales with members who work in the mental health field and volunteered a portion of their time.

One congregational constant is the inclusion of health and healing prayers in daily, Shabbat, and holiday worship. In many communities, these prayers have always been a part of worship. The most significant change in congregational liturgy and worship has been the establishment of separate healing services in many North American congregations and *chavurot* (small prayer and social communities). A healing service differs from the traditional main-sanctuary daily, Shabbat, or holiday prayer service. It can be an informal and interactive gathering of participants who pray, sing, meditate, or sit in silence, as well as study, tell personal stories, and participate in guided ritual activities that derive from Jewish liturgy and practice.[37]

A full, scholarly review of the Jewish healing movement's influence on contemporary North American Jewish communal and personal liturgy and prayer is needed.

Jewish Medical Centers and Jewish Education. The program assessment included a review of twenty historically Jewish hospitals in the United States in order to determine what these medical centers offer the Jewish community in education and service. All hospitals included some form of chaplaincy and spiritual care. An especially robust program was at Barnes-Jewish Hospital in St. Louis, where a rabbi runs a spiritual care department that offers interfaith chaplaincy services, a clinical pastoral education (CPE) program, worship services and rituals, and various educational materials and resources, such as kosher food for Jewish patients, family caregivers, and staff members. Other hospitals, such as Mount Sinai Medical Center in Chicago, have leaner spiritual care staff and few additional resources. Few hospitals offered external Jewish education on health and healing topics to outside community members but focused instead on general topics in health and medicine.

Many leaders of the Judaism and health field work specifically in Jewish healthcare chaplaincy, a subsector that has experienced tremendous growth over the past twenty-five years, during which the larger field of Judaism and health was developing. Chaplains explore many opportunities for research and writing. The 2011 conference of the National Association of Jewish Chaplains focused on professionalizing the field of Jewish chaplaincy.[38] Many Jewish chaplains engaged in discussing standards of care, evidence-based practice, measurement, and evaluation. Study of Jewish chaplaincy efforts occurs in acute-care settings, and in short- and long-term care facilities. Jewish chaplains take advantage of new opportunities for research and writing. They use their research to solidify their positions within their medical centers and to strengthen knowledge and resources to serve the Jewish population, as well as to educate others across faiths and health professions.

A program in development during publication of this book is the Los Angeles–based "Jewish Wisdom and Wellness: A Week of Learning," co-sponsored by Cedars-Sinai Medical Center and the Kalsman Institute.[39] This festival-style, community-wide week of learning for the Jewish community, one portion of the hospital's full census, is a rare offering by a major medical center.

A spot check of Jewish skilled-nursing facilities and centers for multilevel senior care indicated that most offer rabbinic chaplains to help meet the spiritual and emotional needs of residents. Residents received counseling, worship services, education, and rituals. The spot check identified numerous community continuing education programs on general geriatric medicine and psychosocial support but revealed no external community education or programming related to Judaism, health, and medicine.

The program assessment also did a spot check of medical schools to examine whether they provided Jewish students or groups with education or resources related to Judaism, health, and medicine. Some medical schools still have a Maimonides Society or other student groups that foster informal Jewish education. Most U.S. medical schools now offer courses or electives in spirituality in medicine and are working to rehumanize medicine. Offerings focused on specific religions, however, are rarer.

Additional programming for healthcare professionals is occurring throughout North America as congregations reach out to their physicians. Congregations across the country offer programs for healthcare professionals, such as group study sessions, "Dinner for Docs" series, and other opportunities for fellowship and study.

Discussion

What was described more narrowly twenty-five years ago as the Jewish healing movement, centered in Jewish healing centers, has blossomed and grown into a more integrative interdisciplinary and transdenominational effort. The Kalsman Institute surveyed the field by interviewing a sample of key stakeholders and reviewing a large sample of programmatic offerings. Previous unique and grassroots efforts have developed into the field of Judaism and health, focusing on several areas:

- Congregational efforts in liturgical expression, communal programming, education, and lay support efforts with individuals and families
- Community agency offerings, including education, resources, and support for those experiencing illness or celebrating wellness
- Centers for healthcare and medicine providing education and resources for healthcare clinicians
- A robust and growing Jewish chaplaincy movement
- Jewish seminaries providing ever-growing pastoral education through coursework and fieldwork
- Continued scholarly work in the field of Jewish bioethics through academia, centers for healthcare, and Jewish denominational leadership
- Opportunities for social action, social justice, and community organizing around healthcare policy, provision of and access to healthcare, and health and disease-specific education and resources

Barriers to Success and Growth in the Field of Judaism and Health

Key stakeholder interviews revealed the most common barriers to success and growth: (1) funding shortages, (2) overwhelming workloads, (3) lack of time for writing and research, (4) limited marketing efforts, and (5) few new and young leaders.

During his key stakeholder interview, Rabbi Joseph Ozarowski, of JCFS in Chicago, acknowledged that this is a growing field that has slowed not because of the lack of need but because of the economy. In his interview, Rabbi Peter Knobel, of Beth Emet Free Synagogue in Evanston, Illinois, added that this field's greatest weakness is a lack of funding and time for organizations and personnel. Several interviewees expressed gratitude to be working at all, in light of the current recession. That said, many were stretched too thin to achieve the success for which they yearn.

Several stakeholders requested assistance with marketing. Program coordinators needed further knowledge, staff, and financial resources to market the programs themselves. They wanted to increase awareness of programs and get the word out to constituents, targeted participants of the programs, donors, board members, community leaders, and colleagues. Exploration and development of education programs is needed for managers and staff to more effectively publicize programming and to learn more about structuring, pricing, describing, and positioning programs in and outside their organizations.

Another subject that qualifies as a barrier to success and growth in the field of Judaism and health emerged during previous Kalsman Institute gatherings and key stakeholder interviews. Programmatic offerings do not meet the needs of Jews in enough geographical areas. Although programs were available in many cities throughout the United States, there was potential for growth and attention, particularly in the South and Pacific Northwest, where substantial Jewish populations exist.

Recommendations and Conclusions

Overall, the field of Judaism, health, and healing has clearly moved beyond its first organizational "start-up" stage into a more mature stage of organizational life development. Judaism and health organizations, in general, would not necessarily be seen as in a stable or sustaining stage, which is due to the barriers to success, growth, and stability described earlier.[40]

Interdisciplinary contributors to the field will be well served to better understand the "lay of the land" and to affirm the value and need for services, responses, and resources among those struggling with illness and loss and searching for growth, wholeness, and wellness. Further efforts related to outreach, education, and convening stakeholders would ensure that the current leadership and a new generation of Jewish leaders, including clergy and healthcare clinicians, alongside lay leadership, are engaged in expanding the field of Judaism and health.

Rabbi Nancy Epstein, a key stakeholder, suggested during the Kalsman Research Roundtable that field-building efforts in Judaism and health should target three populations: "We are creating a field (1) to serve Jewish individuals (including patients) to help them find sources/resources; (2) to serve Jewish professionals to help them find sources/resources and, for some, find meaning in their work; and (3) to educate non-Jewish professionals on how to best meet the needs of Jews."[41]

Overall field-building recommendations include the following:

1. Maintaining the interdisciplinary and interdenominational collaboration occurring in Judaism and health organizations and among personnel and lay leadership.
2. Maintaining a focus on meeting the needs of those experiencing illness and loss while continuing to build programs and awareness focusing on resiliency and well-being.

Early leaders in the field of Judaism and health have transitioned the focus of their efforts from illness and loss to a focus on spirituality and wellness. Others have shifted to interfaith community building, a natural and understandable outcome of working within interfaith spiritual care and chaplaincy settings. Explorations of these shifts will be useful to continued field building.

Other field-building recommendations include the following:

1. Increasing programming activity, where possible; exploring collaboration to increase activity in underrepresented communities, such as in the South and Pacific Northwest; and continuing to add creative ritual into existing programming and congregational life to acknowledge and respond to shifts in the contemporary family and life cycle, as indicated in other chapters in this book.
2. Continuing to provide education and training for health-care and social service professionals to enhance integrated assessment and provision of care.

The following are especially critical needs in the field of Judaism and health:

1. Fostering emerging leadership among key stakeholders, through mentoring, education, and recruitment.

2. Educating young and established leadership in fundraising and marketing—essential for continued growth of individual programs, institutional advancement, and the field itself.
3. Researching and writing, which are necessary for building a scholarly foundation to validate the programmatic and intellectual efforts of the field of Judaism and health.

Many Jewish nonprofit professionals bring decades of experience in chaplaincy, program development and management, community organizing, and other aspects of Judaism, health, medicine, and healing. Few, however, have written or spread the word about their experiences or shared their models of success and the knowledge developed through trial and error. These professionals are encouraged to carve out time to share this intelligence. A 2012 symposium issue of the *CCAR Journal*, edited by the author and Rabbi Nancy Wiener, illustrates a robust response to a call for articles on the theme of Judaism and health, with twenty articles breaking new ground on the "diverse ways contemporary, liberal Jews respond to the intersections between Jewish teachings and values, our understandings of illness and well-being—and what means we can employ to heal our body and soul when necessary."[42]

Additional questions warrant further exploration: Who else is working in this field and yet does not identify with it, and why? What can be done to promote the field? What do leaders in the field need to do to model best practices? How can the competence of professionals and institutions whose work it is to address the health needs of the Jewish people across the life cycle be improved? Why has the Jewish community, a heavily self-studied community, neglected to study the health and well-being of Jews?

Program review and key stakeholder interviews[43] and analyses explored the strengths, weaknesses, opportunities, and challenges facing the field of Judaism and health and revealed how programmatic offerings have both deepened and broadened in the past twenty-five years. Overall, the field of Judaism and health is more robust, diverse, and far-reaching than in earlier years. The potential exists to celebrate existing successes and to achieve continued entrepreneurial and creative solutions to meet the needs of the Jewish community, grounded in history and scholarship.

Three Jewish Lenses for Work and Health

Rabbi Nancy Epstein, MPH, MAHL,
and Adina Newberg, PhD

In these times, characterized by a feverish pace, constant on-the-go schedules, and unrelenting stresses, how shall we find and nourish relationships and experiences of *shalom* (genuine well-being) and good health? This chapter brings three Jewish lenses to these contemporary challenges, addressing how these affect our work lives, which take up increasingly large amounts of our time, energy, and attention, and our overall health. Grounded in some of the newest and most innovative, fresh-thinking approaches to leadership and organizational health, these Jewish lenses are particularly designed to stimulate the reader's mind about how to bring the holy (*kodesh*) into the everyday (*chol*). Each lens provides a framework for reflection that honors the holiness of our work life pursuits, draws deeply from the Jewish tradition, and is applicable in the day-to-day lives of those who work in the secular and Jewish organizational worlds.

Our Health and Our Organizational Lives: How Are They Related?

At first glance, we might wonder why a chapter on the workplace and organizations belongs in a book on Judaism and health. The answer lies in the fact that what happens at work affects our whole lives. How many of us carry our work stresses with us wherever we go,

---

Rabbi Nancy Epstein, MPH, MAHL, is associate professor of community health and prevention at Drexel University School of Public Health in Philadelphia, Pennsylvania. Adina Newberg, PhD, is director of the Modern Hebrew Language Program and associate professor of Hebrew language at Reconstructionist Rabbinical College in Wyncote, Pennsylvania.

continually checking our phones and e-mail, trying to stay on top of it all, to resolve crises and solve problems? We rarely take a break. The United States has been deemed the "most overworked nation in the developing world," with Americans logging more and more hours at work and even skipping earned vacation days.[1] These unrelenting stresses of time and overwork contribute to a vicious cycle that profoundly impacts our lives, our health, and our relationships.

Tony Schwartz, a leading organizational consultant and well-established author, writes in *The Way We're Working Isn't Working* that this furious pace

> exacts a series of silent costs: less capacity for focused attention, less time for any given task, and less opportunity to think reflectively and long term. We are more frequently anxious, frustrated and irritable as pressures rise. When we finally do get home at night, we have less energy for our families, less time to wind down and relax, and fewer hours of sleep. We return to work each morning feeling less rested, less than fully engaged and less able to focus.[2]

Chronic stresses and sleep deprivation, much of which can be sourced in our work lives, are known to seriously impact our problem-solving abilities and our creativity. In addition, they affect metabolism, hormonal regulation, glucose levels, depression, and brain function and "mimic the effects of aging."[3] As our energy levels are depleted and our health compromised, so, too, are our relationships with ourselves, with others, and with the ineffable spirit that inspires and enervates our very being. While this can certainly be a source of depression, it also has profound impacts for our brains and our connections with others.

Daniel Siegel, a pioneer in neurobiology and psychiatry, has written extensively about the power of relationships to promote health and well-being. His longstanding research has demonstrated that relationships positively affect our brain's development, our energy, and the life information we are able to process.[4] They also add meaning to our lives.

When we shine the light of truth on our lives overall and on our work lives in particular, we find that it is essential to consciously slow down, to engage deeply with our colleagues, to promote receptivity, and to wrestle with how we create meaning, solve problems, and bring creativity into the workplace. Our Jewish tradition provides excellent lenses through which we can examine and respond to these issues. The Hebrew words *shalom* (peace/well-being) and *b'riyut* (health) are both connected to a sense of fullness, completion, and well-being that is broad and deep. How can we create and maintain organizations that reflect the kinds of values and lenses through which we can experience lives of *b'riyut* and *shalom*, fulfilling body, mind, and spirit and counteracting the health-depleting forces of today's overly busy lifestyle?

Our Organizations and Their Leaders: Systems and Shared Leadership

Organizations, too, have lives and are capable of promoting or destroying health. Margaret Wheatley, a renowned organizational consultant, describes organizations as like organisms. They have a method of autopoiesis, or "life's fundamental process for creating and renewing itself for growth and change,"[5] by which "systems and their environments co-create themselves."[6] Accordingly, "no structure stands alone; all organisms are part of a greater living system, all relationships are primary."[7]

This metaphor represents a systems approach that is receiving increasing attention in the organizational literature and in the workplace. It affirms that no part of an organization nor the organization itself exists in isolation; in fact, everything is connected as part of a larger whole and is interrelated with its surrounding environments. Emery and Trist, pathbreaking social systems theorists, established that systems are in a state of constant change characterized by a constant flow of information and energy.[8]

Side by side with this systems approach is a growing understanding that leadership is transforming from a "top-down" hierarchical focus to one that relies on shared leadership cultivated by formal and informal social networks. The *Harvard Business Review* reported in 2010 that new research shows that "meaningful change can be driven from the bottom up," "leadership functions can be spread across multiple individuals," and "leadership can be taken on by those not in formal leadership roles."[9] This approach to shared leadership and a "leaderful organization" is best described by new language, such as "distributive leadership," "connective leadership," and "transformational leadership," all of which emphasize the importance of relationships and social networks, the inherent value of each member of the workplace, and the growing understanding that everyone can play an important role in the work enterprise.

Torah and our Jewish tradition, too, insist that leadership belongs to the many, not the few. Hal Lewis, an authority on Jewish leadership, notes that "all of Israel is *memlekhet kohanim* (a nation in which all are theoretically capable of donning the mantle of leadership),"[10] and these Jewish roots mean that the leader's success "is linked to his or her ability to nurture the leadership capacity in others...."[11]

Embracing the Spiritual Core of Leadership

What is leadership? Where does it come from? How does it relate to our concern?

Leadership is certainly the ability to lead and cultivate others, but it also requires us to know ourselves. It means being able to tap into a spiritual source, embrace our values, and cultivate an essential self-awareness that allows us to lead successfully by engaging others and marshaling everyone's resources for the work at hand. William Isaacs, director of the Dialogue Project at MIT and a consultant to major corporations, confirms that the essence of leadership is mostly invisible. Our effectiveness as leaders depends not only on what we do and how we do it, but also on the inner place from which we operate both individually and collectively. The need to pay attention to this inner place has largely been a blind spot in leadership research.[12]

Marshaling resources and engaging others are crucial, but where would we be if we did not know where we were going or if we did not know the goal of our collective effort? The leader plays an important role in bringing a vision to life, crystallizing it, making it real, and fostering its incorporation into the organization's life so that "all may run with it." As outlined in the Hebrew biblical text, "Record the vision, and inscribe it on tablets, that the one who reads [or proclaims] it may run" (Habakkuk 2:2), the leader must integrate this vision into the daily life of the organization and provide a framework for it to become manifest in the words and actions of everyone in the organization.

Three Jewish Lenses for Work and Health

A key question for organizations and their leaders is how to create intentional strategies of growing and investing in colleagues and employees so that all are energized and inspired to bring the best of themselves to work and simultaneously have the best of themselves for their personal lives. Incorporating the themes of organizational systems, shared leadership, and vision, we offer three Jewish lenses with which to examine, reflect, and respond to our busy work lives and therefore promote improved health for ourselves, our colleagues, and our organizations.

- Lens 1: *Kabbalat panim*—accepting and embracing others
- Lens 2: *Chavruta*—engaging and building relationships through dialogue
- Lens 3: *Shavat vayinafash*—having rest, refreshment, and pleasure

All three lenses are interrelated. The engagement and dialogue of *chavruta* requires the accepting and embracing of others through *kabbalat panim*, and both need the rest and refreshment of *shavat vayinafash*.

Lens 1: *Kabbalat Panim*—Accepting and Embracing Others

Emerging ideas in leadership, organizational development, and neurobiology promote the engagement of all faces that are reflected in an organization. Creativity, innovative problem solving, and strategic thinking require us to fully express ourselves, showing up at work with all of our faces and all of our energy. Hiding or concealing any of our authentic faces results in restriction, retrenchment and a loss of energy, passion, and resources in the organizational system.

Tony Schwartz writes that surprisingly, seeing "and valuing others in the workplace is often overlooked and neglected. Being in relationship with work colleagues is more significant to employees than their work tasks and products. Perhaps no human need is more neglected in the workplace than to feel valued.... The deep need for connection and warm regard persists through our lives and affects our performance to a remarkable degree."[13]

Gallup, known for its polling and strategic leadership consulting, agrees and reports that one of the most important factors for productivity and satisfaction in the workplace is the feeling of engagement.

> Engaged employees work with passion and feel a profound connection to their company. They drive innovation and move the organization forward.... The results of the *GMJ* Employee Engagement Index survey show a strong relationship between worker happiness and workplace engagement. Happy and engaged employees are much more likely to have a positive relationship with their boss, are better equipped to handle new challenges and changes, feel they are more valued by their employers, handle stress more effectively, and are much more satisfied with their lives.[14]

We offer the following proof text (using a text to support a proposition) showing that even God portrayed a willingness to support the idea of *kabbalat panim*: "*Adonai* would speak to Moses face to face [*panim el panim*], as a man speaks with his friend" (Exodus 33:11). God spoke to Moses in a manner that was *b'govah ha'einayim* (eye-to-eye, on the same level), portraying intimacy and eliminating hierarchy. We, too, can speak to each other in such holy and honorable ways, taking the time to look and see each other for who we are, celebrating strengths and talents and finding ways of connecting and engaging that maximize our contributions to the organization.

While there are many individual faces within an organization, we also have different faces within ourselves and show these different faces in different contexts and situations. Interestingly, the Hebrew word for "face" is *panim*—a plural noun that represents one image. *Panim* recognizes the multiplicity of the faces that we each have. *Panim* also urges us to remember that in each situation, we may adapt our face to whichever role we are in and to the particular circumstances of that situation. Each new situation can evoke a different face.

This reminds us of the well-known midrash, "There are seventy faces to the Torah: turn it around and around for everything is in it."[15] The seventy faces serve as metaphors for the innumerable faces and ways that God and Torah are represented in the world. We humans are expressions of God's face in the world. So how shall we welcome and embrace these many faces—our own and those of others—that accompany us in our workplaces? Each of us is unique and *b'tzelem Elohim* (created in the image of the Creator), with value and potential for contribution to the success and well-being of the work enterprise regardless of official status or title.

Rabbi Arthur Green, a preeminent scholar of Jewish thought and spirituality, says it well:

> God wants to dwell *be-tokh* or inside each and every one of us, if we will fashion a proper home for God within our hearts.... We are ever entrusted with this task of *mishkan*-building. Each generation, each community, every single person. Each of us has to do it our own unique way, and yet we have to share that work with another so that the one God, the single One who unites us all, can dwell both within and among us.[16]

Inspired by the Dalai Lama, Will Keepin adds, "It is our job to discover what our unique gift is—our unique role—and for each person to give their gift as skillfully and generously as possible ... [rooting] our actions in both intelligence and compassion—a balance of head and heart...."[17]

Taking the time to be present, to see and relate deeply, face-to-face with our work colleagues, allows us to bring the *kodesh*/holy into the *chol*/everyday. We are reminded that each one of us is created in God's image and carries a God spark within. Investing in relationships, treating each other with honor, respect, and acceptance, brings our fundamental ideals into the practical reality of our lives and our workplaces and allows us to work toward creating a better world.

This lens of *kabbalat panim* reminds us to welcome, accept, and embrace all the faces of others and ourselves, realizing that when we create meaningful relationships in the workplace, we renew passions, counteract the cynicism that can grow from chronic disappointment, and contribute to our own well-being, that of others, and that of the organization as a whole.

As Thomas Merton said, "In the end, it is the reality of personal relationships that saves everything."[18] By attempting to be fully accepting of all our faces and the faces of others, we attempt to emulate the godly premise that we are all made in God's image, and we try to behave in the way God acted with Moses. This is an action that attempts to bring holiness to day-to-day actions and activities in the workplace, thereby improving relationships, increasing feelings of being valued, and having the potential to support and nourish health and well-being.

Lens 2: *Chavruta*—Engaging and Building Relationships through Dialogue

What do we do once we have accepted one another? *Kabbalat panim* provides the foundation for *chavruta*, the dialogue of meeting and engaging with colleagues that promotes reflection, teamwork, and a sense of belonging. It is a variation on studying together and exemplifies values of shared leadership and the most cutting-edge organizational theories today.

Jewish tradition values empowered leadership and the ability of a leader to nourish others' capabilities. *Chavruta*, like *kabbalat panim*, recognizes that everyone is a reflection of God and has something they can contribute to the organization. *Chavruta* is literally relating *b'govah ha-einayim* in the give-and-take of relationships between people who are each *b'tzelem Elohim*. Rabbi David Teutsch, a well-known scholar and organizational consultant, writes that "community building can only happen when we recognize the face of God in every person with whom we work. A community that values, respects, and therefore listens to every individual who is part of the decision-making process will naturally make decisions that genuinely consider the individuals in the community."[19]

Chavruta can engage everyone at all levels of the organization. The ideas and contributions of each person are equally important irrespective of their position, status, knowledge, or expertise. *Chavruta* provides the opportunity for an empowering dialogue and for deep listening between two or more people, who can grapple with a question, a task, or a particular text or examine core values, beliefs, personal experiences, and/or organizational documents, such as an organization's mission statement, a strategic planning document, or a proposal.

Chavruta is an invitation to dialogue with partners as well as an opportunity for reflection on the dialogue itself and on the task being studied. It invites creativity and finding the seventy faces of God. The *chavruta* environment is one in which it is essential to establish openness to express differences without being judged. Each *chavruta* partner is expected to bring his or her many faces and whole self to the conversation and has something valuable to learn from and to teach the other. The outcome of *chavruta* is not predetermined and allows for discovery and innovation to emerge.

Chavruta partners can explore and find meaning and jointly solve problems at a practical and spiritual level while also bringing holiness to the organization's everyday tasks. Such dialogue helps create meaning, a culture of trust, reflection, renewal, and partnership in the organization. The cultivation of meaningful work relationships in tandem with contributing to the organization's endeavors can also help strengthen staff loyalty, employee retention, job satisfaction, and staff compatibility while also reducing stress and promoting health and well-being.

Rabbi Sharon Brous describes *chavruta* as the experience of having a "sparring partner ... to push him beyond what he was comfortable with, what he would naturally come to on his own." She continues, "Jews live dialogically—we argue, we interact, we wrestle. The job of one partner is to help refine and strengthen and hone the other, not through acquiescence but through loving challenge.... Truth emerges through rigorous, loving encounter...."[20]

Chavruta also exemplifies reflection in action, which is an opportunity for meaning making as we constantly learn, adapt, and thrive in ever-changing environments. Donald Schön, the eminent authority on professional reflective learning, wrote about reflection in action as an essential aspect of an organization that learns and renews itself. Only through using reflection as an ongoing process can an organization be a proactive, learning organization, adapting to changes as they occur instead of being reactive and defensive.[21] The leader creates structures and processes that help the whole organization be reflective and continually learning and can facilitate and empower the organization along, just like the music conductor, who does not make a single sound but orchestrates the many voices of the various instruments into one whole.[22]

Drew Gilpin Faust, president of Harvard University, emphasizes that effective leaders help the employees of the whole organization be reflective by creating opportunities for conversations and inquiry into the deeper foundations of leadership, the vision of the organization, and the most meaningful ways to embrace change in an increasingly confusing and volatile world. Faust understands the pivotal role of the leader, who must see the whole picture and ensure that each member understands the core values and vision of the organization while simultaneously respecting and allowing each to have their own version and interpretation of the vision. An effective leader will be open to seeing all members of the organization as real, respected individuals who can contribute to its life and mission in multiple, surprising ways: "An enormous amount of my job is listening to people, trying to understand where they are, and how they see the world so that I can understand how to mobilize their understanding of themselves in service of the institutional priorities."[23]

William Isaacs describes dialogue as a process of listening deeply and thinking together rather than thinking alone. In an interview, he said:

> Adults are moving in a very fast-paced universe, basically. What may be needed more than anything is to stand still and to listen.... Listening to the unfolding music—the creative music—the unfolding order ... listening to what is next wanting to be said ... the unfolding generative order of things ... listening to your own nature ... an inquiry into identity and inquiry into the question, "Who am I?"[24]

This is well supported by Martin Buber, the twentieth-century Jewish philosopher and author of the classic book *I and Thou*, who wrote, "All real living is meeting."[25] Meaning is to be found in neither of the two *chavruta* partners, nor in both together, but only in their dialogue itself, in this "in between" where they live together. Buber says that ultimate meaning is found in the honest, open give-and-take that connects one with another and both with God.

Studying is synonymous in this context with *chavruta*. Lord Jonathan Sacks, former chief rabbi of the United Kingdom, writes, "Before you can lead, you must have a vision of the future and be able to communicate it to others.... Without constant study, leadership lacks direction and depth."[26]

Lens 3: *Shavat Vayinafash*—Rest, Refreshment, and Pleasure

Kabbalat panim and *chavruta* will not be effective in the workplace and make a meaningful difference in one's health without incorporating *shavat vayinafash* (rest, refreshment, and pleasure) into one's life. A Harvard School of Public Health study of over twenty-one thousand female nurses strongly found that job strain is as bad for one's health as smoking and lack of exercise,[27] and a study published in the *American Journal of Epidemiology* found that those who worked fifty-five or more hours per week had less creativity and problem-solving ability and more anxiety and depression than those who worked thirty-five to forty hours per week. They also found that rest results in decreased stress and strain as well as increased cognition, alertness, better mood, improved memory, and increased productivity.[28]

We can also press only so hard without rest and renewal until we run out of steam, lose energy, and become less productive. Renewal comes from nutrition, fitness, fun, the pleasure of relationships, sleep, and rest. Jim Loehr and Tony Schwartz write, "We live in a world that celebrates work and activity, ignores renewal and recovery and fails to recognize that both are necessary for sustained high performance."[29] Moreover, "At the heart of the problem is a fundamental conflict between the demands of our man-made civilization and the very design of the human brain and body,"[30] such that "energy, not time is the fundamental currency of high performance,"[31] and "performance, health and happiness are grounded in the skillful management of energy."[32] As a result, "the capacity to live by our deepest values depends on regularly renewing our spirit—seeking ways to rest and rejuvenate and to reconnect with the values that we find most inspiring and meaningful."[33]

Regularly renewing our spirit is what Jews do on the Sabbath, which is the greatest exemplar of holiness in the Jewish tradition. Bringing Sabbath and also opportunities for weekday renewal and refreshment into our discussion is truly bringing *kodesh* (holiness) into *chol* (everyday). Sabbath is also synonymous with what William Isaacs sees as a quiet time of "standing still" that urges a person to "discover who you are. Recover who you are which is at the most essential level abiding in the source of all things."[34] For millennia, the Jewish people have embraced the commandment to observe the Sabbath: "It will be a sign between me and the Israelites forever, for in six days *Adonai* made the heavens and the earth, and on the seventh day he rested and was refreshed [*shavat vayinafash*]" (Exodus 31:17).

The Hebrew word *vayinafash* is translated as "was refreshed." It comes from the same root as *nefesh* (soul). Rashi, the eleventh-century French rabbi and Talmudic and biblical commentator, said that God's rest on the Sabbath came in the form of breathing and allowing the soul to return to the body as part of the rest. Rest and soul are thus inexorably intertwined.

Opportunities for renewal and reflection in our weekly organizational lives, as well as on the Sabbath, are important. We can practice these in multiple ways during the workweek, such as taking breaks, practicing mindfulness, walking outdoors, on-site massage, and yoga classes; breathing in, engaging in *chavruta*, and intentionally bringing our souls into our daily work lives bring the *kodesh* into *chol*—the holiness into the day-to-day. This aspect of *shavat vayinafash* is so important to integrate into organizational life. Terry Bookman and William Kahn state that refreshment is important in organizations because it builds resilience.[35]

When we add fun into the picture, things get even better. Fun is tied to trust in one's supervisor and co-workers. Productivity can skyrocket when we feel connected to others, happy, full of energy, and optimistic. In his 2008 TED talk, Tim Brown from the IDEO Design Lab reports, "Fun and laughter may be the single most important trait of highly successful workplaces."[36]

Today's organizations need to provide opportunities for workers to refresh and rejuvenate their spirits so that it is easy to reconnect to our core values and purpose, which is, as Loehr and Schwartz write, "what lights us up, floats our boat, feeds our soul."[37]

Conclusion

We have established that it is essential to feel connected to others in the workplace, to engage in dialogue and meaning making, to have opportunities for rest, playfulness and creativity, and to be motivated by one's passions in a way that fulfills a sense of greater purpose in the world. These three lenses offer a unique Jewish approach—rooted in our tradition and inspired by its values—to health, work, and organizational well-being and provide a counterbalance to the rational approach that has prevailed in the past. Each requires engagement, slowing down, and thoughtfulness. All three are intertwined and together provide a relevant antidote to our stressful work lives, the hectic, demanding times in which we live, and our frequently compromised health and well-being. May we each find our path to *b'riyut* (health) and *shalom* (peace and well-being)—one that fully engages us in the passionate pursuit of purpose and meaningful work.

Jewish Ethical Themes That Should Inform the National Healthcare Discussion

A Prolegomenon

Jeff Levin, PhD, MPH

The United States recently endured a couple of years of debate on healthcare reform, culminating in passage of H.R. 3590 and signing of P.L. 111-148,[1] the Patient Protection and Affordable Care Act, which was amended by H.R. 4872 and P.L. 111-152,[2] the Health Care and Education Reconciliation Act of 2010. Numerous secular and religious institutions and organizations, from across the political and religious spectrum, weighed in on putative underlying moral and bioethical issues that argue for or against one or another features of what eventually became these two public laws. Note that the title of this chapter contains the phrase "should inform," not "should have informed." As is becoming clearer each day of the 113th Congress, the national discussion is not over but has just begun. This statement is not made because of the long uncertain status of the act, in light of the passage of H.R. 2[3] and the various court challenges, such as the Eleventh Circuit Court of Appeals' ruling that selected features of the acts are unconstitutional,[4] only recently rejected by the Supreme Court.[5] Nor is it intended to convey a value judgment about the vagaries of congressional opinion or about the worthiness of the law itself, which remains contentious despite the inevitability of its implementation. Rather, the intent is simply to acknowledge that the situation remains fluid and to provide a concise summary overview of key themes from one

---

Jeff Levin, PhD, MPH, is University Professor of Epidemiology and Population Health and director of the Program on Religion and Population Health at the Institute for Studies of Religion at Baylor University in Waco, Texas.

particular bioethical tradition that would valuably contribute to public and legislative discourse as the process continues forward. While the possibility of repeal is no longer looming, nor a formal recasting of debate likely, it is timely and necessary that such discussion be engaged with a depth mostly lacking during the initial iteration of the healthcare reform debate a few years ago.

Systems of values or implied morality, of various flavors and with various ethical programs—utilitarian, communitarian, deontological, libertarian, and so on[6]—underlie implicit stances taken in support of or against particular social legislation, at least presumably. One hopes that the expressed pro and con stances regarding the Democrats' H.R. 3590 and the several alternatives proposed at the time by Republicans (e.g., H.R. 2520, H.R. 3218, H.R. 3400, H.R. 3970, S. 1099) were not solely products of political calculus, although that may be optimistic. Regardless, this chapter is a modest effort to contribute to this discussion by elucidating fundamental themes from the Jewish tradition of medical ethics that would valuably contribute to ongoing national decision making regarding our collective healthcare future, which is far from settled. This includes (a) summary of existing Jewish health policy statements from various sources, (b) review of important biblical and Rabbinic concepts that bear on this issue, and (c) identification of the kinds of policy-related, economic, political, and moral challenges that are likely to be confronted (and that already have been faced, in part) as Washington insiders continue to slog through issues that have arisen in the ongoing healthcare debate. The present discussion is offered as a modest remedy to counter the risk that the same principles that did not feed the contentious public discourse on H.R. 3590 and H.R. 4872 and that did not feed the follow-up dialogue surrounding P.L. 111-148's and P.L. 111-152's failed repeal or modification will also not feed the discussion surrounding its implementation, which, at the time of this writing, is drawing near but still under intense scrutiny and negotiation.

Jewish Health Policy Statements

According to tradition, the Jewish canon begins with Moses at Mount Sinai. It consists of a written Torah (Hebrew Bible) and an orally transmitted counterpart, consisting of the Mishnah, a philosophical legal code redacted in roughly the second century CE; its gloss, known as the *Tosefta*; and two sets of Rabbinic commentaries, known collectively as the Gemara, one from the academies of the Holy Land, originating in about the fourth century, the other from the academies in Babylonia, emerging over the next century. The Mishnah and Gemara together constitute the Talmud, the former version of which is known as the *Yerushalmi*, or Jerusalem Talmud, and the latter as the *Bavli*, or Babylonian Talmud. Additionally, generations of Rabbinic commentaries on the Torah, including both halakhic (legal) and aggadic (philosophical, ethical, and historical) work, were produced, known as the Midrash. Subsequently, commentaries and glosses on much of this work continued to be produced, and legal codes were derived, such as the *Shulchan Arukh*. These latter works codified *halakhah* (Jewish law) for subsequent generations of Jews, providing guidelines for personal and communal behavior. The codes, in turn, spawned their own commentaries, as well as a body of writings known as *t'shuvot*, or the responsa literature—rabbinic rulings on diverse matters that continue to the present day. The rabbis, collectively throughout these centuries of writings, have given considerable attention to the ethics of conduct, especially business and professional conduct, and, within that, especially the obligations of Jews regarding health, healing, medicine, and healthcare.

The rabbis teach that at least two fundamental principles underlie halakhic understanding of our duties regarding medicine and public health: a professional duty to heal and a communal duty to prevent illness. According to Lord Immanuel Jakobovits, the late chief rabbi of the British Commonwealth and a pioneering bioethicist, Jewish law endorses "the unqualified statement that the physician's right to heal is a religious duty and that he who shirks this responsibility is regarded as shedding blood."[7] Further, "Prophylactic hygiene [is] raised to the level of a legal, national and collective institution.... Considered in this perspective, the prevention of disease becomes the major preoccupation of Hebrew medicine."[8]

These principles underlie myriad bioethical and health policy statements issued in recent years by the various Jewish movements (i.e., denominations), by Jewish organizations and institutions, by rabbinic authorities, and by academic scholars in biomedical ethics. These include official statements from the major Jewish movements,[9] health policy white papers or advocacy statements from major Jewish institutions or organizations,[10] and books and monographs on Jewish medical ethics from *poskim* (rabbinic decisors) across movements[11] and from medical or secular academic sources.[12] Important professional symposia[13] and special issues of rabbinic[14] and healthcare[15] journals also have weighed in on this subject.

Concisely summarizing this diverse work is not easy, but we can glean a few points of consensus from the Jewish bioethical tradition on healthcare. First, there is an obligation to vulnerable populations. No explicit positive right to receive healthcare is articulated in Judaism, at least in such terms, but rather explicit obligations to heal and to prevent disease, as noted. Second, society must be mindful and attentive to concerns regarding social justice, however it may be operationalized (e.g., as distributive, egalitarian, utilitarian, or communitarian models of justice). Third, society must endeavor to provide healthcare that is accessible to and affordable for all. Fourth, preserving human life is among the highest ideals.

Yet reading through this work, one is left with the sense that something important is missing. Most rabbinic writing on bioethics, including those works just cited, focuses on clinical decision making and discrete medical issues—for example, abortion, stem cell research, euthanasia, test-tube babies, autopsy, transplantation, and so on. Much less focus, if any, is given to public health issues, such as the nuts and bolts of a putative communal responsibility to provide (preventive) healthcare for the population. Much of the scant Jewish bioethical writing on this topic has come mostly from non-rabbinic sources.[16] Rabbi Elliot Dorff, a leading contemporary *posek* (sing. of *poskim*) in the Conservative movement, underscores this point, noting that while "we do have the clear duty to try to heal, and this duty devolves upon both the physician and society ... Jewish sources on distributing and paying for health care are understandably sparse."[17]

This chapter modestly attempts to construct a contemporary Jewish response to this lacuna. The aim is to produce a concise statement regarding what Judaism has to say about our collective ethical responsibilities when it comes to national healthcare policy in the United States. This statement, it is hoped, is sensitive to and consistent with the historic communitarian and social justice emphases of the public health field—distinctives, incidentally, that mirror Jewish moral-theological emphases of historic long-standing.

A Jewish Theological Lens

Any Jewish discussion or deliberation—whether private study or public meeting—typically begins with some "learning," or text study. We will focus on two texts, one from the Torah and one from the Rabbinic literature.

In the book of Deuteronomy (6:4ff.), the text lays out the famous *Sh'ma* prayer, the basic statement of Jewish faith. It includes a paragraph known as the *V'ahavta*, in which Moses describes in detail how it is that we are to "love *Adonai* your God." The Bible gives us a three-part formula: we are instructed to do so *b'chol l'vav'kha* (with all your heart), *uv'chol nafsh'kha* (and with all your soul), *uv'chol m'odekha* (and with all your might) (Deuteronomy 6:5). In other words, we fulfill our obligations toward God through use of our soul (which the Rabbis also understood as signifying the higher self or mental consciousness—incorporating one's cognitive and intellectual faculties), our heart (that is, through worship and through loving feelings and attitudes), and our might (interpreted as through one's actions, one's labor, and, derived from this, one's financial resources).[18]

The Rabbis expounded on this in Mishnah tractate *Avot*, in two places. Initially, Shimon the Righteous is quoted as saying that "upon three things the world stands" (*al sh'loshah d'varim ha'olam omeid*), just like a three-legged stool: *al hatorah* (upon learning), *v'al ha'avodah* (and upon worship), *v'al g'milut chasadim* (and upon acts of loving-kindness).[19] Later on, his grandson, Rabban Shimon ben Gamliel, is quoted using the same words ("upon three things the world stands"), but this time it is a different set of three things: *al hadin* (upon justice), *v'al ha'emet* (and upon truth), *v'al hashalom* (and upon peace).[20] How could this be? How could two esteemed Rabbinic sages state that the world is sustained by exactly three things, but then come up with two different lists of three things? Which is it: learning, service to God, and acts of loving-kindness, or justice, truth, and peace?

Actually, these two takes on the three-legged stool on which the world stands are easily reconcilable, if understood as respective interpretations of the instructions given in the Bible in the *V'ahavta* paragraph of the *Sh'ma*. These passages from *Avot* explain precisely how we are to love God, along with the consequences if we are successful. They are the respective instructions for and end results of living in accord with Moses's charge to "love *Adonai* your God" (Deuteronomy 6:5). We are to love God with all our soul by way of learning, which will lead us to truth; we are to love God with all our heart through worship and other acts of service, which will lead to peace; and we are to love God with all our might, through acts of loving-kindness to others, which will produce justice. The Rabbis elsewhere explained that *torah* (learning) is the greatest *mitzvah* of all, not because learning is more important than doing but specifically because learning leads to action.[21] The premium here, as throughout Jewish teachings, is on action, on doing, on actively participating in the affairs of the world in order to serve the cause of justice and bring about the world's redemption.

This *d'rash* (commentary) can be summarized, briefly, as follows: (a) we are to love God, (b) we do this in large part through our actions toward others, and (c) these actions matter—they are the way that we attain truth, peace, and justice. These conclusions thus beg the question, just what are the ideas and concepts that should inform our actions? This information is required for a coherent road map for meeting our obligations toward others, whether regarding healthcare or any other topic of social or public policy.

Salient Torah and Rabbinic Themes

Existing Jewish bioethical writing on healthcare has emphasized one or another key concepts or themes. These include thoughtful discussions of justice,[22] *tikkun olam* (repair of the world),[23] the sanctity of human life,[24] and a putative societal obligation to fund medical care.[25] The aim here is to consider these and several other principles in order to construct a uniquely Jewish perspective on this issue. The following ten concepts, derived from Torah and the Rabbis' reading of it, are offered as a start at defining a Jewish ethical perspective on healthcare. These concepts include "covenant," "holiness," "justice," "mercy," "for the sake of peace," "to save a life," "peoplehood," "repair of the world," "repentance," and "jubilee." While these concepts are explicated according to their origination as directives to the Jewish people, they encompass principles that are broadly relevant to the national health-care discussion in the United States and can be applied more widely. It is in that spirit that these concepts are outlined—as a uniquely Jewish prolegomenon to a larger and more focused discussion that is both timely and overdue.

B'rit—Covenant

Implicit in the Jewish covenant or contract with God is a set of social obligations that define and govern responsible human conduct. Rabbi Jonathan Sacks, Lord Jakobovits's successor as British chief rabbi, referred to this as a "covenantal morality,"[26] defined as "an affirmation of mutual obligations on the part of God and humankind."[27] These obligations concern our vertical relationship (*bein adam lamakom*, "between man and God") and our horizontal relationship (*bein adam lachaveiro*, "between man and his fellow man") and are bidirectional and mutual. Through accepting the yoke of the Torah, observing the body of positive and negative *mitzvot* (commandments) that concern the details of life, and living in accord with the collective wisdom of our *chazal* (Rabbinic sages) and the subsequent halakhic codes and *t'shuvot*, religious Jews are immersed in a deep tradition of guidance that communicates what is owed to others and how to go about fulfilling these obligations. To summarize, our obligations to God translate into obligations to our fellow humans.

K'dushah—Holiness

According to the great Jewish mystics, the mission statement of Judaism, if you will, is to "redeem the sparks," to help unlock the innate holiness inside all manifestation, fashioned as it was by a holy God. Reality or metaphor, this is an inspiring take on what we are expected to do while we are here sharing space with other bits of this manifested world. Jewish tradition would say that this redemptive work is achieved by striving to follow the path of *mitzvot* and acting in accordance with eternal moral and ethical principles in our dealings with fellow beings. Every person, after all, is a reflection of God's *k'dushah*, something too easily forgotten. This is why we are implored to love others like we love ourselves—all others, regardless of nationality, social class, ethnicity, or religion—because we are indeed one, we are all "sparks" of the same Source of being. To summarize, respecting the needs of others honors their innate holiness and reverences the God of us all.

Tzedek—Justice

The word *tzedek* is related to the Hebrew word *tzedakah*, a familiar term among Jews that in the vernacular is used for "charity," but that actually means "justice"—a useful meditation in its own right. Other terms for "justice" include *din* and *mishpat*, but they do not imply quite the same thing as *tzedek*. This word is found in the phrase *r'difat tzedek v'shalom* (pursuit of justice and peace), a Jewish legal theme, and in the biblical maxim, "Justice, justice [*tzedek, tzedek*] shall you pursue, that you may live ..." (Deuteronomy 16:20). To summarize, we are obliged to ensure that people who are not as advantaged as we are do not suffer as a result of a lack of something essential to their well-being. To be clear, this does not imply a particular political agenda—a lead role for government or for us as voluntary actors or something entirely different—but simply that the obligation unequivocally exists, however individuals or societies choose to move forward with it.

Chesed—Mercy

The word *chesed* is also sometimes translated as "love" or "loving-kindness" (as in the Rabbinic *g'milut chasadim*, described earlier). The Rabbinic sages and mystics explained that justice must be tempered and balanced by mercy. Too much of one without the other is neither just nor merciful. For the healthcare discussion, this comes into play in two ways. First, we must be merciful to those among us who are in need, including people and families newly among us. The Torah reminds us, "You are to love the stranger in your midst, because you were strangers once" (Deuteronomy 10:19). Second, legislators and policymakers must be civil in their debates and dealings with each other and make certain to listen compassionately, not to proceed forward in a mad dash to pass legislation motivated solely by a tacit presumption that only their way is just. The majority party in the 111th Congress was guilty of that in passing H.R. 3590; the majority party in the 112th Congress was guilty of the same regarding its (temporary) repeal. To summarize, we must be merciful to the less fortunate, as we have been in their shoes, and we must also act compassionately toward others if we are to work together effectively to address the needs of the disadvantaged and oppressed.

Mip'nei Darkhei Shalom—For the Sake of Peace

This ennobling phrase appears throughout the Talmud and Midrash. For example, the Rabbis teach, "All that is written in the Torah was written for the sake of peace."[28] Our actions "for the sake of peace" take precedence over allegiance to any secular ideology. This speaks to the importance and necessity of genuine concern for the well-being of others not to be trumped by the pride, ego, or ideological purity often exhibited by politicians and opinion leaders. It is easy to get lost in the details of debate and the day-to-day machinations of legislative intrigue, and thus lose sight of the ultimate goal, which is to help relieve the suffering of our fellow human beings. To do this, we may have to set aside some of the baggage, intellectual or otherwise, that we are invested in. To summarize, for the sake of peace, we are to forgo focusing solely on ourselves, on our immediate welfare or reputation, on "being right," and instead attend to "doing right."

Pikuach Nefesh—To Save a Life

According to a well-known Rabbinic teaching, "to save a life" supercedes all of the other six hundred–plus *mitzvot* except three (those forbidding idolatry, immoral sexual behavior, and murder). To illustrate with an extreme and fanciful example: if lost, alone, and undeniably starving to death in the desert, even a religious Jew who dutifully observes kashrut (Jewish dietary laws) would be obliged to slaughter and eat a pig, if he or she found one wandering by. Preserving human life takes precedence over exacting orthopraxy, even for the most devout and observant Jew. The biblical admonishment that comes to mind here is "Neither shall you stand idly by the blood of your neighbor" (Leviticus 19:16). This is an influential and guiding principle for Jewish bioethics, with both clinical and public health application. It encompasses the duty to heal, as Jakobovits noted. To summarize, when an innocent life is on the line, little else matters—certainly not one's political ideology, financial well-being, or ritual piety. "Shedding blood" is a terrible *aveirah* (transgression, sin), and its guilt can accrue not only to individuals but collectively, as well, if a people—or a nation—refuses to do what is required to rescue a person or persons, or class of persons, in dire need.

K'lal—Peoplehood

As Jews, we see ourselves as a community, as a people—not as a conglomeration of separate, disconnected individuals linked only by a voluntary social contract. Jews thus operate according to a communal perspective regarding: (a) identity (who we are), (b) redemption/salvation (why we are here), and (c) obligations to others (what we are to do). There are very special responsibilities given to us that are ours to fulfill. According to the Mishnah, "[Rabbi Tarfon] would also say: It is not incumbent upon you to finish the task, but neither are you free to absolve yourself from it."[29] These are special obligations that were agreed to when our ancestors affirmed their covenant with God, and they define the true meaning of "chosenness" that characterizes the Jewish people: that we were chosen for a specific task and that we chose to accept. There are things that we are appointed to do, as a whole people, and so the continued presence of an identified need in our midst reminds us that there remains work to do. To summarize, a central task for us is to labor together to repair the world, to fix the broken, to heal the sick—to be God's active agents in this vital and sacred work.

Tikkun Olam—Repair of the World

The idea of repairing or perfecting the world implies healing and restoration, the kind of work that can only be fulfilled in a communal context. *Tikkun olam* is an especially popular concept among Jewish liberals and progressives and within the Jewish Renewal movement. A notable example is *Tikkun*, the Jewish political magazine edited by Rabbi Michael Lerner. Indeed, this concept is so often identified with Jewish progressives that it is typically forgotten that it is, or at least should be, an essential and defining concept for all Jews—a clarion call to the greater purpose of life. It is regrettable that this idea would be disparaged by any Jewish person—*tikkun olam* represents no less than the social dimension (or some would say sociopolitical dimension) of our divine charge as a people. To summarize, the ongoing presence of the poor or needy among us is a sign of the world's brokenness and of our failure to take seriously God's charge to us to, "Learn to do good, devote yourselves to justice" (Isaiah 1:17).

T'shuvah—Repentance

The word *t'shuvah* also means "return," as in turning back from transgression or aligning oneself with moral and ethical precepts, such as might be derived from *halakhah*. A legal decision in the Jewish responsa literature is also known as a *t'shuvah* (pl. *t'shuvot*). As noted in the description of *k'lal*, above, the ongoing healthcare crisis in the United States could be viewed as a crisis in moral commitment, perhaps as a marker of our collective apostasy. If we truly wish to be obedient to God or to "higher" or more eternal values—and, truth be told, many legislators and policymakers profess to this—then there is a moral program before us that requires our immediate attention. One hopes that these professions of uncompromising commitment to godly or moral values made by politicians and government leaders are not lip service or pandering, but their collective track record as a professional class is not encouraging on this issue. As a professional class of academics, bioethicists, or medical or public health professionals, those of us in that category at least should aspire to a higher standard. To summarize, how we address the issue of healthcare speaks to how we, communally, recognize our pressing need to return to obedience to God or fidelity to our highest values, however each of us cares to conceptualize this charge.

Yoveil—Jubilee

At its heart, *yoveil* (jubilee) references a communal obligation to restore things to God's original, created order (Leviticus 25). All things belong to God—more so, they are made up of and infused by godliness—and are only on loan to us for a season. After a time, everything of this world must be restored to God, including our bodies, which are recycled into dust. This may be an inspiring or a depressing theme, depending on one's perspective! It is also evocative of several themes already described: (a) the presence of a moral gold standard, (b) our covenantal obligations to the poor, (c) pursuit of "justice, justice" superseding most else, and (d) the communal dimension of personhood. To summarize, if some people's essential healthcare needs are not being met, through no fault of their own or even otherwise, then God requires of us, voluntarily at least, a redistributive justice bolder than any secular government would dare to legislate. Whether we are speaking of federal government involvement, private- or philanthropic-sector involvement, or something else entirely is not the issue here. But, however we choose as individuals, as communities, or as a nation to work that out, a Jewish understanding is that we most certainly are obliged to act, without reservation.

Lekh L'kha: How Do We "Go Forth"?

> *Adonai* said to Abram, "Go forth from your native land and from your father's house to the land that I will show you. I will make of you a great nation, and I will bless you; I will make your name great, and you shall be a blessing. I will bless those who bless you and curse him that curses you; and all the families of the earth shall bless themselves by you." Abram went forth [*vayeilech Avram*] as *Adonai* had commanded him.... (Genesis 12:1–4)

When God established a *b'rit* with Abram, Abram sealed it by going forth—he became an actor in the world, an agent of God's intentions for humankind. That, then, is what we are to do. This discussion is not just an academic exercise; the Torah teaches that we are to put these ideas into practice.

In going forth, we can expect to encounter certain barriers, some more resistant than others, depending on the intransigence or pliability of the major players. Four nested challenges can be identified, involving policy-related issues, economic and political considerations, and matters of morality. The intention here is not to propose specific solutions—to quote a well-known public figure, that charge is above the present author's pay grade—but rather simply to identify issues that Jewish ethical teachings direct us to confront.

First, there are *policy-related challenges*. Couched in conventional bioethical terms, the challenge here is how to meet obligations of justice and beneficence without violating principles of non-maleficence and autonomy. This is meant not solely in a clinical or individual context, but in the communal context of population health. That is, how do we improve access to healthcare for underserved or vulnerable populations without threatening that of everyone else? How do we foster social justice for historically oppressed people without sacrificing it for others? How do we provide care for less advantaged people without creating permanent entitlements that put others at financial risk? The Rabbis, for example, taught that there is a limit to charity, to giving—namely the point at which we put our own family/house at risk and are in need of charity ourselves.[30] The calculus involved in answering such questions is complex, and the temptation, on both sides of the aisle, has been to ignore them and press ahead anyway.

Second, these challenges, in turn, produce considerable *economic challenges*. In the debate and lead-up to passage of H.R. 3590, the discourse on healthcare reform on Capitol Hill and in the mass media was obnoxiously polarized. Some opponents of the bill, on the political right, stereotyped supporters as conscious agents of a nefarious plot to overthrow our liberties; ostensible moral and economic considerations in favor of the bill were not treated seriously. Likewise, the reaction to this narrative, from some on the political left, was itself stereotype driven, presuming that opposition was invariably driven by overt hostility to the needs of the uninsured. An earnest critique of P.L. 111-148 and P.L. 111-152, however, was offered from the right on economic grounds, from the perspectives of the classical-liberal Austrian school and the neoclassical Chicago school. These include among them economists concerned that the plan supported by the current administration, once implemented, will only exacerbate a bad situation because it is based on faulty economic principles. Such concerns include, for example, the inefficiencies of central planning and command economies, abrogation of the market's discovery process, the inevitability of shortages and rationing, and the possibility of a most-favored status for political allies, such as through the granting of waivers. Disregarding the possibility of market-based solutions, this perspective holds, will hinder eradication of systemic poverty, which is instrumental to improving population health. True or false, such a critique is over the proper role of the state, not over the imperative to reach out to the underserved.

This chapter is not the place to debate these ideas. Moreover, it is not being suggested that this critique is entirely on-base, nor that all conservative opponents of the current administration's efforts have been motivated by genuine concerns such as these. For some opponents, regrettably, their opposition has been over the substance of the moral program to help the structurally underserved. Yet, rather than facing the possibility that some of this market-based economic critique may have a point, it has been much easier to stereotype and demonize all of the legislation's opposition, a strategy that, besides being uncivil, has not been conducive to the kind of sophisticated economic deliberation that this issue ideally required and that was not forthcoming from 2009 to 2012. The resulting resonance of these two types of concerns, pragmatic and ideological, no matter the validity of either type of concern, thus presents additional barriers to constructive change.

Third, these challenges, in turn, produce *political challenges*. Notwithstanding the arguments that can be and were marshaled for healthcare reform, moral or ethical or otherwise, there are distinct and visible threats to effectively addressing these issues in the current political environment, still, even as implementation of the new act draws near. These include a woeful polarization of discourse; an intransigent Congress, which refused to read its own legislation; an ideological House leadership unwilling to negotiate; a disengaged White House so eager to sign a bill, any bill, into public law that it compromised on issues that undercut its own supporters in Congress; a news blackout on earnest minority-party proposals; and decision making based on nonce political calculus rather than on careful policy deliberation, economic realities, or moral principles. These are not looming threats; they already affected the healthcare debate in the 111th Congress. Nor did this situation change much with the 112th Congress; the players simply reversed roles. There is thus a plentiful supply of blame to be shared by both major parties. Without a subsequent change of course, this drama has continued to be reenacted and exacerbated in the 113th Congress and threatens to do so into the foreseeable future.

Fourth, these challenges, in turn, produce *moral challenges*. How these will be addressed and whether they will be addressed at all depend in part on whether there is success in negotiating the policy-related, economic, and political challenges that will continue to arise.

Otherwise, we will continue to lament the continued estrangement of bioethics and public health[31] and "the mystery of the missing moral momentum"[32] related to healthcare reform. For religiously committed Jews, however, there is no mystery, and the outline of the moral program is clear.

To summarize what has been stated up to now, there is an identifiable Jewish consensus on certain basic points regarding the healthcare reform discussion. Do moral values and principles influence health policy? Yes. Should they? Yes. Are we obliged to work for constructive social change? Yes. According to only certain ideological perspectives? No. Are we in breach of our covenantal obligations if we eschew this responsibility? Yes. Should concern for justice, mercy, saving life, and preserving peace take precedence over political calculation and expediency? Yes. But just because these things should happen does not mean that they will. The danger is that these issues will continue not to be engaged and that not only will this discourse suffer, but the lives of many Americans will be jeopardized as a result.

The take-home point here is straightforward: regardless of our political or economic preferences, or our level of halakhic observance, we cannot ignore the Rabbis' clear and nearly unanimous support of an obligation to provide for the healthcare of those unable to afford it or provide it on their own. The *mitzvah* of preserving a life (*pikuach nefesh*) is paramount. This is a red-letter moral issue for Judaism. It is hard to imagine any organized Jewish religious entity—denominational, communal, or rabbinic—that would sanction a purely laissez-faire or social Darwinist or Randian approach or something similar, to consider examples from one of the far ends of the spectrum of political economy, albeit one that is not likely to be popular within public health circles. Such a view might even be considered a *chillul HaShem* (desecration of God's name) in some quarters. A libertarian or minimal-state or classical-liberal perspective on political economy may have much to recommend it as a general approach to federal governing, according to many people, a minority of Jews included. But when it comes specifically to issues of healthcare access, public health preparedness, and primary prevention, such a perspective would likely have close to zero traction among observant Jews, regardless of denominational affiliation or political preference. The commandments regarding "saving a life" and "shedding blood," alone, would seem to be unequivocal. The concepts reviewed in this chapter make clear that the health of populations is a communal responsibility and that when any of us suffer we are all suffering and we all must join together to marshal an effective response.

In closing, Rabbi Dorff emphasizes this point clearly:

> The Jewish demand that everyone have access to health care does not necessarily mandate a particular form of delivery, such as socialized medicine: any delivery system that does the job will meet these Jewish standards.... However, the fact that more than forty million Americans have no health insurance whatsoever is, from a Jewish point of view, an intolerable dereliction of society's moral duty.... While the specific form of health care system may vary, Jewish ethics definitely demands that American Jews work to ensure that the United States, as a society, provides health care to everyone in some way.[33]

Notes

Foreword

1. I develop more of these fundamental principles through which Judaism's view of life affects healthcare in chapter 2 of my book *Matters of Life and Death: A Jewish Approach to Modern Medical Ethics.*

Introduction: Judaism and Health, by Jeff Levin, PhD, MPH, and Michele F. Prince, LCSW, MAJCS

1. Martin E. Marty, "Tradition and the Traditions in Health/Medicine and Religion," in *Health/Medicine and the Faith Traditions: An Inquiry into Religion and Medicine*, ed. Martin E. Marty and Kenneth L. Vaux (Philadelphia: Fortress Press, 1982), 3.
2. See, e.g., Harold G. Koenig, Dana E. King, and Verna Benner Carson, *Handbook of Religion and Health*, 2nd ed. (New York: Oxford University Press, 2012), including its preface, by Jeff Levin, xiii–xv.
3. Two representative works, both by leading Christian physicians, are Dale A. Matthews with Connie Clark, *The Faith Factor: Proof of the Healing Power of Prayer* (New York: Viking, 1998), and Harold G. Koenig, *The Healing Power of Faith: Science Explores Medicine's Last Great Frontier* (New York: Simon & Schuster, 1999).
4. The finest scholarly critique of this work, especially the numerous research studies, can be found in Joel James Shuman and Keith G. Meador, *Heal Thyself: Spirituality, Medicine, and the Distortion of Christianity* (New York: Oxford University Press, 2003).
5. A good sourcebook for theory, research, and conceptual issues related to the intersection of spirituality and health and the larger subject of integral healing is Marilyn Schlitz and Tina Amorok, with Marc S. Micozzi, eds., *Consciousness and Healing: Integral Approaches to Mind-Body Medicine* (St. Louis: Elsevier Churchill Livingstone, 2005).
6. Harold G. Koenig, Elizabeth G. Hooten, Erin Lindsay-Calkins, and Keith G. Meador, "Spirituality in Medical School Curricula: Findings from a National Survey," *International Journal of Psychiatry in Medicine* 40 (2010): 391–98.

7. See Jeff Levin and Keith G. Meador, eds., *Healing to All Their Flesh: Jewish and Christian Perspectives on Spirituality, Theology, and Health* (West Conshohocken, PA: Templeton Press, 2012).
8. Helpful historical perspectives can be found in various chapters throughout Marty and Vaux, *Health/Medicine and the Faith Traditions.*
9. Fred Rosner, *Contemporary Biomedical Ethical Issues and Jewish Law* (Jersey City, NJ: Ktav, 2007), ix.
10. Fred Rosner, "Moses Maimonides (1135–1204)," *Annals of Internal Medicine* 62 (1965): 374.
11. Nisson E. Shulman, "Contemporary Specialists in Jewish Medical Ethics," in *Pioneers in Jewish Medical Ethics*, ed. Fred Rosner (Northvale, NJ: Jason Aronson, 1997), 203–30.
12. Fred Rosner, preface to Rosner, *Pioneers in Jewish Medical Ethics*, xiii.
13. Shimon Glick, foreword to Rosner, *Pioneers in Jewish Medical Ethics*, xv.
14. See the excellent collection of essays found in Herman Branover and Ilana Coven Attia, eds., *Science in the Light of Torah: A* B'Or Ha'Torah *Reader* (Northvale, NJ: Jason Aronson, 1994).
15. Immanuel Jakobovits, foreword to *Jewish Answers to Medical Ethics Questions*, ed. Nisson E. Shulman (Northvale, NJ: Jason Aronson, 1998), xv.
16. Notable recent historical works include Natalia Berger, ed., *Jews and Medicine: Religion, Culture, Science* (Philadelphia: Jewish Publication Society, 1995); Frank Heynick, *Jews in Medicine: An Epic Saga* (Hoboken, NJ: Ktav, 2002); and Mitchell B. Hart, *The Healthy Jew: The Symbiosis of Judaism and Modern Medicine* (New York: Cambridge University Press, 2007). Academic papers on the mental and physical health of Jews are plentiful and are summarized in the chapters "Jewish Religious Coping and Trust in God: A Review of the Empirical Literature" and "Population Research on Judaism, Health, and Well-Being," respectively, in this book.
17. See the essays in Rabbi William Cutter's two edited works, *Healing and the Jewish Imagination: Spiritual and Practical Perspectives on Judaism and Health* (Woodstock, VT: Jewish Lights, 2007) and *Midrash and Medicine: Healing Body and Soul in the Jewish Interpretive Tradition* (Woodstock, VT: Jewish Lights, 2011), as well as Rabbi Samuel E. Karff's book review of the latter in *Journal of Religion and Health* 50 (2011): 869–71. See also the wonderful anthology by David Freeman and Judith Z. Abrams, eds., *Illness and Health in the Jewish Tradition: Writings from the Bible to Today* (Philadelphia: Jewish Publication Society, 1999). The most recent and most comprehensive resource is Michele Prince and Rabbi Nancy H. Wiener, eds., "Symposium Issue on Judaism, Health, and Healing," special issue, *CCAR Journal: The Reform Jewish Quarterly*, Summer 2012, 1–264.

18. Jeff Levin and Michele F. Prince, "Judaism and Health: Reflections on an Emerging Scholarly Field," *Journal of Religion and Health* 50 (2011): 765–77.
19. Dayle A. Friedman, *Jewish Pastoral Care: A Practical Handbook from Traditional and Contemporary Sources*, 2nd ed. (Woodstock, VT: Jewish Lights, 2005).
20. Dayle A Friedman, *Jewish Visions for Aging: A Professional Guide for Fostering Wholeness* (Woodstock, VT: Jewish Lights, 2008).
21. Stephen B. Roberts, *Professional Spiritual and Pastoral Care: A Practical Clergy and Chaplain's Handbook* (Woodstock, VT: SkyLight Paths, 2012).
22. The Kalsman Institute's website, besides describing the work of the institute, is also an outstanding resource for all things Judaism-and-health: http://huc.edu/kalsman/. A spin-off project, initiated by the two editors of this book, is the Archive of Judaism and Health Research, a collaborative project between the Kalsman Institute and Baylor University's Institute for Studies of Religion: www.ajhr.org/.

History of Jews in Medicine and Healthcare, by Fred Rosner, MD, MACP

The author is indebted to Mrs. Miriam Rodriguez for typing the manuscript and to librarians Timothy Omaxa and Deborah Gass for providing reference material.

1. Shimon Glick, foreword to *Pioneers in Jewish Medical Ethics*, ed. Fred Rosner (Northvale, NJ: Jason Aronson, 1997), xv.
2. Immanuel Jakobovits, *Jewish Medical Ethics: A Comparative and Historical Study of the Jewish Religious Attitude to Medicine and Its Practice*, 2nd ed. (New York: Philosophical Library, 1975), viii.
3. For a historical overview of medical practice in biblical and Talmudic times, see Samuel S. Kottek, "The Practice of Medicine in the Bible and Talmud," in Rosner, *Pioneers in Jewish Medical Ethics*, 7–26.
4. Fred Rosner, introduction to *Contemporary Biomedical Ethical Issues and Jewish Law* (Jersey City, NJ: Ktav, 2007), ix–xxi.
5. Jeff Levin and Michele F. Prince, "Judaism and Health: Reflections on an Emerging Scholarly Field," *Journal of Religion and Health* 50 (2011): 765–77.
6. Norman R. Goodman, Jeffrey L. Goodman, and Walter I. Hofman, "Autopsy: Traditional Jewish Laws and Customs 'Halacha,'" *American Journal of Forensic and Medical Pathology* 32 (2011): 300–303.
7. Marios Loukas, Ester Bilinsky, Samuel Bilinsky, Peter Abrahams, Mark Diamond, Mohammadali M. Shoja, and R. Shane Tubbs, "Surgery in Early Jewish History," *Clinical Anatomy* 24 (2011): 151–54.
8. Gary H. Brandeis and Daniel J. Oates, "The Judaic-Christian Origin of Nursing Homes," *Journal of the American Medical Directors Association* 8 (2007): 279–83.

9. Y. Michael Barilan, "From Imago Dei in the Jewish-Christian Traditions to Human Dignity in Contemporary Jewish Law," *Kennedy Institute of Ethics Journal* 19 (2009): 231–59.
10. Goedele Baeke, Jean-Pierre Wils, and Bert Broeckaert, "There Is a Time to Be Born and a Time to Die (Ecclesiastes 3:2a): The Jewish Perspective on Euthanasia," *Journal of Religion and Health* 50 (2011): 778–95.
11. Daniel B. Sinclair, "Dealing with Death in the Jewish Legal Tradition," *Journal of Bioethical Inquiry* 6 (2009): 297–305.
12. Benjamin O. Gesundheit, Reuven Or, Chanoch Gamliel, Fred Rosner, and Avraham Steinberg, "Treatment of Depression by Maimonides (1138–1204): Rabbi, Physician, and Philosopher," *American Journal of Psychiatry* 165 (2008): 425–28.
13. Donna Evleth, "The Ordre des Médicines and the Jews in Vichy France, 1940–1944," *French History* 20 (2006): 204–24.
14. Benjamin Gesundheit, Avraham Steinberg, Shraga Blazer, and Alan Jotkawits, "The Groningen Protocol—The Jewish Perspective," *Neonatology* 96 (2009): 6–10.
15. Zohar Amar and Efraim Lev, "An Early Glimpse at Western Medicine in Jerusalem 1700–1840: The Case of the Jews and the Franciscans' Medical Activity," *Vesalius: Acta Internationales Historiae Medicinae* 11 (2005): 81–87.
16. Fred Rosner, "An Observant Jewish Physician Working in a Secular Society: Ethical Dilemmas," *Israel Medical Association Journal* 7 (2005): 53–57.
17. William P. Cheshire Jr., "Twigs of Terebinth: The Ethical Origins of the Hospital in the Judeo-Christian Tradition," *Ethics and Medicine* 19 (2003): 143–53.
18. Avraham Steinberg, "Medical-Halachic Decisions of Rabbi Shlomo Zalman Auerbach (1910–1995)," *Assia—Jewish Medical Ethics* 3, no. 1 (1997): 30–43.
19. See, e.g., Fred Rosner, *The Medical Legacy of Moses Maimonides* (Hoboken, NJ: Ktav, 1988); Immanuel Jakobovits, "Medical Experimentation on Humans in Jewish Law," *Proceedings of the Association of Orthodox Jewish Scientists* 1 (1970): 1–7, reprinted in *Jewish Bioethics*, ed. Fred Rosner and J. David Bleich (New York: Hebrew Publishing Co., 1979), 377–83; Avraham Steinberg, comp., *Encyclopedia of Jewish Medical Ethics* [Hebrew] (Jerusalem: Schlesinger Institute, 1994); Fred Rosner and Moshe D. Tendler, *Practical Medical Halachah*, 3rd ed. (Hoboken, NJ: Ktav, 1990), 90; J. David Bleich, *Judaism and Healing: Halakhic Perspectives* (New York: Ktav, 1981), 116–22; Yaakov Weinder, *Ye Shall Surely Heal: Medical Ethics from a Halachic Perspective* (Jerusalem: Center for Research, 1995), 145–61; David M. Feldman and Fred Rosner, eds., *Compendium on Medical Ethics: Jewish Moral, Ethical and Religious Principles in Medical Practice*, 6th ed. (New York: Federation of Jewish Philanthropies, 1984), 94–100; J. David Bleich, *Contemporary Halakhic Problems*, 4 vols. (New York: Ktav

and Yeshiva University Press, 1977–1995; and Abraham S. Abraham, *Nishmat Avraham*, 4 vols. (Jerusalem: Schlesinger Institute of the Shaare Zedek Medical Center, 1993–2005).

20. Jakobovits, *Jewish Medical Ethics*.

21. Quoted in Stephen Goodwin, "Inside Parliament: Lords Cherish Spiritual Roots: Peers Debate Sunday Trading—Jakobovits Says Sabbath 'Proclaims Equality of All Men'—Commons Considers Bosnia Troop Numbers," *The Independent* (March 9, 1994), www.independent.co.uk/news/uk/politics/inside-parliament-lords-cherish-spiritual-roots-peers-debate-sunday-trading-jakobovits-says-sabbath-proclaims-equality-of-all-men-commons-considers-bosnia-troop-numbers-1427873.html.

22. Quoted in Fred Rosner, "Immanuel Jakobovits: Grandfather of Jewish Medical Ethics," *Israel Medical Association Journal* 3 (2001): 305.

23. See, e.g., Rosner, "Immanuel Jakobovits: Grandfather of Jewish Medical Ethics"; Benjamin Gesundheit, Avraham Steinberg, Shimon Glick, Reuven Or, and Alan Jotkowitz, "Bioethics: Euthanasia: An Overview and the Jewish Perspective," *Cancer Investigation* 24 (2006): 621–29; Masahiro Morioka, "When Did 'Bioethics' Begin in Each Country? A Proposal of a Comparative Study," *Eubios Journal of Asian and International Bioethics* 13, no. 2 (2003): 51; Orit Navot, "A Historical Overview of the Developing Medical Ethics Culture in the New Jewish Settlement in Israel during 1840–1914," *Eubios Journal of Asian and International Bioethics* 13, no. 2 (2003): 51–53; Sussmann Muntner, "Hebrew Medical Ethics and the Oath of Asaph," *Journal of the American Medical Association* 205 (1968): 967; and S. Levin, "Jewish Ethics in Relation to Medicine," *South African Medical Journal* 47 (1973): 924–30.

24. Immanuel Jakobovits, "Medicine and Judaism: An Overview," *Assia—Jewish Medical Ethics* 7, nos. 3–4 (1980): 57–78.

25. Samuel S. Kottek, "The Physician in the Talmudic Period: Between Technie and Halakhah" [French], *Medicina Nei Secoli* 9 (1997): 313–30.

26. Mordechai Halperin, "Milestones in Jewish Medical Ethics: Medical-Halachic Literature in Israel, 1948–1998," *Assia—Jewish Medical Ethics* 4, no. 2 (2004): 4–19.

27. Michael A. Grodin, "Halakhic Dilemmas in Modern Medicine," *Journal of Clinical Ethics* 6 (1995): 218–21.

28. Etienne Lepicard, "The Embryo in Ancient Rabbinic Literature: Between Religious Law and Didactic Narratives; An Interpretive Essay," *History and Philosophy of the Life Sciences* 32 (2010): 21–41.

29. Robert J. Joling, "Abortion—The Breath of Life," *Medical Trial Technique Quarterly* 21 (1974): 199–232.

30. Kalman J. Kaplan and Matthew B. Schwartz, "Hippocrates, Maimonides and the Doctor's Responsibility," *Omega* 40 (1999–2000): 17–26.

31. Harry Friedenwald, *The Jews and Medicine: Essays* (Baltimore: Johns Hopkins University Press, 1944), 1:27.
32. Harry A. Savitz, "Jacob Zahalon, and His Book, 'The Treasure of Life,'" *New England Journal of Medicine* 213 (1935): 167–76.
33. Freidenwald, *The Jews and Medicine*, 295–321.
34. Fred Rosner, "The Physician's Prayer Attributed to Moses Maimonides," *Bulletin of the History of Medicine* 41 (1967): 440–54.

At the Bedside in the Babylonian Talmud: Reflections on Classical Rabbinic Healers and Their Approaches to Helping the Suffering, by Rabbi Simkha Y. Weintraub, LCSW

1. *Pirkei Avot* 2:2.
2. Talmud, *B'rakhot* 5b.
3. See, e.g., Talmud, *N'darim* 40a.
4. Ruhama Weiss, "Neither Suffering nor Its Rewards: A Story about Intimacy and Dealing with Suffering and with Death," in *Midrash and Medicine: Healing Body and Soul in the Jewish Interpretive Tradition*, ed. William Cutter (Woodstock, VT: Jewish Lights, 2011), 109.
5. A note about the metaphor of prison: to many people, "prison" suggests crime and culpability, and most of us do not accept that illness results from ethical misconduct, certainly not in any clear, perceivable cause-effect relationship. But many who suffer and have studied this text have expressed that they do *feel* that they are being punished, regardless of theology or philosophy.
6. See Galia Benziman, Ruth Kannai, and Ayesha Ahmad, "The Wounded Healer as Cultural Archetype," *CLCWeb: Comparative Literature and Culture* 14, no. 1 (2012), http://docs.lib.purdue.edu/clcweb/vol14/iss1/11.
7. Tsvi Blanchard, "To Join Heaven and Earth: Maimonides and the Laws of *Bikur Cholim*," *The Outstretched Arm* 4, no. 1 (1994), www.ncjh.org/downloads/BikurJoinHeavenEarth.doc.
8. *Song of Songs Rabbah* 2:46 (probably from fifth to sixth centuries CE). The last few words, about lilies, refer to those whose heart is pliant to God's will and ready to accept suffering.
9. The Hebrew root *'rv* can also refer to the co-signer of a covenant.
10. See, e.g., Talmud, *N'darim* 39b and *Leviticus Rabbah* 34:1.
11. Talmud, *B'rakhot* 34b. The words about the servant to the king mean: Who has permission to come and go at will, as he serves the king. The words about the nobleman mean: Who appears only at times fixed in advance.
12. See, e.g., *Shulchan Arukh, Yoreh De'ah* 335:3–6, or chap. 193 in *Kitzur Shulchan Arukh*, 3.

13. These words were understood as referring to the Torah.
14. Talmud, *K'tubot* 77b.
15. *Avot d'Rabbi Natan* 4:1 (probably compiled in the geonic era, 700–900 CE).
16. Rabbi Moshe Leib of Sassov, 1745–1807, quoted in Simkha Y. Weintraub, "*Bikur Cholim* over the Long Haul: Challenges and Opportunities with Chronic Illness; Some Materials for Our Exploration" (workshop at Turn to Me: Faces and Phases of *Bikur Cholim*, 19th Annual *Bikur Cholim* Conference, New York, November 12, 2006), 2.

An Overview of Jewish Bioethics, by Rabbi David A. Teutsch, PhD

Most of this chapter is excerpted from David A. Teutsch, *Bioethics: Reinvigorating the Practice of Contemporary Jewish Ethics* (Wyncote, PA: Reconstructionist Rabbinical College Press, 2005); and David A. Teutsch, *A Guide to Jewish Practice*, vol. 1, *Everyday Living* (Wyncote, PA: Reconstructionist Rabbinical College Press, 2011).

1. Reconstructionist Rabbinical College, *Behoref Hayamim: In the Winter of Life, A Values-Based Jewish Guide for Decision Making at the End of Life* (Wyncote, PA: Reconstructionist Rabbinical College Press, 2002).
2. Teutsch, *A Guide to Jewish Practice*.

Words Worth Healing, by Rabbi William Cutter, PhD, and Ronald M. Andiman, MD

1. John Keats, "The Fall of Hyperion. A Dream" [1856–57], in *John Keats: The Complete Poems*, 2nd ed., ed. John Barnard (New York: Penguin Classics, 1977), 440.
2. T. Carmi, "Empty for the Time Being," from "Poems (and Images) in Spite of Myself," in *Shirim: Selected Poems 1951–1994* [Hebrew] (Tel Aviv, Israel: Dvir, 1994), 316 (unofficial translation by William Cutter).
3. "Final Orders," in Carmi, *Shirim*, 311 (unofficial translation by William Cutter).
4. Malka Shaked, *Libi Pose'a le'achor (My Heart Steps Backwards)* (Tel Aviv: Hakibbutz Hameuhad, 2009), 27.
5. Zelda Schneurson Mishkovsky, "Then My Soul Cried Out," in *The Spectacular Difference: Selected Poems of Zelda*, trans. Marcia Falk (Detroit: Wayne State University Press, 2004), 71.
6. Abba Kovner, "Sloan-Kettering," in *Sloan-Kettering: Poems* [1987], trans. Eddie Levenston (New York: Schocken Books, 2002), 11–12.
7. Mishovsky, "When a horse is sold in the marketplace," in *The Spectacular Difference*, 239.
8. Mishovsky, "When the woman," in *The Spectacular Difference*, 247.

9. Kovner, "Visiting time is over," in *Sloan-Kettering*, 56.
10. Kovner, "Nine o'clock. Norma," in *Sloan-Kettering*, 53–54.
11. Ibid., 53.
12. Yehuda Amichai, "The Precision of Pain and the Blurriness of Joy: The Touch of Longing Is Everywhere," in *Open Closed Open: Poems*, trans. Chana Block and Chana Kronfeld (New York: Harcourt, 2000), 105.
13. Herbert Leibowitz, *"Something Urgent I Have to Say to You": The Life and Works of William Carlos Williams* (New York: Farrar, Straus and Giroux, 2011), 329–30.
14. Ibid.

Spiritual Resources for Jewish Healthcare Professionals, by Elizabeth Feldman, MD

1. See Sameer S. Chopra, Wayne M. Sotile, and Mary O. Sotile, "Physican Burnout," *Journal of the American Medical Association* 291 (2004): 633; and Salley A. Santen, Danielle B. Holt, Jean D. Kemp, and Robin R. Hemphill, "Burnout in Medical Students: Examining the Prevalence and Associated Factors," *Southern Medical Journal* 103 (2010): 758–63.
2. A large body of Jewish texts, from ancient to contemporary, address topics such as the meaning of suffering, dealing with illness and death, end-of-life decisions, and even self-care for healthcare providers. A helpful online resource is the "Resources" page on the Kalsman Institute website: http://huc.edu/kalsman/SpiritualityHealing/resources/. Another online resource is the "Tools and Resources" page on the National Center for Jewish Healing website: www.jewishhealing.org/bibliographies.html#1.
3. Talmud, *Ta'anit* 7a.
4. E.g., *Pirkei Avot* 3:14.
5. Talmud, *Sanhedrin* 37a.
6. *Sifre Deuteronomy* 49.
7. A project of the Jewish United Fund/Jewish Federation of Metropolitan Chicago.
8. Abraham Joshua Heschel, *The Sabbath: Its Meaning for Modern Man* [1951] (New York: Farrar, Straus and Giroux, 1979), 17.
9. Rashi on Genesis 47:29.
10. From the *Birkhot Hashachar* (morning blessings) in the *siddur*; originates in Talmud, *B'rakhot* 60b.
11. From the *Shacharit* (morning service) in the *siddur*; originates in Psalm 150:6.
12. See "ASSAF: Judaism, Health and Healing for Clinicians," Kalsman Institute (2008 and 2010), http://huc.edu/kalsman/SpiritualityHealing/activities/.

Jewish Healthcare Chaplaincy: Professionalizing Spiritual Caregiving, by Rabbi Naomi Kalish, BCC

1. See Rashi on Genesis 18:1.
2. Talmud, *N'darim* 39a, 39b, 40a. Moses Maimonides codified the practice of visiting the sick in *Mishneh Torah, Hilkhot Bikkur Cholim.*
3. See "Chaplain" and other articles at IACC: International Association of Christian Chaplains, www.christianchaplains.com/pages.php?pagina=pg_chaplain.php.
4. See M. G. Maness, "Meaning of 'Chaplain': 'Traditional' & 'Professional,' www.preciousheart.net/chaplaincy/Meaning_Chaplain.htm.
5. Robert Tabak, "The Emergence of Jewish Health-Care Chaplaincy: The Professionalization of Spiritual Care," *American Jewish Archives Journal* 62, no. 2 (2010): 89–109. Tabak's article is the first in-depth historical study of the Jewish healthcare chaplaincy profession.
6. T. Andrew Dodds, "Richard Cabot: Medical Reformer during the Progressive Era (1890–1920)," *Annals of Internal Medicine* 119 (1993): 417–22; and Anton T. Boisen, "Clinical Training for Theological Students," *Chicago Theological Seminary Register* 35 (1945): 16–19.
7. Will Herberg, *Protestant-Catholic-Jew: An Essay in American Religious Sociology* (Chicago: University of Chicago Press, 1955).
8. Deborah Dash Moore, *GI Jews: How World War II Changed a Generation* (Cambridge, MA: Harvard University Press, 2004).
9. Much consensus exists among sociologists and historians as to the hallmarks of the professions: "1. the use of skills based on theoretical knowledge; 2. education and training in these skills; 3. the competence of professionals is ensured by examinations; 4. a code of conduct to ensure professional integrity; 5. performance of a service that is for the common good; and 6. a professional activity which organizes its members ... ; 7. members have a feeling of identity, sharing common values; 8. within the profession a common language is used which can be only partially understood by outsiders; and 9. with the selection of students, the profession is reproduced" (Thomas Brante, "Sociological Approaches to the Professions," *Acta Sociologica* 31 [1988]: 122).
10. While the majority of Jewish chaplains affiliate with NAJC (approximately 300 professional chaplains and 300 supporters [as per conversation with Cecille Asekoff, executive vice president, NAJC]), some Jews who are chaplains choose to affiliate either in addition or instead with the Association for Professional Chaplain (APC). With historically Protestant origins as the College of Chaplains, APC separated from its parent group, the American Protestant Healthcare Association, with a commitment to become more interfaith and multicultural (see www.professionalchaplains.org). Further study is needed to understand better how Jewish chaplains choose their professional associations and how they use them.

11. The Jewish community took these steps to build their profession alongside other minorities who, too, sought to establish religiously and/or culturally specific professional contexts. These include the National Association of Catholic Chaplains, founded in 1965 (see www.nacc.org/aboutnacc/history.aspx); the Racial Ethnic Multicultural (REM) Network of the Association of Clinical Pastoral Education (ACPE), founded in the 1980s (see www.acpe.edu/index.html); and the Zen Center for Contemplative Care, founded in 2006 (see http://zencare.org/our-vison).
12. Quoted in Tabak, "The Emergence of Jewish Health-Care Chaplaincy," 97.
13. Naomi Kalish, "Evidence-Based Spiritual Care: A Literature Review," *Current Opinion in Supportive and Palliative Care* 6 (2012): 242–46.
14. Christina Puchalski, Betty Ferrell, Rose Virani, Shirley Otis-Green, Pamela Baird, Janet Bull, Harvey Chochinov, George Handzo, Holly Nelson-Becker, Maryjo Prince-Paul, Karen Pugliese, and Daniel Sulmasy, "Improving the Quality of Spiritual Care as a Dimension of Palliative Care: The Report of the Consensus Conference," *Journal of Palliative Medicine* 12 (2009): 887.
15. Ibid., 891.
16. See "Our History," NAJC: The National Association of Jewish Chaplains, www.najc.org/about/history/.
17. Ibid.
18. Salvatore R. Cutolo, *Bellevue Is My Home* (Philadelphia: Curtis, 1956), 241.
19. Phyllis B. Toback, "A Theological Reflection on Baptism by a Jewish Chaplain," *Journal of Pastoral Care* 47 (1993): 315–17.
20. "May a Jewish Chaplain Perform a Baptism?" (CCAR Responsa 5755.9), in *Teshuvot for the Nineties: Reform Judaism's Answers to Today's Dilemmas*, ed. W. Gunther Plaut and Mark Washofsky (New York: CCAR Press, 1997), 154.
21. Ibid., 157.
22. Bethamie Horowitz, "Reframing the Study of Contemporary American Jewish Identity," *Contemporary Jewry* 23 (2002): 28.
23. Ibid., 29.
24. Marion Shulevitz and Mychal Springer, "Assessment of Religious Experience: A Jewish Approach," *Journal of Pastoral Care* 48 (1994): 399–406. Also see Zahara Davidowitz-Farkas, "Jewish Spiritual Assessment," in *Jewish Pastoral Care: A Practical Handbook from Traditional and Contemporary Sources*, ed. Dayle A. Friedman (Woodstock, VT: Jewish Lights, 2001), 104–24; and Zahara Davidowitz-Farkas and George Handzo, "Using Religious Resources in Clinical Ministry," in *The Guide to Pastoral Counseling and Care*, ed. Gary Ahlskog and Harry Sands (Madison, CT: Psychosocial Press, 2000), 323–59.
25. Neil Gillman, *Sacred Fragments: Recovering Theology for the Modern Jew* (Philadelphia: Jewish Publication Society, 1990), xvii.

26. Horowitz, "Reframing the Study of Contemporary American Jewish Identity," 23–24.
27. Wendy Cadge, "A Profession in Process," *Chaplaincy Today* 25, no. 2 (2009): 26, www.wendycadge.com/assets/Cadge2009ChaplaincyToday.pdf. See also Wendy Cadge, *Paging God: Religion in the Halls of Medicine* (Chicago: University of Chicago Press, 2013).

Jewish Pastoral Care, by Rabbi Mychal B. Springer

This chapter draws heavily on my chapter "Jewish Spiritual Care" in *Multifaith Views in Spiritual Care*, ed. Daniel S. Schipani (Kitchener, ON: Pandora Press, 2013).

1. Excerpted from Yehuda Amichai, "God Full of Mercy," from "Two Hopes Away: Poems" [1960], in *Yehuda Amichai: A Life of Poetry, 1948–1994*, trans. Benjamin and Barbara Harshav (New York: HarperCollins, 1994), 31.
2. Talmud, *Sotah* 14a. Also *Genesis Rabbah* 8. See Joseph S. Ozarowski, "*Bikur Cholim*: A Paradigm for Pastoral Caring," in *Jewish Pastoral Care: A Practical Handbook from Traditional and Contemporary Sources*, 2nd ed., ed. Dayle A. Friedman (Woodstock, VT: Jewish Lights, 2005), 57.
3. Nahum M. Sarna, ed., *Genesis*, The JPS Torah Commentary (Philadelphia: Jewish Publication Society, 1989), 128.
4. Rashi on Genesis 18:1.
5. Israel Kestenbaum, "The Gift of Healing Relationship: A Theology of Jewish Pastoral Care," in *Jewish Pastoral Care: A Practical Handbook from Traditional and Contemporary Sources*, ed. Dayle A. Friedman (Woodstock, VT: Jewish Lights, 2001), 4.
6. Edward Feld, ed., *Mahzor Lev Shalem for Rosh Hashanah and Yom Kippur* (New York: Rabbinical Assembly, 2010), 93.
7. Robert Alter, trans., *The Book of Psalms: A Translation with Commentary* (New York: W.W. Norton, 2007), 92.
8. Ibid.: 93.
9. See Numbers 6:25.
10. Maimonides, *Mishneh Torah, Hilkhot Eivel* 14:1, 4–6; and *Shulchan Arukh, Yoreh De'ah* 335.
11. Talmud, *N'darim* 40a. See Ozarowski, "*Bikur Cholim*," 65.
12. Michael Fishbane, "The Sacred Center: The Symbolic Structure of the Bible," in *Texts and Responses: Studies Presented to Nahum N. Glatzer on the Occasion of His Seventieth Birthday by His Students*, ed. Michael Fishbane and Paul R. Mendes-Flohr (Leiden, Netherlands: E.J. Brill, 1975), 23. This paragraph draws on Mychal B. Springer, "Exile and Return Retold: Theology Theory," *Journal of Supervision and Training in Ministry* 18 (1997), 166–67.

13. Neil Gillman, *Sacred Fragments: Recovering Theology for the Modern Jew* (Philadelphia: Jewish Publication Society, 1990), 265.
14. Talmud, *M'gillah* 29a.
15. Jules Harlow, ed., *Siddur Sim Shalom* (New York: Rabbinical Assembly, 1985), 201. See also Abraham Joshua Heschel, *Heavenly Torah: As Refracted through the Generations*, ed. and trans. Gordon Tucker (New York: Continuum, 2005), 107. This line is based on an early midrash taught by Rabbi Meir on Exodus 14:30.
16. Harlow, *Siddur Sim Shalom*, 201. I would like to thank Rabbi Jason Rubenstein for first calling my attention to these lines. See Heschel, *Heavenly Torah*, 110–11.
17. Gershom Scholem, *On the Kabbalah and Its Symbolism*, trans. Ralph Manheim (New York: Schocken Books, 1969), 116.
18. Quoted in Estelle Frankel, *Sacred Therapy: Jewish Spiritual Teachings on Emotional Healing and Inner Wholeness* (Boston: Shambhala, 2003), 15.
19. Ibid., 21.
20. I would like to acknowledge that I am drawing from David Kraemer's phenomenal annual teaching about Tisha B'Av to the clinical pastoral education students at the Jewish Theological Seminary.
21. Kathleen M. O'Connor, *Lamentations and the Tears of the World* (Maryknoll, NY: Orbis Books, 2002), 84. See Lamentations 3:44.
22. Ibid., 85.
23. Ibid., 96.
24. Ibid., 94.
25. Ibid., 107.
26. Ibid., 108–9.
27. Edward Feld, ed., *Mahzor Lev Shalem for Rosh Hashanah and Yom Kippur* (New York: Rabbinical Assembly, 2010), 227.
28. Marcus Jastrow, comp., *Dictionary of the Targumim, Talmud Babli, Yerushalmi and Midrashic Literature* [1903] (New York: Judaica Press, 1985), 868.
29. Talmud, *Eruvin* 13b.
30. Jonathan Sacks, trans., *The Koren Siddur* (Jerusalem: Koren Publishers, 2009), 724.

Pastoral Care in a Postmodern World: Promoting Spiritual Health across the Life Cycle, by Rabbi Nancy Wiener, DMin, and Barbara Breitman, DMin

1. Pamela Cooper-White, "Human Development in Relational and Cultural Context," in *Human Development and Faith: Life-Cycle Stages of Body, Mind and Soul*, ed. Felicity B. Kelcourse (St. Louis: Chalice Press, 2004), 108–9.

2. Alan Fontana and Robert Rosenheck, "The Role of Loss of Meaning in the Pursuit of Treatment for Posttraumatic Stress Disorder," *Journal of Traumatic Stress* (18) 2005: 135.
3. Friedrich L. Schweitzer, *The Postmodern Life Cycle: Challenges for Church and Theology* (St. Louis: Chalice Press, 2004): 8–9.
4. World Health Organization, *Health Promotion Glossary* (Geneva, Switzerland: World Health Organization, 1998), 13.
5. The case of the androgenous or intersex individual, in Jewish literature known as the *tumtum*, is a case in point. For further information, see the website of the HUC–JIR Institute for Judaism and Sexual Orientation (http://huc.edu/ijso) or Judith Plaskow, "Dismantling the Gender Binary within Judaism: The Challenge of Transgender and Compulsory Heterosexuality," in *Heterosexism in Contemporary World Religion: Problem and Prospect*, ed. Marvin E. Ellison and Judith Plaskow (Cleveland: Pilgrim Press, 2007), 13–36.
6. Lawrence A. Hoffman, "Life Cycle Liturgy as Status Transformation," in *Eulogema: Studies in Honor of Robert Taft, S.J.*, ed. E. Carr, S. Parenti, A. A. Theirmeyer, and E. Velkovska (Rome: Centro Studi San Anselmo, 1993), 161–77.
7. See *Pirkei Avot* 5:21.
8. According to Jewish law, males, not females, have an obligation to be fruitful and multiply (see *Mishnah Y'vamot* 6:6).
9. *Pirkei Avot* 5:21 provides the first articulation of a male's significant milestones and ties them to specific ages: "At five [one should begin the study of] Scriptures; at ten, Mishnah; at thirteen [one becomes obligated in] the commandments; at fifteen [the study of] Talmud; at eighteen the wedding canopy...." The list continues from age twenty to ninety with achievements, but none are tied to any specific ceremonies.
10. Indeed, building on the biblical identification of a lifespan being three score and ten, a growing number of Jews celebrate their second bar/bat mitzvah at age eighty-three.
11. Cooper-White, "Human Development in Relational and Cultural Context," 106.
12. See http://huc.edu/ijso and http://ritualwell.org for rituals. For information about the history and development of such rituals, see Christie Balka and Andy Rose, eds., *Twice Blessed: On Being Lesbian or Gay and Jewish* (Boston: Beacon Press, 1989).
13. Martin Buber, *I and Thou*, trans. Walter Kaufmann (New York: Charles Scribner's Sons, 1970), 69.
14. Ibid., 67.
15. Erik H. Erikson, *Childhood and Society* (New York: W.W. Norton, 1950).
16. Schweitzer, *The Postmodern Life Cycle*, 49.

17. Reuben Zellman, "Making Your Community More Transgender-Friendly: Guidelines for Individuals and Congregations," Jewish Mosaic: The National Center for Sexual and Gender Diversity, www.jewishmosaic.org/page/file/113.
18. See Stephen M. Cohen, Jacob J. Ukeles, and Ron Miller, "Diverse Jewish Communities," in *Jewish Community Study of New York: 2011; Comprehensive Report* (New York: UJA-Federation of New York, 2012), 211–52, www.ujafedny.org/jewish-community-study-of-new-york-2011.
19. Diane Tobin, "1 in 4 New York Jewish Households Identify as Non-White or Sephardic," *Huffington Post*, June 20, 2012, http://behcollashon.org/media/news/6-20-2012.php.
20. Tom W. Smith, *Religious Switching among American Jews* (New York: American Jewish Committee, 2009), 10.
21. Tobin Belzer, "Fluid Identification: San Francisco's Mission Minyan," *Sh'ma: A Journal of Jewish Ideas*, December 1, 2011, www.shma.com/2011/12/fluid-identification-san-francisco's-mission-minyan/.
22. Schweitzer, *The Postmodern Life Cycle*, 51.

Seminary-Based Jewish Pastoral Education, by Rabbi Nancy Wiener, DMin, Rabbi Julie Schwartz, and Michele F. Prince, LCSW, MAJCS

1. Michael A. Meyer, *Hebrew Union College–Jewish Institute of Religion: A Centennial History 1875–1975* (Cincinnati: HUC Press, 1976), 9–10.
2. Ibid., 21, 30–31.
3. Ibid., 91–92.
4. From its inception, the Jewish Institute of Religion (JIR) had a strong emphasis on practical courses and field experiences.
5. Psalms 23, 78:52.
6. All of these verbs appear in the psalms.
7. For more information, see the website of the ACPE: The Association for Clinical Pastoral Education, http://acpe.edu.
8. Many Christian seminaries are named "theological schools" or "theological seminaries," so their emphasis on practical theology is a natural outgrowth of this label.
9. In the late 1990s, as HUC-JIR (New York) prepared a proposal to establish the pastoral care center that became known as the Jacob and Hilda Blaustein Center for Pastoral Counseling, it joined with the Central Conference of American Rabbis to conduct a survey of rabbinic and cantorial alumni of the New York campus.
10. Each HUC-JIR campus, by that point, had developed its own distinctive terminology.
11. Each HUC-JIR campus has its own personality and ethos and, thus, a distinctive way of providing supervision for pastoral training.

12. From Rabbi Julie Schwartz, who provided anecdotal information from this survey.
13. Ibid.
14. Rabbi A.B., class of 1998.
15. At the four campuses of HUC-JIR, this multifaceted approach is the hallmark of all of our programs for Jewish professionals—including Jewish Education, Jewish Non-Profit Management, etc.
16. Arthur W. Frank, *The Wounded Storyteller: Body, Illness, and Ethics* (Chicago: University of Chicago Press, 1995).

Judaism and Caregiving, by Rabbi Stephanie Dickstein, LMSW

1. James Gorman, "Ancient Bones That Tell a Story of Compassion," *New York Times*, December 17, 2012, www.nytimes.com/2012/12/18/science/ancient-bones-that-tell-a-story-of-compassion.html.
2. A small selection of such books includes Richard F. Address and Hara E. Person, eds., *That You May Live Long: Caring for Our Aging Parents, Caring for Ourselves* (New York: UAHC Press, 2003); Gerald J. Blidstein, *Honor Thy Father and Mother: Filial Responsibility in Jewish Law and Ethics* (New York: Ktav, 1975); Dayle A. Friedman, *Jewish Visions for Aging: A Professional Guide for Fostering Wholeness* (Woodstock, VT: Jewish Lights, 2008); and Martin S. Cohen and Michael Katz, eds., *The Observant Life: The Wisdom of Conservative Judaism for Contemporary Jews* (New York: Rabbinical Assembly, 2012).
3. Cohen and Katz, *The Observant Life*, 685.
4. Gerald C. Skolnik, "Between Grandparents and Grandchildren," in Cohen and Katz, *The Observant Life*, 709–12.
5. David M. Greenstein, "Between Siblings," in Cohen and Katz, *The Observant Life*, 693–708.
6. National Alliance for Caregiving in collaboration with AARP, "Caregiving in the U.S. 2009," November 2009, www.caregiving.org/data/Caregiving_in_the_US_2009_full_report.pdf.
7. Ibid.
8. Stephen M. Cohen, Ron Miller, and Jacob B. Ukeles, "People in Need and Access to Support," in *Jewish Community Study of New York: 2011; Comprehensive Report* (New York: UJA-Federation of New York, 2012), 83–109.
9. National Alliance for Caregiving in collaboration with AARP, "Caregiving in the U.S. 2009."
10. Susan C. Reinhard, Lynn Feinberg, and Rita Choula, "A Call to Action: What Experts Say Needs to Be Done to Meet the Challenges of Family Caregiving," *Spotlight* (AARP Public Policy Institute) 1, 2012, www.aarp.org/content/dam/

aarp/research/public_policy_institute/ltc/2012/Spotlight-Paper-Meeting-the-Challenges-of-Family-Caregiving-AARP-ppi-ltc.pdf.

11. Friedman, *Jewish Visions for Aging*, 77.
12. Stephanie Dickstein, *With Sweetness from the Rock: A Jewish Spiritual Companion for Caregivers* (New York: National Center for Jewish Healing, 2006).
13. Stephanie Dickstein, "Finding Solace and Meaning in the Psalms," *The Outstretched Arm* 4, no. 1 (2002–3): 6–7.
14. Jerusalem Talmud, *Pe'ah* 1:1.

The Jewish Professional as Personal Caregiver, by Rabbi Stephen B. Roberts, MBA, BCC

1. Stephen B. Roberts, Kevin L. Ellers, and John C. Wilson, "Compassion Fatigue," in *Disaster Spiritual Care: Clergy Responses to Community, Regional and National Tragedy*, ed. Stephen B. Roberts and Willard W. C. Ashley, Sr. (Woodstock, VT: SkyLight Paths, 2008), 209. See also Charles R. Figley, ed., *Compassion Fatigue: Coping with Secondary Traumatic Stress Disorder in Those Who Treat the Traumatized* (New York: Brunnel/Mazel, 1995). Figley defines compassion fatigue as "a state of tension and preoccupation with the individual or cumulative trauma of clients as manifested in one or more ways: reexperiencing the traumatic events, avoidance/numbing of reminders of the traumatic event, and persistent arousal" (Charles R. Figley, ed., *Treating Compassion Fatigue* [New York: Routledge, 2002]: 157).
2. "Understanding Compassion Fatigue: Helping Public Health Professionals and Other Front-Line Responders Combat the Occupational Stressors and Psychological Injuries of Bioterrorism Defense for a Strengthened Public Health Response" is a course that has been offered by the Florida Center for Public Health Preparedness at the College of Public Health, University of South Florida; course manual: www.fcphp.usf.edu/courses/content/ucf/UCF_manual.pdf.

Tradition, Texts, and Our Search for Meaning, by Rabbi Richard Address, DMin

1. Irvin Yalom, *The Gift of Therapy: An Open Letter to a New Generation of Therapists and Their Patients* (New York: Harper, 2002), 133.
2. Richard F. Address and Andrew L. Rosenkranz, *To Honor and Respect: A Program and Resource Guide for Congregations on Sacred Aging* (New York: URJ Press, 2005), 61.
3. Martin Buber, *The Way of Man: According to the Teaching of Hasidism* (Secaucus, NJ: Citadel Press, 1964), 16.

Bad Things Happen: On Suffering, by Rabbi Rachel Adler, PhD

1. Viktor E. Frankl, *Man's Search for Meaning* [1959] (New York: Washington Square Press, 1984).
2. Anthony Giddens, *Capitalism and Modern Social Theory: An Analysis of the Writings of Marx, Durkheim and Max Weber* (London: Cambridge University Press, 1971), 79–81.
3. Elaine Scarry, *The Body in Pain: The Making and Unmaking of the World* (New York: Oxford University Press, 1985).
4. Ibid., 30.
5. Ibid., 172.
6. Rachel Adler, "For These I Weep: A Theology of Lament," Dr. Samuel Atlas Memorial Lecture, *The Chronicle* 68 (2006): 10–15.
7. "Lament across Cultures," part 3 in *Lamentations in Ancient and Contemporary Cultural Contexts*, ed. Nancy C. Lee and Carleen Mandolfo (Atlanta: Society for Biblical Literature, 2008), 115–217.
8. Nancy C. Lee, "The Singers of Lamentations: (A)Scribing (De)Claiming Poets and Prophets," in Lee and Mandolfo, *Lamentations in Ancient and Contemporary Cultural Contexts*, 33–46; and Rachel Adler, "Rabbinic Dirges and the Voices of Women in Lament," in *Making a Difference: Essays on the Bible and Judaism in Honor of Tamara Cohn Eskenazi*, ed. David J. A. Clines, Kent Harold Richards, and Jacob L. Wright (Sheffield, UK: Sheffield Phoenix Press, 2012).
9. Walter Brueggeman, "The Costly Loss of Lament," *Journal for the Study of the Old Testament* 36 (1986): 59.
10. Clifford Geertz, "Religion as a Cultural System," in *The Interpretation of Cultures* (New York: Basic Books, 1973), 100.
11. Talmud, *Bava Kamma* 60a.
12. Talmud, *Shabbat* 32a.
13. Emanuel Levinas, "Useless Suffering," in *Entre Nous: Thinking-of-the-Other*, trans. Michael B. Smith and Barbara Harshav (New York: Columbia University Press, 1998), 91–101.

Judaism and Disability: *R'fuat Hanefesh*—The Healing of Our Souls, Individual and Communal, by Rabbi Lynne F. Landsberg and Shelly Thomas Christensen, MA

Portions of the first section of this chapter originally appeared in Lynne Landsberg, "No Jew Should Be Left Behind," *The Forward*, February 26, 2010), http://forward.com/articles/125903/no-jew-should-be-left-behind/.

1. Ibn Ezra on Deuteronomy 25:18 ("*hanecheshalim*").

2. Rashi on Deuteronomy 25:18 ("*hanecheshalim*").
3. Matthew W. Brault, *Americans with Disabilities: 2010: Household Economic Studies*, Current Population Reports, P70–131 (Washington, DC: U.S. Department of Commerce, U.S. Census Bureau, 2012), 5.
4. Quoted in Lynne Landsberg, "Reflecting on 5768: A Victorious Year in Disability Rights," Religious Action Center of Reform Judaism blog, October 7, 2008, http://blogs.rj.org/rac/2008/10/07.
5. *Mishneh Torah*, *Hilkhot Talmud Torah* 10.
6. Bradley Shavit Artson, "Shabbat Parashat Naso—4 Sivan 5765—God's Healing Angels," June 11, 2006, Ziegler School of Rabbinic Studies, http://ziegler.ajula.edu/Default.aspx?id=5505.
7. *Pirkei Avot* 2:5.
8. From the Passover Haggadah.
9. Moses Nachmanides, *Sefer Torat Ha-Adam: 'Al Divrat Bene Ha-Adam U'Vet Mo'ed le-Khol Hai* (Venice: Giovanni de Gara, 1595).
10. Talmud, *B'rakhot* 34b.
11. Alexander Schindler, Letter in the UAHC 1993–94 Yearbook, archived at "Frequently Asked Questions on Reform/Progressive Judaism" (Question 18.3.12: "Reform's Position on ... The role of women"), www.faqs.org/faqs/judaism/FAQ/10-Reform/.

Judaism and Resiliency, by Rabbi Shira Stern, DMin, BCC

1. See "Resilience," Dictionary.com, Random House, Inc., http://dictionary.reference.com/browse/resilience.
2. Ibid.
3. Ibid.
4. Carole Radziwill, *What Remains: A Memoir of Fate, Friendship, and Love* (New York: Scribner, 2005).
5. Viktor Frankl, *Man's Search for Meaning* (Boston: Beacon Press, 1959), 36.
6. The quotation, widely attributed to Frankl, is not from his book but is referenced in numerous book reviews and thousands of websites.
7. Sheldon Zimmerman, "A Prayer for Prayer," in *Healing of Soul, Healing of Body: Spiritual Leaders Unfold the Strength and Solace in Psalms*, ed. Simkha Y. Weintraub (Woodstock, VT: Jewish Lights, 1994), 104.
8. *B'shem amra*, Rabbi Liz Rolle, my colleague and friend, who opened my eyes to the critical first moments of the chaplaincy encounter.
9. Douglas L. Carver, "From the Chief," in "Spiritual Resilience: Renewing the Soldier's Mind," special issue, *The Army Chaplaincy* PB-16-09-2 (Summer–Fall 2009): 2.

10. Frankl, *Man's Search for Meaning*, 131.
11. *Genesis Rabbah* 56:8.
12. Friedrich Nietzsche, "Notebook 10, Autumn 1887," in *Nietzsche: Writings from the Late Notebooks*, ed. Rüdiger Bittner, trans. Kate Sturge (Cambridge: Cambridge University Press, 2003), 188.
13. See Zahara Davidowitz-Farkas and George Handzo, "Using Religious Resources in Clinical Ministry," in *The Guide to Pastoral Counseling and Care*, ed. Gary Ahlskog and Harry Sands (Madison, CT: Psychosocial Press, 2000), 323–59; especially 327–28.
14. "Who We Are," ACPE: The Association for Clinical Pastoral Education, www.acpe.edu, accessed August 27, 2013.

Doing *Kaddish* to Turn Mourning into Dancing, by Rabbi Anne Brener, LCSW

1. See Shlomo Ganzfried, chap. 6 in *Kitzur Shulchan Arukh*, vol. 1 [1870], trans. Avrohom Davis (Lakewood, NJ: Metsudah, 2006), 25–33.
2. Anne Brener, *Mourning & Mitzvah: A Guided Journal for Walking the Mourner's Path through Grief to Healing*, 2nd ed. (Woodstock, VT: Jewish Lights, 2001).
3. Ibid.
4. Ibid.
5. It should be noted that the Bible contains several words that all translate into English with the one word "dance." Not all of these words carry the exuberant image of dancing more often implied by the English. There can be dances, such as dirge dances, that reflect a spectrum of human emotions. In Psalm 30:12, the word used, *machol*, implies a ritual circle dance, such as those performed by women in the Jerusalem Temple; see Maria-Gabriele Wosien, *Sacred Dance: Encounter with the Gods* (New York: Avon, 1974).
6. Minor Tractate *S'machot* 6:12 (on mourning).
7. Mathew Fox, *Original Blessing: A Primer in Creation Spirituality Presented in Four Paths, Twenty-Six Themes, and Two Questions* (New York: Jeremy P. Tarcher/Putnam, 2000), 139.
8. Ernest Becker, *The Denial of Death* (New York: The Free Press, 1973), ix.
9. Ibid.
10. Ibid.
11. Melinda Henneberger, "Elizabeth Edwards' Unflinching Acknowledgment of Mortality," *Huffington Post*, March 28, 2007, www.huffingtonpost.com/melinda-henneberger/elizabeth-edwards-unflinc_b_44452.html.
12. Becker, *The Denial of Death*, ix.

13. This phrase is from the prayer, *Yotzer Or*, in the morning liturgy. This is one of the first three blessings that surround the *Sh'ma* and the *V'ahavta*. It is concerned with the idea that all things, both light and dark, hence good and bad, ultimately come from God.
14. See the work of Elisabeth Kübler-Ross, *On Grief and Grieving: Finding the Meaning of Grief through the Five Stages of Loss* (New York: Scribner, 2005).
15. Barbara Charlesworth Gelpi and Albert Gelpi, eds., *Adrienne Rich's Poetry and Prose* (New York: W.W. Norton, 1975), 21.
16. Francis Brown, S. R. Driver, and Charles A. Briggs, *Hebrew and English Lexicon of the Old Testament* (Oxford, UK: Clarendon Press, 1951), 245–46.
17. *Mochin d'gadlut, mochin d'katnut* (Aramaic): "Mature and immature intellect or mindsets, respectively. *Mochin d'gadlut* is a state of expanded intellectual understanding or maturity. *Mochin d'katnut* is a state of restricted or immature intellectual understanding—the higher intellectual faculties, *chochma* and *bina*, are immature or inactive. *Mochin d'katnut* is restrictive and pedantic, exhibiting primarily *middat hadin* (austerity tending toward severity).... *Mochin d'gadlut*, on the other hand, is a state of intellect in which the higher intellectual faculties, *chochma* and *bina* are mature and active. *Mochin d'gadlut* is magnanimous and tolerant, exhibiting primarily *middat harachamim* (compassion)." Kabbalah Online, Dictionary of Terms, www.kabbalaonline.org/kabbalah/article_cdo/aid/472782/jewish/Glossary.htm.
18. Brown, Driver, and Briggs, *Hebrew and English Lexicon of the Old Testament*, 296–97. See also Michael Fishbane, *The Exegetical Imagination: On Jewish Thought and Theology* (Cambridge, MA: Harvard University Press, 1998), 173–76.
19. Fishbane, *The Exegetical Imagination*, 173–76; Brown, Driver, and Briggs, *Hebrew and English Lexicon of the Old Testament*, 296–97.
20. Brown, Driver, and Briggs, *Hebrew and English Lexicon of the Old Testament*, 296–97.
21. Wosien, *Sacred Dance*.
22. See Talmud, *Sotah* 14a; and Ganzfried, chap. 205 in *Kitzur Shulchan Arukh*, vol. 2, 1237–39.
23. See Brener, *Mourning & Mitzvah*; and Simcha Paul Raphael, *Jewish Views of the Afterlife*, 2nd ed. (Lanham, MD: Rowman & Littlefield, 2009).
24. Brener, *Mourning & Mitzvah*.
25. Talmud, *Bava Batra* 16b.
26. Quoted in Samuel Dresner, *Heschel, Hasidism, and Halakha* (New York: Fordham University Press, 2002), 2.

27. Cited in Matityahu Clark, *Etymological Dictionary of Biblical Hebrew: Based on the Commentaries of Samson Raphael Hirsch* (Jerusalem: Feldheim, 1999), xi. Choosing words to describe and contain the experiences of those making the passage through the wilderness of grief is a humbling task. Languaging an empty space has biblical antecedents. According to Genesis 1:1–31, the world was created out of chaos through the words of God. Interestingly, there is an etymological connection between the Hebrew words for "wilderness" (*midbar*) and "to speak" (*l'daber*). According to Gershon Sholem, in medieval Jewish philosophy, human beings were referred to as *midaber*, or "creatures who speak" (see Gershom Sholem, *Kabbalah* [New York: Quadrangle, 1974]: 423–26). It was in the wilderness that the Ten Utterances and the Torah, words that were to shape behavior, were given. Imagining ourselves in the wilderness is to imagine ourselves at a time of great vulnerability, and this is certainly true for those passing through the crucible of liminality.
28. *Shulchan Arukh, Yoreh De'ah* 341:1. See also Chaim Binyamin Goldberg, *Mourning in Halachah: The Laws and Customs of the Year of Mourning*, ed. Meir Zlotowitz and trans. Shlomo Fox-Ashrei (Brooklyn, NY: Mesorah, 1991), 62.
29. *Shulchan Arukh, Yoreh De'ah* 340:1 and 374:4.
30. Brener, *Mourning & Mitzvah*; and *Shulchan Arukh, Yoreh De'ah* 340:1 and 374:4.
31. This is attributed to Reb Shlomo Carlebach, and is often cited (e.g., by Rabbi David Wolpe in his keynote address at "Funeral Practices *Yom Iyun*," Board of Rabbis of Southern California, Los Angeles, October 23, 2012).
32. Bob Dylan, "Knockin' on Heaven's Door" (song), copyright Ram's Horn Music, 1973.
33. Dresner, *Heschel, Hasidism, and Halakha*, 1–2.

Creativity and Healing in a Jewish Context, by Judith Margolis

1. From an interview conducted in 1934 by Giovanni Papini (1881–1956), Italian pragmatist philosopher and writer, reprinted as "A Visit to Freud," *Review of Existential Psychology and Psychiatry* 9, no. 2 (1969): 130–34. Also quoted in James Hillman, *Healing Fiction* (Barrytown, NY: Stanton Hill Press, 1983), 3.
2. Carl Gustav Jung, *Modern Man in Search of a Soul* [1933] (London: Routledge Classics, 2001), 157.
3. From Rachel Naomi Remen, "The Will to Live and Other Mysteries" (2-CD series) (Louisville, CO: Sounds True, 2001), quoted in Judith Margolis, "Choose Life: Three Creative Women Dance with Death," *Nashim: A Journal of Jewish Women's Studies & Gender Issues* 12 (2006): 242–43.

4. This project was supported by a grant from Cornell University Council on the Arts, Ithaca, NY, awarded in 1983.
5. See Judith Margolis, "A Life in Art," *Nashim: A Journal of Jewish Women's Studies & Gender Issues* 7 (2004): 217–28.
6. "Living in the Moment: Contemporary Artists Celebrate Jewish Time," an exhibit at Hebrew Union College–Jewish Institute of Religion, New York, September 2000 to June 2001, featured the works of 144 international artists and craftspeople, who were invited to create contemporary and innovative works of Jewish ceremonial art in order to "sanctify life and spiritual experience."
7. Margolis, *Life Support, Invitation to Prayer.*
8. At Art Night at the 18th Street Arts Center in Santa Monica, California, where I was an artist in residence, visitors to the display gathered and spoke to each other in an open manner, unusual for art openings. Many wept recounting ways they had used needlework for such honoring of the departed. For example, one woman had cut heart-shaped pieces from her father's sweaters and appliquéd them to the inside of her family members' sweaters, right over the heart. Another person had made pillowcases from her husband's shirts, certain that the cloth retained his fragrance.
9. Abraham Joshua Heschel, *God in Search of Man: A Philosophy of Judaism* (New York: Farrar, Straus & Giroux, 1955), 7.
10. Shirley Faktor was a senior lecturer at Bezalel, Academy of Arts and Design in Jerusalem, Israel, between 1980 and 2003. Her work can be seen at www.shirleyfaktor.com/; in *A Matter of Spirit*, the catalog from her 2012 exhibit of the same name, published by Jerusalem Artists House; and in Judith Margolis, "A Worthy Opponent: The Later Works of Janet Shafner and Shirley Faktor," *Nashim: A Journal of Jewish Women's Studies & Gender Issues* 23 (2012): 169–82.
11. Jeff Camhi's most recent book is *A Dam in the River: Releasing the Flow of University Ideas* (New York: Algora Publications, 2013). More information about Professor Camhi and his publications can be found at www.bio.huji.ac.il/eng/staff_in.asp?staff_id=31.
12. Miriam Lippel Blum is a freelance writer, poet, and educator living in Tucson, Arizona. Her published essays and poems are found in Margolis, "Choose Life"; "Fishing on One Leg in Sedona," *Wheelin' Sportsmen Magazine*, Spring 2005, 43–45; "Meditation on the Sukkah," in Robin B. Zeiger, "Reflections on Infertility," in *Jewish Women Speak Out: Expanding the Boundaries of Psychology*, eds. Kayla Weiner and Arinna Moon (Seattle: Canopy Press, 1995), 77–98; and "Recollection of the Heart: A Personal Memoir," in *Jewish Values in Health and Medicine*, ed. Levi Meier (Lanharn, MD: University Press of America, 1991), 3–27. Her CaringBridge blog site is located at http://m.caringbridge.org/visit/Miriamlippelblum.

13. This quotation is from a catalog (p. 4) that accompanied Chana Cromer's show of mixed-media works called "The Hollow of His Thigh," held in the Small Room, Elul, in Jerusalem (November 7–December 24, 1999).
14. Susan Sontag, *Illness as Metaphor* (New York: Farrar, Straus & Giroux, 1978).
15. To learn more about photographer and writer Albert J. Winn's work including *My Life Until Now*, which chronicles his life as a gay Jewish man, and *Blood on the Doorpost ... the Aids Mezuzah*, go to his website: www.albertjwinn.com/.
16. Susan Kaplow, *Hard Blessings: Jewish Ways Through Illness* is available for on-demand printing. For more information about this and Kaplow's other art projects, including *Wisdom of the Mothers* and *Abomination: Wrestling with Leviticus 18:22*, visit her website: www.susankaplow.com/.
17. Robert Kirschbaum is professor of fine arts at Trinity College in Hartford, Connecticut, and recipient of numerous grants and awards, including three Fulbright Awards. His work can be seen at http://artspacenh.org/artists/robertkirschbaum.
18. To learn more about Rebecca Newman and to see images of her art and read her illustrated lectures, visit her website: http://rebeccanewman.com/.
19. Art therapist Nehama Grenimann Bauch, developed the *Faraway Places* project and oversaw its installation. Its website is http://farawayplaceshadassah.blogspot.com/.
20. From Shlomo Mor-Yosef, "The Healing Power of Art," *Hadassah News*, January 3, 2011, www.hadassah.org/site/apps/nlnet/content3.aspx?c=keJNIWOvElH&b=7657019&ct=8992107.

Judaism and Addiction, by Rabbi Abraham J. Twerski, MD

1. Shais Taub, *God of Our Understanding: Jewish Spirituality and Recovery from Addiction* (Jersey City, NJ: Ktav, 2011), 7.
2. Talmud, *K'dushin* 30b.
3. Bob Smith and Bill Wilson, *The Big Book of Alcoholics Anonymous* [1939] (Lexington, KY: Lark Publishing, 2013), 32.
4. Abraham J. Twerski, *Self-Improvement?—I'm Jewish: Overcoming Self-Defeating Behavior* (Brooklyn: Mesorah, 1995).
5. Abraham J. Twerski, *Happiness and the Human Spirit: The Spirituality of Becoming the Best You Can Be* (Woodstock, VT: Jewish Lights, 2007).
6. Quoted in "Spiritus contra Spiritum: The Bill Wilson/C. G. Jung Letters: The Roots of the Society of Alcoholics Anonymous," *Parabola: The Magazine of Myth and Tradition* 12, no. 2 (1987): 68–71.
7. Twerski, *Happiness and the Human Spirit*, 34–35.
8. See Alcoholics Anonymous, "Step Three," in *Twelve Steps and Twelve Traditions* [1952] (New York: Alcoholics Anonymous World Services, 1981), 34–41.

9. See, e.g., Elijah ben Solomon, *The Vilna Gaon Views Life: Even Shlaima, the Classic Collection of the Gaon of Vilna's Wisdom*, trans. Yaacov Singer and Chaim Dovid Ackerman (Jerusalem: n.p., 1974).
10. Abraham J. Twerski, *Compulsive Gambling—More Than Dreidle* (Pittsburgh: Mirkov, 2006).
11. Howard J. Shaffer and Matthew N. Hall, "Estimating Prevalence of Adolescent Gambling Disorders: A Quantitative Synthesis and Guide Toward Standard Gambling Nomenclature," *Journal of Gambling Studies* 12 (1996): 193–214.
12. Henry R. Lesieur and Richard J. Rosenthal, "Pathological Gambling: A Review of the Literature (Prepared for the American Psychiatric Association Task Force on DSM-IV Committee on Disorders of Impulse Control Not Elsewhere Classified)," *Journal of Gambling Studies* 7 (1991): 5–39.
13. Durand F. Jacobs, "Illegal and Undocumented: A Review of Teenage Gambling and the Plight of Children of Problem Gamblers in America," in *Compulsive Gambling: Theory, Research, and Practice*, ed. Howard J. Shaffer, Sharon A. Stein, Blase Gambino, and Thomas N. Cummings (Lexington, MA: Lexington Books, 1989), 249–92.
14. Personal communication.
15. Personal communication.
16. Abraham J. Twerski, *Addictive Thinking: Understanding Self-Deception* (Center City, MN: Hazelden, 1990).

Gratitude: Perspectives from Positive Psychology and Judaism, by David Pelcovitz, PhD

1. Christopher Peterson and Martin Seligman, *Character Strengths and Virtues: A Handbook and Classification* (New York: Oxford University Press, 2004).
2. Alex M. Wood, Jeffrey J. Froh, and Adam W. A. Geraghty, "Gratitude and Well-Being: A Review and Theoretical Integration," *Clinical Psychology Review* 30 (2010): 890–905.
3. Alex M. Wood, John Maltby, Neil Stewart, and Stephen Joseph, "Conceptualizing Gratitude and Appreciation as a Unitary Personality Trait," *Personality and Individual Differences* 44 (2008): 621–32.
4. Kenneth S. Kendler, Xiaio-Qing Liu, Charles Gardner, Michael E. McCullough, David Larson, and Carol A. Prescott, "Dimensions of Religiosity and Their Relationship to Lifetime Psychiatric and Substance Use Disorders," *American Journal of Psychiatry* 160 (2010): 496–503.
5. Robert A. Emmons and Michael E. McCullough, "Counting Blessings Versus Burdens: An Experimental Investigation of Gratitude and Subjective Well-Being in Daily Life," *Journal of Personality and Social Psychology* 84 (2003): 377–89.

6. Neal Krause, "Gratitude Toward God, Stress, and Health in Late Life," *Research on Aging* 28 (2006): 163–83.

7. Alex Wood, Stephen Joseph, Joanna Lloyd, and Stephen Atkins, "Gratitude Influences Sleep through the Mechanism of Pre-sleep Cognitions," *Journal of Psychosomatic Research* 66 (2009): 43–48.

8. Robert Emmons, *Thanks! How Practicing Gratitude Can Make You Happier* (New York: Houghton Mifflin, 2007), 33.

9. Rollin McCraty and Doc Childre, "The Grateful Heart: The Psychophysiology of Appreciation," in *The Psychology of Gratitude*, ed. Robert A. Emmons and Michael E. McCullough (New York: Oxford University Press, 2004), 230–55.

10. Todd Kashdan, "Gratitude and Hedonic and Eudaimonic Well-Being in Vietnam War Veterans," *Behaviour Research and Therapy* 44 (2006): 177–99.

11. Linda Skitka, Christopher Bauman, and Elizabeth Mullen, "Political Tolerance and Coming to Psychological Closure following September 11, 2001: An Integrative Approach," *Personality and Social Psychology Bulletin* 30 (2004): 743–56.

12. Todd B. Kashdan, Gitendra Uswatte, and Terri Julian, "Gratitude and Hedonic and Eudaimonic Well-Being in Vietnam War Veterans," *Behaviour Research and Therapy* 44 (2006): 177–99.

13. Glen Affleck, Howard Tennen, and Sydney Croog, "Causal Attribution, Perceived Benefits, and Morbidity After a Heart Attack: An 8-Year Study," *Journal of Consulting and Clinical Psychology* 55 (1987): 29–35.

14. Bill E. Peterson and Abigail J. Stewart, "Antecedents and Contexts of Generativity," *Psychology and Aging* 11 (1996): 21–33.

15. Alex M. Wood, P. Alex Linley, John Maltby, Michael Baliousis, and Stephen Joseph, "The Authentic Personality: A Theoretical and Empirical Conceptualization and the Development of the Authenticity Scale," *Journal of Counseling Psychology* 55 (2008): 385–99.

16. Edward L. Deci and Richard M. Ryan, "Human Autonomy: The Basis for True Self-Esteem," in *Efficacy, Agency and Self-Esteem*, ed. Michael H. Kernis (New York: Plenum, 1995), 31–49.

17. Jeffrey J. Froh, Robert A. Emmons, Noel A. Card, Giacomo Bono, and Jennifer A. Wilson, "Gratitude and the Reduced Cost of Materialism in Adolescents," *Journal of Happiness Studies* 12 (2011): 289–302.

18. Emily L. Polak and Michael E. McCullough, "Is Gratitude an Alternative to Materialism?" *Journal of Happiness Studies* 7 (2006): 343–60.

19. Portions of this section are adapted from Raphael Pelcovitz and David Pelcovitz, *Life in the Balance: Torah Perspectives on Positive Psychology* (NY: ArtScroll, in press).

20. Rashi on Genesis 29:35.

21. *Leviticus Rabbah* 9.
22. Sforno on Leviticus 7:12.
23. Talmud, *Shabbat* 88a.
24. *Tiferes Shimshon Al HaTorah, Chukas.*
25. Yitzhak Hutner, *Pachad Yitzchak,* Rosh Hashanah #3, as translated and cited in Shai Held, "The Spiritual Life Begins in Gratitude and Culminates in Compassion: A Jewish Vision of Spirituality and Generosity," presentation at 2012 Jewish Seminary Pastoral Educator Conference, HUC-JIR and UJA-Federation of New York, New York (January 10, 2012), 3.
26. *Gur Aryeh* on Genesis 2:5 ("*veayn maker betovosom*").
27. Emmons and McCullough, *The Psychology of Gratitude.*
28. Bachya ben Joseph ibn Pakuda, "Section Two: The Gate of Reflection," *Duties of the Heart (Chovos HaLevavos),* trans. Daniel Haberman (Jerusalem: Feldheim, 1996), 163.
29. Ibid.
30. *Genesis Rabbah* 14:9.
31. Gregg Krech, *Naikan: Gratitude, Grace, and the Japanese Art of Self-Reflection* (Berkeley, CA: Stone Bridge Press, 2002).
32. Wood, Froh, and Geraghty, "Gratitude and Well-Being."
33. John M. Gottman and Nan Silver, *The Seven Principles for Making Marriage Work: A Practical Guide from the Nation's Foremost Relationship Expert* (New York: Three Rivers Press, 1999).
34. Martin E. P. Seligman, Tracy A. Steen, Nansook Park, and Christopher Peterson, "Positive Psychology Progress: Empirical Validation of Interventions," *American Psychologist* 60 (2005): 410–21.

Jewish Religious Coping and Trust in God: A Review of the Empirical Literature, by David H. Rosmarin, PhD, Devora Greer Shabtai, Steven Pirutinsky, MS, and Kenneth I. Pargament, PhD

1. For instance, William James, *The Varieties of Religious Experience: A Study in Human Nature* [1902] (New York: Collier-Macmillan, 1961).
2. Albert Ellis, "Is Religiosity Pathological?," *Free Inquiry* 18 (1988): 27–32; H. J. Eysenck, *A Model for Personality* (New York: Springer, 1981); and Sigmund Freud, *A General Introduction to Psychoanalysis* (Garden City, NY: Garden City Publishing, 1943).
3. Kenneth I. Pargament, ed., *APA Handbook of Psychology, Religion, and Spirituality* (Washington, DC: American Psychological Association, 2013).

4. Harold G. Koenig, Stephen M. Ford, Linda K. George, Dan G. Blazer, and Keith G. Meador, "Religion and Anxiety Disorder: An Examination and Comparison of Associations in Young, Middle-Aged, and Elderly Adults," *Journal of Anxiety Disorders* 7 (1993): 321–42; Timothy B. Smith, Michael E. McCullough, and Justin Poll, "Religiousness and Depression: Evidence for a Main Effect and the Moderating Influence of Stressful Life Events," *Psychological Bulletin* 129 (2003): 614–36; and David R. Williams, David B. Larson, Robert E. Buckler, Richard C. Heckmann, and Caroline M. Pyle, "Religion and Psychological Distress in a Community Sample," *Social Science and Medicine* 32 (1991): 1257–62.
5. Myleme O. Harrison, Harold G. Koenig, Judith C. Hays, Anedi G. Eme-Akwari, and Kenneth I. Pargament, "The Epidemiology of Religious Coping: A Review of Recent Literature," *International Review of Psychiatry* 13 (2001): 86–93; and Kenneth I. Pargament, *Spiritually Integrated Psychotherapy: Understanding and Addressing the Sacred* (New York: Guilford Press, 2007).
6. Julie J. Exline, "Religious and Spiritual Struggles," in Pargament, *APA Handbook of Psychology, Religion, and Spirituality*; Kenneth I. Pargament, Nichole Murray-Swank, Gina M. Magyar, and Gene Ano, "Spiritual Struggle: A Phenomenon of Interest to Psychology and Religion," in *Judeo-Christian Perspectives on Psychology: Human Nature, Motivation, and Change*, ed. William R. Miller and Harold D. Delaney (Washington, DC: American Psychological Association, 2005), 245–68; Steven Pirutinsky, David H. Rosmarin, Kenneth I. Pargament, and Elizabeth Midlarsky, "Does Negative Religious Coping Accompany, Precede, or Follow Depression among Orthodox Jews?" *Journal of Affective Disorders* 132 (2011): 401–5; Kelley M. McConnell, Kenneth I. Pargament, Christopher G. Ellison, and Kevin J. Flannelly, "Examining the Links between Spiritual Struggles and Symptoms of Psychopathology in a National Sample," *Journal of Clinical Psychology* 62 (2006): 1469–84.
7. Barry A. Kosmin, and Seymour P. Lachman, *One Nation Under God: Religion in Contemporary American Society* (New York: Harmony, 1993).
8. Sergio DellaPergola, Uzi Rebhun, and Mark Tolts, "Contemporary Jewish Diaspora in Global Context: Human Development Correlates of Population Trends," *Israel Studies* 10 (2005): 61–95.
9. Robert Kohn, Itzhak Levav, Stacey Zolondek, and Michaele Richter, "Affective Disorders among Jews: A Historical Review and Meta-Analysis," *History of Psychiatry* 10 (1999): 245–67; and Itzhak Levav, Robert Kohn, Jacqueline M. Golding, and Myrna M. Weissman, "Vulnerability of Jews to Affective Disorders," *American Journal of Psychiatry* 154 (1997): 941–47.
10. Peter C. Hill and Kenneth I. Pargament, "Advances in the Conceptualization and Measurement of Religion and Spirituality," *American Psychologist* 58 (2003): 64–74.
11. Kenneth I. Pargament, *The Psychology of Religion and Coping: Theory, Research, Practice* (New York: Guilford Press, 1997).

12. Todd W. Hall and Keith J. Edwards, "The Initial Development and Factor Analysis of the Spiritual Assessment Inventory," *Journal of Psychology and Theology* 24 (1996): 233–46.
13. Kenneth I. Pargament and Annette Mahoney, "Sacred Matters: Sanctification as a Vital Topic for the Psychology of Religion," *International Journal for the Psychology of Religion* 15 (2005): 179–98.
14. Julie J. Exline, Ann M. Yali, and William C. Sanderson, "Guilt, Discord, and Alienation: The Role of Religious Strain in Depression and Suicidality," *Journal of Clinical Psychology* 56 (2000): 1481–96.
15. Adam B. Cohen and Peter C. Hill, "Religion as Culture: Religious Individualism and Collectivism among American Catholics, Jews, and Protestants," *Journal of Personality* 75 (2007): 709–42.
16. Pargament, *The Psychology of Religion and Coping*; and Jeremy P. Cummings and Kenneth I. Pargament, "Medicine for the Spirit: Religious Coping in Individuals with Medical Conditions," *Religions* 1 (2010): 28–53.
17. Kenneth Pargament, Bruce Smith, Harold G. Koenig, and Lisa Perez, "Patterns of Positive and Negative Religious Coping with Major Life Stressors," *Journal for the Scientific Study of Religion* 37 (1998): 710–24.
18. Exline, "Religious and Spiritual Struggles"; and Pargament et al., "Spiritual Struggle."
19. Kenneth I. Pargament, Harold G. Koenig, and Lisa M. Perez, "The Many Methods of Religious Coping: Development and Initial Validation of the RCOPE," *Journal of Clinical Psychology* 56 (2000): 519–43.
20. Harold G. Koenig, Michael E. McCullough, and David B. Larson, *Handbook of Religion and Health* (New York: Oxford University Press, 2001).
21. McConnell et al., "Examining the Links between Spiritual Struggles and Symptoms of Psychopathology in a National Sample"; and Smith et al., "Religiousness and Depression."
22. Kenneth I. Pargament, Brian J. Zinnbauer, Allie B. Scott, Eric M. Butter, Jill Zerowin, and Patricia Stanik, "Red Flags and Religious Coping: Identifying Some Religious Warning Signs among People in Crisis," *Journal of Clinical Psychology* 59 (2003): 1335–48.
23. Irene I. Harris, Christopher R. Erbes, Brian E. Engdahl, Raymond H. Olson, Ann M. Winskowski, and Joelle J. McMahill, "Christian Religious Functioning and Trauma Outcomes," *Journal of Clinical Psychology* 64 (2008): 17–29.
24. Gene G. Ano and Erin B. Vasconcelles, "Religious Coping and Psychological Adjustment to Stress: A Meta-Analysis," *Journal of Clinical Psychology* 61 (2005): 461–80.
25. Kenneth I. Pargament, Harold G. Koenig, Nalini Tarakeshwar, and June Hahn, "Religious Struggle as a Predictor of Mortality among Medically Ill Elderly

Patients: A Two-year Longitudinal Study," *Journal of Clinical Psychology* 161 (2001): 1881–85.

26. Kelley M. Trevino, Kenneth I. Pargament, Sian Cotton, Anthony C. Leonard, June Hahn, Carol A. Caprini-Faigin, and Joel Tsevat, "Religious Coping and Physiological, Psychological, Social, and Spiritual Outcomes in Patients with HIV/AIDS: Cross-Sectional and Longitudinal Findings," *AIDS Behavior* 14 (2010): 379–89.
27. Andrew P. Tix and Patricia A. Frazier, "The Use of Religious Coping during Stressful Life Events: Main Effects, Moderation, and Mediation," *Journal of Consulting and Clinical Psychology* 66 (1998): 411–22.
28. Elizabeth J. Krumrei, Annette Mahoney, and Kenneth I. Pargament, "Spiritual Stress and Coping Model of Divorce: A Longitudinal Study," *Journal of Family Psychology* 25 (2011): 973–85.
29. Eric F. Dubow, Kenneth I. Pargament, Paul Boxer, and Nalini Tarakeshwar, "Initial Investigation of Jewish Early Adolescents' Ethnic Identity, Stress and Coping," *Journal of Early Adolescence* 20 (2000): 418–41.
30. Kate M. Loewenthal, Andrew K. MacLeod, Vivienne Goldblatt, Guy Lubitsh, and John D. Valentine, "Comfort and Joy? Religion, Cognition, and Mood in Protestants and Jews under Stress," *Cognition and Emotion* 14 (2000): 355–74.
31. Pargament, Koenig, and Perez, "The Many Methods of Religious Coping."
32. Adam B. Cohen, "The Importance of Spirituality in Well-Being for Jews and Christians," *Journal of Happiness Studies* 3 (2002): 287–310; and Adam B. Cohen, Joel I. Siegal, and Paul Rozin, "Faith versus Practice: Different Bases for Religiosity Judgments by Jews and Protestants," *European Journal of Social Psychology* 33 (2003): 287–95.
33. David H. Rosmarin, Kenneth I. Pargament, Elizabeth J. Krumrei, and Kevin J. Flannelly, "Religious Coping Among Jews: Development and Initial Validation of the JCOPE," *Journal of Clinical Psychology* 65 (2009): 1–14.
34. Harold S. Himmelfarb, "Measuring Religious Involvement," *Social Forces* 53 (1975): 606–18.
35. David H. Rosmarin, Kenneth I. Pargament, and Kevin J. Flannelly, "Do Spiritual Struggles Predict Poorer Physical/Mental Health among Jews?" *International Journal for the Psychology of Religion* 19 (2009): 244–58.
36. Steven Pirutinsky, David H. Rosmarin, and Cheryl Holt, "Does Positive Religious Coping Moderate the Relationship between Emotional Functioning and Obesity?" *Health Psychology* 31 (2011): 394–97.
37. Kenneth I. Pargament, "Wrestling with the Angels: Religious Struggles in the Context of Mental Illness" (paper presented at the American Psychiatric Association Institute for Psychiatric Services, New York, October 2009).

38. Pirutinsky et al., "Does Negative Religious Coping Accompany, Precede, or Follow Depression among Orthodox Jews?"

39. Harold S. Kushner, *Who Needs God?* (New York: Fireside, 2002).

40. Bahya ibn Pakuda, *The Duties of the Heart* [1040], trans. Yaakov Feldman (Northvale, NJ: Jason Aronson, 1996).

41. David H. Rosmarin, Kenneth I. Pargament, and Annette Mahoney, "The Role of Religiousness in Anxiety, Depression, and Happiness in a Jewish Community Sample: A Preliminary Investigation," *Mental Health, Religion and Culture* 12 (2009): 97–113.

42. David H. Rosmarin, Elizabeth Krumrei, and Gerhard Andersson, "Religion as a Predictor of Psychological Distress in Two Religious Communities," *Cognitive Behavior Therapy* 38 (2009): 54–64.

43. David H. Rosmarin, Steven Pirutinsky, and Kenneth I. Pargament, "A Brief Measure of Core Religious Beliefs for Use in Psychiatric Settings," *International Journal of Psychiatry in Medicine* 41 (2011): 253–61.

44. David H. Rosmarin, Steven Pirutinsky, Randy P. Auerbach, Thrötur Björgvinsson, Joseph Bigda-Peyton, Gerhard Andersson, Kenneth I. Pargament, and Elizabeth J. Krumrei, "Incorporating Spiritual Beliefs into a Cognitive Model of Worry," *Journal of Clinical Psychology* 67 (2011): 1–10.

45. Judith S. Beck, *Cognitive Therapy: Basics and Beyond* (New York: Guilford Press, 1995).

46. Michel J. Dugas, Mark H. Freeston, and Robert Ladouceur, "Intolerance of Uncertainty and Problem Orientation in Worry," *Cognitive Therapy and Research* 21 (1997): 593–606.

47. Rosmarin et al., "Incorporating Spiritual Beliefs into a Cognitive Model of Worry."

48. David H. Rosmarin, Kenneth I. Pargament, Steven Pirutinsky, and Annette Mahoney, "A Randomized Controlled Evaluation of a Spiritually-Integrated Treatment for Subclinical Anxiety in the Jewish Community, Delivered via the Internet," *Journal of Anxiety Disorders* 24 (2010): 799–808.

49. Pargament, *Spiritually Integrated Psychotherapy.*

50. Doug Oman, John Hedberg, and Carl E. Thoresen, "Passage Meditation Reduces Perceived Stress in Health Professionals: A Randomized, Controlled Trial," *Journal of Consulting and Clinical Psychology* 74 (2006): 714–19; L. Rebecca Propst, Richard Ostram, Philip Watkins, Terri Dean, and David Mashburn, "Comparative Efficacy of Religious and Nonreligious Cognitive Behavioral Therapy for the Treatment of Clinical Depression in Religious Individuals," *Journal of Consulting and Clinical Psychology* 60 (1992): 94–103; Mark S. Rye, Kenneth I. Pargament, Wei Pan, David W. Yingling, Karrie A. Shogren, and Masako Ito, "Can Group Interventions Facilitate Forgiveness of an Ex-Spouse? A Randomized Clinical

Trial," *Journal of Consulting and Clinical Psychology* 73 (2005): 880–92; and Amy B. Wachholtz and Kenneth I. Pargament, "Migraines and Meditation: Does Spirituality Matter?" *Journal of Behavioral Medicine* 31 (2009): 351–66.

51. Michael E. McCullough, "Research on Religion-Accommodative Counseling: Review and Meta-Analysis," *Journal of Counseling Psychology* 46 (1999): 92–98; Joshua N. Hook, Everett L. Worthington, Jr., Don E. Davis, David J. Jennings II, Aubrey L. Gartner, and Jan P. Hook, "Empirically Supported Religious and Spiritual Therapies," *Journal of Clinical Psychology* 66 (2010): 46–72.
52. See "Increase Your Trust in God," JPSYCH: Research on Judaism and Mental Health (2010), http://www.jpsych.com/increase_your_trust_in_god.html.
53. Elizabeth J. Krumrei, Steven Pirutinsky and David H. Rosmarin, "Jewish Spirituality, Depression and Health: An Empirical Test of a Conceptual Framework," *International Journal of Behavioral Medicine* (online prepublication), http://www.springerlink.com/content/13mq4p514m578336/fulltext.html.
54. Cohen and Hill, "Religion as Culture"; Cohen, Siegel, and Rozin, "Faith versus Practice"; and Adam B. Cohen and Paul Rozin, "Religion and the Morality of Mentality," *Journal of Personality and Social Psychology* 81 (2001): 697–710.
55. Pargament, *Spiritually Integrated Psychotherapy*.
56. David H. Rosmarin, Kenneth I. Pargament, and Harold B. Robb III, "Introduction," *Cognitive and Behavioral Practice* 17 (2010): 343–7.
57. David Greenberg, "Is Psychotherapy Possible with Unbelievers? The Care of the Ultra-Orthodox Communities," *Israel Journal of Psychiatry and Related Sciences* 28 (1991): 19–30.
58. Steven Pirutinsky, David H. Rosmarin, and Kenneth I. Pargament, "Community Attitudes towards Culture-Influenced Mental Illness: Scrupulosity vs. Non-Religious OCD among Orthodox Jews," *Journal of Community Psychology* 37 (2009): 949–58.
59. Ibn Pakuda, *The Duties of the Heart*.
60. Farr A. Curlin, John D. Lantos, Chad J. Roach, Sarah A. Sellergren, and Marshall H. Chin, "Religious Characteristics of U.S. Physicians: A National Survey," *Journal of General Internal Medicine* 20 (2005): 629–34.
61. Steven J. Haggbloom, Renee Warnick, Jason E. Warnick, Vinessa K. Jones, Gary L. Yarbrough, Tenea M. Russell, Chris M. Borecky, Reagan McGahhey, John L. Powell III, Jamie Beavers, and Emmanuelle Monte, "The 100 Most Eminent Psychologists of the 20th Century," *Review of General Psychology* 6: 139–52.

Population Research on Judaism, Health, and Well-Being, by Jeff Levin, PhD, MPH

1. See Jeff Levin, *God, Faith, and Health: Exploring the Spirituality-Healing Connection* (New York: John Wiley & Sons, 2001), and Harold G. Koenig, *The*

Healing Power of Faith: Science Explores Medicine's Last Great Frontier (New York: Simon & Schuster, 1999).

2. Jeff Levin and Harold G. Koenig, "Faith Matters: Reflections on the Life and Work of Dr. David B. Larson," in *Faith, Medicine, and Science: A Festschrift in Honor of Dr. David B. Larson* (New York: Haworth Pastoral Press, 2005), 3–25, especially 3–7.
3. Harold G. Koenig, Dana E. King, and Verna Benner Carson, *Handbook of Religion and Health*, 2nd ed. (New York: Oxford University Press, 2012).
4. The earliest comprehensive review of these epidemiologic studies of physical health outcomes was Jeffrey S. Levin and Preston L. Schiller, "Is There a Religious Factor in Health?" *Journal of Religion and Health* 26 (1987): 9–36. The most recent review and most comprehensive overview ever published, including studies of mental health, is Koenig, King, and Carson, *Handbook of Religion and Health*.
5. For example, Neal Krause, "Religion and Health: Making Sense of a Disheveled Literature," *Journal of Religion and Health* 50 (2011): 20–35; Linda K. George, Christopher G. Ellison, and David B. Larson, "Explaining the Relationships between Religious Involvement and Health," *Psychological Inquiry* 13 (2002): 190–200, especially the section "Research on Religion and Health: What It Does and Does Not Tell Us," 190–92; Jeffrey S. Levin, "How Religion Influences Morbidity and Health: Reflections on Natural History, Salutogenesis and Host Resistance," *Social Science and Medicine* 43 (1996): 849–64; and Jeff Levin, "'And Let Us Makes Us a Name': Reflections on the Future of the Religion and Health Field," *Journal of Religion and Health* 48 (2009): 125–45.
6. See Levin and Schiller, "Is There a Religious Factor in Health?"
7. Ibid.
8. Ibid.
9. Benjamin Travers, "Observations on the Local Diseases Termed Malignant," *Medico-Chirurgical Transactions* 17 (1837): 337, cited in Levin and Schiller, "Is There a Religious Factor in Health?," 9.
10. See, e.g., the superb review by E. L. Kennaway, "The Racial and Social Incidence of Cancer of the Uterus," *British Journal of Cancer* 2 (1948): 177–212.
11. Joseph Menczer, "The Low Incidence of Cervical Cancer in Jewish Women: Has the Puzzle Finally Been Solved?" *Israel Medical Association Journal* 5 (2003): 120–23.
12. Kate Miriam Loewenthal, Vivienne Goldblatt, Tessa Gorton, Guy Lubitsch, Helen Bicknell, Deborah Fellowes, and Amanda Sowden, "The Social Circumstances of Anxiety and Its Symptoms among Anglo-Jews," *Journal of Affective Disorders* 46 (1997): 87–94.

13. Kate Loewenthal, Vivienne Goldblatt, Tessa Gorton, Guy Lubitsch, Helen Bicknell, Deborah Fellowes, and Amanda Sowden, "Gender and Depression in Anglo-Jewry," *Psychological Medicine* 25 (1995): 1051–63.
14. Kate Miriam Loewenthal, Andrew K. MacLeod, Vivienne Goldblatt, Guy Lubitsch, and John D. Valentine, "Comfort and Joy? Religion, Cognition, and Mood in Protestants and Jews under Stress," *Cognition and Emotion* 14 (2000): 355–74.
15. Ann Bowling, Morag Farquhar, and Jane Leaver, "Jewish People and Ageing: Their Emotional Well-Being, Physical Health Status and Use of Services," *Nursing Practice* 5, no. 4 (1992): 5–16.
16. Isaac W. Eberstein and Kathleen M. Heyman, "Jewish Identity and Self-Reported Health," in *Religion, Families, and Health: Population-Based Research in the United States*, ed. Christopher G. Ellison and Robert A. Hummer (New Brunswick, NJ: Rutgers University Press, 2010), 349–67.
17. Ibid., 362.
18. Jeremy D. Kark, Galia Shemi, Yechiel Friedlander, Oz Martin, Orly Manor, and S. H. Blondheim, "Does Religious Observance Promote Health? Mortality in Secular versus Religious Kibbutzim in Israel," *American Journal of Public Health* 86 (1996): 341–46.
19. Yechiel Friedlander, Jeremy D. Kark, and Yechezkiel Stein, "Religious Orthodoxy and Myocardial Infarction in Jerusalem—A Case-Control Study," *International Journal of Cardiology* 10 (1986): 33–41.
20. Ofra Anson, Aaron Antonovsky, and Shira Sagy, "Religiosity and Well-Being among Retirees: A Question of Causality," *Behavior, Health, and Aging* 1 (1990): 85–97.
21. For example, Ofra Anson, Arieh Levenson, Benyamin Maoz, and Dan Y. Bonneh, "Religious Community, Individual Religiosity, and Health: A Tale of Two Kibbutzim," *Sociology* 25 (1991): 119–32; Amir Shmueli, "Health and Religiosity among Israeli Jews," *European Journal of Public Health* 17 (2006): 104–11; and Noa Vilchinsky and Shlomo Kravetz, "How Are Religious Belief and Behavior Good for You? An Investigation of Mediators Relating Religion to Mental Health in a Sample of Israeli Jewish Students," *Journal for the Scientific Study of Religion* 44 (2005): 459–71.
22. For example, Karin Amit, "Determinants of Life Satisfaction Among Immigrants from Western Countries and from the FSU in Israel," *Social Indicators Research* 96 (2010): 515–34; Itzhak Levav, Robert Kohn, and Miriam Billig, "The Protective Effect of Religiosity Under Terrorism," *Psychiatry* 71 (2008): 46–58; and Tamar Shkolnik, Chava Weiner, Lea Malik, and Yoel Festinger, "The Effect of Jewish Religiosity of Elderly Israelis on Their Life Satisfaction, Health,

Function and Activity," *Journal of Cross-Cultural Gerontology* 16 (2011): 201–19.

23. Anson et al., "Religiosity and Well-Being among Retirees"; Dov Shmotkin, "Subjective Well-Being as a Function of Age and Gender: A Multivariate Look for Differentiated Trends," *Social Indicators Research* 23 (1990): 201–30; and Simha F. Landau, Benjamin Beit-Hallahmi, and Shlomit Levy, "The Personal and the Political: Israelis' Perception of Well-Being in Times of War and Peace," *Social Indicators Research* 44 (1998): 329–65.
24. Maya Kritchman Lupo and Rael D. Strous, "Religiosity, Anxiety and Depression among Israeli Medical Students, *Israel Medical Association Journal* 13 (2011): 613–18.
25. Ellen L. Idler, "Self-Rated Health," in *Encyclopedia of the Life Course and Human Development*, vol. 3, *Later Life*, ed. Deborah Carr (Detroit: Macmillan Reference USA, 2009), 354–58.
26. For example, in the United States: Eberstein and Heyman, "Jewish Identity and Self-Reported Health"; and in Israel: Shmueli, "Health and Religiosity among Israeli Jews."
27. Barry Kosmin, "The Need for a Systematic Comparative Approach to National Population Surveys of Jews," *Contemporary Jewry* 25 (2005): 33–49.
28. Linda K. George and Richard Landerman, "Health and Subjective Well-Being: A Replicated Secondary Data Analysis," *International Journal of Aging and Human Development* 19 (1984): 133–56.
29. Jeff Levin, "Health Impact of Jewish Religious Observance in the USA: Findings from the 2000–01 National Jewish Population Survey," *Journal of Religion and Health* 50 (2011): 852–68.
30. Jeff Levin, "Religion and Positive Well-Being among Israeli and Diaspora Jews: Findings from the World Values Survey," *Mental Health, Religion, and Culture* 15 (2012): 689–707.
31. Jeff Levin, "Religion and Psychological Well-Being and Distress in Israeli Jews: Findings from the Gallup World Poll," *Israel Journal of Psychiatry and Related Sciences* 48 (2011): 252–61.
32. Two papers were published using the SHARE data, one addressing physical health and one addressing mental health: Jeff Levin, "Religion and Physical Health among Older Israeli Jews: Findings from the SHARE-Israel Study," *Israel Medical Association Journal* 14 (2012): 595–601; and Jeff Levin, "Religion and Mental Health Among Israeli Jews: Findings from the SHARE-Israel Study," *Social Indicators Research*.
33. Jeff Levin, "Religious Behavior, Health, and Well-Being Among Israeli Jews: Findings from the European Social Survey," *Psychology of Religion and Spirituality*, 2013 (online prepublication).

34. Jeff Levin, "Religion and Happiness Among Israeli Jews: Findings from the ISSP Religion III Survey," *Journal of Happiness Studies*, 2013 (online prepublication).
35. Jeff Levin, "Religious Observance and Well-Being among Israeli Jewish Adults: Findings from the Israel Social Survey," *Religions* (under review).
36. Levin, "Health Impact of Jewish Religious Observance in the USA."
37. Levin, "Religion and Positive Well-Being among Israeli and Diaspora Jews."
38. See the following papers by Levin: "Religion and Psychological Well-Being and Distress in Israeli Jews," "Religion and Physical Health among Older Israeli Jews," "Religion and Mental Health Among Israeli Jews," "Religious Behavior, Health, and Well-Being Among Israeli Jews," "Religion and Happiness among Israeli Jews," and "Religious Observance and Well-Being Among Israeli Jewish Adults."
39. Jeffrey S. Levin and Harold Y. Vanderpool, "Is Frequent Religious Attendance *Really* Conducive to Better Health? Toward an Epidemiology of Religion," *Social Science and Medicine* 24 (1987): 589–600.
40. See, e.g., Jeffrey S. Levin, "How Religion Influences Morbidity and Health"; Ellen L. Idler, "Religious Involvement and the Health of the Elderly: Some Hypotheses and an Initial Test," *Social Forces* 66 (1987): 226–38; Daniel McIntosh and Bernard Spilka, "Religion and Physical Health: The Role of Personal Faith and Control Beliefs," *Research in the Social Scientific Study of Religion* 2 (1990): 167–94; Linda K. George, Christopher G. Ellison, and David B. Larson, "Explaining the Relationship between Religious Involvement and Health," *Psychological Inquiry* 13 (2002): 190–200; Michael E. McCullough and Brian L. B. Willoughby, "Religion, Self-Regulation, and Self-Control: Associations, Explanations, and Implications," *Psychological Bulletin* 135 (2009): 69–93; and others in sociology, psychology, medicine, and epidemiology.
41. Jeff Levin, "Religion, Health Benefits of," in *Encyclopedia of Lifestyle Medicine and Health*, ed. James Rippe (Thousand Oaks, CA: Sage Publications, 2012), 978.
42. Norman Porritt, *Religion and Health: Their Mutual Relationship and Influence* (London: Sheffington & Son, 1905), 68.
43. Jeff Levin, "How Faith Heals: A Theoretical Model," *EXPLORE: The Journal of Science and Healing* 5 (2009): 82.
44. Ibid. See also the thousands of references to Torah, Mishnah, *Tosefta*, *Bavli*, *Yerushalmi*, Midrash, and *Targums* in Julius Preuss, *Biblical and Talmudic Medicine* [1911], trans. Fred Rosner (Northvale, NJ: Jason Aronson, 1993).
45. Jeff Levin, "Restoring the Spiritual: Reflections on Arrogance and Myopia—Allopathic and Holistic," *Journal of Religion and Health* 48 (2009): 487.
46. See, e.g., Esther M. Sternberg, *The Balance Within: The Science Connecting Health and Emotions* (New York: W. H. Freeman, 2001), especially chap. 9, "Can Believing Make You Well," 159–79; and the classic work by Blair Justice,

Who Gets Sick: How Beliefs, Moods, and Thoughts Affect Your Health (Los Angeles: Jeremy Tarcher, 1987).

47. As in the *mitzvah* of *shiluach hakan* (sending away a mother bird before taking her young), from Deuteronomy 22:6–7.
48. *Pirkei Avot* 4:2.
49. See the many excellent articles in two special journal issues devoted to the National Jewish Population Survey: "The National Jewish Population Survey 2000–1," special issue, *Sociology of Religion* 67, no. 4 (2006); and *Contemporary Jewry* 25, no. 1 (2005).
50. This idea has been mentioned in several places: e.g., in Jeff Levin and Michele F. Prince, "Judaism and Health: Reflections on an Emerging Scholarly Field," *Journal of Religion and Health* 50 (2011): 765–77; Levin, "Health Impact of Jewish Religious Observance in the USA"; Levin, "Religion and Psychological Distress and Well-Being in Israeli Jews"; and Levin, "Religion and Positive Well-Being among Israeli and Diaspora Jews."

A Program Assessment of the Field of Judaism and Health: Program Review and Key Stakeholder Interviews, by Michele F. Prince, LCSW, MAJCS

1. The author publicly thanks Adina Bodenstein, MSW, previously assistant director of the Kalsman Institute, who partnered on this project to perform the program assessment key stakeholder interviews and gather program and institutional data.
2. Michele Prince and Adina Bodenstein, *A Program Assessment: Exploration of the Field of Judaism, Health, and Healing through Program Review and Key Stakeholder Interviews; A Report by the Kalsman Institute on Judaism and Health* (Los Angeles: Kalsman Institute on Judaism and Health, Hebrew Union College–Jewish Institute of Religion, 2011), www.bjpa.org/Publications/details.cfm?PublicationID=11225.
3. Michele Prince, "The Kalsman Institute Research Roundtable: Building a Field of Judaism and Health," *CCAR Journal: The Reform Jewish Quarterly*, Summer 2012, 34.
4. Jeff Levin and Michele F. Prince, "Judaism and Health: Reflections on an Emerging Scholarly Field," *Journal of Religion and Health* 50 (2011): 765–77.
5. David L. Freeman and Judith Z. Abrams, eds., *Illness and Health in the Jewish Tradition: Writings from the Bible to Today* (Philadelphia: Jewish Publication Society, 1999).
6. Avraham Y. Finkel, *In My Flesh I See God: A Treasury of Rabbinic Insights about the Human Anatomy* (Northvale, NJ: Jason Aronson, 1995).
7. Julius Preuss, *Biblical and Talmudic Medicine* [1911], trans. Fred Rosner (Northvale, NJ: Jason Aronson, 1993).

8. Fred Rosner and Samuel S. Kottek, eds., *Moses Maimonides: Physician, Scientist, and Philosopher* (Northvale, NJ: Jason Aronson, 1993).
9. For example, David M. Feldman, *Health and Medicine in the Jewish Tradition: L'Hayyim—To Life* (New York: Crossroad, 1986); David J. Bleich, *Judaism and Healing: Halakhic Perspectives* (New York: Ktav, 1981); and Elliot N. Dorff, *Matters of Life and Death: A Jewish Approach to Modern Medical Ethics* (Philadelphia: Jewish Publication Society, 1998).
10. Richard F. Address and Hara E. Person, eds., *That You May Live Long: Caring for Our Aging Parents, Caring for Ourselves* (New York: UAHC Press, 2003); Zev Harel, David E. Biegel, and David Guttman, eds., *Jewish Aged in the United States and Israel: Diversity, Programs, and Services* (New York: Springer, 1994); and Dayle A. Friedman, *Jewish Visions for Aging: A Professional Guide for Fostering Wholeness* (Woodstock, VT: Jewish Lights, 2008).
11. Tzvi G. Schur, *Illness and Coping: Coping the Jewish Way* (New York: NCSY/Orthodox Union, 1987); and Dayle A. Friedman, ed., *Jewish Pastoral Care: A Practical Handbook from Traditional and Contemporary Sources*, 2nd ed. (Woodstock, VT: Jewish Lights, 2005).
12. Michele F. Prince, "Judaism, Health, and Healing: How a New Jewish Communal Field Took Root and Where It Might Grow," *Journal of Jewish Communal Service* 84, nos. 3/4 (2009): 280–91.
13. William Cutter, ed., *Healing and the Jewish Imagination: Spiritual and Practical Perspectives on Judaism and Health* (Woodstock, VT: Jewish Lights, 2007).
14. Howard Silverman, "A Physician's Reflection on the Jewish Healing Movement," in Cutter, *Healing and the Jewish Imagination*, 11.
15. Simkha Y. Weintraub, ed., *Healing of Soul, Healing of Body: Spiritual Leaders Unfold the Strength and Solace in Psalms* (Woodstock, VT: Jewish Lights, 1994).
16. Prince and Bodenstein, *A Program Assessment*.
17. Susan Rosenthal, *Jewish Healing Programs: Best Practices Sampler 2008*, National Center for Jewish Healing of the Jewish Board of Family and Children's Services (New York: UJA-Federation of New York, 2008), http://www.ncjh.org/2008bestpractices.pdf.
18. "Jewish Wisdom and Wellness: A Week of Learning," Kalsman Institute and Cedars-Sinai (April 21–27, 2013), http://jewishwisdomandwellness.com/.
19. Each internal interview remains confidential, and transcripts are not attached. Highlights are shared. Several interviewees have new professional titles since the interview process was conducted.
20. Excerpted from Sergio DellaPergola, *World Jewish Population, 2010*, Berman Institute–North American Jewish Data Bank, Current Jewish Population Reports No. 2 (Storrs, CA: North American Jewish Data Bank, 2010), 21, http://www.jewishdatabank.org/Reports/World_Jewish_Population_2010.pdf.

21. Ellen Hermanson, "Our Charter," *The Outstretched Arm* 1, no. 1 (1991): 1.
22. These concepts are described in Judith Sharken Simon, *The Five Life Stages of Nonprofit Organizations: Where You Are, Where You're Going, and What to Expect When You Get There* (St. Paul, MN: Fieldstone Alliance, 2001).
23. See Prince, "Judaism, Health, and Healing," 280–91.
24. Jack Wertheimer, *Generation of Change: How Leaders in Their Twenties and Thirties Are Reshaping American Jewish Life* (New York: Avi Chai Foundation, 2010), http://avichai.org/wp-content/uploads/2010/08/Generation-of-Change-FINAL.pdf.
25. Shira Stern, quoted in Prince and Bodenstein, *A Program Assessment*, 22.
26. "2012 Jewish Seminary Pastoral Educator Conference," Kalsman Institute and UJA-Federation of New York, New York (January 10–11, 2012), http://huc.edu/kalsman/PastoralEducation/schedule/.
27. "Models of Cooperation: Reflections on the Jewish Healing Movement," Bay Area Jewish Healing Center, HUC-JIR, and UCSF, Burlingame, CA (December 14–16, 2003), http://huc.edu/kalsman/projects/coop/coopbroc.pdf.
28. "Midrash & Medicine: Imagining Wholeness," Kalsman Institute and Bay Area Jewish Healing Center, Pacific Grove, CA (May 11–13, 2009), http://huc.edu/kalsman/Midrash-and-Medicine/.
29. Hiddur: The Center for Aging and Judaism, under the direction of Rabbi Friedman, was located at the Reconstructionist Rabbinical College. After eight years of operations, it closed in 2011: www.rrc.edu/Hiddur.
30. "Mental Illness in the Jewish Community: Help, Hope and Healing," Bay Area Jewish Healing Center and the Kalsman Institute, San Francisco (October 20, 2002).
31. Rabbi Eleanor Steinman, personal communication, November 1, 2010.
32. "A Loss Worthy of Grief: Jewish Approaches to Bringing Comfort after Miscarriage, Stillbirth, and Neonatal Death," National Center for Jewish Healing, New York (April 23, 2009), www.ncjh.org/downloads/LWG-Brochure.pdf.
33. See Rosenthal, *Jewish Healing Programs*.
34. Sally Weber, "The Rabbi/Social Worker Roundtable," *Journal of Jewish Communal Service* 82, nos. 1/2 (2007): 39–47.
35. Tracey Lipsig Kite and Susan Rosenthal, "Bridges to Wholeness: Jewish Family Services and Jewish Healing," *Journal of Jewish Communal Service* 82, nos. 1/2 (2007): 7–14.
36. Sally Kaplan, personal communication, October 27, 2010.
37. Susan Starr Sered, "Healing and Religion: A Jewish Perspective," *Yale Journal for Humanities in Medicine*, January 28, 2002, http://yjhm.yale.edu/archives/spirit2003/healing/ssered.htm.

38. "Professionalism: Promoting and Advancing Chaplaincy through Membership, Education and Advocacy," National Association of Jewish Chaplains 2011 Conference, Scottsdale, AZ (January 16–19, 2011).
39. "Jewish Wisdom and Wellness."
40. Simon, *The Five Life Stages of Nonprofit Organizations.*
41. Rabbi Nancy Epstein, personal communication, February 15, 2011.
42. Michele Prince and Nancy H. Wiener, "Introduction to this Issue from the Guest Editors," *CCAR Journal: The Reform Jewish Quarterly*, Summer 2012, 3.
43. Key Stakeholder Interviewees:

    Rabbi Richard Address, DMin, Mkor Shalom, Cherry Hill, New Jersey

    Adi Bodenstein, MSW, assistant director, Kalsman Institute on Judaism and Health, Hebrew Union College–Jewish Institute of Religion (HUC-JIR), Los Angeles, California

    Rabbi Anne Brener, LCSW, psychotherapist, author, and rabbi, Yedidya, Los Angeles, California

    Rabbi William Cutter, PhD, Steinberg Emeritus Professor of Human Relations and emeritus professor of modern Hebrew literature and education, HUC-JIR, and founding director, Kalsman Institute on Judaism and Health, Los Angeles, California

    Rabbi Nancy Epstein, MPH, Jewish Reconstructionist Federation, Jenkintown, Pennsylvania

    Rabbi Natan Fenner, Bay Area Healing Center, San Francisco, California

    Rabbi Dayle Friedman, MAJCS, MSW, director, Hiddur: The Center for Aging and Judaism of the Reconstructionist Rabbinical College, Wyncote, Pennsylvania

    Michelle Friedman, MD, chair, Department of Pastoral Counseling, Yeshivat Chovevei Torah, New York, New York

    Barbara Glickstein, RN, MPH, MS, co-director, Center for Health, Media and Policy, New York, New York

    Rabbi Naomi Kalish, president, National Association of Jewish Chaplains, Whippany, New Jersey

    Sally Kaplan, planning executive for spiritual and end of life care, UJA-Federation of New York, New York, New York

    Rabbi Peter S. Knobel, Beth Emet, The Free Synagogue, Evanston, Illinois

    Debra Kolodny, president, ALEPH: Alliance for Jewish Renewal, Philadelphia, Pennsylvania

    Roberta Leiner, managing director, UJA-Federation of New York, New York, New York

Rabbi Daniel E. Levin, Temple Beth El of Boca Raton, Boca Raton, Florida

Jeff Levin, PhD, MPH, University Professor of Epidemiology and Population Health and director of the Program on Religion and Population Health, Institute for Studies of Religion, Baylor University, Waco, Texas

Rabbi Richard Litvak, Temple Beth El, Aptos, California

Rabbi Sheldon Marder, chaplain, Jewish Home, San Francisco, California

Rabbi Yocheved Mintz, president, OHALA, Las Vegas, Nevada

Rabbi Joseph Ozarowski, DMin, rabbinic chaplain, Jewish Child and Family Services, Jewish Healing Network of Chicago, Chicago, Illinois

Michele F. Prince, LCSW, MAJCS, director, Kalsman Institute on Judaism and Health, HUC-JIR, Los Angeles, California

Rabbi Debbie Prinz, director of program and member services, Central Conference for American Rabbis (CCAR), New York, New York

Susan J. Rosenthal, LCSW, coordinator, National Center for Jewish Healing (JBFCS), New York, New York

Marjorie Sokoll, BSW, director, Jewish Healing Connections, Jewish Family and Children's Services, Waltham, Massachusetts

Rabbi Shira Stern, Center for Pastoral Counseling, Marlborough, New Jersey

Rabbi Ute Steyer, Jewish Theological Seminary (JTS), New York, New York

Rabbi David Teutsch, PhD, director, Levin-Leiber Program in Jewish Ethics and the Center for Jewish Ethics, Reconstructionist Rabbinical College, Wyncote, Pennsylvania

Rabbi Nancy Wiener, DMin, clinical director, Jacob and Hilda Blaustein Center for Pastoral Counseling, HUC-JIR, New York, New York

Rachel Yoskowitz, BSN, MPH, director, Health and Healing Initiatives, Jewish Family Service of Metropolitan Detroit, Detroit, Michigan

Malka Young, director, Healing Partners, Jewish Family Service, Framingham, Massachusetts

Three Jewish Lenses for Work and Health, by Rabbi Nancy Epstein, MPH, MAHL, and Adina Newberg, PhD

1. Michael Janati, "A Nation Overworked: Abandoning Happiness and Health for Paychecks," *Washington Times*, April 22, 2012, http://communities.washingtontimes.com/neighborhood/life-line-healthful-habits-made-simple/2012/apr/22/nation-overworked-abandoning-happiness-and-health-/.

2. Tony Schwartz, *The Way We're Working Isn't Working: The Four Forgotten Needs That Energize Great Performance* (New York: Simon and Schuster, 2010), 3.
3. "Lack of Sleep Alters Hormones, Metabolism, Stimulates Effects of Aging," University of Chicago Medicine Communications (October 21, 1999), www.uchospitals.edu/news/1999/19991021-sleepdebt.html.
4. Daniel J. Siegel, *The Neurobiology of "We": How Relationships, the Mind, and the Brain Interact to Shape Who We Are* (audiobook) (Sounds True Audio Learning Course, 2008).
5. Margaret J. Wheatley, *Leadership and the New Science: Learning about Organization from an Orderly Universe* (San Francisco: Berrett-Koehler Publishers, 1994), 20.
6. Ibid., 30.
7. Christian D. Boyd, "Church and Organizational Development," *The Hound and Hare: Theological Musings and Other Oddities* (October 10, 2011), http://celtichoundblog.wordpress.com/2011/10/10/church-and-organizational-development-part-2/.
8. Fred E. Emery and Eric L. Trist, "The Causal Texture of Organizational Environments," *Human Relations* 18 (1965): 21–32.
9. Deborah Ancona and Elaine Backman, "It's Not All About You," HBR Blog Network/Imagining the Future of Leadership, *Harvard Business Review*, (April 26, 2010), http://blogs.hbr.org/imagining-the-future-of-leadership/2010/04/its-not-all-about-me-its-all-a.html.
10. Hal M. Lewis, *From Sanctuary to Boardroom: A Jewish Approach to Leadership* (New York: Rowman and Littlefield Publishers, 2006), 143.
11. Ibid., 148.
12. William Isaacs, "Listen to What You Love Most: Conversation with Bill Isaacs," *People Edge*, December 21, 2001, http://peopleedge.mindtouch.us/@api/deki/files/252/Listen_to_what_you_love_most.pdf.
13. Schwartz, *The Way We're Working Isn't Working*, 15–20.
14. "Gallup Study: Feeling Good Matters in Workplace," *Gallup Business Journal*, January 12, 2006, http://businessjournal.gallup.com/content/20770/gallup-study-feeling-good-matters-in-the.aspx.
15. *Numbers Rabbah* 13:15.
16. Arthur Green, "Making a Home for God," in *On Sacred Ground: Jewish and Christian Clergy Reflect on Transformative Passages from the Five Books of Moses*, ed. Jeff Bernhardt (New York: Blackbird Books, 2012): 122–23.
17. Quoted in Will Keepin, "Principles of Spiritual Leadership," *Shavano Letter*, Winter 1997, http://willowbear.tripod.com/rainbow_builder/metagnosis/satyana/spiritual_principles_2.html.
18. Thomas Merton, quoted in Margaret J. Wheatley, "Eight Fearless Questions," excerpted from "A Call to Fearlessness for Gentle Leaders" (address at the

Shambhala Institute Core Program, Halifax, NS, June 2006), http://www.margaretwheatley.com/articles/eightfearlessquestions.html.

19. David A. Teutsch, *Spiritual Community: The Power to Restore Hope, Commitment and Joy* (Woodstock, VT: Jewish Lights, 2005), 30.
20. Sharon Brous, "What Love Is," in Bernhardt, *On Sacred Ground*, 22–23.
21. Donald A. Schön, *The Reflective Practitioner: How Professionals Think in Action* (London: Temple Smith, 1983), 32.
22. Benjamin Zander, "Classical Music with Shining Eyes: Benjamin Zander on TED.com" (video) June 25, 2008, http://blog.ted.com/2008/06/25/benjamin_zander/.
23. Drew Gilpin Faust, "Leadership without a Secret Code" (Interview), *New York Times*, October 31, 2009, www.nytimes.com/2009/11/01/business/01corner.html?pagewanted=all.
24. Isaacs, "Listen to What You Love Most," 3.
25. Martin Buber, *I and Thou* [1923] (New York: Touchstone, 1970), 26.
26. Jonathan Sacks, "Seven Principles of Leadership," June 14, 2012, www.chiefrabbi.org/2012/06/14/seven-principles-of-jewish-leadership-written-for-the-adam-science-foundation-leadership-programme/.
27. Yawen Cheng, Ichiro Kawachi, Eugenie H. Coakley, Joel Schwartz, and Graham Colditz, "Association between Psychosocial Work Characteristics and Health Functioning in American Women: Prospective Study," *British Medical Journal* 320 (2000): 1432–36.
28. Marianna Virtanen, Archana Singh-Manoux, Jane E. Ferrie, David Gimeno, Michael G. Marmot, Marko Elovainio, Markus Jokela, Jussi Vahtera and Mika Kivimäki, "Long Working Hours and Cognitive Function: The Whitehall II Study," *American Journal of Epidemiology* 169 (2008): 596–605.
29. Jim Loehr and Tony Schwartz, *The Power of Full Engagement: Managing Energy, Not Time, Is the Key to High Performance and Personal Renewal* (New York: Free Press, 2003), 37.
30. Martin Moore-Ede, *The Twenty-Four Hour Society: Understanding Human Limits in a World That Never Stops* (New York: Addison-Wesley, 1994), quoted in Loehr and Schwartz, *The Power of Full Engagement*, 37.
31. Loehr and Schwartz, *The Power of Full Engagement*, 4.
32. Ibid., 5.
33. Ibid., 110.
34. Isaacs, "Listen to What You Love Most," 4.
35. Terry Bookman and William Kahn, *This House We Build: Lessons for Healthy Synagogues and the People Who Dwell There* (Washington, DC: Alban Institute, 2007).

36. Tim Brown, "Tim Brown: Tales of Creativity and Play" (video), November 2008, www.ted.com/talks/tim_brown_on_creativity_and_play.html.
37. Loehr and Schwartz, *The Power of Full Engagement*, 131.

Jewish Ethical Themes That Should Inform the National Healthcare Discussion: A Prolegomenon, by Jeff Levin, PhD, MPH

This chapter is adapted from an identically named article published in *Journal of Religion and Health* 51 (2012): 589–600. An earlier version of this paper was presented at Human Dignity and the Future of Health Care, the 2010 Baylor Symposium on Faith and Culture, Waco, TX, October 30, 2010.

1. "Patient Protection and Affordable Care Act," P.L. 111-148, 124 STAT. 119 (March 23, 2010), www.gpo.gov/fdsys/pkg/PLAW-111publ148/pdf/PLAW-111publ148.pdf.
2. "Health Care and Education Reconciliation Act of 2010," P.L. 111–152, 124 STAT. 1029 (March 30, 2010), www.gpo.gov/fdsys/pkg/PLAW-111publ152/pdf/PLAW-111publ152.pdf.
3. "Repealing the Job-Killing Health Care Law Act," H.R. 2, 112th Congress, 1st Session, Calendar No. 3 (January 26, 2011), http://www.gpo.gov/fdsys/pkg/BILLS-112hr2pcs/pdf/BILLS-112hr2pcs.pdf.
4. United States Court of Appeals for the Eleventh Circuit, Nos. 11-11021 & 11-11067, D.C. Docket No. 3:10-cv-00091-RV-EMT (August 12, 2011), www.uscourts.gov/uscourts/courts/ca11/201111021.pdf.
5. Supreme Court of the United States, "National Federation of Independent Business et al. v. Sebelius, Secretary of Health and Human Services, et al.: Certiorari to the United States Court of Appeals for the Eleventh Circuit," 567 U.S. ___, Slip Op., No. 11-393, 11-398, and 11-400 (2012) (July 28, 2012), www.supremecourt.gov/opinions/11pdf/11-393c3a2.pdf.
6. See Tom L. Beauchamp and James F. Childress, *Principles of Biomedical Ethics*, 6th ed. (New York: Oxford University Press, 2009).
7. Immanuel Jakobovits, *Jewish Medical Ethics: A Comparative and Historical Study of the Jewish Religious Attitude to Medicine and Its Practice* (New York: Bloch, 1959), 7.
8. Ibid., xxi–xxii.
9. United Synagogue of Conservative Judaism, "Judaism and Health Care Reform," April 1993, www.uscj.org/images/judaism_and_health_care_reform.pdf; Rabbinical Council of America, "Health Care Reform 1999," June 1, 1999, www.rabbis.org/news/article.cfm?id=100998; Union for Reform Judaism, "Health Care Initiative: Health Care for All," December 15, 2007, http://urj.org/socialaction/issues/healthcare; Agudath Israel of America, "Health Care Reform" (letter to President

Obama), August 19, 2009, http://daledamos.blogspot.com/2009/08/agudath-israel-weighs-in-on-health-care.html; and Kenneth B. Frisof, Linda Hannah Walling, and Marie Frisof, *Seeking Justice in Health Care: A Guide for Advocates in Faith Communities* (Cleveland: Faithful Reform in Health Care, 2010).

10. For example, Jewish Council for Public Affairs, "JCPA Resolution on Health Care Coverage" (adopted by the 2003 JCPA Plenum), www.jewishpublicaffairs.org/www.e-guana.net/organizations/org/HealthCare-1.doc; American Jewish Congress, "American Jewish Congress Urges Senate Rejection of New Restrictions on Reproductive Health Care in Health Care Reform Legislation," 2009, http://www.ajcongress.org/site/News2?page=NewsArticle&id=7087; National Council of Jewish Women, "Health Care Reform Talking Points, August 2009, www.ncjw.org/media/PDFs/rsrcehealthcarereformtps0809.pdf; Jewish Federations of North America, "Health & Long-Term Care Reform Documents and Information," 2011, www.jewishfederations.org/page.aspx?id=235364; and B'nai B'rith International, "Healthcare Repair: A B'nai B'rith Agenda for Reform" (n.d.), www.bnaibrith.org/uploads/7/8/5/9/7859990/repairhealthcare.pdf.

11. For example, Jakobovits, *Jewish Medical Ethics*; Fred Rosner and Moshe D. Tendler, *Practical Medical Halacha* (Jerusalem: Feldheim Publishers, 1980); Solomon B. Freehof, *New Reform Responsa* (Cincinnati: Hebrew Union College Press, 1981); Moshe Feinstein, *Responsa of Rav Moshe Feinstein*, vol. 1, *Care of the Critically Ill*, trans. Moshe Dovid Tendler (Hoboken, NJ: Ktav, 1985); Walter Jacob, *Contemporary American Reform Responsa* (New York: Central Conference of American Rabbis Press, 1987); UAHC Committee on Bio-Ethics, *Bioethics Program Guide VII: Allocation of Scarce Medical Resources* (New York: UAHC Department of Jewish Family Concerns, 1994); W. Gunther Plaut and Mark Washofsky, eds., *Teshuvot for the Nineties: Reform Judaism's Answers to Today's Dilemmas* (New York: Central Conference of American Rabbis Press, 1997); Elliot N. Dorff, *Matters of Life and Death: A Jewish Approach to Modern Medical Ethics* (Philadelphia: Jewish Publication Society, 1998); David Golinkin, *Responsa in a Moment* (Jerusalem: Institute of Applied Halakhah at the Schechter Institute of Jewish Studies, 2000); and Reconstructionist Rabbinical College, *Behoref Hayamim: In the Winter of Life: A Values-Based Jewish Guide for Decision-Making at the End of Life* (Wyncote, PA: Reconstructionist Rabbinical College, 2002).

12. For example, J. David Bleich, *Judaism and Healing: Halakhic Perspectives* (New York: Ktav, 1981); J. David Bleich, *Bioethical Dilemmas: A Jewish Perspective* (Hoboken, NJ: Ktav, 1998); David M. Feldman, *Health and Medicine in the Jewish Tradition:* L'Hayyim—*To Life* (New York: Crossroad, 1986); Noam J. Zohar, *Alternatives in Jewish Bioethics* (Albany, NY: State University of New York Press, 1997); Benjamin Freedman, *Duty and Healing: Foundations of a Jewish Bioethics* (New York: Routledge, 1999); Laurie Zoloth, *Health Care and*

the Ethics of Encounter: A Jewish Discussion of Social Justice (Chapel Hill, NC: University of North Carolina Press, 1999); Fred Rosner and J. David Bleich, eds., *Jewish Bioethics*, augmented ed. (Hoboken, NJ: Ktav, 2001); Fred Rosner, *Biomedical Ethics and Jewish Law* (Hoboken, NJ: Ktav, 2001); Fred Rosner, *Contemporary Biomedical Ethical Issues and Jewish Law* (Jersey City, NJ: Ktav, 2007); and Avraham Steinberg, *Encyclopedia of Jewish Medical Ethics*, trans. Fred Rosner (Jerusalem: Feldheim Publishers, 2003).

13. "Medicine, Money and Morals: The Jewish Obligation to Heal Confronts Healthcare Economics," Second Annual Conference of the Academic Coalition of Jewish Bioethics, Philadelphia (April 3–4, 2005).
14. "Health Care: Right or Privilege? Moral and Religious Values in Health Care Reform," special issue, *Conservative Judaism* 51, no. 4 (1999); and "Caring and Healing," special issue, *The Reconstructionist* 63, no. 2 (1999).
15. "Judaism and Health Care," special issue, *Bulletin of the Park Ridge Center* 14 (2000).
16. For example, Zoloth, *Health Care and the Ethics of Encounter.*
17. Dorff, *Matters of Life and Death*, 281.
18. An alternative interpretation is also possible. It could be that "*b'chol l'vav'kha*" corresponds not to emotions but to cognition (as in the ancient Near East tradition to view the heart as the seat of the mind) and "*uv'chol nafsh'kha*" corresponds not to higher mind but to spirit. Accordingly, it would be the spirit (*nefesh*), in turn, that engages in *avodah* and achieves *shalom*, and the mind (i.e., heart: *leivav*) that pursues *torah* and realizes *emet*. But, no matter, the general scheme holds—the three psychological functions of mind, emotions, and behavior as highlighted in the *V'ahavta*—as well as the exegetical application of the Mishnaic passages to the *pasukim* in Deuteronomy. Thanks to Rabbi Gordon Fuller for this additional insight.
19. *Pirkei Avot* 1:2.
20. *Pirkei Avot* 1:18.
21. *Mishnah Pe'ah* 1:1.
22. Aaron L. Mackler, "Judaism, Justice and Access to Health Care," *Kennedy Institute of Ethics Journal* 1, no. 2 (1991): 143–61.
23. Noam J. Zohar, "A Jewish Perspective on Access to Healthcare," *Cambridge Quarterly of Healthcare Ethics* 7 (1998): 260–65.
24. Immanuel Jakobovits, "Jewish Medical Ethics—A Brief Overview," *Journal of Medical Ethics* 9 (1983): 109–12.
25. David Novak, "A Jewish Argument for Socialized Medicine," *Kennedy Institute for Ethics Journal* 13 (2003): 313–28.

26. Jonathan Sacks, *A Letter in the Scroll: Understanding Our Jewish Identity and Exploring the Legacy of the World's Oldest Religion* (New York: Free Press, 2000).
27. Jeff Levin, "Divine Love in the World's Religious Traditions," in *Divine Love: Perspectives from the World's Religious Traditions*, ed. Jeff Levin and Stephen G. Post (West Conshohocken, PA: Templeton Press, 2010), 16.
28. *Tanchuma Shof'tim* 18.
29. *Pirkei Avot* 2:16.
30. Jerusalem Talmud, *Pe'ah* 1:1.
31. Daniel B. Rubin, "A Role for Moral Vision in Public Health," *Hastings Center Report* 40, no. 6 (2010): 20–22.
32. Lawrence D. Brown, "Health Reform in America: The Mystery of the Missing Moral Momentum," *Cambridge Quarterly of Healthcare Ethics* 7 (1998): 239–46.
33. Dorff, *Matters of Life and Death*, 307–9.

Suggested Reading

Berger, Natalia, ed., *Jews and Medicine: Religion, Culture, Science* (Philadelphia: Jewish Publication Society, 1995).

Cutter, William, ed., *Healing and the Jewish Imagination: Spiritual and Practical Perspectives on Judaism and Health* (Woodstock, VT: Jewish Lights, 2007).

Cutter, William, ed., *Midrash and Medicine: Healing Body and Soul in the Jewish Interpretive Tradition* (Woodstock, VT: Jewish Lights, 2011).

Dorff, Elliot N., *Matters of Life and Death: A Jewish Approach to Modern Medical Ethics* (Philadelphia: Jewish Publication Society, 2003).

Feldman, David M., *Health and Medicine in the Jewish Tradition:* L'Hayyim—*to Life* (New York: Crossroad, 1986).

Freeman, David L. and Judith Z. Abrams, eds., *Illness and Health in the Jewish Tradition: Writings from the Bible to Today* (Philadelphia: Jewish Publication Society, 1999).

Friedman, Dayle A., ed., *Jewish Pastoral Care: A Practical Handbook from Traditional and Contemporary Sources*, 2nd ed. (Woodstock, VT: Jewish Lights, 2005).

Hart, Mitchell B., *The Healthy Jew: The Symbiosis of Judaism and Modern Medicine* (New York: Cambridge University Press, 2007).

Heynick, Frank, *Jews and Medicine: An Epic Saga* (Hoboken, NJ: KTAV Publishing House, 2002).

Jakobovits, Immanuel, *Jewish Medical Ethics: A Comparative and Historical Study of the Jewish Religious Attitude to Medicine and its Practice* (1959) (New York: Bloch Publishing Co., 1975).

Person, Hara E., ed., *The Mitzvah of Healing: An Anthology of Essays, Jewish Texts, Personal Stories, Meditations, and Rituals* (New York: Women of Reform Judaism/UAHC Press, 2003).

Preuss, Julius, *Biblical and Talmudic Medicine* (1911), trans. and ed. by Fred Rosner (Northvale, NJ: Jason Aronson, 1993).

Prince, Michele and Nancy H. Weiner, eds., "Symposium Issue on Judaism, Health, and Healing," special issue, *CCAR Journal: The Reform Jewish Quarterly* 49, no. 3 (2012):1-264.

Schur, Tsvi G., *Illness and Crisis: Coping the Jewish Way* (New York: NCSY/ Orthodox Union, 1987).

Weintraub, Simkha Y., ed., *Healing of Soul, Healing of Body: Spiritual Leaders Unfold the Strength and Solace in Psalms* (Woodstock, VT: Jewish Lights, 1994).

Credits

"An Overview of Jewish Bioethics": Adapted with permission from two previous publications by David A. Teutsch: *A Guide to Jewish Practice: Bioethics* (Wyncote, PA: Reconstructionist Rabbinical College Press, 2005) and *A Guide to Jewish Practice: Everyday Living* (Wyncote, PA: Reconstructionist Rabbinical Press, 2011).

"The Precision of Pain": from *Open Closed Open: Poems* by Yehuda Amichai, translated from the Hebrew by Chana Block and Chana Kronfeld. Copyright © 2000 by Chana Bloch and Chana Kronfeld. Reprinted by permission of Houghton Mifflin Harcourt Publishing Company. All rights reserved.

From "God Full of Mercy": from Yehuda Amichai, *Yehuda Amichai: A Life of Poetry, 1948–1994.* Reprinted with the permission of the estate of Yehuda Amichai.

With kind permission from Springer Science+Business Media: "Jewish Ethical Themes That Should Inform the National Healthcare Discussion: A Prolegomenon," *Journal of Religion and Health* 51 (2012): 589–600, © Springer Science+Business Media, LLC 2012.

"Judaism and Disability: *R'fuat Hanefesh*—The Healing of Our Souls, Individual and Communal": A version of this article originally appeared in *The Forward* (February 26, 2010).

"When a Horse Is Sold in the Marketplace" and "When the Woman": excerpted from *The Spectacular Difference: Selected Poems of Zelda*, translated from the Hebrew by Marcia Falk, Hebrew Union College Press. © 2004 by Marcia Lee Falk. Reprinted by permission of the translator.

From *Life in the Balance*: forthcoming (New York: ArtScroll). Reprinted by permission.

From "Sloan-Kettering," "Visiting Time Is Over," and "Nine O'Clock. Norma," by Abba Kovner: from *Sloan-Kettering Poems* (New York: Schocken, 2002), © Michael Kovner. Reprinted by permission.

From "A Recipe for Visiting the Sick": from *Libbi Pose 'a le'achor* by Malka Shaked. Reprinted by permission of Malka Shaked and of HaKibbutz HaMe'uchad.

From "Jewish Spiritual Care": from *Multifaith Views in Spiritual Care*, edited by Daniel S. Schipani, forthcoming at Pandora Press. Material adapted with permission.

Index

AVAILABLE FROM BETTER BOOKSTORES. TRY YOUR BOOKSTORE FIRST.

Bible Study / Midrash

Passing Life's Tests: Spiritual Reflections on the Trial of Abraham, the Binding of Isaac *By Rabbi Bradley Shavit Artson, DHL*
Invites us to use this powerful tale as a tool for our own soul wrestling, to confront our existential sacrifices and enable us to face—and surmount—life's tests.
6 x 9, 176 pp, Quality PB, 978-1-58023-631-7 **$18.99**

The Messiah and the Jews: Three Thousand Years of Tradition, Belief and Hope *By Rabbi Elaine Rose Glickman; Foreword by Rabbi Neil Gillman, PhD; Preface by Rabbi Judith Z. Abrams, PhD*
Explores and explains an astonishing range of primary and secondary sources, infusing them with new meaning for the modern reader.
6 x 9, 192 pp, Quality PB, 978-1-58023-690-4 **$16.99**

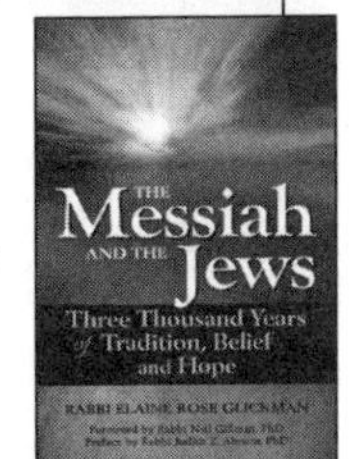

Speaking Torah: Spiritual Teachings from around the Maggid's Table—in Two Volumes *By Arthur Green, with Ebn Leader, Ariel Evan Mayse and Or N. Rose*
The most powerful Hasidic teachings made accessible—from some of the world's preeminent authorities on Jewish thought and spirituality.
Volume 1—6 x 9, 512 pp, Hardcover, 978-1-58023-668-3 **$34.99**
Volume 2—6 x 9, 448 pp, Hardcover, 978-1-58023-694-2 **$34.99**

Masking and Unmasking Ourselves: Interpreting Biblical Texts on Clothing & Identity *By Dr. Norman J. Cohen*
Presents ten Bible stories that involve clothing in an essential way, as a means of learning about the text, its characters and their interactions.
6 x 9, 240 pp, HC, 978-1-58023-461-0 **$24.99**

The Genesis of Leadership: What the Bible Teaches Us about Vision, Values and Leading Change *By Rabbi Nathan Laufer; Foreword by Senator Joseph I. Lieberman*
6 x 9, 288 pp, Quality PB, 978-1-58023-352-1 **$18.99**

Hineini in Our Lives: Learning How to Respond to Others through 14 Biblical Texts and Personal Stories *By Rabbi Norman J. Cohen, PhD* 6 x 9, 240 pp, Quality PB, 978-1-58023-274-6 **$16.99**

The Modern Men's Torah Commentary: New Insights from Jewish Men on the 54 Weekly Torah Portions *Edited by Rabbi Jeffrey K. Salkin*
6 x 9, 368 pp, HC, 978-1-58023-395-8 **$24.99**

Moses and the Journey to Leadership: Timeless Lessons of Effective Management from the Bible and Today's Leaders *By Rabbi Norman J. Cohen, PhD*
6 x 9, 240 pp, Quality PB, 978-1-58023-351-4 **$18.99**; HC, 978-1-58023-227-2 **$21.99**

The Other Talmud—*The Yerushalmi*: Unlocking the Secrets of The Talmud of Israel for Judaism Today *By Rabbi Judith Z. Abrams, PhD*
6 x 9, 256 pp, HC, 978-1-58023-463-4 **$24.99**

Sage Tales: Wisdom and Wonder from the Rabbis of the Talmud *By Rabbi Burton L. Visotzky* 6 x 9, 256 pp, HC, 978-1-58023-456-6 **$24.99**

The Torah Revolution: Fourteen Truths That Changed the World *By Rabbi Reuven Hammer, PhD* 6 x 9, 240 pp, HC, 978-1-58023-457-3 **$24.99**

The Wisdom of Judaism: An Introduction to the Values of the Talmud *By Rabbi Dov Peretz Elkins* 6 x 9, 192 pp, Quality PB, 978-1-58023-327-9 **$16.99**

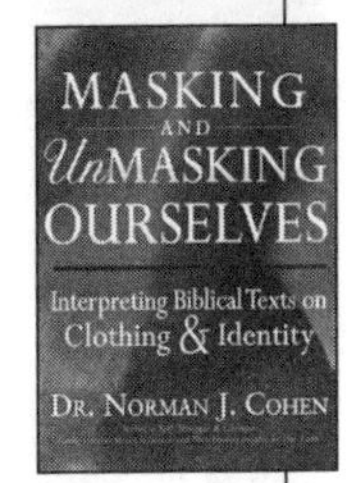

Or phone, fax, mail or e-mail to: **JEWISH LIGHTS Publishing**
Sunset Farm Offices, Route 4 • P.O. Box 237 • Woodstock, Vermont 05091
Tel: (802) 457-4000 • Fax: (802) 457-4004 • www.jewishlights.com
Credit card orders: **(800) 962-4544** (8:30AM–5:30PM EST Monday–Friday)
Generous discounts on quantity orders. SATISFACTION GUARANTEED. Prices subject to change.

Congregation Resources

Jewish Megatrends: Charting the Course of the American Jewish Future
By Rabbi Sidney Schwarz; Foreword by Ambassador Stuart E. Eizenstat
Visionary solutions for a community ripe for transformational change—from fourteen leading innovators of Jewish life.
6 x 9, 288 pp, HC, 978-1-58023-667-6 **$24.99**

Relational Judaism: Using the Power of Relationships to Transform the Jewish Community *By Dr. Ron Wolfson*
How to transform the model of twentieth-century Jewish institutions into twenty-first-century relational communities offering meaning and purpose, belonging and blessing.
6 x 9, 288 pp, HC, 978-1-58023-666-9 **$24.99**

Revolution of Jewish Spirit: How to Revive *Ruakh* in Your Spiritual Life, Transform Your Synagogue & Inspire Your Jewish Community
By Rabbi Baruch HaLevi, DMin, and Ellen Frankel, LCSW; Foreword by Dr. Ron Wolfson
A practical and engaging guide to reinvigorating Jewish life. Offers strategies for sustaining and expanding transformation, impassioned leadership, inspired programming and inviting sacred spaces.
6 x 9, 224 pp, Quality PB Original, 978-1-58023-625-6 **$19.99**

Building a Successful Volunteer Culture: Finding Meaning in Service in the Jewish Community *By Rabbi Charles Simon; Foreword by Shelley Lindauer; Preface by Dr. Ron Wolfson*
6 x 9, 192 pp, Quality PB, 978-1-58023-408-5 **$16.99**

The Case for Jewish Peoplehood: Can We Be One?
By Dr. Erica Brown and Dr. Misha Galperin; Foreword by Rabbi Joseph Telushkin
6 x 9, 224 pp, HC, 978-1-58023-401-6 **$21.99**

Empowered Judaism: What Independent Minyanim Can Teach Us about Building Vibrant Jewish Communities *By Rabbi Elie Kaunfer; Foreword by Prof. Jonathan D. Sarna*
6 x 9, 224 pp, Quality PB, 978-1-58023-412-2 **$18.99**

Finding a Spiritual Home: How a New Generation of Jews Can Transform the American Synagogue *By Rabbi Sidney Schwarz*
6 x 9, 352 pp, Quality PB, 978-1-58023-185-5 **$19.95**

Inspired Jewish Leadership: Practical Approaches to Building Strong Communities
By Dr. Erica Brown 6 x 9, 256 pp, HC, 978-1-58023-361-3 **$27.99**

Jewish Pastoral Care, 2nd Edition: A Practical Handbook from Traditional & Contemporary Sources *Edited by Rabbi Dayle A. Friedman, MSW, MAJCS, BCC*
6 x 9, 528 pp, Quality PB, 978-1-58023-427-6 **$35.00**

Jewish Spiritual Direction: An Innovative Guide from Traditional and Contemporary Sources
Edited by Rabbi Howard A. Addison, PhD, and Barbara Eve Breitman, MSW
6 x 9, 368 pp, HC, 978-1-58023-230-2 **$30.00**

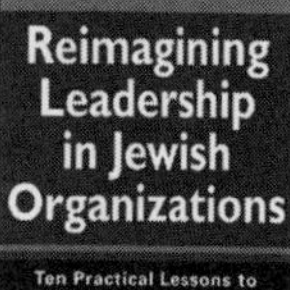

A Practical Guide to Rabbinic Counseling
Edited by Rabbi Yisrael N. Levitz, PhD, and Rabbi Abraham J. Twerski, MD
6 x 9, 432 pp, HC, 978-1-58023-562-4 **$40.00**

Professional Spiritual & Pastoral Care: A Practical Clergy and Chaplain's Handbook
Edited by Rabbi Stephen B. Roberts, MBA, MHL, BCJC
6 x 9, 480 pp, HC, 978-1-59473-312-3 **$50.00**

Reimagining Leadership in Jewish Organizations: Ten Practical Lessons to Help You Implement Change and Achieve Your Goals *By Dr. Misha Galperin*
6 x 9, 192 pp, Quality PB, 978-1-58023-492-4 **$16.99**

Rethinking Synagogues: A New Vocabulary for Congregational Life
By Rabbi Lawrence A. Hoffman, PhD 6 x 9, 240 pp, Quality PB, 978-1-58023-248-7 **$19.99**

Spiritual Community: The Power to Restore Hope, Commitment and Joy
By Rabbi David A. Teutsch, PhD
5½ x 8½, 144 pp, HC, 978-1-58023-270-8 **$19.99**

Spiritual Boredom: Rediscovering the Wonder of Judaism *By Dr. Erica Brown*
6 x 9, 208 pp, HC, 978-1-58023-405-4 **$21.99**

The Spirituality of Welcoming: How to Transform Your Congregation into a Sacred Community *By Dr. Ron Wolfson* 6 x 9, 224 pp, Quality PB, 978-1-58023-244-9 **$19.99**

Theology / Philosophy

Believing and Its Tensions: A Personal Conversation about God, Torah, Suffering and Death in Jewish Thought
By Rabbi Neil Gillman, PhD
Explores the changing nature of belief and the complexities of reconciling the intellectual, emotional and moral questions of Gillman's own searching mind and soul.
5½ x 8½, 144 pp, HC, 978-1-58023-669-0 **$19.99**

God of Becoming and Relationship: The Dynamic Nature of Process Theology *By Rabbi Bradley Shavit Artson, DHL*
Explains how Process Theology breaks us free from the strictures of ancient Greek and medieval European philosophy, allowing us to see all creation as related patterns of energy through which we connect to everything.
6 x 9, 208 pp, HC, 978-1-58023-713-0 **$24.99**

The Other Talmud—*The Yerushalmi*: Unlocking the Secrets of The Talmud of Israel for Judaism Today *By Rabbi Judith Z. Abrams, PhD*
A fascinating—and stimulating—look at "the other Talmud" and the possibilities for Jewish life reflected there. 6 x 9, 256 pp, HC, 978-1-58023-463-4 **$24.99**

The Way of Man: According to Hasidic Teaching
By Martin Buber; New Translation and Introduction by Rabbi Bernard H. Mehlman and Dr. Gabriel E. Padawer; Foreword by Paul Mendes-Flohr
An accessible and engaging new translation of Buber's classic work—*available as an e-book only*. E-book, 978-1-58023-601-0 Digital List Price **$14.99**

The Death of Death: Resurrection and Immortality in Jewish Thought
By Rabbi Neil Gillman, PhD 6 x 9, 336 pp, Quality PB, 978-1-58023-081-0 **$18.95**

Doing Jewish Theology: God, Torah & Israel in Modern Judaism *By Rabbi Neil Gillman, PhD*
6 x 9, 304 pp, Quality PB, 978-1-58023-439-9 **$18.99**; HC, 978-1-58023-322-4 **$24.99**

From Defender to Critic: The Search for a New Jewish Self
By Dr. David Hartman 6 x 9, 336 pp, HC, 978-1-58023-515-0 **$35.00**

The God Who Hates Lies: Confronting & Rethinking Jewish Tradition
By Dr. David Hartman with Charlie Buckholtz 6 x 9, 208 pp, HC, 978-1-58023-455-9 **$24.99**

A Heart of Many Rooms: Celebrating the Many Voices within Judaism
By Dr. David Hartman 6 x 9, 352 pp, Quality PB, 978-1-58023-156-5 **$19.95**

Jewish Theology in Our Time: A New Generation Explores the Foundations and Future of Jewish Belief *Edited by Rabbi Elliot J. Cosgrove, PhD; Foreword by Rabbi David J. Wolpe; Preface by Rabbi Carole B. Balin, PhD* 6 x 9, 240 pp, Quality PB, 978-1-58023-630-1, **$19.99**; HC, 978-1-58023-413-9 **$24.99**

Maimonides—Essential Teachings on Jewish Faith & Ethics: The Book of Knowledge & the Thirteen Principles of Faith—Annotated & Explained
Translation and Annotation by Rabbi Marc D. Angel, PhD
5½ x 8½, 224 pp, Quality PB Original, 978-1-59473-311-6 **$18.99***

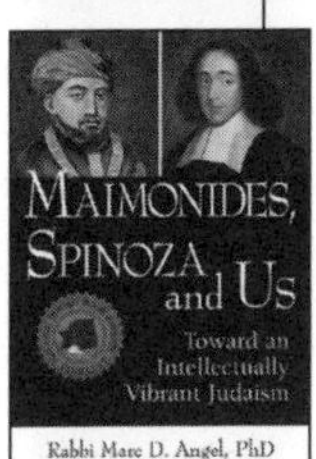

Maimonides, Spinoza and Us: Toward an Intellectually Vibrant Judaism
By Rabbi Marc D. Angel, PhD 6 x 9, 224 pp, HC, 978-1-58023-411-5 **$24.99**

Our Religious Brains: What Cognitive Science Reveals about Belief, Morality, Community and Our Relationship with God
By Rabbi Ralph D. Mecklenburger; Foreword by Dr. Howard Kelfer; Preface by Dr. Neil Gillman
6 x 9, 224 pp, HC, 978-1-58023-508-2 **$24.99**

Your Word Is Fire: The Hasidic Masters on Contemplative Prayer
Edited and translated by Rabbi Arthur Green, PhD, and Barry W. Holtz
6 x 9, 160 pp, Quality PB, 978-1-879045-25-5 **$16.99**

I Am Jewish

Personal Reflections Inspired by the Last Words of Daniel Pearl

Almost 150 Jews—both famous and not—from all walks of life, from all around the world, write about many aspects of their Judaism.
Edited by Judea and Ruth Pearl 6 x 9, 304 pp, Deluxe PB w/ flaps, 978-1-58023-259-3 **$19.99**
Download a free copy of the *I Am Jewish Teacher's Guide* at www.jewishlights.com.

**A book from SkyLight Paths, Jewish Lights' sister imprint*

Social Justice

Where Justice Dwells
A Hands-On Guide to Doing Social Justice in Your Jewish Community
By Rabbi Jill Jacobs; Foreword by Rabbi David Saperstein
Provides ways to envision and act on your own ideals of social justice.
7 x 9, 288 pp, Quality PB Original, 978-1-58023-453-5 **$24.99**

There Shall Be No Needy
Pursuing Social Justice through Jewish Law and Tradition
By Rabbi Jill Jacobs; Foreword by Rabbi Elliot N. Dorff, PhD; Preface by Simon Greer
Confronts the most pressing issues of twenty-first-century America from a deeply Jewish perspective. 6 x 9, 288 pp, Quality PB, 978-1-58023-425-2 **$16.99**

There Shall Be No Needy Teacher's Guide 8½ x 11, 56 pp, PB, 978-1-58023-429-0 **$8.99**

Conscience
The Duty to Obey and the Duty to Disobey
By Rabbi Harold M. Schulweis
Examines the idea of conscience and the role conscience plays in our relationships to government, law, ethics, religion, human nature, God—and to each other.
6 x 9, 160 pp, Quality PB, 978-1-58023-419-1 **$16.99**; HC, 978-1-58023-375-0 **$19.99**

Judaism and Justice
The Jewish Passion to Repair the World
By Rabbi Sidney Schwarz; Foreword by Ruth Messinger
Explores the relationship between Judaism, social justice and the Jewish identity of American Jews. 6 x 9, 352 pp, Quality PB, 978-1-58023-353-8 **$19.99**

Spirituality / Women's Interest

New Jewish Feminism
Probing the Past, Forging the Future
Edited by Rabbi Elyse Goldstein; Foreword by Anita Diamant
Looks at the growth and accomplishments of Jewish feminism and what they mean for Jewish women today and tomorrow.
6 x 9, 480 pp, HC, 978-1-58023-359-0 **$24.99**

The Divine Feminine in Biblical Wisdom Literature
Selections Annotated & Explained
Translation & Annotation by Rabbi Rami Shapiro
5½ x 8½, 240 pp, Quality PB, 978-1-59473-109-9 **$16.99**
(A book from SkyLight Paths, Jewish Lights' sister imprint)

The Quotable Jewish Woman
Wisdom, Inspiration & Humor from the Mind & Heart
Edited by Elaine Bernstein Partnow
6 x 9, 496 pp, Quality PB, 978-1-58023-236-4 **$19.99**

The Women's Haftarah Commentary
New Insights from Women Rabbis on the 54 Weekly Haftarah Portions, the 5 Megillot & Special Shabbatot
Edited by Rabbi Elyse Goldstein
Illuminates the historical significance of female portrayals in the Haftarah and the Five Megillot. 6 x 9, 560 pp, Quality PB, 978-1-58023-371-2 **$19.99**

The Women's Torah Commentary
New Insights from Women Rabbis on the 54 Weekly Torah Portions
Edited by Rabbi Elyse Goldstein
Over fifty women rabbis offer inspiring insights on the Torah, in a week-by-week format.
6 x 9, 496 pp, Quality PB, 978-1-58023-370-5 **$19.99**; HC, 978-1-58023-076-6 **$34.95**

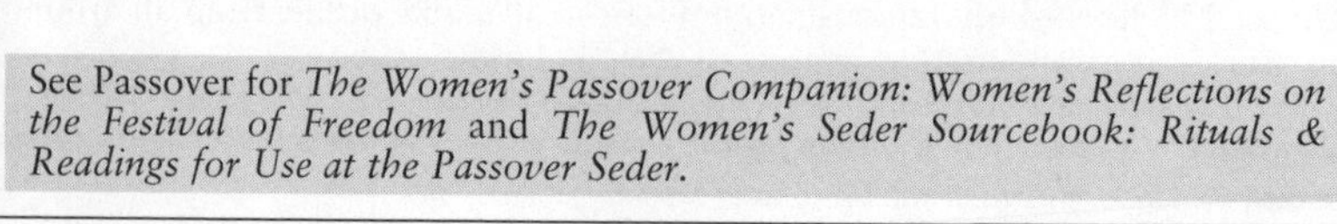
See Passover for *The Women's Passover Companion: Women's Reflections on the Festival of Freedom* and *The Women's Seder Sourcebook: Rituals & Readings for Use at the Passover Seder.*

Ecology / Environment

A Wild Faith: Jewish Ways into Wilderness, Wilderness Ways into Judaism
By Rabbi Mike Comins; Foreword by Nigel Savage 6 x 9, 240 pp, Quality PB, 978-1-58023-316-3 **$16.99**

Ecology & the Jewish Spirit: Where Nature & the Sacred Meet
Edited by Ellen Bernstein 6 x 9, 288 pp, Quality PB, 978-1-58023-082-7 **$18.99**

Torah of the Earth: Exploring 4,000 Years of Ecology in Jewish Thought
Vol. 1: Biblical Israel & Rabbinic Judaism; Vol. 2: Zionism & Eco-Judaism
Edited by Rabbi Arthur Waskow Vol. 1: 6 x 9, 272 pp, Quality PB, 978-1-58023-086-5 **$19.95**
Vol. 2: 6 x 9, 336 pp, Quality PB, 978-1-58023-087-2 **$19.95**

The Way Into Judaism and the Environment *By Jeremy Benstein, PhD*
6 x 9, 288 pp, Quality PB, 978-1-58023-368-2 **$18.99**; HC, 978-1-58023-268-5 **$24.99**

Graphic Novels / Graphic History

The Adventures of Rabbi Harvey: A Graphic Novel of Jewish Wisdom and Wit in the Wild West *By Steve Sheinkin* 6 x 9, 144 pp, Full-color illus., Quality PB, 978-1-58023-310-1 **$16.99**

Rabbi Harvey Rides Again: A Graphic Novel of Jewish Folktales Let Loose in the Wild West *By Steve Sheinkin* 6 x 9, 144 pp, Full-color illus., Quality PB, 978-1-58023-347-7 **$16.99**

Rabbi Harvey vs. the Wisdom Kid: A Graphic Novel of Dueling Jewish Folktales in the Wild West *By Steve Sheinkin*
6 x 9, 144 pp, Full-color illus., Quality PB, 978-1-58023-422-1 **$16.99**

The Story of the Jews: A 4,000-Year Adventure—A Graphic History Book
By Stan Mack 6 x 9, 288 pp, Illus., Quality PB, 978-1-58023-155-8 **$16.99**

Grief / Healing

Judaism and Health: A Handbook of Practical, Professional and Scholarly Resources *Edited by Jeff Levin, PhD, MPH, and Michele F. Prince, LCSW, MAJCS*
Foreword by Rabbi Elliot N. Dorff, PhD
Explores the expressions of health in the form of overviews of research studies, first-person narratives and advice. 6 x 9, 448 pp, HC, 978-1-58023-714-7 **$50.00**

Facing Illness, Finding God: How Judaism Can Help You and Caregivers Cope When Body or Spirit Fails *By Rabbi Joseph B. Meszler*
6 x 9, 208 pp, Quality PB, 978-1-58023-423-8 **$16.99**

Grief in Our Seasons: A Mourner's Kaddish Companion *By Rabbi Kerry M. Olitzky*
4½ x 6½, 448 pp, Quality PB, 978-1-879045-55-2 **$15.95**

Healing and the Jewish Imagination: Spiritual and Practical Perspectives on Judaism and Health *Edited by Rabbi William Cutter, PhD*
6 x 9, 240 pp, Quality PB, 978-1-58023-373-6 **$19.99**

Healing from Despair: Choosing Wholeness in a Broken World
By Rabbi Elie Kaplan Spitz with Erica Shapiro Taylor; Foreword by Abraham J. Twerski, MD
5½ x 8½, 208 pp, Quality PB, 978-1-58023-436-8 **$16.99**

Healing of Soul, Healing of Body: Spiritual Leaders Unfold the Strength & Solace in Psalms *Edited by Rabbi Simkha Y. Weintraub, LCSW*
6 x 9, 128 pp, 2-color illus. text, Quality PB, 978-1-879045-31-6 **$16.99**

Midrash & Medicine: Healing Body and Soul in the Jewish Interpretive Tradition
Edited by Rabbi William Cutter, PhD; Foreword by Michele F. Prince, LCSW, MAJCS
6 x 9, 352 pp, Quality PB, 978-1-58023-484-9 **$21.99**

Mourning & Mitzvah, 2nd Edition: A Guided Journal for Walking the Mourner's Path through Grief to Healing *By Rabbi Anne Brener, LCSW*
7½ x 9, 304 pp, Quality PB, 978-1-58023-113-8 **$19.99**

Tears of Sorrow, Seeds of Hope, 2nd Edition: A Jewish Spiritual Companion for Infertility and Pregnancy Loss *By Rabbi Nina Beth Cardin*
6 x 9, 208 pp, Quality PB, 978-1-58023-233-3 **$18.99**

A Time to Mourn, a Time to Comfort, 2nd Edition: A Guide to Jewish Bereavement *By Dr. Ron Wolfson; Foreword by Rabbi David J. Wolpe*
7 x 9, 384 pp, Quality PB, 978-1-58023-253-1 **$21.99**

When a Grandparent Dies: A Kid's Own Remembering Workbook for Dealing with Shiva and the Year Beyond *By Nechama Liss-Levinson, PhD*
8 x 10, 48 pp, 2-color text, HC, 978-1-879045-44-6 **$15.95** *For ages 7–13*

Meditation

The Magic of Hebrew Chant: Healing the Spirit, Transforming the Mind, Deepening Love
By Rabbi Shefa Gold; Foreword by Sylvia Boorstein
Introduces this transformative spiritual practice as a way to unlock the power of sacred texts and make prayer and meditation the delight of your life. Includes musical notations. 6 x 9, 352 pp, Quality PB, 978-1-58023-671-3 **$24.99**

The Magic of Hebrew Chant Companion—The Big Book of Musical Notations and Incantations
8½ x 11, 154 pp, PB, 978-1-58023-722-2 **$19.99**

Jewish Meditation Practices for Everyday Life
Awakening Your Heart, Connecting with God
By Rabbi Jeff Roth
Offers a fresh take on meditation that draws on life experience and living life with greater clarity as opposed to the traditional method of rigorous study.
6 x 9, 224 pp, Quality PB, 978-1-58023-397-2 **$18.99**

Discovering Jewish Meditation, 2nd Edition
Instruction & Guidance for Learning an Ancient Spiritual Practice
By Nan Fink Gefen, PhD 6 x 9, 208 pp, Quality PB, 978-1-58023-462-7 **$16.99**

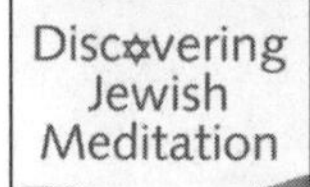

The Handbook of Jewish Meditation Practices
A Guide for Enriching the Sabbath and Other Days of Your Life
By Rabbi David A. Cooper 6 x 9, 208 pp, Quality PB, 978-1-58023-102-2 **$16.95**

Meditation from the Heart of Judaism
Today's Teachers Share Their Practices, Techniques, and Faith
Edited by Avram Davis 6 x 9, 256 pp, Quality PB, 978-1-58023-049-0 **$16.95**

Ritual / Sacred Practices

God in Your Body: Kabbalah, Mindfulness and Embodied Spiritual Practice
By Jay Michaelson
The first comprehensive treatment of the body in Jewish spiritual practice and an essential guide to the sacred. 6 x 9, 272 pp, Quality PB, 978-1-58023-304-0 **$18.99**

The Book of Jewish Sacred Practices: CLAL's Guide to Everyday & Holiday Rituals & Blessings *Edited by Rabbi Irwin Kula and Vanessa L. Ochs, PhD*
6 x 9, 368 pp, Quality PB, 978-1-58023-152-7 **$18.95**

The Jewish Dream Book: The Key to Opening the Inner Meaning of Your Dreams
By Vanessa L. Ochs, PhD, with Elizabeth Ochs; Illus. by Kristina Swarner
8 x 8, 128 pp, Full-color illus., Deluxe PB w/ flaps, 978-1-58023-132-9 $16.95

Jewish Ritual: A Brief Introduction for Christians
By Rabbi Kerry M. Olitzky and Rabbi Daniel Judson
5½ x 8½, 144 pp, Quality PB, 978-1-58023-210-4 **$14.99**

The Rituals & Practices of a Jewish Life: A Handbook for Personal Spiritual Renewal *Edited by Rabbi Kerry M. Olitzky and Rabbi Daniel Judson*
6 x 9, 272 pp, Illus., Quality PB, 978-1-58023-169-5 **$18.95**

The Sacred Art of Lovingkindness: Preparing to Practice
By Rabbi Rami Shapiro 5½ x 8½, 176 pp, Quality PB, 978-1-59473-151-8 **$16.99**
(A book from SkyLight Paths, Jewish Lights' sister imprint)

Mystery & Detective Fiction

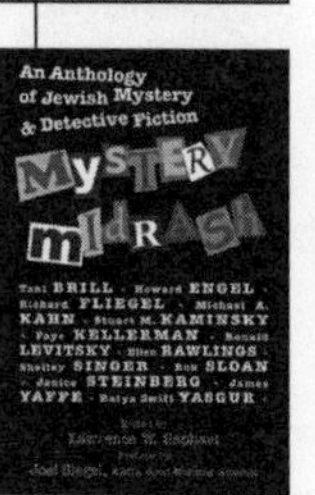

Criminal Kabbalah: An Intriguing Anthology of Jewish Mystery & Detective Fiction *Edited by Lawrence W. Raphael; Foreword by Laurie R. King*
All-new stories from twelve of today's masters of mystery and detective fiction—sure to delight mystery buffs of all faith traditions.
6 x 9, 256 pp, Quality PB, 978-1-58023-109-1 **$16.95**

Mystery Midrash: An Anthology of Jewish Mystery & Detective Fiction
Edited by Lawrence W. Raphael; Preface by Joel Siegel
6 x 9, 304 pp, Quality PB, 978-1-58023-055-1 **$16.95**

Inspiration

Into the Fullness of the Void: A Spiritual Autobiography *By Dov Elbaum*
The spiritual autobiography of one of Israel's leading cultural figures that provides insights and guidance for all of us. 6 x 9, 304 pp, Quality PB Original, 978-1-58023-715-4 **$18.99**

Saying No and Letting Go: Jewish Wisdom on Making Room for What Matters Most
By Rabbi Edwin Goldberg, DHL; Foreword by Rabbi Naomi Levy
Taps into timeless Jewish wisdom that teaches how to "hold on tightly" to the things that matter most while learning to "let go lightly" of the demands and worries that do not ultimately matter. 6 x 9, 192 pp, Quality PB, 978-1-58023-670-6 **$16.99**

The Bridge to Forgiveness: Stories and Prayers for Finding God and Restoring Wholeness *By Rabbi Karyn D. Kedar* 6 x 9, 176 pp, Quality PB, 978-1-58023-451-1 **$16.99**

The Empty Chair: Finding Hope and Joy—Timeless Wisdom from a Hasidic Master, Rebbe Nachman of Breslov *Adapted by Moshe Mykoff and the Breslov Research Institute*
4 x 6, 128 pp, Deluxe PB w/ flaps, 978-1-879045-67-5 **$9.99**

A Formula for Proper Living: Practical Lessons from Life and Torah
By Rabbi Abraham J. Twerski, MD 6 x 9, 144 pp, HC, 978-1-58023-402-3 **$19.99**

The Gentle Weapon: Prayers for Everyday and Not-So-Everyday Moments—Timeless Wisdom from the Teachings of the Hasidic Master, Rebbe Nachman of Breslov
Adapted by Moshe Mykoff and S. C. Mizrahi, together with the Breslov Research Institute
4 x 6, 144 pp, Deluxe PB w/ flaps, 978-1-58023-022-3 **$9.99**

The God Upgrade: Finding Your 21st-Century Spirituality in Judaism's 5,000-Year-Old Tradition *By Rabbi Jamie Korngold; Foreword by Rabbi Harold M. Schulweis*
6 x 9, 176 pp, Quality PB, 978-1-58023-443-6 $15.99

God Whispers: Stories of the Soul, Lessons of the Heart *By Rabbi Karyn D. Kedar*
6 x 9, 176 pp, Quality PB, 978-1-58023-088-9 **$15.95**

God's To-Do List: 103 Ways to Be an Angel and Do God's Work on Earth
By Dr. Ron Wolfson 6 x 9, 144 pp, Quality PB, 978-1-58023-301-9 **$16.99**

Happiness and the Human Spirit: The Spirituality of Becoming the Best You Can Be
By Rabbi Abraham J. Twerski, MD
6 x 9, 176 pp, Quality PB, 978-1-58023-404-7 **$16.99**; HC, 978-1-58023-343-9 **$19.99**

Life's Daily Blessings: Inspiring Reflections on Gratitude and Joy for Every Day, Based on Jewish Wisdom *By Rabbi Kerry M. Olitzky* 4½ x 6½, 368 pp, Quality PB, 978-1-58023-396-5 **$16.99**

The Magic of Hebrew Chant: Healing the Spirit, Transforming the Mind, Deepening Love *By Rabbi Shefa Gold; Foreword by Sylvia Boorstein*
6 x 9, 352 pp, Quality PB, 978-1-58023-671-3 **$24.99**

Restful Reflections: Nighttime Inspiration to Calm the Soul, Based on Jewish Wisdom
By Rabbi Kerry M. Olitzky and Rabbi Lori Forman-Jacobi 5 x 8, 352 pp, Quality PB, 978-1-58023-091-9 **$16.99**

Sacred Intentions: Morning Inspiration to Strengthen the Spirit, Based on Jewish Wisdom
By Rabbi Kerry M. Olitzky and Rabbi Lori Forman-Jacobi 4½ x 6½, 448 pp, Quality PB, 978-1-58023-061-2 **$16.99**

The Seven Questions You're Asked in Heaven: Reviewing and Renewing Your Life on Earth *By Dr. Ron Wolfson* 6 x 9, 176 pp, Quality PB, 978-1-58023-407-8 **$16.99**

Kabbalah / Mysticism

Ehyeh: A Kabbalah for Tomorrow
By Rabbi Arthur Green, PhD 6 x 9, 224 pp, Quality PB, 978-1-58023-213-5 **$18.99**

The Gift of Kabbalah: Discovering the Secrets of Heaven, Renewing Your Life on Earth
By Tamar Frankiel, PhD 6 x 9, 256 pp, Quality PB, 978-1-58023-141-1 **$16.95**

Jewish Mysticism and the Spiritual Life: Classical Texts, Contemporary Reflections *Edited by Dr. Lawrence Fine, Dr. Eitan Fishbane and Rabbi Or N. Rose*
6 x 9, 256 pp, HC, 978-1-58023-434-4 **$24.99**; Quality PB, 978-1-58023-719-2 **$18.99**

Seek My Face: A Jewish Mystical Theology *By Rabbi Arthur Green, PhD*
6 x 9, 304 pp, Quality PB, 978-1-58023-130-5 **$19.95**

Zohar: Annotated & Explained *Translation & Annotation by Dr. Daniel C. Matt; Foreword by Andrew Harvey* 5½ x 8½, 176 pp, Quality PB, 978-1-893361-51-5 **$16.99**
(A book from SkyLight Paths, Jewish Lights' sister imprint)

See also *The Way Into Jewish Mystical Tradition* in The Way Into… Series.

Spirituality

Amazing *Chesed*: Living a Grace-Filled Judaism
By Rabbi Rami Shapiro Drawing from ancient and contemporary, traditional and non-traditional Jewish wisdom, reclaims the idea of grace in Judaism.
6 x 9, 176 pp, Quality PB, 978-1-58023-624-9 **$16.99**

Jewish with Feeling: A Guide to Meaningful Jewish Practice
By Rabbi Zalman Schachter-Shalomi with Joel Segel
Takes off from basic questions like "Why be Jewish?" and whether the word God still speaks to us today and lays out a vision for a whole-person Judaism.
5½ x 8½, 288 pp, Quality PB, 978-1-58023-691-1 **$19.99**

Perennial Wisdom for the Spiritually Independent: Sacred Teachings—Annotated & Explained *Annotation by Rami Shapiro; Foreword by Richard Rohr*
Weaves sacred texts and teachings from the world's major religions into a coherent exploration of the five core questions at the heart of every religion's search.
5½ x 8½, 336 pp, Quality PB Original, 978-1-59473-515-8 **$16.99**

Aleph-Bet Yoga: Embodying the Hebrew Letters for Physical and Spiritual Well-Being
By Steven A. Rapp; Foreword by Tamar Frankiel, PhD, and Judy Greenfeld; Preface by Hart Lazer
7 x 10, 128 pp, b/w photos, Quality PB, Lay-flat binding, 978-1-58023-162-6 **$16.95**

A Book of Life: Embracing Judaism as a Spiritual Practice
By Rabbi Michael Strassfeld 6 x 9, 544 pp, Quality PB, 978-1-58023-247-0 **$19.99**

Bringing the Psalms to Life: How to Understand and Use the Book of Psalms
By Rabbi Daniel F. Polish, PhD 6 x 9, 208 pp, Quality PB, 978-1-58023-157-2 **$16.95**

Does the Soul Survive? A Jewish Journey to Belief in Afterlife, Past Lives & Living with Purpose *By Rabbi Elie Kaplan Spitz; Foreword by Brian L. Weiss, MD*
6 x 9, 288 pp, Quality PB, 978-1-58023-165-7 **$18.99**

Entering the Temple of Dreams: Jewish Prayers, Movements and Meditations for the End of the Day *By Tamar Frankiel, PhD, and Judy Greenfeld*
7 x 10, 192 pp, illus., Quality PB, 978-1-58023-079-7 **$16.95**

First Steps to a New Jewish Spirit: Reb Zalman's Guide to Recapturing the Intimacy & Ecstasy in Your Relationship with God *By Rabbi Zalman M. Schachter-Shalomi with Donald Gropman* 6 x 9, 144 pp, Quality PB, 978-1-58023-182-4 **$16.95**

Foundations of Sephardic Spirituality: The Inner Life of Jews of the Ottoman Empire
By Rabbi Marc D. Angel, PhD 6 x 9, 224 pp, Quality PB, 978-1-58023-341-5 **$18.99**

God & the Big Bang: Discovering Harmony between Science & Spirituality
By Dr. Daniel C. Matt 6 x 9, 216 pp, Quality PB, 978-1-879045-89-7 **$18.99**

God in Our Relationships: Spirituality between People from the Teachings of Martin Buber *By Rabbi Dennis S. Ross* 5½ x 8½, 160 pp, Quality PB, 978-1-58023-147-3 **$16.95**

The Jewish Lights Spirituality Handbook: A Guide to Understanding, Exploring & Living a Spiritual Life *Edited by Stuart M. Matlins*
6 x 9, 456 pp, Quality PB, 978-1-58023-093-3 **$19.99**

Judaism, Physics and God: Searching for Sacred Metaphors in a Post-Einstein World
By Rabbi David W. Nelson 6 x 9, 352 pp, Quality PB, inc. reader's discussion guide, 978-1-58023-306-4 **$18.99**; HC, 352 pp, 978-1-58023-252-4 **$24.99**

Meaning & Mitzvah: Daily Practices for Reclaiming Judaism through Prayer, God, Torah, Hebrew, Mitzvot and Peoplehood *By Rabbi Goldie Milgram*
7 x 9, 336 pp, Quality PB, 978-1-58023-256-2 **$19.99**

Repentance: The Meaning and Practice of Teshuvah
By Dr. Louis E. Newman; Foreword by Rabbi Harold M. Schulweis; Preface by Rabbi Karyn D. Kedar
6 x 9, 256 pp, HC, 978-1-58023-426-9 **$24.99** Quality PB, 978-1-58023-718-5 **$18.99**

The Sabbath Soul: Mystical Reflections on the Transformative Power of Holy Time
Selection, Translation and Commentary by Eitan Fishbane, PhD
6 x 9, 208 pp, Quality PB, 978-1-58023-459-7 **$18.99**

***Tanya*, the Masterpiece of Hasidic Wisdom:** Selections Annotated & Explained
Translation & Annotation by Rabbi Rami Shapiro; Foreword by Rabbi Zalman M. Schachter-Shalomi
5½ x 8½, 240 pp, Quality PB, 978-1-59473-275-1 **$16.99**

These Are the Words, 2nd Edition: A Vocabulary of Jewish Spiritual Life
By Rabbi Arthur Green, PhD 6 x 9, 320 pp, Quality PB, 978-1-58023-494-8 **$19.99**

About Jewish Lights

People of all faiths and backgrounds yearn for books that attract, engage, educate, and spiritually inspire.

Our principal goal is to stimulate thought and help all people learn about who the Jewish People are, where they come from, and what the future can be made to hold. While people of our diverse Jewish heritage are the primary audience, our books speak to people in the Christian world as well and will broaden their understanding of Judaism and the roots of their own faith.

We bring to you authors who are at the forefront of spiritual thought and experience. While each has something different to say, they all say it in a voice that you can hear.

Our books are designed to welcome you and then to engage, stimulate, and inspire. We judge our success not only by whether or not our books are beautiful and commercially successful, but by whether or not they make a difference in your life.

For your information and convenience, at the back of this book we have provided a list of other Jewish Lights books you might find interesting and useful. They cover all the categories of your life:

- Bar/Bat Mitzvah
- Bible Study / Midrash
- Children's Books
- Congregation Resources
- Current Events / History
- Ecology / Environment
- Fiction: Mystery, Science Fiction
- Grief / Healing
- Holidays / Holy Days
- Inspiration
- Kabbalah / Mysticism / Enneagram
- Life Cycle
- Meditation
- Men's Interest
- Parenting
- Prayer / Ritual / Sacred Practice
- Social Justice
- Spirituality
- Theology / Philosophy
- Travel
- Twelve Steps
- Women's Interest

Stuart M. Matlins, Publisher

Or phone, fax, mail or e-mail to: **JEWISH LIGHTS Publishing**
Sunset Farm Offices, Route 4 • P.O. Box 237 • Woodstock, Vermont 05091
Tel: (802) 457-4000 • Fax: (802) 457-4004 • www.jewishlights.com
Credit card orders: **(800) 962-4544** (8:30AM–5:30PM EST Monday–Friday)